Ontology-Driven Software Development

Jeff Z. Pan • Steffen Staab • Uwe Aßmann
Jürgen Ebert • Yuting Zhao
Editors

Ontology-Driven
Software Development

 Springer

Editors

Jeff Z. Pan
Department of Computing Science
University of Aberdeen
Aberdeen
United Kingdom

Steffen Staab
Insitute for Computer Science
University of Koblenz-Landau
Koblenz
Germany

Uwe Aßmann
Institute for Software-
  and Multimedia-Technology
Technical University of Dresden
Dresden
Germany

Jürgen Ebert
Institute for Software Technology
University of Koblenz-Landau
Koblenz
Germany

Yuting Zhao
Department of Computing Science
University of Aberdeen
Aberdeen
United Kingdom

ISBN 978-3-642-42895-1   ISBN 978-3-642-31226-7 (eBook)
DOI 10.1007/978-3-642-31226-7
Springer Heidelberg New York Dordrecht London

ACM Computing Classification (1998): D.2, I.2

Printed on acid-free paper

Springer is part of Springer Science+Business Media (www.springer.com)

Foreword

We live in exciting times. Easier than ever before, thanks to the Web, we can cross any geographical, cultural, or organizational borders. It is so easy to be in touch not only with family, friends, but also with authorities or organizations we work with. Social software indeed taught us an important lesson, we'd somehow forgotten, that we are still social beings. We like to play together. We are more creative together. We can only solve hard problems if we act together. *How many of us realize the central role that software play in modern technologies for dealing with grand challenges in areas like health care, engineering, and climate change?* As most of us can use and play with software, we need more and more of it. What software we daydream now, it is just a miniature fragment of what will be present in the 2020s. But, who is going to develop all that software?

At the transition of millennia, as a new grad student looking into what the "world peace" problem that one can solve, I was early introduced to *ontologies*, by my mentor. He first made sure to convince me that ontologies are not a philosophical elaboration. How would I otherwise even consider ontologies, when I was busy working on the pragmatic solution to the world peace problem, right? It was easy to realize that *communication* is the key activity in software development and use. We first talk to those who need the software. We then talk to other members of software development teams. We also talk to computers to encode the elicited ideas into software. Finally, our pieces of software need to talk to each other. How many times, in our lives we got lost in translation? And, here we have just mentioned at least four places of translation. How could we ensure our software can perform correctly according to what we initially wanted? Not to mention the need to communicate correctly with other software systems. So, the main question is how we make sure that the critical ideas and concepts for a system under development are consistently communicated throughout all these steps of communication.

Ontologies offer a promising solution to this everlasting communication problem. Ontologies allow for defining a shared "language" about the domain for which we develop some software. Ontologies also offer a formal representation about *relationships* between *concepts* of our domain language. This way we automatically check if our "language" is consistently used and if all our sentences when we talk to other humans or computers are correctly written.

We cannot build our software only with ontologies though; we need many other languages. Complexity of today's software needs to be adequately addressed. Software engineering and information systems offer many promising approaches to managing software complexity. Model-driven engineering, domain-specific languages, meta-programming, business process management, or software product lines are just some examples. Yet, all these approaches require some way of facilitating communication. Bridging ontologies as one technological space, and software engineering languages as another one(s), is certainly the most critical task for present and future software engineering.

So, I found my "world peace" problem to solve. Bridging between technological spaces is a problem that is far from being solved even today. Conversely, it is even harder. I haven't found any projects (no matter if they are related to workflow management, e-health, e-government, e-learning, or social networking), organizations or companies in which the bridging of some kind of ontologies and software technologies has *not* been at the very source of most of problems.

When I first learned about the MOST project, which this book is built upon, I was sure that the project must certainly be in the right direction to help in solving the problem. "Most" in my native language exactly means "bridge."

The book about the "Bridge" project offers a nice balance supporting creative thinking via *low thresholds, high ceilings, and wide walls*. The book starts from the foundational concepts of model-driven software engineering, ontologies and description logics. This offers a very didactic learning opportunity with low thresholds of foreknowledge for all of those who are not familiar with those concepts. Once the foundational concepts are mastered, readers can easily sail through the remaining sections covering the issues of bridging between ontologies and software technologies. From then on, the only constraint is one's imagination to reach the highest ceilings.

This book advances the coverage of the topic as compared to my coauthored book *Model Driven Engineering and Ontology Development* (also published by Springer): not only does the current book (in its second and third parts) improve the reasoning and transformation with in-depth coverage, but it also provides a number of practical aspects of use of ontologies and automated reasoning over the two critical aspects of any modern software—structure and behavior. Many practitioners and researchers (such as those working on conceptual modeling, language engineering, business process and workflow management, and software architectures) can find many useful solutions and know-how.

In its final part, the book outlines a novel ontology-driven software development approach. What I find especially exciting about it is the concept of ontology-guided development. Not only are ontologies used to integrate diverse software artifacts to improve traceability, but they also guide software engineers throughout the process of the software development activities such as requirements engineering and business process modeling. All real software engineers will especially appreciate this part of the book, as they will also be able to experiment with the toolset implementing all the explained ideas in the book. This is accompanied by concrete case studies from industry. Even better, the people from industry are also coauthors here who validate the discussed solutions.

It is my great pleasure to recommend this book to all computing science students, professionals, and researchers interested in the relevant technological landscape. The book is suited for those who are yet to learn about basics of ontologies and software development in their undergrad days. It is equally suited for those who look for exciting research questions, sound solutions to practical problems, or promising business opportunities.

Dragan Gašević
Vancouver, Canada
September 2011

Contents

1   Introduction 1
Uwe Aßmann, Jürgen Ebert, Jeff Z. Pan, Steffen Staab, and
Yuting Zhao
1.1   Vision: From Type-Safe to Consistency-Based
and Guided Software Development 2
1.2   This Book: From Model-Driven to ODSD 4
1.3   Who This Book Is for 11
1.3.1   I Know About Software Development, What
Can I Learn from This Book? 11
1.3.2   I Know About Ontology, What Can I Learn
from This Book? 12
1.3.3   The Website of This Book 12
1.4   How to Read This Book 12
1.4.1   Part I: Ontology and Software Technology 13
1.4.2   Part II: Foundational Technologies for ODSD 14
1.4.3   Part III: Consistency Checking in ODSD 14
1.4.4   Part IV: ODSD with Process Guidance................... 14

Part I   Ontology and Software Technologies

2   Model-Driven Software Development 21
Fernando Silva Parreiras, Gerd Gröner, Tobias Walter,
Andreas Friesen, Tirdad Rahmani, Jens Lemcke, Hannes
Schwarz, Krzysztof Miksa, Christian Wende, and Uwe
Aßmann
2.1   Introduction of MDE 21
2.1.1   Models 22
2.1.2   Metamodels 22
2.1.3   Modelling Languages 22

2.2   MDE Languages...   23
       2.2.1   UML Class Diagram   23
       2.2.2   Metamodelling Language   24
       2.2.3   Process Modelling Languages   26
       2.2.4   Domain-Specific Language   28
       2.2.5   Graph-Based Languages   29
       2.2.6   Feature Modelling Languages   33
2.3   Two-Dimensional Modelling   36
2.4   Model Transformation Languages...................................   37
       2.4.1   Atlas Transformation Language   38
       2.4.2   Graph Repository Transformation Language$^{(*)}$ 39
2.5   Constraint and Query Languages...................................   43
       2.5.1   The Object Constraint Language   43
       2.5.2   Graph Repository Query Language$^{(*)}$ 44
       2.5.3   Process Algebra...   48
2.6   Conclusion...   50

3   **Ontology Languages and Description Logics**.........................   51
    Yuting Zhao, Jeff Z. Pan, Edward Thomas, Nophadol
    Jekjantuk, and Yuan Ren
    3.1   Description Logics   51
           3.1.1   The Basic Description Language $\mathcal{AL}$ 52
           3.1.2   The Family of $\mathcal{AL}$ Languages   53
           3.1.3   Reasoning Tasks in Description Logics   54
           3.1.4   Computational Properties for Description Logics.........   55
    3.2   The OWL Family of Ontology Languages and Related
           Others   57
           3.2.1   OWL 2 Web Ontology Language (OWL 2)   57
           3.2.2   OWL 2 Profiles   59
           3.2.3 $\mathcal{EL}^{++}$ 60
           3.2.4   DL-Lite...   61
           3.2.5   OWL DL   64
    3.3   Conclusion..   67

4   **Case Studies for Marrying Ontology and Software Technologies**.....   69
    Krzysztof Miksa, Pawel Sabina, Andreas Friesen, Tirdad
    Rahmani, Jens Lemcke, Christian Wende, Srdjan Zivkovic,
    Uwe Aßmann, and Andreas Bartho
    4.1   Case Studies on Domain Engineering............................   69
           4.1.1   Problem Description.....................................   70
           4.1.2   Implementation   72
           4.1.3   Results   74
    4.2   Case Studies on Process Modelling and Refinement   74
           4.2.1   Introduction..   75
           4.2.2   Case Study: Process Refinement.........................   78

	4.2.3	Case Study: Querying Tasks and Artefacts	87
	4.2.4	Process Refinement Validation: Implementation and Results	90
	4.2.5	Querying Tasks and Artefacts: Implementation and Results	90
4.3		Case Study on Software Product Line Engineering	91
	4.3.1	Problem Description	91
	4.3.2	Case Study Implementation	92
	4.3.3	Results	93
4.4		Conclusion	94

Part II   Foundational Technologies for Ontology-Driven Software Development

5   Scalable Ontology Reasoning Services 99
Edward Thomas, Yuan Ren, Jeff Z. Pan, Yuting Zhao, and
Nophadol Jekjantuk

5.1	TrOWL: Tractable Reasoning Infrastructure for OWL 2	99
	5.1.1	Applications	100
	5.1.2	Technology	101
	5.1.3	Query Answering Using Semantic Approximation[*]	103
	5.1.4	Scalable Reasoning Using Syntactic Approximation[*]	107
	5.1.5	Local Closed World Reasoning with NBox[*]	110
5.2	Justification of Reasoning Results	113
	5.2.1	Justification in General	113
	5.2.2	Justification on OWL 2 EL[*]	116
	5.2.3	Justification on OWL 2 QL[*]	116
5.3	Conclusion	120

6   Traceability 121
Hannes Schwarz and Jürgen Ebert

6.1	Fields of Application	121
	6.1.1	Change Management	122
	6.1.2	Maintenance	122
	6.1.3	Project Management	122
	6.1.4	Quality Assurance	122
	6.1.5	Requirements Management	123
	6.1.6	Reuse	123
	6.1.7	Reverse Engineering	123
6.2	Traceability-Related Activities	124
	6.2.1	Definition	124
	6.2.2	Identification	125
	6.2.3	Recording	125
	6.2.4	Retrieval	126

		6.2.5	Utilisation	126
		6.2.6	Maintenance	127
	6.3	An Universal Traceability Concept		127
		6.3.1	The Traceability Relationship Type Template	128
		6.3.2	Traceability Retrieval Patterns	130
	6.4	Implementation Based on Ecore[*]		132
		6.4.1	Mapping of TRTT Properties	132
		6.4.2	Transformation-Based Identification	135
		6.4.3	Technologies for Recording	135
		6.4.4	Querying Conforming to the Retrieval Patterns	136
	6.5	Implementation Based on the TGraph Approach[*]		137
		6.5.1	Mapping of TRTT Properties	138
		6.5.2	Transformation-Based Identification	140
		6.5.3	Technologies for Recording	141
		6.5.4	Querying Conforming to the Retrieval Patterns	141
	6.6	Implementation Based on OWL[*]		143
		6.6.1	Mapping of TRTT Properties	143
		6.6.2	Technologies for Recording	147
		6.6.3	Querying Conforming to the Retrieval Patterns	147
	6.7	Discussions		149
	6.8	Conclusion		150

7 Metamodelling and Ontologies[*] 151
Gerd Gröner, Nophadol Jekjantuk, Tobias Walter, Fernando
Silva Parreiras, and Jeff Z. Pan

	7.1	Metamodelling for Ontologies		151
		7.1.1	Ontology Definition Metamodel	152
		7.1.2	NeOn OWL Metamodel	154
		7.1.3	OWL 2 Metamodel	156
	7.2	Ontologies for Metamodelling: OWL FA		157
		7.2.1	Motivating Example	157
		7.2.2	OWL FA Syntax and Semantics	159
		7.2.3	Metamodelling with OWL FA	162
		7.2.4	Reasoning in OWL FA	163
		7.2.5	Preprocessing	163
		7.2.6	Consistency Checking	165
		7.2.7	Instance Retrieval	165
		7.2.8	Justification on OWL FA	166
	7.3	Metamodelling in Ontologies and Metamodelling in MOF		167
		7.3.1	Open and Closed World Assumptions	168
		7.3.2	Ensuring Integrity Constraints in a Closed Domain	170
	7.4	Conclusion		174

Part III   Consistency Checking in Ontology-Driven Software Development (ODSD)

8   Ontology and Bridging Technologies 179
Uwe Aßmann, Jürgen Ebert, Tobias Walter, and Christian
Wende
   8.1   Ontology Services 179
          8.1.1   Pattern for Specification of Ontology Services 180
          8.1.2   Specification of Ontology Services 180
   8.2   Transformation Bridges[*] 183
          8.2.1   Transformation Services 183
          8.2.2   Example: OWLizer 184
   8.3   Integration Bridge[*] 185
          8.3.1   Integration Bridge Establishment 186
          8.3.2   Integration Bridge Use 188
          8.3.3   Example: M3 Integration Bridge 190
   8.4   Conclusion 192

**9   Ontology Reasoning for Consistency-Preserving
    Structural Modelling** 193
Christian Wende, Katja Siegemund, Edward Thomas, Yuting
Zhao, Jeff Z. Pan, Fernando Silva Parreiras, Tobias Walter,
Krzysztof Miksa, Pawel Sabina, and Uwe Aßmann
   9.1   Reasoning for Requirement Engineering 194
          9.1.1   The ODRE Approach 194
          9.1.2   Rules for Consistency Checking 194
          9.1.3   Rules for Completeness Checking 197
          9.1.4   Verification of the Requirement Specification Base 198
          9.1.5   Results 199
   9.2   Reasoning for Feature Model Analysis 199
          9.2.1   Ontology-Based Formalisation of Feature Models 199
          9.2.2   Application of Ontology Services for Feature
                   Analysis 201
          9.2.3   Results 203
   9.3   Reasoning for Domain Engineering 204
          9.3.1   Physical Devices Ontology 204
          9.3.2   Integrating PDDSL and OWL 2 207
          9.3.3   Metamodel Integration 207
          9.3.4   Reasoning with Integrated PDDSL and
                   OWL 2 Models 211
          9.3.5   Results 214
   9.4   Reasoning for UML Class Diagrams 214
          9.4.1   TwoUse 214
          9.4.2   Results 217
   9.5   Conclusion 217

10   Ontology Reasoning for Process Models 219
Yuan Ren, Gerd Gröner, Tirdad Rahmani, Jens Lemcke,
Andreas Friesen, Srdjan Zivkovic, Yuting Zhao, and Jeff Z.
Pan
10.1   A Running Example 220
10.2   Reasoning for Process Modelling and Retrieval 221
 10.2.1   Semantic Representation of Process Models 221
 10.2.2   Reasoning for Process Retrieval 223
10.3   Reasoning for Process Refinement in BPMN [*] 224
 10.3.1   Defining Valid Process Refinement 225
 10.3.2   Constraints on Refinement Relations 229
 10.3.3   Validating Parallel-Free Process Refinement
    with Ontology 232
 10.3.4   Extending Specific Process with Parallel Gateways 234
 10.3.5   Extending Abstract Process with Parallel Gateways 235
 10.3.6   Validating Grounding with Ontology 237
 10.3.7   Pinpointing and Explaining Sources of
    Invalidity with Ontology Reasoning 240
 10.3.8   Efficient Refinement Validation with
    Approximate Ontology Reasoning 242
10.4   Reasoning for Process Guidance 244
 10.4.1   Concepts and Knowledge Assets of a
    Modelling Scenario 244
 10.4.2   Formalising Guidance Knowledge into Ontologies 246
 10.4.3   Retrieving Tasks by Query Answering 248
 10.4.4   Generalised Solution for Representation and Retrieval ... 250
 10.4.5   Computational Properties 250
10.5   Conclusion 251

**Part IV   Ontology-Driven Software Development (ODSD)
    with Process Guidance**

**11   Ontology-Driven Metamodelling for Ontology-Integrated
Modelling**[*] 257
Uwe Aßmann, Jürgen Ebert, Tobias Walter, and Christian
Wende
11.1   Reasoning for Language Engineering and Use 257
 11.1.1   Defining an M3 Integration Bridge 258
 11.1.2   Using an M3 Integration Bridge 261
11.2   OWLText 265
 11.2.1   ODMM with OWLText 265
 11.2.2   Realisation and Application of the M3
    Bridges and M2 Bridges in OWLText 267
 11.2.3   An Exemplary Application of OWLText 270
11.3   Conclusion 273

12   A Platform for ODSD: The MOST Workbench 275
Srdjan Zivkovic, Christian Wende, Edward Thomas,
Fernando Silva Parreiras, Tobias Walter, Krzysztof Miksa,
Harald Kühn, Hannes Schwarz, and Jeff Z. Pan
   12.1   Towards ODSD Tool Environments 275
           12.1.1   Current Tool Environments 276
           12.1.2   ODSD Tool Environments 278
           12.1.3   Developing a Family of ODSD Tool Environments 280
   12.2   Configurable and Tractable Ontology Reasoning
           Infrastructure for ODSD 283
           12.2.1   Closed-World Reasoning in NBox 283
           12.2.2   Justification and Explanation 284
           12.2.3   Tractability 284
           12.2.4   Configurability 284
   12.3   Integrated Queries for ODSD 285
   12.4   Validation and Explanation in ODSD 287
           12.4.1   Validation and Explanations for Process Refinements 287
           12.4.2   Validation and Explanations for Domain Engineering 288
           12.4.3   Model Repair 289
   12.5   Traceability in ODSD 290
           12.5.1   Using the Integration Infrastructure for Traceability 290
           12.5.2   Benefiting from Transformations Between
                    Modelling and Ontology Languages...................... 291
   12.6   Conclusion 292

**13   Ontology-Guided Software Engineering in the MOST
       Workbench** 293
Uwe Aßmann, Srdjan Zivkovic, Krzysztof Miksa, Katja
Siegemund, Andreas Bartho, Tirdad Rahmani, Edward
Thomas, and Jeff Z. Pan
   13.1   Ontology-Based Guidance Engine 293
           13.1.1   The Generic Guidance................................... 293
           13.1.2   The Generic Guidance Ontology 296
           13.1.3   Implementation Technologies............................ 298
   13.2   Guidance for Process Refinement Engineering 300
           13.2.1   Guidance as a Service for Refinement................... 301
           13.2.2   Guidance as a Process for Refinement................... 302
   13.3   Guidance for Domain Engineering 305
           13.3.1   Consistency Guidance 305
           13.3.2   Process Guidance 306
   13.4   Guidance for Requirements Engineering.......................... 309
           13.4.1   Requirements Guidance Ontology 310
           13.4.2   Guidance for Requirement Engineering 312
   13.5   Guidance for Documentation Engineering 314
   13.6   Conclusion 318

14 Conclusion and Outlooks 319
Jeff Z. Pan, Steffen Staab, Uwe Aßmann, Jürgen Ebert,
Yuting Zhao, and Daniel Oberle
14.1 Key questions for Ontology-Driven Software
Development (ODSD) 320
14.2 Where to Go from Here? 320
14.2.1 Things to Keep in Mind When Adopting ODSD 321
14.2.2 Contributing to the Linked Software Data 321
14.2.3 Further Visions in Software Engineering 322

References 323

Index 335

Contributors

Uwe Aßmann Technical University Dresden, Dresden, Germany

Andreas Bartho Technical University Dresden, Dresden, Germany

Jürgen Ebert University of Koblenz-Landau, Koblenz, Germany

Andreas Friesen SAP Research, Karlsruhe, Germany

Gerd Gröner University of Koblenz-Landau, Koblenz, Germany

Nophadol Jekjantuk University of Aberdeen, King's College, Aberdeen, UK

Harald Kühn BOC Information Systems GmbH, Vienna, Austria

Jens Lemcke SAP Research, Karlsruhe, Germany

Krzysztof Miksa COMARCH S.A., Kraków, Poland

Daniel Oberle SAP Research, Karlsruhe, Germany

Jeff Z. Pan University of Aberdeen, King's College, Aberdeen, UK

Tirdad Rahmani SAP Research, Karlsruhe, Germany

Yuan Ren University of Aberdeen, King's College, Aberdeen, UK

Pawel Sabina COMARCH S.A., Kraków, Poland

Hannes Schwarz University of Koblenz-Landau, Koblenz, Germany

Katja Siegemund Technical University Dresden, Dresden, Germany

Fernando Silva Parreiras FUMEC University, Minas Gerais, Brazil

Steffen Staab University of Koblenz-Landau, Koblenz, Germany

Edward Thomas University of Aberdeen, King's College, Aberdeen, UK

Tobias Walter University of Koblenz-Landau, Koblenz, Germany

Christian Wende DevBoost GmbH, Berlin, Germany

Yuting Zhao University of Aberdeen, King's College, Aberdeen, UK

Srdjan Zivkovic BOC Information Systems GmbH, Vienna, Austria

Chapter 1
Introduction

Uwe Aßmann, Jürgen Ebert, Jeff Z. Pan, Steffen Staab, and Yuting Zhao

> *That's one small step for [a] man, one giant leap for mankind.*
> *[Neil Armstrong]*

> *A technical space is a model management framework*
> *accompanied by a set of tools that operate on the models*
> *definable within the framework.*
> *[Jean Bézivin and Ivan Kurtev] [24]*

Abstract This book is about a significant step forward in software development. The starting point for this book has been the project "marrying ontology and software technology (MOST)"[1], a European Commission information and communication technologies (ICT) research project in the 7th Research Framework Programme. Its goal has been to improve software engineering by leveraging ontology and reasoning technology. It has aimed at developing a seamless integration technology for ontologies into model-driven software development (MDSD), often referred to as model-driven architecture (MDA), and other software development processes, resulting in ontology-driven software development (ODSD). In this book, we share our experience from the MOST project. We will travel together with the readers through the vision of ODSD, bridges between ontology technologies and MDSD and various practical technologies for building the ODSD infrastructure.

In this chapter, we first introduce our vision of where software development is heading for (Sect. 1.1), before presenting an overview (Sect. 1.2) of our contribution on ODSD. Some reader guidance information is also available, including who this book is for (Sect. 1.3) and how to read this book (Sect. 1.4). Figure 1.9 (p. 13) is the roadmap of this book.

---

[1] Web site at http://project.odsd.eu/most/

J.Z. Pan et al. (eds.), *Ontology-Driven Software Development*,
DOI 10.1007/978-3-642-31226-7_1, © Springer-Verlag Berlin Heidelberg 2013

1.1   Vision: From Type-Safe to Consistency-Based and Guided Software Development

This book is about entering a new level of quality for software products, and, related, a new level of efficiency for their development. It is best if we explain this step advance with a figure showing the progress of software development over time, Fig. 1.1. In the 1950s, assembler languages were basically untyped (level 1). Errors in programming were discovered during or after running the program. With the advent of higher-level programming languages, types were introduced, which helped programmers to discover bugs at compile time (level 2). While types usually only constrain single variables and check their consistent assignments and use, constraint languages allow for the specification of more powerful, also context-sensitive constraints (level 3). Languages such as *object constraint language (OCL)* or Alloy help to constrain software models, making the work with the code more convenient and safe, safer than with type systems alone. One may say that constraint languages exploit the power of logic to prove the well-formedness of models with regard to logical constraints.

This book is about bringing further results of logic into mainstream software development and its languages. Ontologies, based on description logics, have been introduced to capture the knowledge of domains, to evaluate constraints over domain data, to prove consistency of domain data, and to guide domain engineers while developing domain models [11]. Ontologies can be used to check the consistency of a type schema, its constraints (both located in the TBox, the schema part of an ontology) to a set of objects (individuals in the ABox, the data part of an ontology). Ontologies can also be used to generate proposals about how to complete a specification in a reasonable way, so that the developer may continue if he got stuck. Now, the question is: can we use these powerful capabilities, *consistency checking* and *guidance*, not only for domain engineering but also for software construction? Will the reasoning power of ontologies be available also for software models and programs? *How can we marry ontologies and software engineering* to help the programmer to write more consistent specifications, models, and programs? How can we extend the MDSD to integrate ontologies at any time during modelling and programming?

Figure 1.2 (p. 4) shows another argument for why ontologies are important for software development. Usually, four aspects of software development are distinguished: *domain modelling*, which models the application domains and brings their knowledge into the software; *structural* or *syntactic modelling*, which describes the interfaces, architecture, and coarse-grain structure of an application; *static semantics*, which ensures well-formedness of the specifications, models, and programs with regard to language semantics; and *dynamic semantics*, which gives a behavioural meaning and interpretation to all involved software artefacts. While ontologies have been introduced for domain modelling, they have the advantage that usually they are modelled in decidable languages, so that it is possible to check the specifications in finite time. This immediately creates the idea of exploiting ontologies also for static semantics of specifications, models, and programs, which is what

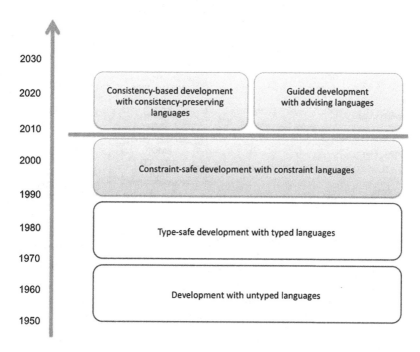

Fig. 1.1 The development of software over time

this book is about: it proposes an extended MDSD process with integrated use of ontologies, and resulting in Ontology-Driven Software Development (ODSD), so that all involved specifications, models, and programs can statically be checked for *consistency* and that developers are *guided* on how to continue. In this process, software models and ontologies are partners: we will see examples for ontologies not only used in structural modelling but also employed for advanced tasks in static semantics. Only in dynamic semantics do ontologies find their limitations: usually, languages to specify dynamic semantics should be undecidable; otherwise, they are too restricted.

We do not believe that the integration of ontologies into software development will provide the ultimate and final approach for consistency-based (stage 1 of level 4 in Fig. 1.1) and guided development (stage 2 of level 4 in Fig. 1.1). More technologies will be added to these stages of software development; for instance, model checking, real-time model checking, probabilistic model checking, abstract interpretations, or other static checking techniques based on formal frameworks. Each of these approaches, which are currently being investigated in the research community, has its advantages; they are not competing, but rather contributing approaches for *consistency-based* and *guided* software development. However, we hope this book will convince you that ontologies will also have their share: marrying ontologies and software technology, bridging between the technical spaces of ontologies and software models, has many advantages to get the software clean, bug free and faster to the market.

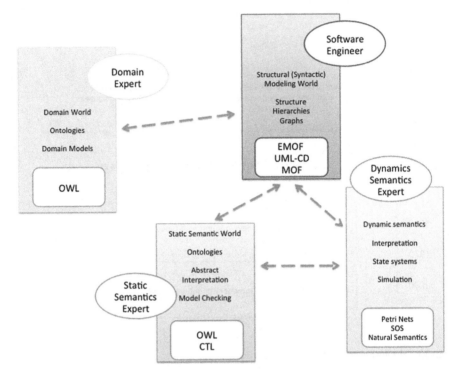

Fig. 1.2 The four aspects of software development, their interaction, and influence on software quality

1.2 This Book: From Model-Driven to ODSD

In this book, our journey starts from Model-Driven Software Development (MDSD).

In the 2000s, MDSD has focused on the work with structural models, e.g., models that describe the structure of software applications, designs, or components. Important software modelling environments, such as Eclipse *eclipse modelling framework (EMF)*, have been built for the quick-and-easy management of simple, structural models, basically equivalent to graphs. While this is a clear advance over the tree-based development environments of the 1980s and the 1990s, structural modelling only deals with syntactical modelling of graphs, not with their static nor dynamic semantics. On the other hand, in the 2000s domain modelling with typed logic also became popular, based on ontologies in description logic [11]. Ontologies offer many more services, e.g., automatic classification or consistency checking for models. Languages, such as the *web ontology language (OWL)*, have been developed as a structured family of language dialects, clearly demarcated from each other, and are already standardised by the *world wide web consortium (W3C)*. So,

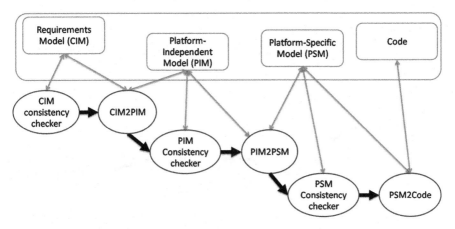

Fig. 1.3 A sketch of the standard MDSD process from CIM to PIM to PSM. Besides transformers, consistency checkers are employed

how can we employ the power of ontologies and their well-elaborated languages for the development of graph-based models in MDSD? Is it possible to reason about the static and dynamic semantics of software models made in *essential MOF (EMOF)* or UML class diagrams (UML-CD)? Can we use a reasoner to help us to causally connect *platform-independent model (PIM)* with *platform-specific model (PSM)*, as shown in Fig. 1.3? Can we employ ontologies for domain models or requirements specifications, filling the "black hole" of the *computation independent model (CIM)* in the MDSD process?

This book will answer some of these questions, hopefully some of your particular questions too. We believe that ontologies should be tightly integrated into an MDSD process or development environment to *check consistency* of the involved models; that they should *drive* the software development by *guiding* software developers about which steps to do or which proof obligations still being open; and that they should causally connect different specifications in the development process, e.g., requirements specifications and domain models. This is what we call in this book Ontology-Driven Software Development (ODSD), the leveraging of the MDSD with the power of ontologies.

At the moment, ontologies can already be used in the software development process, but in a rather restricted way (Fig. 1.4). From the code level, domain ontologies and other ontologies, such as those representing business rules or business models, can be queried. To this end, state-of-the-art reasoners offer an *application programming interface (API)* to access the ontology and to provide reasoning services. However, this only works on the code level; during modelling the ontologies cannot be accessed, nor applied to the models in question. It would be much nicer to have ontology services *invisibly available* also for the modeller.

However, several obstacles have to be removed, before ontologies become *transparent* to developers, i.e., tightly integrated with structural modelling. Firstly, all

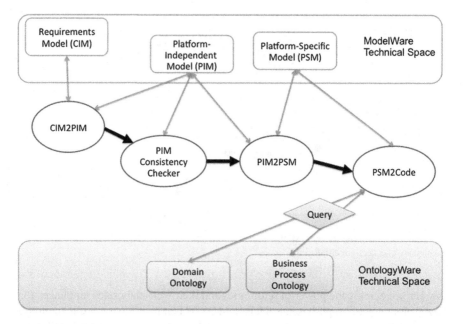

Fig. 1.4 The standard MDSD process may access some ontologies, e.g., domain ontologies, by querying them. However, this is mostly done from the platform-specific or implementation level

ontology services should be accessible, in a simple and integrated way, as common *ontology-integrated services (OIS)*. It is hoped that, eventually, for all models in the MDSD chain (upper half of Fig. 1.5), ontology services can be invoked (lower half of Fig. 1.5). Because the ontology world is a separate technical space [24], it has to be smoothly integrated with the system modelling space (Fig. 1.6). For this integration, bridges between the software modelling (called *ModelWare*) and ontology world (called *OntologyWare*) have to be built, on the one hand, on the language level (e.g., mapping *meta object facility (MOF)* to *RDF schema (RDFS)* with an *integration bridge*), on the other hand, on the model level, e.g., transforming models from an EMF repository to a reasoner with a *transformation bridge,* or by adapting model access from a reasoner to an EMF tool with an *adapter bridge* (see the vertical block arrows in Fig. 1.7). Then, with a bridge, structural models from the software world should be automatically transported to the ontology world so that ontology services can be executed on them (Fig. 1.7). For instance, checking consistency of a CIM or PIM could be done very well by a reasoner, however, then they have first to be transported into the ontology world.

Since these bridges between several technical spaces are necessary for smoothly integrated ontology services, this book deals to a large extent with their construction. Luckily, it turns out that the building of bridges can largely be automated, by employing generators (Chap. 8). Technical spaces are structured into several levels (Fig. 1.8), starting with M0 (individuals or objects), M1 (models or programs), M2

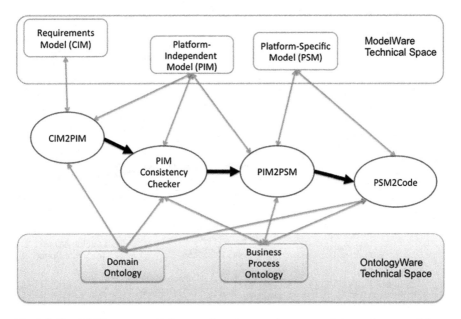

Fig. 1.5 The MDSD process with integrated ontology services accessed from software models

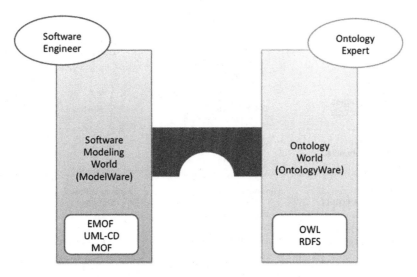

Fig. 1.6 Bridging the two technological spaces of structural software modelling and ontology modelling is a prerequisite for ODSD

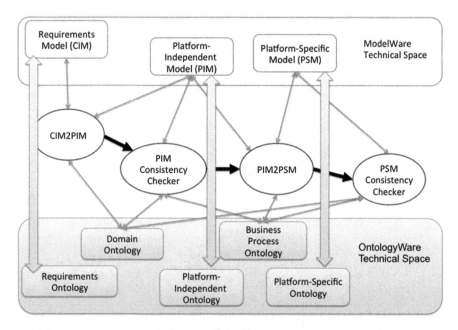

Fig. 1.7 The MDSD process with integrated ontology services (OIS) for all kinds of software models. Integration is done by technical space bridges

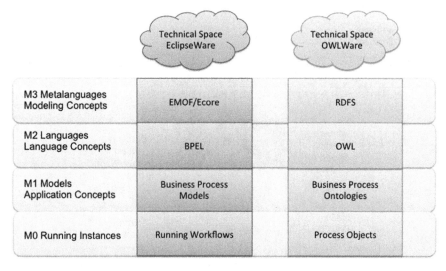

Fig. 1.8 The layers of technical spaces M0-M3. EclipseWare is a typical software modelling space, with metalanguage EMOF (Ecore). OWLWare is a typical ontology technical space for ontologies, with RDFS as metalanguage. Other examples are found in this book

(metamodels or languages), and M3 (metalanguages). Depending on the form of bridge that is required, mappings have to be constructed, either on M3 between two metalanguages, or on M2, between two languages. From these mappings, bridges can be generated. And with the bridges, ontologies can invisibly be integrated into the model-driven software development process.

Motivational Example: Consistency Preservation of Requirements Specifications and Domain Models

Requirements engineering (RE) usually is the first task of a software development process. The usual approach identifies, analyses, prioritises, and documents customer demands in a requirements specification, an important part of the contract eventually to be signed between customer and developer. It is well known that a consistent and complete *requirements specification base (RSB)* is the indispensable basis for the successful development of software [128]. One significant problem faced by requirements engineers is inconsistency in the raw information collected from the customers. Such inconsistencies may result from the acquisition of goals and requirements from multiple stakeholder and different sources [207]. Also, changes of requirements have a particularly significant impact on the consistency of specifications. In order to regain consistency, conflicting requirements may be removed from the specification, but removal often leads to its incompleteness. Therefore, the ability to detect and repair inconsistent requirements and the ability to discover incomplete requirements are crucial for all following development tasks.

Although all following steps in design and implementation of the software product are based on this initial requirements specification, in practice this specification is often not sufficiently connected to them. In these later phases, it is usually not clear anymore from which requirements certain parts of the design models and code originated or how they are related. Also, questions may arise, e.g., why certain requirements have been refined or which alternatives exist, and if decisions are made addressing these open questions, they are often not reintegrated with the initial requirements specification. Thus, the value of the requirements specification for the subsequent development phases continuously decreases.

Finally, the plethora and high customisability of software development methods make it hard to decide which of them to apply, how to sort individual tasks, and how to keep track of the development progress. For instance, products of a product line have to be shown to be consistent not only with requirements specification but also with the domain model of the product line. Complex domain constraints can be violated by design and code, if no causal connection to the domain model exists. Checking domain constraints, however, is a tedious task which should be done incrementally, in a step-by-step fashion until every inconsistency has been removed. The order and time when these steps should be executed can be very difficult to remember for a developer and difficult to record if extensive documentation for certification is needed. Thus, help for the ordering and the completion of the consistency preservation process of domain model constraints would be very welcome.

What ODSD Delivers to Your Requirements Engineering

In the following, we will exemplify how ODSD can help to address the aforementioned challenges. Ontologies provide a formal representation of knowledge and the relationships between concepts. Thus, they are well suited to tracking and analysing the relationship between various kinds of software development artefacts ranging from requirements to implementation code. Reasoning services like consistency and completeness checking allow for validation of incomplete requirements specifications, consistency preservation of design models, and continuous evolution of the involved artefacts.

For requirements engineering, we suggest to use a domain-independent ontology to specify the general concepts, requirements and relationships to be captured during requirements elicitation (Chap. 9). This domain-independent ontology can later be instantiated with the requirement artefacts (goals, requirements, obstacles, etc.) for a particular project and becomes an integral part of the RSB. Then, reasoning techniques are applied for consistency checking, whereas query techniques validate the completeness of individual requirements.

This approach, the ontological representation, validation, and consistency preservation of development artefacts, can not only be applied to requirements specifications but also in later phases of software development to both platform-independent and platform-specific design models. In order to track the impact of requirements on later development artefacts, we suggest to use *traceability relation ontologies* to store dependencies among various specifications and development phases (Chap. 6). Again, reasoning and query services help to analyse these dependencies and assist software developers in understanding artefact relations and the impact of changes. By tracing relations of development artefacts along the whole development life cycle, software designers are supported in understanding decisions during requirements engineering, validating their design for consistency with the requirements specification, and propagating design decisions affecting requirements back to the requirements specification. Programmers are enabled to recognise which requirements and designs they are currently implementing and which use-cases, metrics, etc. might be connected with it then.

Thirdly, ontologies can be used for the checking of static semantics constraints in domain-specific languages (DSL), in which domain models are often specified. Many areas of software development are domain specific and need DSL. Chap. 11 shows how domain-specific languages can be developed with ontologies describing their statics semantics. An ontology provides a clean and standardised way to express the static semantics of such a DSL, and the language environment can hide the complexity of the checking process for the developer. Therefore, ODSD facilitates the specification of domain models using domain-specific languages backing them up with ontology-based semantics. Together, this extends the applicability of ontology reasoning and querying to the whole software development life cycle, defining *consistency-preserving software development (CPSD)* (Fig. 1.1).

Finally, ontologies can be used to model a software development method and its associated software processes. We suggest to represent the tasks of a development method, their interdependencies, and the status of a concrete process in a *guidance ontology* (Chap. 13). This ontology can again be analysed to check the current process status, and it can be queried for next development tasks, guiding programmers through the development process. Also, individual development artefacts may become part of the guidance ontology. For example, the computation of the next development task may depend on the current content of the Requirements Ontology and may change when adding, modifying, or deleting particular requirements. Furthermore, software tools and their interactions can be specified in the guidance ontology. Then, the ontology can notify the developer about errors resulting from running a checking, testing, or verification tool against the requirements specification, and it can explain which steps to take to remedy them. Thus, a guidance ontology can flexibly guide the software developer through the development process, when consistency of artefacts with the requirements should be ensured, when requirements change over time, or complex tool interactions have to be resolved. We call this application of ontologies in software process modelling *guided software development (GSD)*.

1.3   Who This Book Is for

This book is for undergraduate and postgraduate students, professionals, as well as researchers who are interested in the connections of the technological spaces of ontology and software engineering.

This book can be helpful for undergraduate students and professionals who are interested in studying how ontologies and related semantic reasoning can be applied to the software development process. It can serve as a useful source for a undergraduate course on topics related to semantics-enabled software engineering.

This book can also be helpful for postgraduate students, professionals, and researchers who are going to embark on their research in these areas. It can serve as a useful source for a postgraduate course on advanced topics that are related to semantics-enabled software engineering. The chapters/sections/subsections that are more suitable for postgraduate courses have (*) added to the end of their titles; they could also be considered as optional contents for an undergraduate course.

1.3.1   *I Know About Software Development, What Can I Learn from This Book?*

For readers who are familiar with software development, this book provides an introduction of ontology and their reasoning services. Most importantly, it shows how ontology and reasoning services can be applied in software development, with clear benefits of providing new methodologies and infrastructures to improve quality of the models and productivity of software development activities. These readers will find the included industrial case studies useful to help understand the ODSD technologies presented in this book.

1.3.2   *I Know About Ontology, What Can I Learn from This Book?*

For readers who are familiar with ontology, this book provides an introduction of MDSD and how ontology can be applied to improve it, resulting in taking software development to a new level. The recent years have witnessed many applications of ontology technologies in different areas. What remains to be answered is whether ontology can play a more profound role in software engineering in general. These readers will find some answers in this book.

1.3.3   *The Website of This Book*

The homepage of the book is http://book.odsd.eu/odsd/, where you could find some information about the book, such as:

- Slides and teaching materials for this book
- Related scientific publications and documents
- Related ontologies and ontology patterns
- Standardisation initiatives
- Related events

1.4   How to Read This Book

As a roadmap of the book, Fig. 1.9 is used across this book to remind you where you are in the journey. The first part of this book makes sure you are ready. By the time you are done with it, you will have been introduced to MDSD; you will have been exposed to an introduction of ontology languages, as well as their formal underpinnings—description logics. These introductions will be followed by several industrial case studies that will be revisited again and again in later chapters.

The next part takes you through the enabling technologies for ODSD. This part starts with the responsive ontology reasoning services that one will need to meet the requirements of industrial case studies for ontology reasoning. It then covers how to keep track of dependencies among software artefacts in ODSD. Finally, it shows you the role of metamodels in ODSD, as well as existing challenges and solutions.

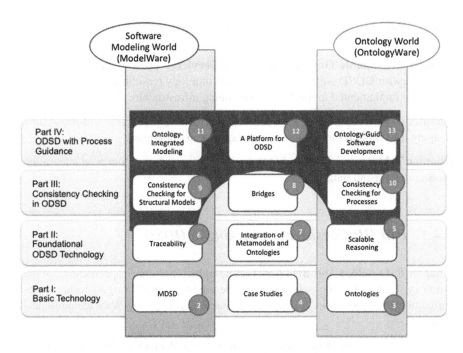

Fig. 1.9 The roadmap of this book: all steps to realise the bridge of Fig. 1.6

The final two parts of this book present detailed techniques, based on the enabling technologies introduced in the second part, in ODSD for stages 1 and 2 of level 4 of software development in Fig. 1.1 (p. 3), namely consistency checking and process guidance in ODSD. The discussions start from bridging techniques of the two (ontology and software engineering) technological spaces and conclude with a platform for ODSD—the MOST ODSD Workbench.

1.4.1 Part I: Ontology and Software Technology

Chapter 2 (Model-Driven Software Development—MDSD) introduces, with examples, MDSD, a software development methodology, in which models are used to describe software on an abstract level.

Chapter 3 (Ontology Languages and Description Logics) introduces ontology, as well as the state of the art of ontology languages and their underpinnings description logics.

Chapter 4 (Case Studies for Marrying Ontology and Software Technologies) presents some industrial case studies to motivate ODSD.

1.4.2   Part II: Foundational Technologies for ODSD

Chapter 5 (Scalable Ontology Reasoning Services) presents the key enabling technology for ODSD—effective and efficient ontology reasoning services, most of which are implemented in the TrOWL reasoning infrastructure (http://trowl.eu/).

Chapter 6 (Traceability) gives a detailed overview of traceability and shows how to apply it to support model-driven engineering and ontologies.

Chapter 7 (Metamodelling and Ontologies) presents technologies on integrating metamodelling and ontologies.

1.4.3   Part III: Consistency Checking in ODSD

Chapter 8 (Ontology and Bridging Technologies) presents a specification of the ontology services and shows how they can be used to support bridging technologies for combining ModelWare technological spaces and OntologyWare technological spaces.

Chapter 9 (Ontology Reasoning for Consistency-Preserving Structural Modelling) presents concrete applications of ontology and reasoning technology for the analysis and validation of structural models such as requirements models, feature models, and UML models.

Chapter 10 (Ontology Reasoning for Process Models) presents applications of ontology and reasoning technology for behavioural models, especially business process models (such as BPMN).

1.4.4   Part IV: ODSD with Process Guidance

Chapter 11 (Ontology-Driven Metamodelling for Ontology-Integrated Modelling) presents an ontology-driven metamodelling approach to incremental, interactive consistency checking for DSL (domain-specific language) editors.

Chapter 12 (A Platform for ODSD: The MOST Workbench) presents the MOST ODSD Workbench, the first platform for ODSD, in which process guidance is realised with the so-called *Guidance Engines*, which are configured based on guidance ontologies.

Chapter 13 (Ontology-Guided Software Engineering in the MOST Workbench) presents how to develop guidance engines, such as those for process refinement, domain engineering for product lines, requirements engineering, and documentation engineering, on top of the MOST ODSD Workbench.

Chapter 14 (Conclusion and Outlooks) discusses the challenges in adopting semantic technologies in Software Engineering and our vision on the way forward.

We hope you will enjoy "marrying ontologies with software technology", as we have been enjoying it.

Part I
Ontology and Software Technologies

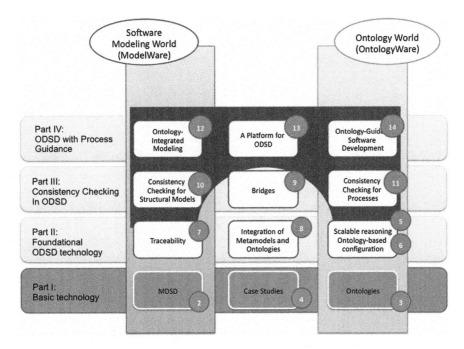

Fig. RoadMap.1 The roadmap of Part I

The first part of this book introduces basic background knowledge about model-driven software development (Chap. 2) and ontology (Chap. 3). For readers who are familiar with both of them, they could jump directly to Chap. 4, which presents a few industrial case studies, which motivate the consistency-preserving and guided software development, namely, the two stages of level 4 in Fig. 1.1 (page 3).

Part I contains the following chapters:

Chapter 2: Model-Driven Software Development (MDSD)
Chapter 3: Ontology Languages and Description Logics
Chapter 4: Case Studies for Marrying Ontology and Software Technologies

Chapter 2
Model-Driven Software Development

Fernando Silva Parreiras, Gerd Gröner, Tobias Walter, Andreas Friesen, Tirdad Rahmani, Jens Lemcke, Hannes Schwarz, Krzysztof Miksa, Christian Wende, and Uwe Aßmann

Abstract Since ontology-driven software development (ODSD) is an integration of ontology technologies and model-driven software development (MDSD), it is necessary to identify and analyse technologies applied in MDSD. We define basic concepts, such as model-driven engineering, metamodelling, model transformation and technological space, and describe the state-of-the-art implementations of these concepts.

In this chapter, we start with the notion of *model-driven engineering (MDE)* in Sect. 2.1 and a set of *modelling languages* in Sect. 2.2. We introduce the notion of *two-dimensional modelling* in Sect. 2.3. In Sect. 2.4 we continue with *model transformation languages*, and in Sect. 2.5 we introduce *constraint languages*.

2.1 Introduction of MDE

Model-driven techniques provide management, transformation and synchronisation of different software artefacts. This is motivated by the objective of factorising complexity into different levels of abstraction and concern, from high-level conceptual models down to the individual aspects of target platforms.

There is a consensus in the literature about the cornerstones of MDE: (1) modelling languages comprising models that represent real-world elements, metamodels to describe the structure of models and language semantics; (2) and transformations between languages. Schmidt [180] argues that MDE technologies should combine domain-specific modelling languages (DSML) and transformation engines to address platform complexity. For Kent [117], MDE requires a family of languages, transformations between languages and a process associated with the conception of languages and transformations. In this chapter, we concentrate on the structural specification of MDE.

J.Z. Pan et al. (eds.), *Ontology-Driven Software Development*,
DOI 10.1007/978-3-642-31226-7_2, © Springer-Verlag Berlin Heidelberg 2013

An instance of MDE is the *model-driven architecture (MDA)*[133], which is based on object management group (OMG's) meta-object facility (MOF). It frequently includes *unified modelling language (UML)* as its modelling language and a common pipeline of managing and transforming models according to MDA [119]: A *platform independent model (PIM)* is transformed into a *platform specific model (PSM)* and eventually into an executable representation (code), being the target platform.

2.1.1 Models

The notion of model accepted in MDE is that a *model* is a simplification of a physical system. Apostel [6] uses the word *simplification* to denote a viewpoint of a system from a certain scale where the system is controlled with a certain purpose in mind.

The UML specification [151] corroborates this notion describing a model as an abstraction of a physical system. Bezivin [22] uses the association representByM or representationOf to connect the system under study to a model. Thus, a system can have multiple models depending on the viewpoint.

2.1.2 Metamodels

Whereas models describe a specific abstraction of reality, metamodels define models. *Metamodels* are models of languages used to define models.

Metamodel-based approaches are working on a staged architecture of models and metamodels, where the structure of lower level models is defined by higher-level metamodels. This staged architecture defines a four-layered structure, which is applied to define domain-specific languages (DSLs), including the UML.

At the top level (M3), the MOF [149] is situated, which is a class-based modelling language that defines itself. Language specifications like the UML specification are viewed as instances [7] of MOF situated on the metamodel level (M2). The model level (M1) contains concrete models defined by metamodels on M2. These models represent real-world systems situated on M0.

2.1.3 Modelling Languages

Kurtev et al. define the role of a language in mega-modelling as an abstract system comprising a set of elements or a set of coordinated models [27].

In the realm of modelling languages, i.e., languages for defining models, we identify two categories of languages according to the purpose of usage: *general-purpose modelling languages (GPML)* and Domain- Specific Modelling languages (DSML).

A GPML provides constructs to represent multiple aspects of a system. For example, the UML and the *extensible markup language (XML)* are GPML used to model a wide variety of systems.

In contrast to GPML, DSML captures the essential concepts of a limited domain. They address specific applications. Examples of DSMLs are HTML and MATLAB.

A modelling language consists of a syntactic notation and its semantics.

2.2   MDE Languages

In this section we describe class diagram languages. We start with the UML class diagram language in Sect. 2.2.1. Then we introduce metamodelling languages where class diagrams are designed to design the abstract syntax of a new modelling language.

2.2.1   UML Class Diagram

MDE as promoted by the OMG is mostly based on UML diagrams as model descriptions. The UML [151] is a visual design notation for designing software systems. UML is a GPML, capable of capturing information about different views of systems like static structure and dynamic behaviour.

UML class diagrams are a means for describing application domains and software systems in the *instance-schema-metaschema dimension* (ISM-dimension). Instances are described as schemas, where schemas in turn are described by metaschemas. UML class diagrams have their roots in *entity-relationship* (ER) descriptions of database schemas on the one hand and in design notations for object-oriented programs on the other hand. These two areas use class diagrams for different purposes. In the context of database schemas, the usage is primarily descriptive in the sense that diagrams model concrete domains by describing concepts and their relationships. In the context of program design, the usage is primarily prescriptive in order to supply a basis for implementation.

Depending on the purpose of the diagrams, there are different semantics associated with them. In the case of a descriptive usage, an extensional semantics seems appropriate to describe the set of possible instances (the so-called extension) of a given diagram. For a prescriptive usage, the semantics of the target language is to be transferred to the diagram, which is usually an intensional semantics, since it describes the properties and the behaviour of their potential instances.

It is important to distinguish the notion of snapshot. A snapshot is the static configuration of a system at a given point in time. It consists of objects, values and links.

A class-based vocabulary $V_p = (\mathcal{D}, D)$ is a 2-tuple where $\mathcal{D}$ is a schema and D is a snapshot of $\mathcal{D}$.

Definition 1 (Schema).

$\mathcal{D}$ is a schema of the form $\mathcal{D} = (\mathcal{T}_\mathcal{D}, \mathcal{A}_\mathcal{D}, <_\mathcal{D}, \mathcal{R}_\mathcal{D}, \mathcal{O}_\mathcal{D})$ where:

1. $\mathcal{T}_\mathcal{D}$ is a set of types t of the form: $t \leftarrow \text{Class}(C) \mid \text{Datatype}(D)$ where $C, D \in \mathcal{T}_\mathcal{D}$.
2. $<_\mathcal{D}$ is a set of subtype relations in the form $C_1 < C_2$ where $C_1, C_2 \in \mathcal{T}_\mathcal{D}$.
3. $\mathcal{A}_\mathcal{D}$ is a set of functions F_a of attributes a of the form $F_a : C \rightarrow S_r$ where $C \in \mathcal{T}_\mathcal{D}$ is the domain and $S_r \in \mathcal{T}_\mathcal{D}$ is the range of a.
4. $\mathcal{R}_\mathcal{D}$ is a set of functions F_r of references r of the form: if $multiplicity(e2) > 1$, then $F_{r,e1,e2} : C \rightarrow Set(S_2)$; if $multiplicity(e2) = 1$, then $F_{r,e1,e2} : C \rightarrow S_2$ where r is an association; e_1, e_2 are association ends attached to classes; $F_{r,e1,e2} \in \mathcal{R}_\mathcal{D}$; $C \in \mathcal{T}_\mathcal{D}$ is the domain of r; $S_2 \in \mathcal{T}_\mathcal{D}$ is the range of r.
5. $\mathcal{O}_\mathcal{D}$ is a set of functions F_o of operations o of the form $F_o : S \times S_1 \times \cdots \times S_k \rightarrow S'$ where S is the domain of o; $S_{i,i\in\{1,\ldots,k\}}$ is parameter type of o; S' is result type of o; $F_o \in \mathcal{O}_\mathcal{D}$.

Definition 2 (Snapshot).

A snapshot D is a snapshot of the form $D = (I_D, V_D, L_D, AI_D, AV_D, AL_D)$ where:

1. I_D, V_D, L_D are sets of objects, values and links, respectively.
2. AI_D is a set of class assertions in the form $InstanceOf(i, C)$ where $i \in I_D$ and $C \in \mathcal{T}_\mathcal{D}$.
3. AV_D is a set of value assertions in the form $InstanceOf(v, D)$ where $v \in V_D$ and $D \in \mathcal{T}_\mathcal{D}$.
4. AL_D is a set of association assertions in the form $InstanceOf(l, R)$ where $l \in L_D$ and $R \in \mathcal{R}_\mathcal{D}$.

2.2.2 Metamodelling Language

In this section we introduce metamodelling languages used to design metamodels. In particular, we consider the MOF and the Ecore metamodelling languages.

Meta-Object Facility

The MOF is OMG's standard for defining metamodels. It provides a language for defining the abstract syntax of modelling languages. MOF is in general a minimal set of concepts which can be used for defining other modelling languages. The version 2.0 of MOF provides two metametamodels, namely *Essential MOF (EMOF)* and *Complete MOF* (CMOF).

The core of EMOF provides the capability to describe classes in the metamodel and for defining specialisation hierarchies. EMOF allows for defining properties of classes which are used either for attributing the classes (here, the property has a data type) or to define references to other classes (here, the property has a class as type).

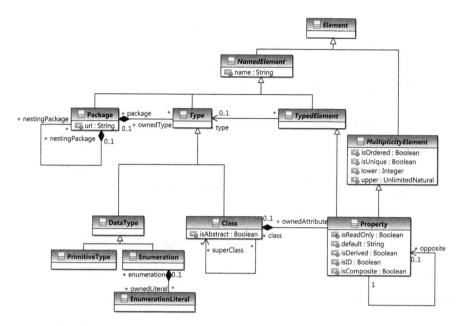

Fig. 2.1 EMOF metametamodel

Figure 2.1 depicts an excerpt of the EMOF metametamodel. Here, Classes
are NamedElements which have a number of properties and can be related by a
specialisation relationship. Each Property is an element with a multiplicity and can
be related to opposite properties. In addition, properties are TypedElements which
refer to a Type, where types are either Classes or Datatypes. Datatypes either
are PrimitiveTypes or Enumerations with literals. All types may be contained by
Packages which can be nested.

To support the attribution of associations and relations between association
types in hierarchies, MOF provides CMOF. In addition to EMOF, the CMOF
metametamodel provides the concept Association. Associations in CMOF are
classifiers which classify an object, they can be attributed and have at least two
ends, that are described by the class Property. Since associations are classifiers,
again they can be connected by associations.

Ecore

Another metametamodel is provided by the Ecore metamodelling language, which
is used in the eclipse modelling framework [39]. Ecore is an implementation of
EMOF and provides four basic constructs: (1) Class—used for representing a
modelled class. It has a name, zero or more attributes, and zero or more references.
(2) Attribute—used for representing a modelled attribute. Attributes have a name
and a type. (3) Reference—used for representing an association between classes.
(4) DataType—used for representing attribute types.

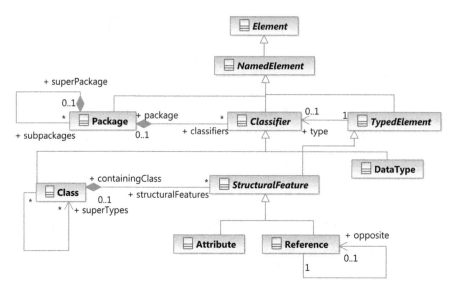

Fig. 2.2 Ecore metametamodel

An excerpt of the Ecore metametamodel is depicted in Fig. 2.2. Here, each Package consists of Classifiers which are either Classes or Datatypes. Classes contain StructuralFeatures, which are either Attributes or References. StructuralFeatures are TypedElements which refer to a Classifier as a type. In the case of References the type is a Class; in the case of Attributes, the type is a Datatype.

2.2.3 Process Modelling Languages

There are many process modelling languages existing in the MDE field. Prominent examples are *event process chains (EPC)*, UML Activity Diagrams, *yet another workflow language (YAWL)*, Petri nets and the *business process management notation (BPMN)*. For the process refinement case study in the MOST project, BPMN is chosen as the basic modelling language considered in all theoretical analysis and investigations as well as the prototype development later on (cf. Chap. 4). This is due to several reasons that will be explained in the following. These explanations also give insight about some of the languages and include a summary of comparisons of them in order to better understand the requirements which led to the choice of BPMN.

Generally one could say that EPC were one of the most used process modelling languages to design business processes in business applications since the early 1990s. At that time the *architecture integrated information systems* (ARIS) from IDS Scheer[1] were developed in a tight cooperation with SAP. Consequently, most

---

[1]http://www.ids-scheer.com/international/en

of the processes in SAP's business applications are captured and documented as EPCs. Although EPCs are widespread, the lack of standardisation and formal specification are major reasons for their dwindling in the model engineering community these days.

On the other hand, Petri nets[2] rely on a formal specification which is quite suitable for process verification and simulation. But the problem with Petri nets is their complexity for modelling roles working on a high abstraction level. In the process refinement case study many roles are addressed and it is intended to bridge the gap between Business and IT. Hence, Petri nets would meet the requirements on the IT level but would fail to fulfil the needs on the business level.

The language YAWL[3] is a very powerful modelling language and business process management system which integrates almost every concept of existing control flow-based languages. Furthermore, it extends the Petri Net theoretical foundation with additional concepts and provides modellers with strong verification and monitoring support. Unfortunately, it is not a standardised language and open source with special licences which are burdens for the use of YAWL in software companies.

After the discussion above the two remaining candidates for the process refinement case study are UML activity diagrams and BPMN[4] processes, which are both standardised by the OMG[5].

The basic difference between BPMN and UML activity diagrams can be summarised as follows: UML activity diagrams are an execution-oriented language. Their execution semantics is defined in quite some level of details, and various formal semantics of UML activity diagrams have been defined. It is feasible to build an execution engine for UML activity diagrams. On the other hand, BPMN has been designed originally with the aim of being a notation for high-level modelling. As a result in the beginnings, several constructs in BPMN, e.g., complex gateways and or-joins do not have a fully defined execution semantics, which makes the direct execution impossible if the full set of modelling entities are used.

However, recently and as a part of the strategy to bridge the gap between business and IT, SAP's endeavour was to make BPMN processes executable (at least when a core set of elements are used) without any intermediary transformation to any other execution language like BPEL. The rationale behind this decision is that BPMN can then be used by business experts, process analysts and process developers homogeneously through the entire company. By doing so, firstly, education efforts will be reduced in a company and its ecosystem of partners and customers. Furthermore, unnecessary model transformations from high-level models to detailed execution specific models which are often based on different metameta- and metamodels become superfluous.

---

[2]http://www.informatik.uni-hamburg.de/TGI/PetriNets/

[3]http://www.yawl-system.com

[4]http://www.bpmn.org

[5]http://www.omg.org

2.2.4 Domain-Specific Language

DSLs are used to model and develop systems of particular application domains. Such languages are high-level and provide abstractions and notations for better understanding and easier modelling using concepts and notations that are familiar to domain experts. Often, a variety of different DSLs is used simultaneously to describe the system from several viewpoints [116]. In the context of MDE, DSL models may be combined with other models in standardised languages to form a complete and consistent overall model of the system under development.

Domain-specific modelling aims to raise the level of abstraction beyond programming languages and source code by modelling the solution in a language that directly uses concepts and rules from a specific problem domain.

Like other modelling languages DSLs must be defined formally to be supported by tools. Here, metamodelling is used as well-known way to describe languages. An important framework for defining languages is the OMG four-layer modelling architecture [23]. In such a modelling architecture the M0-layer represents the real-world objects and systems. Domain models are defined at the M1-layer, a simplification and abstraction of the M0-layer. Models at the M1-layer are defined using domain concepts which are described by metamodels at the M2-layer. Furthermore, metamodels are annotated with constraints and rules to restrict the use of concepts it provides. Thus, each metamodel at the M2-layer determines how expressive its models can be. Analogously, metamodels are defined by using concepts described as metametamodels at the M3-layer.

The metamodel defines the abstract syntax of a DSL. The concrete syntax is used to make models readable and more easily understandable by humans. Here, the syntax varies between textual concrete syntaxes and graphical concrete syntaxes. Each concept defined in the metamodel should have one representation in the concrete syntax. In the case of textual concrete syntaxes, models are created by textual editors. Different frameworks (e.g., [92]) exist to parse and print these models to represent them as an abstract syntax model (the instances of the metamodel). In the case of graphical concrete syntaxes, the abstract syntax models are visualised by graphical elements.

Model transformations are used to translate models represented in one language into models represented in another language. In particular, code generators produce code from domain models. This helps in raising the abstraction, as mentioned above, moving away from (general purpose) programming languages towards modelling languages with concepts and rules of a particular domain [116].

For modelling the static structure of a system under study structural DSLs are considered. Popular structural modelling languages are those for modelling data structures or database schemas or to model the application structure. Furthermore, the UML provides some prominent structural modelling languages, e.g., for class diagrams or component diagrams.

2.2.5   Graph-Based Languages

Before the advent of current metamodelling languages such as MOF or Ecore (see Sect. 2.2.2), graphs have been identified as suitable data structure for the representation of software engineering artefacts [141]. Thus, various graph-based modelling approaches together with respective *repository tools*, serving to hold the abstract syntax of artefacts, have evolved. One of them is the *TGraph approach* [62, 63], whose modelling part, consisting of TGraphs themselves and the metamodelling language *grUML* [28] (*graph UML*), is presented in the following. This section is concluded by a short comparison to similar approaches.

The TGraph approach has been successfully applied in various fields, such as the development of meta-case tools [64], the definition of metamodels for visual languages [220], reengineering [65], or the storage of traceability information [185].

TGraphs

TGraphs are a very general kind of graphs and are underpinned by a formal mathematical definition (see Definition 3). In particular, TGraphs are:

- *Typed*, i.e., vertices, edges and the graph itself have a type.
- *Attributed*, i.e., vertices, edges and the graph itself can carry attribute–value pairs.
- *Directed*, i.e., edges have a start and an end vertex.
- *Ordered*, i.e., vertices and edges are globally ordered within the graph. Further, the incident edges of a vertex are ordered.

A further distinctive feature of TGraphs is that edges are first-class citizens, meaning that they are granted the same status as vertices. They can be explicitly referred to and stored in variables, for instance.

Definition 3 (TGraph). Let:

- *Vertex* be the universe of *vertices*
- *Edge* be the universe of *edges*
- *TypeId* be the universe of *type identifiers*
- *AttrId* be the universe of *attribute identifiers*
- *Value* be the universe of *attribute values*

Assuming two finite sets:

- A *vertex set* $V \subseteq Vertex$
- An *edge set* $E \subseteq Edge$

be given. $G = (Vseq, Eseq, Aseq, type, value)$ is a *TGraph* iff:

- $Vseq \in \text{iseq } V$ is a *permutation* of V.
- $Eseq \in \text{iseq } E$ is a *permutation* of E.

Fig. 2.3 BPMN diagram in concrete syntax

- Λseq : $V \rightarrow$ iseq($E \times \{in, out\}$) is an *incidence function* where
  $\forall e \in E : \exists!v, w \in V : (e, out) \in \text{ran } \Lambda seq(v) \wedge (e, in) \in \text{ran } \Lambda seq(w)$.
- $Type : V \cup E \rightarrow TypeId$ is a *type function.*
- $Value : V \cup E \rightarrow (AttrId \twoheadrightarrow Value)$ is an *attribute function* where $\forall x, y \in$
  $V \cup E : type(x) = type(y) \Rightarrow \text{dom}(value(x)) = \text{dom}(value(y))$.

Explanation:

- iseq S: the set of duplicate-free sequences over the set S
- ran R: the range of the binary relation R
- dom R: the domain of the binary relation R
- $X \twoheadrightarrow Y$: a finite partial function from X to Y

For an example, consider Fig. 2.3, which shows a simple process model represented in BPMN (business process modelling notation) is a standardised language for process modelling [145]. The example model shows a possible process of some organisation for hiring new staff. Starting at the *start event* (represented by the circle with the thin border), the *sequence flow* (represented by the arrows) goes to the first *task* of the process, HR-Approval. This task is concerned with the decision of whether new staff is to be hired at all. The following *exclusive gateway* (the diamond) denotes that depending on the outcome of that decision, the process may either continue with the tasks Interview Approval and Hiring or directly proceed to the *end event* (the circle with the thick border), where the process is terminated.

Figure 2.4 shows a TGraph representing the abstract syntax of the BPMN diagram. Although only a single BPMN model is depicted here, such graphs shall serve to represent BPMN refinement chains where more specific process models refine the tasks of more abstract models. Therefore, the type of the graph itself is called BPMNRefinementChain. Its vertices are of different types: the BPMNModel itself, containing the individual diagram objects, as well as the object types Task, Event and Gateway. Similarly, edges are either instances of SequenceFlow or of Contains, with the latter denoting the containment relationship between the BPMNModel and its objects. Depending on their type, graph elements possess different attributes. While the names of the BPMNModel and of the Tasks are of type String, the type attributes of Event and Gateway vertices are of user-defined enumeration types.

Edge directions are displayed as arrowheads. For illustrative purposes, the global orders of vertices and edges are represented by their identifiers v1–v8 and e1–e14. The order of the vertices' incident edges is annotated by the numbers in parentheses. While not being important for the BPMN example, incidence orders may play a

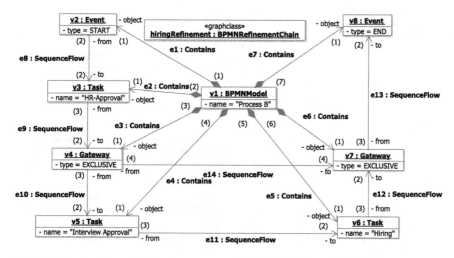

Fig. 2.4 TGraph representing the abstract syntax of the BPMN diagram in Fig. 2.3

significant role in other applications. For a source code statement, the sequence of its contained keywords and expressions may be represented by the incidence order of the edges connecting the statement vertex to its parts, for instance.

grUML

Analogous to MOF, the TGraph approach follows a four-layered meta-hierarchy, with TGraphs themselves being situated on the M1 layer (with run-time instances on M0). Their metamodels, the so-called *schemas*, are represented in grUML, reside on the M2 layer and conform to the fixed grUML *metaschema* on M3.

grUML is actually a subset of UML class diagrams, adopting those concepts which feature a graph-like semantics. In detail, vertex types and their attributes are modelled by classes with attributes. Edge types are represented by associations, potentially adorned by a transparent or opaque diamond in the case aggregation or composition semantics are exhibited, respectively. For edge types possessing attributes, association classes are used. Note, that association classes must not be connected by associations. The direction of edges is denoted by the reading direction of associations representing their edge classes. Multiplicities are used to specify degree restrictions, i.e., they limit the number of vertices a given vertex may be connected to by edges of the respective type.

In addition, it is allowed to model generalisation relationships between vertex classes as well as between edge classes. In doing so, the specialisations inherit the attributes of their supertypes. Furthermore, instances of a specialising vertex class may be incident to edges being instance of an edge class actually connecting to the super vertex classes. Analogously, instances of a specialising edge class may also relate vertices which are instances of the vertex classes connected to the super edge class.

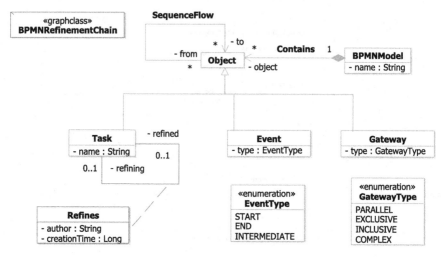

Fig. 2.5 grUML schema for BPMN

Finally, a dedicated class with the stereotype graphclass is employed to specify the type of the graphs conforming to a schema.

Figure 2.5 shows a schema for the sample graph in Fig. 2.4. Note that in order to represent refinement relationships between Tasks, the schema includes the Refines edge class, which are not used in Fig. 2.4.

In Fig. 2.6, a simplified version of the grUML metaschema is shown. Besides the already mentioned concepts of VertexClass, EdgeClass and GraphClass, generalised by AttributedElementClass, some further metaclasses are defined. They include the Schema itself which contains the other elements via a mandatory default Package and, optionally, other sub-Packages used for structuring purposes. The edge classes depicted as associations in grUML are actually the concrete syntax for an instance of EdgeClass together with two Incidences as starting and ending points. For reasons of brevity, the specialisations of the abstract metaclass Domain, representing the domains of Attributes, are omitted in the figure. They include simple domains such as Boolean, Integer or String, as well as the composite domains Set, List or Record, for instance.

A TGraph conforms to a grUML schema if the following conditions are met. First, the types and attribute assignments of the graph, its vertices and edges have to adhere to the specifications of the schema. Second, edges must be incident to instances of the vertex classes prescribed by the schema. Finally, vertex degrees have to respect the given multiplicities.

Comparison to Other Modelling Approaches

Examples for other graph-based approaches combined with a respective toolset are LEDA [130], GRAS [118] and its successor DRAGOS [29]. The graphs used by

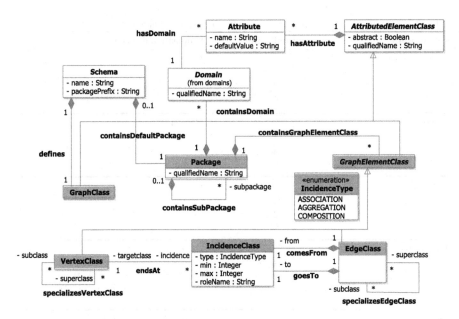

Fig. 2.6 grUML metaschema (simplified)

these approaches are of varying expressiveness: while LEDA supports directed and ordered graphs, GRAS features a type system and attributes for vertices but lacks an edge ordering. DRAGOS extends these capabilities by allowing edge attributes. Regarding these aspects, all three approaches fail to achieve the expressiveness of TGraphs. However, DRAGOS offers a rudimentary concept for nesting graphs within each other, which is not yet supported by the TGraph approach.

Compared to EMOF and Ecore, it can be stated that the expressiveness of the TGraph approach is somewhat higher. In particular, while TGraphs treat edges as first-class objects, EMOF and Ecore model relations between two objects as two special properties, one belonging to each object, representing references to the respective other object. Unlike TGraph edges, these connections do not have an identity and cannot be typed or attributed. Another benefit of TGraphs is that they feature orderings for their elements, i.e., a global ordering of vertices, a global ordering of edges and orderings of the incident edges at each vertex.

2.2.6   Feature Modelling Languages

Feature models are important structural modelling languages particularly used in software product line engineering (SPLE) [165] . They support the systematic analysis and specification of variability amongst a set of related software products. Using features and various relationships amongst them, feature models describe common and variable functionality or properties and constrain allowed feature

Table 2.1 Feature relationships and their semantics in propositional logic

Relationship	Visualisation	Propositional formula
Parent–Child	P — C	$C \rightarrow P$
Mandatory	P — M	$P \rightarrow M$
Optional	P — O	–
Alternative	P — $A_1 \cdots A_n$	$P \rightarrow$ $((A_1 \wedge (\neg A_2 \wedge \cdots \wedge \neg A_n)) \vee$ $(A_2 \wedge (\neg A_1 \wedge \cdots \wedge \neg A_n)) \vee \cdots \vee$ $(A_n \wedge (\neg A_1 \wedge \cdots \wedge \neg A_{n-1})))$
Or	P — $O_1 \cdots O_n$	$P \rightarrow (O_1 \vee \cdots \vee O_n)$
Requires	F → R	$F \rightarrow R$
Conflicts	C_1 ◄/► C_2	$\neg C_1 \vee \neg C_2$

combinations that apply for all product variants. For the specification of a single, concrete variant, *variant models* select a subset of the features in a product line's feature model. Using this variant model a variant-specific product can be derived from software components that implement the respective features. Thus, feature modelling provides a foundation for the efficient mass-customisation of customer-specific software variants.

In the context of this book, feature models are used for two purposes: First, the simple basic structure and the expressive but intuitive semantics of feature relationships (cf. Table 2.1) make feature analysis an interesting case study to explore the potential and contributions of ontology technology for semantics validation of structural modelling languages. Second, we will apply the notion of feature models to characterise and manage variability found for the application of ontology technology in MDSD.

Feature Model Notation

There exists a variety of feature modelling languages that are built around the concept of features and feature relationships. The first feature model was introduced by Kang et al. [114] and denotes a hierarchically organised set of features. The following relations are typically used to build and restrict the feature hierarchy:

Parent–Child Relationship   Every feature model has a root feature with a set of child features. Each feature can again have children and so on. Using these simple parent–child relationships, feature models build a tree structure. These parent–child relationships implicitly require the inclusion of the parent feature when its child feature(s) is meant to be included in variant.

Mandatory Features   Each feature is either mandatory or optional w.r.t its parent feature. Mandatory means that the feature needs to be included in every variant its parent is included in.

Optional Features   An optional feature can be optionally included when their parents are selected for a variant.

Alternative Features   A set of child features can be in an alternative relationship which means that exactly one of the features has to be included in the variant model if their common parent is included.

Or Features   A set of child features can be in an or relationship which means that at least on of the features has to be included in the variant model if their common parent is included.

Besides these basic relationships a feature model can be complemented by additional cross-tree relationships. They are used to express implications and conflicts between features that are not related hierarchically.

Requires   A pair of features can be in a requires relationship which means that the inclusion of the first feature requires the inclusion of the second feature.

Conflicts   A pair of features can be in a conflict relationship which means that the inclusion of either feature prohibits inclusion of the other feature.

A general way to describe the semantics of feature relations are propositional formulas [18]. Table 2.1 introduces a graphical notation for the discussed relationships and concludes their semantics using propositional formulas.

In addition, various extensions to the original feature modelling constructs, e.g., cardinality-based features, feature groups [53] and feature attributes [52], were suggested. As their benefit and meaning is still discussed controversially, in practice, we will focus on the basic relations introduced above.

Feature Analysis

In practice, feature models can become very large. Detecting, understanding and repairing inconsistencies in feature models and variant models with a various number of explicit and implicit relationships make the automated analysis of feature models and variant models an important but complex task. The following questions are of particular importance during feature analysis.

Q1: Feature Model Validity: Does a given feature model allow for building at least a single variant or does it contain relationships that impose conflicting constraints?

Q2: Feature Model Debugging: If a given feature model is invalid which particular constraints cause such invalidity?

Q3: Feature Model Repair: Given a set of causes for invalidity how can the feature model be repaired?

Q4: Variant Model Validity: Does a given variant model conform to all implicit and explicit constraints imposed by the corresponding feature model?

Q5: Variant Model Debugging: If a given variant model is invalid, which constraints are unsatisfied and which features are causing the invalidity?

Q6: Variant Model Repair: Given a set of features and constraints that cause invalidity, how can the variant model be repaired?

Q7: Variant Model Completion: If a given variant model and is invalid and considered incomplete, are there inclusion or exclusions of features that could complete the variant model to a valid configuration?

Wang et. al [215] already explored the application of description logics to provide a formalisation for feature models and to use ontology reasoning for validation and debugging of feature and variant specifications. In Sect. 9.2 we will discuss an extension of this approach and demonstrate the potential and benefits of applying ontology technology and reasoning to answer the introduced questions Q1–Q7.

2.3   Two-Dimensional Modelling

The physical devices DSL language, introduced in Sect. 4.1, contains both the concepts that refer to the types of the devices (e.g., the Cisco 7603 router model) as well as the instances of these types (e.g., a concrete Cisco 7603 router operating in the network). Therefore, the case study relates to the *two-dimensional metamodelling architecture*, with both the *linguistic instantiation* and the *ontological instantiation* (see Fig. 2.7).

The diagram consists of the two *linguistic* layers:

* The M2 layer contains the PDDSL metamodel.
* The M1 layer contains the PDDSL model.

   Also, the two *ontological* layers are outlined:

* The O2 layer describes the types of the physical devices.
* The O1 layer describes the instances of the physical devices.

The `instance_of` relationship between elements of the layers M1 and M2 is the *linguistic* instantiation relationship (specifies a linguistic type of the modelling object), e.g., `Cisco7603` is the instance of the `DeviceType` metaconcept. The M1 layer `hasType` relationship between elements of the layers O1 and O2 is

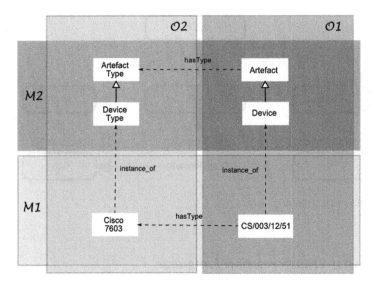

Fig. 2.7 Two-dimensional metamodelling in the PDDSL case

ontological instantiation relationship (specifies the domain type of the modelling object), e.g., the Cisco7603 is the domain type of the ''CS/003/12/51'' device.

The similar hasType association on the M2 layer represents the *linguistic* definition of the *ontological* instantiation relationship. It connects two classes, the Artefact and the ArtefactType, on M2. These two classes are fundamental for the PDDSL metamodel, which is depicted in Fig. 2.7. The Artefact is a common supertype for all classes that constitute the O1 layer, such as Slot, Card and Device. The ArtefactType is a common supertype for all classes that constitute the O2 layer, such as SlotType, CardType and DeviceType.

The reason why we define the hasType relationship explicitly in the metamodel is that our case does not fit into a single type/instance level architecture. However, despite the metamodel definition containing the hasType relationship, such an association has no specific meaning to the modelling tools. For instance, the model elements located in the layers M2, O2 have no role in determining whether their instances in the layers M1, O1 are well formed.

2.4   Model Transformation Languages

In this section we present model transformation languages. In particular, we introduce the atlas transformation language in Sect. 2.4.1 and the graph repository transformation language (GReTL) in Sect. 2.4.2.

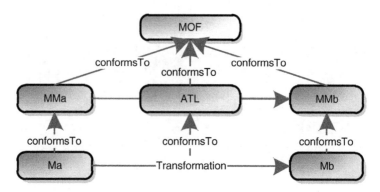

Fig. 2.8 Model Transformation with ATL

2.4.1 Atlas Transformation Language

The *atlas transformation language (ATL)* is developed as a part of the *ATLAS model management architecture (AMMA)* platform [25]. ATL is a hybrid language, ,i.e., it is a mix of declarative and imperative constructs. ATL is used to transform a source model Ma into a target model Mb. The transformation is defined by a transformation definition written in the ATL language and follows the transformation pattern defined in Fig. 2.8. Here, the transformation definition is a model. The source and target models and the transformation definition conform to their metamodels MMa, MMb and ATL, respectively. In the case of ATL, all metamodels conform to the MOF metametamodel [108].

ATL transformations are unidirectional, operating on read-only source models and producing a write-only target model. During the execution of a transformation the source model may be navigated but changes are not allowed. Target model cannot be navigated.

Transformation definitions in ATL consist of modules. A module contains a mandatory header section, import section and a number of helpers and transformation rules. Header section gives the name of a transformation module and declares the source and target models. Helpers are used to perform navigation over the source models. They are specified in OCL. The basic construct of ATL are rules. Rules express the transformation logic. A rule is composed of a source pattern and of a target pattern. Rule source pattern specifies a set of source types (coming from source metamodels and the set of collection types available in OCL) and a guard (as a Boolean expression in OCL). A source pattern is evaluated to a set of matches in source models. The target pattern is composed of a set of elements. Each of these elements specifies a target type (from the target metamodel) and a set of bindings. A binding refers to a feature of the type (i.e., an attribute, a reference or association end) and specifies an expression whose value is used to initialise the feature.

2.4.2   *Graph Repository Transformation Language*[*]

The *graph repository transformation language (GReTL)*, [96] is a language for transforming TGraphs *and* TGraph schemas. In contrast to other transformation languages, the target schemas of GReTL transformations do not need to be predefined, but can be created in the course of the transformations. GReTL not only comes with a Java framework for the programmatic development of transformations, but also provides a concrete syntax that is independent of the programming language.

In the following, GReTL is introduced by giving an overview of the GReTL Java framework and by describing the elementary transformation operations. Finally, GReTL is shortly compared to ATL and QVT Operational Mappings.

Transformations as Java Objects

GReTL is based on a Java framework that is integrated with the *JGraLab* library for handling TGraphs (see Sect. 2.2.5). In detail, the GReTL framework provides an abstract class **Transformation** and a set of concrete subclasses that implement a set of elementary transformation operations. Transformation developers may write their own transformations by specifying their own subclasses of **Transformation**. These subclasses override the abstract transform() method of **Transformation** and call elementary operations to appropriately realise the intended behaviour. When instantiating a **Transformation** subclass, an instance of the helper class **Context** has to be passed to the constructor. It specifies the source schema and graph(s) and will contain a reference to the target graph after the execution of the transformation. GReTL's concrete syntax basically uses similar constructs, but does without syntactical details of the Java programming language, such as parentheses, commas and semicolons.

Realising GReTL transformations in Java facilitates their efficient reuse. First, it is possible to further subclass concrete transformations in order to inherit from them and extend their behaviour. Second, already existing transformations may be called out of a given transformation, thus giving the possibility to factor out frequently used fragments. Since the mappings between a transformation's source and target elements are centrally held by the **Context** object, these mappings are also available outside a specific transformation object and can be used amongst nested transformations.

The bijective mappings between a transformation's source and target elements, called *archetypes* and *images*, respectively, are centrally retained by the **Context** object. In detail, the bijection img_T maps archetypes to their images and $arch_T$ maps images to archetypes, with T being the schema element the target elements conform to. These mappings can be accessed by elementary transformation operations other than that which created the mappings. The mappings are also available outside a specific transformation object and can be used amongst nested transformations. An export operation allows to persist the mappings in an XML file.

Transformation Operations

As mentioned above, subclasses of the abstract Transformation class provide elementary transformation operations to be used in transformations, e.g., CreateVertexClass, CreateEdgeClass or CreateAttribute. These classes are derived from the grUML metaschema (see Sect. 2.2.5) and are used to create the elements of the target schema together with their instances. The static properties of the schema element to be created, such as the name or, in the case of an edge class, the start and end vertex classes, are passed as parameters to the constructors of these classes. Furthermore, a so-called semantic expression is passed, corresponding to a Graph repository query language (GReQL) expression specifying the set of instances to be created for the given schema element. Usually, the expression returns a set of source graph elements so that for each of those elements a new element in the target graph is created. The elements of the set returned by the semantic expression are the archetypes.

Analogous to the creation of new schema elements together with their instances, it is possible to create instances of already existing schema classes. The according subclasses of Transformation are createVertices(), createEdges() and SetAttributes(). Besides the semantic expression, they take only the name of an existing schema element as parameter.

Consider the following example for an illustration of the described concepts. It is based on the BPMN refinement example introduced in Sect. 2.2.5. In Fig. 2.5, page 32, a TGraph schema for BPMN refinement chains is introduced. To assist developers in the identification of Refines edges between Tasks contained by a more abstract and a more specific process model in a BPMN refinement chain, i.e., if some (manually created) Refines edges already exist between two Tasks, additional Refines edges between two Tasks of the same name shall be automatically generated. This implies that the Task in the more specific model has been adopted unchanged from the more abstract model.

Figure 2.9 shows the GReTL implementation of the transformation described above. While the constructor passes the Context instance holding information on the source and target graph to the constructor of the superclass Transformation, the actual transformation is specified in the method transform(). In lines 7–8, a predefined copy transformation is called. It copies the source graph to the target graph without any changes. The additional Refines edges are created in lines 10–18. Since the Refines edge class, created by the copy transformation, already exists in the target schema, the CreateEdges() class is used. The GReQL query passed as semantic expression returns a set of triples. Such a triple consists of the archetype of the created edge itself, its start vertex and its end vertex. In this case, the archetypes are pairs of Tasks denoted by the variables refining and refined. In addition to the conditions described above, i.e., the names of refining and refined must be identical (line 12) and the model containing refining contains another Task refining a Task contained by the model of refined (lines 13–14), it is ensured that refining and refined are not already connected by a Refines edge (line 15).

```
1   public class RefinementIdentification extends Transformation {
2
3       public RefinementIdentification(Context context) { super(context); }
4
5       @Override
6       protected void transform() {
7                   Transformation copy = new CopyTransformation(context);
8                   copy.execute();
9
10                  new CreateEdges(context, ec("Refines"),
11                  "from refining, refined: V{Task},                          "
12                + "with refining.name = refined.name                        "
13                + "     and refining <--{Contains} -->{Contains} -->{Refines} "
14                + "                   <--{Contains} -->{Contains} refined      "
15                + "     and not refining -->{Refines} refined                "
16                + "reportSet tup(refining, refined), refining, refined       "
17                + "end                                                       "
18              );
19
20          new SetAttributes(context, attr("Refines.author"),
21                + "from key: keySet(img_Refines) "
22                + "reportMap key, \"generated\"   "
23                + "end                            "
24              );
25
26          long currentTime = System.currentTimeMillis();
27
28          new SetAttributes(context, attr("Refines.creationTime"),
29                + "from key: keySet(img_Refines) "
30                + "reportMap key,                " + currentTime
31                + "end                           "
32              );
33      }
34  }
```

Fig. 2.9 GReTL transformation example

The method calls in lines 20–24 and 28–32 are responsible for setting the values of the author and creationTime attributes of the Refines edges. The attribute values are set according to the map returned by the GReQL queries passed as parameter. They map each member of the archetype set of Refines to the appropriate values, i.e., the String generated for the author attribute and the current time as value of domain Long for creationTime.

An example BPMN diagram serving as source for this transformation is shown in Fig. 2.10. The figure shows an abstract process model whose task Hiring has been refined by the tasks Select Applicant and Hire Applicant in the specific model. The respective Refines edges have been created manually. Now, the RefinementIdentification transformation is applied to automatically generate the Refines edges between the unchanged tasks. The resulting target diagram is illustrated in Fig. 2.11 (using the BPMN concrete syntax).

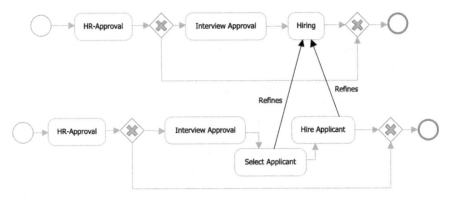

Fig. 2.10 BPMN diagram serving as transformation source

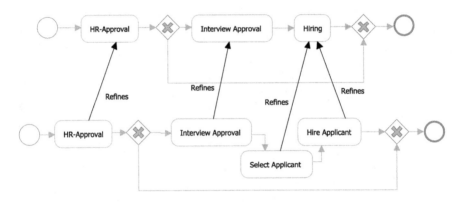

Fig. 2.11 BPMN diagram resulting from transformation

Comparison to Other Transformation Languages

The transformation approach pursued by GReTL is quite different from that taken by ATL. ATL transformations are specified in the form of declarative rules, whose order of application is determined by the ATL transformation machine. In contrast, GReTL transformations adhere to the Java execution semantics. To allow an ATL rule to access the elements created by other rules, various techniques have to be considered by the developers, while GReTL provides uniform access to this information via the img_T and $arch_T$ mappings.

Another important difference stems from the treatment of relations in the underlying modelling languages. While in TGraphs, edges are first-class objects, the equivalent concepts in the EMOF/Ecore technological space are references which are part of the entities to be related. Consequently, TGraph edges are explicitly created by GReTL transformations, but EMOF/Ecore references are created along with the ATL transformation rules responsible for the generation of the entities.

With GReTL, it is always possible to create all edges after all vertices have been created. The ATL approach may cause cyclic dependencies which have to resolved using the delayed assignment of references.

Comparing GReTL to *operational QVT language (QVTO)*, it is discernible that due to the operational semantics of QVTO, these two languages have more in common than GReTL with ATL. However, similar to ATL, accessing target elements of other transformation operations in QVTO is more complicated than with using GReTL. Furthermore, QVTO also suffers from the possibility of cyclic dependencies due to the representation of relations as references in EMOF/Ecore, making delayed assignment of references necessary. A benefit of QVTO is the availability of various extensions which ease developers' work in creating transformations by facilitating reuse.

2.5   Constraint and Query Languages

In this section we introduce constraint languages. Constraint languages are used to restrict the structure of instance models by annotating respective metamodel/schema elements with respective constraints.

2.5.1   *The Object Constraint Language*

UML class diagrams alone are not expressive enough to describe the behaviour of operations. For example, developers might want to define an operation that queries whether a given sales order is duty free or not. In common UML modelling practice, a textual query language such as *object constraint language (OCL)* [148] may be used to specify such a query.

Beyond querying, OCL may also be used to specify invariants on classes and types in the class model, to describe pre- and post-conditions on operations and methods and to specify initial and derived rules over a UML model [148].

The OCL syntax differs from well-known query languages like SQL and SPARQL. Indeed, SQL and SPARQL do not require a starting point for querying, i.e., it takes a global point of view. OCL, on the other hand, takes the object-oriented point of view, starting the queries from one given instance.

In OCL, expressions are written "in the context of an instance of an specific type" [148]. The reserved word **self** is used to denote this instance.

OCL expressions may be used to specify the body of query operations. Since OCL is a typed language, i.e., each OCL expression is evaluated to a value, expressions may be chained to specify complex queries or invariants.

OCL defines a predefined class called `OclAny`, which acts as a superclass for all the types except for the OCL predefined `collection` types. Hence, features of `OclAny` are available on each object in all OCL expressions, and all classes in a UML model inherit all operations defined on OclAny. We highlight two of these operations:

- oclIsTypeOf(typespec: OclType): Boolean. Evaluates to true if the given object is of the type identified by typespec
- oclIsKindOf(typespec: OclType): Boolean. Evaluates to true if the object is of the type identified by typespec or one of its subtypes

Let us exemplify these operations. The first one evaluates to true if we have an instance of SalesOrder and ask whether it is an instance of SalesOrder. The second one evaluates to true if the prior example evaluates to true or if we have an instance of USSalesOrder and ask whether it is an instance of SalesOrder, *but not the opposite.*

Semantics

The specification of OCL is given in natural language, although an informative formal semantics is annexed to the specification. Despite this informative formal semantics based on [177], other strategies have been used to define the semantics of OCL.

Roe et al.[178] have proposed mappings between UML models incorporating OCL constraints and Object-Z[197]. Object-Z prescribes a formal specification for object-orientation extending the language Z.

Schmitt et al.[181] propose a model theoretic Semantics of UML class diagrams and OCL. It defines the semantics of model properties and excludes the previous values of properties in post-conditions. This work was extended later to deal with this issue, when translating OCL into dynamic logic.

Additionally, Beckert *et al.* proposes a translation of OCL into first-order predicate logic [19].

Bucker presents a representation of the semantics of OCL in higher-order logic [36]. The proof calculi allowing the implementation of an OCL reasoner is defined in [37].

Complexity

In spite of the available semantics of OCL described above, reasoning with OCL is undecidable in worst case scenario.

2.5.2   Graph Repository Query Language(*)

GReQL [61, 122] is part of the TGraph approach and allows to query TGraphs, but also supports access to TGraph schemas. GReQL is an expression language, meaning that its basic language elements are expressions which can be combined to form more complex expressions. GReQL also provides a user-extensible function library of about 100 functions from different domains, including logics, arithmetics and operations on collections such as lists or sets, as well as from graph analysis. A parser and evaluator for GReQL is part of the JGraLab library (see Sect. 2.2.5).

Due to the multitude of different language constructs, only the most important ones can be described in the following introduction to the GReQL language. They include *regular path expressions* (*RPEs*), from-with-report (*FWR*) expressions and *quantified* expressions. At the end of this section, a short comparison of GReQL to other query languages, most importantly OCL, can be found.

Regular Path Expressions

RPEs serve to describe the structure of paths in graphs. They are used as stand-alone expressions, but embedded in other kinds of expressions. Examples are *path existence* expressions to return a Boolean value depending on whether there is a path conforming to the RPE between two vertices or not, *backward vertex set* expressions to compute the set of vertices from which a given vertex can be reached by paths conforming to the RPE or *forward vertex set* expressions to determine the set of vertices reachable from a given vertex. The examples given below refer to the graph in Fig. 2.4. For illustrative purposes, identifiers in the examples such as v2 or e5 act as variables referring to the respective graph elements. In "real" GReQL expressions, this binding of variables to elements has to be conducted by the users.

The elementary constructs of RPEs are *simple path descriptions* describing single edges which may be directed or otherwise restricted.

```
1   v5 <-> v7
2   <-- v3
3   v4 -->{SequenceFlow}
```

The path existence expression in line 1 tests if v5 and v7 are connected by any single edge (*false*). The backward vertex set expression in line 2 gives back all vertices from which v3 is reachable by following any edge in backward direction ({v4}). Finally, the forward vertex set expression in line 3 features an *edge restriction* and returns the set of vertices reachable from v4 via a SequenceFlow edge in forward direction ({v5, v7}).

By using regular expression operations, i.e., concatenation, option, grouping, alternation and iteration, simple path descriptions can be combined to form more complex expressions.

```
4   v6 --> <--{SequenceFlow} [<--]
5   (-->{Contains} | -->{SequenceFlow}) v5
6   v1 -->{SequenceFlow}+ v8
```

The forward vertex set expression in line 4 returns the set of vertices reachable from v7 by first following any edge in forward direction, then a SequenceFlow edge in backward direction, and optionally again any edge in backward direction ({v1, v3, v5}). Line 5 yields those vertices from which v5 is reachable by following either a Contains edge or a SequenceFlow edge in forward direction ({v1, v4}). Line 6 checks whether there exists a path of one or more SequenceFlow edges in forward direction from v1 to v8 (*true*).

Other RPE features worth mentioning are *start vertex restrictions* and *goal vertex restrictions* which constrain the start and end vertices of path expressions, respectively. Furthermore, by using *intermediate vertex path descriptions*, it is possible to refer to specific vertices on paths. Analogously, *edge path restrictions* allow to refer to specific edges.

```
7   {BPMNModel @ thisVertex.name = "Process B"}&<-- v3
8   v4 <--{SequenceFlow}&{Object}*
9   v3 -->{SequenceFlow}&{Gateway} -->{SequenceFlow} v5
10  v4 --e14-> v7 <-e13-> v8
```

The start vertex restriction in line 7 ensures that the backward vertex set to be computed only includes instances of BPMNModel with name = "Process B" ({v1}). Line 8 uses a goal vertex restriction to get the set of vertices reachable from v4 by a sequence of any number of SequenceFlows, traversed in backward direction and each one ending at an instance of Object ({v2, v3}). The expression in line 9 (*true*) shows the usage of vertex restrictions in the middle of a path expression. In this example, it is checked whether there is a path from v3 via a SequenceFlow to a Gateway and another SequenceFlow to v5 (*true*). By using an intermediate vertex path description and two edge path descriptions, the expression in line 10 checks if there is a path from v4 via e14–v7 and further via e13–v8. While e14 must be traversed in forward direction, the direction of e13 is insignificant (*true*).

from-with-report Expressions

FWR expressions return a bag, i.e., a multiset of tuples, with their elements for most applications being vertices, edges or attribute values. In particular, an FWR expression's from part binds variables to domains. In the with part, a Boolean expression specifies constraints which have to be met by variable values eligible to be included in the returned bag. Finally, the report part determines the structure of the returned bag. In place of report, reportSet can be used to return a set instead of a bag.

```
from m:V{BPMNModel}, o:V{Object}
with m -->{Contains} o
report m, o
end
```

This query returns a bag of tuples (*m*, *o*) with *m* and *o* being instances of BPMN-Model and Object, respectively. *m* must be connected to *o* by a Contains edge. For the graph in Fig. 2.4, the resulting bag would be {(v1, v2), (v1, v3), ..., (v1, v8)}.

Since TGraphs treat edges as first-class citizens, the above FWR expression could be rewritten to an equivalent expression which only uses a single variable, bound to the set of instances of the Contains edge class. The start and end vertices of those edges are accessed by the functions startVertex() and endVertex(), respectively:

```
from c:E{Contains}
report startVertex(c), endVertex(o)
end
```

Quantified Expressions

Quantified expressions are categorised into universally, existentially and uniquely quantified expressions. They check whether all, some or exactly one element(s) of a given collection fulfils a specific Boolean expression, respectively.

The example below illustrates the structure of quantified expressions: subsequently to one of the keywords forall, exists or exists!, one or more variable declarations are following. The domains of the variables may be further restricted by an optional Boolean expression following a comma. The Boolean expression which has to be checked is then specified after an @-sign. Line 1 asserts that all Event vertices with type = START do not have any incoming Sequence-Flow edges (*true*). Line 2 ensures that there does not exist any BPMNModel instance with the empty string as value for name (*true*). Finally, line 3 ensures that there is exactly one Task with name = "Interview" (*false*).

```
1  forall e:V{Event}, e.type = START @ inDegree{SequenceFlow}(e) = 0
2  not exists m:V{BPMNModel} @ e.name = ""
3  exists! t:V{Task} @ t.name = "Interview"
```

Path Systems and Slices

Essentially, *path systems* and *slices* can be regarded as subgraphs of a queried TGraph. Path systems are determined with respect to a given vertex and an RPE. For each vertex that is reachable from the given vertex by a path conforming to the RPE, the path system contains exactly one of these paths. Slices, on the other hand, are computed based on a set of vertices and an RPE and include all paths that start at some vertex in the set and conform to the RPE.

The following example GReQL expressions for the computation of path systems and slices refer to the graph in Fig. 2.4:

```
1  pathSystem(v4, (-->{SequenceFlow} | --> --> -->))
2  slice({v4}, (-->{SequenceFlow} | --> --> -->))
```

The path system determined by the function call in line 1 includes only one path from v4 to v7, e.g., (v4, e14, v7), although there is a second one conforming to the given RPE: (v4, e10, v5, e11, v6, e12, v7). Both paths are contained in the slice computed in line 2.

Comparison to Other Query Languages

There exist various query languages which are comparable to GReQL as they operate on graph-like data structures. Amongst the most popular ones are the XML query language *XPath* [21] and the RDF query language *SPARQL* [167]. Examples for other, less known languages are *Gram* [4], *GraphQL* [89] and *PQL* [95]. Although these languages use different data structures, and possess different constructs, arguably GReQL with its RPEs offers the most expressive form of describing path structures [61].

Compared to OCL, GReQL is of similar expressiveness, so that it is possible to transform queries between both languages in a rather straightforward manner. However, both languages possess some features not available in the respective other language. On the one hand, it is not possible in GReQL to define expression contexts. In addition, GReQL lacks a generic iteration operation which iterates over collections and stores intermediate results which can be used in the next iteration. On the other hand, OCL does not support the handling of graph structures such as paths and does not offer a concept equivalent to RPEs. Although most regular expression operations can be emulated by employing logical operators, this results in more cumbersome expressions. Furthermore, it is impossible to mimic iterated path descriptions, i.e., the computation of transitive closure over path descriptions, with OCL.

2.5.3   Process Algebra

This subsection gives a short overview of process algebra and the usage of process algebra in process modelling and management.

Process algebra or process calculi is a higher-level description for a formal modelling of concurrent systems in general and for processes in particular. We identify the following general key properties of process algebra (cf. [161]): (1) It provides a formal definition of algebraic structures and rules for process operations in order to allow the manipulation of process descriptions, i.e., to allow the representation of a changing system. (2) Process representations consist of a few primitives and a simple syntax only. Process representations can be combined and composed with each other and are usually defined recursively. (3) Interaction between processes is represented by process communication like message passing. We distinguish calculi in this section according to the kind of communication they provide.

According to Milner et al. [136], a process calculus has an infinite set of names (or channels) $\mathcal{N}$ and a set $\mathcal{K}$ of agent identifies each with an integer arity (≥ 0). In the following, u, v, w, x, y, z range over $\mathcal{N}$ and P, Q, R range over agents $\mathcal{K}$ or over process expressions. While a process describes the behaviour of a complex dynamic system, an agent is a part of such a system. Then, a process behaviour expression is defined according to the following behaviour operators:

- A summation $P_1 + \cdots + P_n$ defines the behaviour of the agent according to one of the process or agent P_i.
- A prefix indicates input and output ports: A negative prefix $\bar{y}x.P$ describes an output port with the output name x and afterwards the agents behaves like P. Positive prefixes describe input ports.
- A composition is represented by the expression $P_1 \mid P_2$. The behaviour of the agent is defined by a parallel execution of P_1 and P_2.
- A restriction $(x)P$ defines the agent's behaviour like P, but the actions at ports $\bar{x}$ and x are prohibited.
- A match is described by $[x = y]P$. If the names x and y are identical, the agent behaves like P otherwise the agent does nothing.
- $A(y_1, \ldots, y_n)$ is a defined agent for an agent identifier A with arity n. This definition (including recursive definitions) requires an equation like $P = A(x_1, \ldots, x_n)$. Hence, the agent $A(y_1, \ldots, y_n)$ behaves like $P\{y_1/x_1, \ldots, y_n/x_n\}$ where x_i are distinct and free names of P.

A transition of the system is represented in the process calculus by a binary relation $\rightarrow$ over behaviour expressions. These relations are called inference or reduction rules. The definitions of these inference rules depend on the concrete calculus. They are defined with respect to the above behaviour expressions, i.e., they describe how a transition is affected by applying one of the introduced behaviour operators. For instance, there are rules for composition like a transition $P_1 \rightarrow P_1\prime$ results in the transition $P_1 \mid P_2 \rightarrow P_1\prime \mid P_2$ by applying a composition rule.

In [179], process calculi are categorised into *first-order calculi* and *higher-order calculi*. The π-calculus [136] belongs to the category of first-order calculi. It is a calculus of communicating systems to describe changing structures. The calculus also allows modelling of communication between the components (agents) of a system. It is an extension of the process algebra CCS. The π-calculus (or first-order calculi in general) allows only communication between names (or channels) within the system.

The group of higher-order calculi contains the λ-calculus and the higher-order π-calculus. The λ-calculus [31] defines the way how specified functions are applied to their arguments, i.e., it basically consists of function term (λ expression) and function applications. A key property of the λ-calculus is to distinguish between bound and unbound variables in the λ expression. The function applications are described by reduction rules.

The higher-order π-calculus enriches the π-calculus by higher-order communications, i.e., not only names (or channels) can communicate with each other but also agents.

Once, processes are represented with process algebra, this formal representation can be used to analyse process properties like the bisimulation of processes which is called observation equivalence in [134]. Bisimulation describes an equivalent behaviour of two processes (or agents).

We adopt the following definition (Definition 4) on bisimulation from [135]. In the definition, a is an action and $\hat{a}$ is the corresponding label.

Definition 4. A binary relation $\mathcal{S} \subseteq \mathcal{P} \times \mathcal{P}$ over agents is a (weak) bisimulation if $(P, Q) \in \mathcal{S}$ implies:

- If $P \xrightarrow{a} P\prime$, then for some $Q\prime$, $Q \xRightarrow{\hat{a}} Q\prime$ and $(P\prime, Q\prime) \in \mathcal{S}$.
- If $Q \xrightarrow{a} Q\prime$, then for some $P\prime$, $P \xRightarrow{\hat{a}} P\prime$ and $(P\prime, Q\prime) \in \mathcal{S}$.

According to the definition, we call two agents P and Q bisimular or observation-equivalent, if for every action a and the a-descendant of P ($P\prime$) is bisimular to an a descendant of Q ($Q\prime$).

2.6 Conclusion

In this chapter, we introduced MDSD. We presented the main components of MDSD, namely modelling languages and model transformations. Modelling languages are used to design models representing the real world. The structure of models is described by metamodels which may be annotated by additional constraints. Model transformations are used to transform source models to models conforming to some other modelling language. Query languages in MDSD can be used to query models in order to retrieve facts from them.

In the next chapter, we will introduce the ontology languages and their underpinnings—description logics. In Chap. 4, we will present some industrial use cases to motivate why we need to go beyond MDSD.

Chapter 3
Ontology Languages and Description Logics

Yuting Zhao, Jeff Z. Pan, Edward Thomas, Nophadol Jekjantuk,
and Yuan Ren

Abstract Ontology-driven software technology is expected to improve MDSD
with better facilities for modelling, better understanding of relationships between
artefacts and better handling of complexity, via ontology-based knowledge representation (KR) techniques and reasoning techniques. The term ontology originates
from philosophy, where it refers to a unique description of the universe or 'things
that are'. In modern information technology, especially in the Semantic Web, an
ontology is a model of (some aspects of) the world, which introduces key vocabulary
(such as concepts and relations) of a target domain and their meanings. This chapter
introduces the standard ontology language family web ontology language (OWL)
and its underpinnings—description logics.

In this chapter, we first introduce description logics (DL) [11] and some simple
DL languages in Sect. 3.1. Then in Sect. 3.2 we present the web ontology language
(OWL) family, which is endorsed by the world wide web consortium (W3C) .
We pay special attention to OWL 2 profiles, which are tractable sub-languages in
the OWL family. They play an important role in scalable reasoning services (cf.
Chap. 5). Section 3.3 concludes this chapter.

3.1 Description Logics

DL [11] is a family of KR formalisms that represent the knowledge structure of an
application domain, in terms of *concepts*, *roles*, *individuals*, and their relationships.

In the DLs formalisms, the intensional knowledge which describes the general
cases about the application domain is always included in the "*TBox*", and the
extensional knowledge specifying a particular problem is kept in the "*ABox*". A DL
knowledge base (KB) is typically composed by two components—a *TBox* and an
ABox.

The TBox stands for terminology box, which is a collection of declarations (also
called *axioms*) describing general properties of concepts and roles. In TBox one
can use an "IS-A" relationship to state the link between concepts. For example, the

J.Z. Pan et al. (eds.), *Ontology-Driven Software Development*,
DOI 10.1007/978-3-642-31226-7_3, © Springer-Verlag Berlin Heidelberg 2013

knowledge "birds are animals" is formalised in DLs, by treating `Bird` and `Animal` as two concepts, and a statement in TBox "`Bird ⊑ Animal`".

The ABox stands for assertional box, which contains assertions of specific individuals in a problem domain. For example, one can announce some fact like "Tweety is a bird" by an assertion "`TWEETY:Bird`" in ABox. In DL roles are used as a binary predicates to state a relationship between individuals. For example, `hasMonther(TOM,ALICE)` indicates the knowledge "ALICE is the mother of TOM".

In TBox, we always use *general concept inclusion (GCI)* to denote those axioms of the form

$$C \sqsubseteq D$$

where C and D are concept expressions and *role inclusion (RI)* the axioms of the form

$$R \sqsubseteq S$$

where R and S are roles.

In DL languages, *atomic concepts* and *atomic roles* are the elementary descriptions. *Constructors* are used to build complex descriptions (*complex concepts* and *complex roles*). In general, in abstract notation, we use the letters A and B for atomic concepts, the letter R for atomic roles, and the letters C and D for concept descriptions.

DLs languages are distinguished by the constructors they are applying. In the following we use a basic description language $\mathcal{AL}$ as an example, to briefly introduce the syntax and semantics of DL languages. Readers can refer [11] for more details of DLs and DL languages.

3.1.1 The Basic Description Language $\mathcal{AL}$

In $\mathcal{AL}$ concept expressions are formed according to the following syntax rule:

$$
\begin{array}{rll}
C, D & \rightarrow \quad A \mid & \text{(atomic concept)} \\
 & \top \mid & \text{(universal concept)} \\
 & \bot \mid & \text{(bottom concept)} \\
 & \neg A \mid & \text{(atomic negation)} \\
 & C \sqcap D \mid & \text{(intersection)} \\
 & \forall R.C \mid & \text{(value restriction)}
\end{array}
$$

$$\exists R.\top \qquad \text{(limited existential quantification)}.$$

An $\mathcal{AL}$ knowledge base $\mathcal{O} = <\mathcal{T}, \mathcal{A}>$ is composed of a TBox $\mathcal{T}$ and an ABox $\mathcal{A}$, where $\mathcal{T}$ is a set of GCI axioms of the form

$$C \sqsubseteq D$$

where C and D are concept expressions, and $\mathcal{A}$ is a finite set of assertion axioms, in which:

- A *concept assertion* is a statement of the form $a{:}C$, where a is an individual and C is a concept.
- A *role assertion* is a statement of the form $(a,b){:}R$, where a, b are individuals and R is a role.

The formal semantics of $\mathcal{AL}$ is given by its model theory. An *interpretation* $\mathcal{I}$ consists of a non-empty set Δ^I as its domain and an interpretation function, which:

- Assigns to every individual a a element $a^I \in \Delta^I$
- Assigns to every atomic concept A a set $A^I \subseteq \Delta^I$
- Assigns to every atomic role R a binary relation $R^I \subseteq \Delta^I \times \Delta^I$

Furthermore, Table 3.1 shows the inductive definition of the semantics of concept expressions.

If an interpretation $\mathcal{I}$ satisfies all axioms in a DL knowledge base O, we say $\mathcal{I}$ is a *model* of O.

3.1.2   The Family of $\mathcal{AL}$ Languages

$\mathcal{AL}$ is a very basic description language. By adding further constructors we get more expressive languages:

- $\mathcal{U}$: *Union* of concepts, $C \sqcup D$.
  $$(C \sqcup D)^I = C^I \cup D^I$$
- $\mathcal{E}$: *Full existential quantification*, $\exists R.C$.
  $$(\exists R.C)^I = \{a \mid \exists b, (a, b) \in R^I \wedge b \in C^I\}$$
- $\mathcal{N}$: *Number restrictions*, $\geq nR$ and $\leq nR$.
  $$(\geq nR)^I = \{a \mid \sharp\{b \mid (a, b) \in R^I\} \geq n\}, \text{ and}$$
  $$(\leq nR)^I = \{a \mid \sharp\{b \mid (a, b) \in R^I\} \leq n\}$$
- $\mathcal{C}$: *Complement*, $\neg C$.
  $$(\neg C)^I = \Delta^I \setminus C^I$$

So $\mathcal{AL}$ languages are named by a string of the form

$$\mathcal{AL}[\mathcal{U}][\mathcal{E}][\mathcal{N}][\mathcal{C}]$$

Table 3.1 $\mathcal{AL}$ Semantics

Syntax	Semantics
$\top$	Δ^I
$\bot$	$\varnothing$
$\neg A$	$\Delta^I \setminus A^I$
$C \sqcap D$	$C^I \cap D^I$
$\exists R.\top$	$\{a \mid \exists b, (a, b) \in R^I\}$
$\forall R.C$	$\{a \mid \forall b, (a, b) \in R^I \rightarrow b \in C^I\}$
$C \sqsubseteq D$	$C^I \subseteq D^I$
$a : C$	$a^I \in C^I$
$(a, b) : R$	$(a^I, b^I) \in R^I$

Table 3.2 $\mathcal{AL}$ families

	Syntax	Semantics	$\mathcal{AL}$	$\mathcal{ALU}$	$\mathcal{ALE}$	$\mathcal{ALN}$	$\mathcal{ALC}$
Concepts	$\top$	Δ^I	✓	✓	✓	✓	✓
	$\bot$	$\varnothing$	✓	✓	✓	✓	✓
	$\neg A$	$\Delta^I \setminus A^I$	✓	✓	✓	✓	✓
	$C \sqcap D$	$C^I \cap D^I$	✓	✓	✓	✓	✓
	$\exists R.\top$	$\{a \mid \exists b, (a, b) \in R^I\}$	✓	✓	✓	✓	✓
	$\forall R.C$	$\{a \mid \forall b, (a, b) \in R^I \rightarrow b \in C^I\}$	✓	✓	✓	✓	✓
	$\mathcal{U} : C \sqcup D$	$(C \sqcup D)^I = C^I \cup D^I$		✓			✓
	$\mathcal{E} : \exists R.C$	$(\exists R.C)^I = \{a \mid \exists b, (a, b) \in R^I \text{ and } b \in C^I\}$			✓		✓
	$\mathcal{N} : \geq nR$	$(\geq nR)^I = \{a \mid \sharp\{b \mid (a, b) \in R^I\} \geq n\}$				✓	
	$\leq nR$	$(\leq nR)^I = \{a \mid \sharp\{b \mid (a, b) \in R^I\} \leq n\}$				✓	
	$\mathcal{C} : \neg C$	$(\neg C)^I = \Delta^I \setminus C^I$					✓
TBox	$C \sqsubseteq D$	$C^I \subseteq D^I$	✓	✓	✓	✓	✓
ABox	$a : C$	$a^I \in C^I$	✓	✓	✓	✓	✓
	$(a, b) : R$	$(a^I, b^I) \in R^I$	✓	✓	✓	✓	✓

Because of the semantical equivalences $C \sqcup D \equiv \neg(\neg C \sqcap \neg D)$ and $\exists R.C \equiv \neg \forall R.\neg C$, we always use the letter $\mathcal{C}$ instead of the letters $\mathcal{UE}$ in language names. Table 3.2 shows the $\mathcal{AL}$ families of DL languages.

3.1.3 Reasoning Tasks in Description Logics

In general reasonings detect implicit knowledge in logic-based information systems. Here we briefly explain the basic reasoning tasks in DL. They make up the foundations of the ontology services presented in Sect. 8.1 under the chapter "Ontology and Bridging Technologies".

TBox Reasoning

- *Satisfiability checking*: if a concept description is satisfiable (i.e. non-contradictory). For example, to check if concept $Vegetarian \sqcap Non-vegetarian$ is satisfiable in O
- *Subsumption checking*: if one description is more general than another one. For example, to check if concept $Professor \sqsubseteq Vegetarian$ is entailed from O

ABox Reasoning

- *Consistency checking*: if there is a model for O. For example, if O entails $Vegetarian \sqsubseteq \perp$, and also *peter : vegetarian*, then O is inconsistent.
- *Instance retrieval*: if a particular individual is an instance of a given concept description. For example, to find all instances of *Professor*.

Query Answering

- *Query answering*: Return all answer sets to a query. For example, to find all of the postgraduate students and their supervisors who both like swimming, the query could be:

$$Q(x, y) \leftarrow student(x), teacher(y), supervising(y, x),$$
$$likes(x, swimming), habit(y, swimming)$$

SPARQL Protocol and RDF Query Language (SPARQL) [167] is an RDF query language proposed by the *RDF data access working group (DAWG)* of the *W3C*, and now it is an official W3C Recommendation. SPARQL allows several kinds of queries, which will be detailed in later chapters.

3.1.4 Computational Properties for Description Logics

For each language in the DL family, there is trade-offs between the expressivity of the language and the efficiency of the most relevant reasoning tasks. In this book, we always consider reasoning tasks introduced in Sect. 3.1.3.

Following common understanding we use *computational complexity* to evaluate the efficiency of a DL (or ontology) language in this book. Here we explain the terms on computational complexities we used in this book.

In general there are two popular types of complexity: the *time complexity* of a problem equal to the number of steps that it takes to solve an instance of the problem as a function of the size of the input (e.g. facts in one ontology), using the most efficient algorithm, and the *space complexity* of a problem equal to the volume of the memory used by the algorithm that it takes to solve an instance of the problem as a function of the size of the input, using the most efficient algorithm. The complexity classes introduced in here cover both of them.

In computational complexity theory , the complexity class *P* is the set of decision problems that can be solved by a deterministic Turing machine in polynomial time. The complexity class *NP* is the set of decision problems that can be solved by a non-deterministic Turing machine in polynomial time. For example, the *Boolean satisfiability problem* and the *Hamiltonian path problem* are typical *NP* problems.

In general a computational problem is *complete* for a complexity class when it is one of the "hardest" or "most expressive" problems in the complexity class. Formally, a problem that is complete for a class *C* is said to be *C-complete*, and the class of all problems complete for *C* is denoted *C-complete*. The first complete class to be defined and the most well known is *NP-complete*. In this book, sometimes, we also use "-comp." as a short of "-complete".

A problem X belongs to complexity class *co-NP* if and only if its complement $\bar{X}$ is in complexity class *NP*.

LogSpace is the complexity class containing decision problems which can be solved by a deterministic Turing machine using a logarithmic amount of memory space. *PSPACE* is the class of all problems which can be solved by programs which only need a polynomial (in the number of facts in one ontology) amount of memory to run.

In computational complexity theory, the complexity class *EXPTIME* (sometimes called EXP) is the set of all decision problems solvable by a deterministic Turing machine in $O(2^{p(n)})$ time, where $p(n)$ is a polynomial function of n. The complexity class *2-EXPTIME* (sometimes called 2-EXP) is the set of all decision problems solvable by a deterministic Turing machine in $O(2^{2^{p(n)}})$ time, where $p(n)$ is a polynomial function of n. The complexity class *NEXPTIME* (sometimes called NEXP) is the set of decision problems that can be solved by a non-deterministic Turing machine using time $O(2^{p(n)})$ for some polynomial $p(n)$ and unlimited space. The complexity class *2NEXPTIME* (sometimes called 2NEXP) is the set of decision problems that can be solved by a non-deterministic Turing machine using time $O(2^{2^{p(n)}})$ for some polynomial $p(n)$ and unlimited space.

Specially on DL-based ontology reasonings, when evaluating then efficiency people, consider the following kinds of complexities [139]:

- The *Taxonomic Complexity* is the complexity measured with respect to the size of the axioms in the ontology.
- The *Data Complexity* is the complexity of evaluating a query on the number of facts in the ontology, when the query is fixed. We express the complexity as a function of the size of the ontology.
- The *Query Complexity* is the complexity measured with respect to the number of conjuncts in the conjunctive query.
- The *Combined Complexity* is the complexity measured with respect to both the size of the axioms and the number of facts. In the case of conjunctive query

answering, the combined complexity also includes the query complexity.

3.2 The OWL Family of Ontology Languages and Related Others

The state of the art ontology language for the Semantic Web with formal semantics is OWL 2 [143]. Currently it enjoys the W3C Recommendation status. OWL 2 is an extension of OWL, which was the most famous ontology language. The aim is to extend the expressiveness of OWL specification by introducing new constructs.

Although the full language of *OWL 2* is very powerful in the sense of expressiveness, its computational cost is also high. So *OWL 2* working group also provides three important profiles—*OWL 2 EL*, *OWL 2 QL*, and *OWL 2 RL*—for different application scenarios. In this book, the $\mathcal{EL}^{++}$, which is the core language of *OWL 2 EL*, and the *DL-Lite*, which is the core language of *OWL 2 QL*, are most used in our ontology-driven software development (ODSD) practicals. So in this section, after a brief introduction on *OWL 2* and its three profiles—*OWL 2 EL*, *OWL 2 QL*, and *OWL 2 RL*—we will introduce the $\mathcal{EL}^{++}$ and the *DL-Lite*; we will also introduce *OWL DL* which was a representative profile of *OWL*.

3.2.1 OWL 2 Web Ontology Language (OWL 2)

OWL 2 is an extension of OWL , by adding many useful features that have been requested by users. The new features include extra syntactic sugar, additional property and qualified cardinality constructors, extended data-type support, simple metamodelling, and extended annotations [139].

For example, OWL 2 allows user-defined data types, using a syntax similar to the one used in Protégé [120]. This ability can be used in defining new data types that can be used in the ontology. For example, the customised data type 'atLeast18' can be used in the following definition of the class 'Adult':

```
        SubClassOf(Adult DataSomeValuesFrom(age
DatatypeRestriction(xsd:integer minInclusive "18"8sd:integer))),
```

which says that an `Adult` is a `Person` whose *age* is at least 18.

OWL 2 can express things that are not expressible in current OWL. For example,

```
SubObjectPropertyOf(SubObjectPropertyChain(parent brother)
                          uncle)
```

Which says that `brother` of `parent` is `uncle`.

An overview of *OWL 2* features is given in Table 3.3.

Table 3.3 OWL 2 summary

OWL 2	
Language information	
Reference	http://www.w3.org/TR/owl2-primer/
Purpose	Addresses deficiencies identified by users and developers
Language dependency	
Dependencies	OWL 2 is an extension of OWL 1
Language evaluation	
Advantages	Extra syntactic sugar, additional property and qualified cardinality constructors, extended data-type support, simple metamodelling, and extended annotations
Deficiencies	OWL 2 does not have an RDF-compatible semantics

Table 3.4 Additional syntax and semantics in OWL 2

Construct name	DL syntax	Semantics	
Universal role	U	$\Delta^{\mathcal{I}} \times \Delta^{\mathcal{I}}$	
Role hierarchy	$R \sqsubseteq S$	$R^{\mathcal{I}} \subseteq S^{\mathcal{I}}$	
Generalised role inclusion axioms	$R_1 \circ \ldots \circ R_n \sqsubseteq R$	$R_1^{\mathcal{I}} \circ \ldots \circ R_n^{\mathcal{I}} \sqsubseteq R^{\mathcal{I}}$	$\mathcal{R}$
Self-concept	$\exists S.C$	$\{x \in \Delta^{\mathcal{I}} \mid (x, x) \in S^{\mathcal{I}}\}$	
At least restriction	$\leq nS.C$	$\{x \in \Delta^{\mathcal{I}} \mid \sharp\{y \in \Delta^{\mathcal{I}} \mid (x, y) \in S^{\mathcal{I}} \wedge y \in C^{\mathcal{I}}\} \geq n\}$	
At most restriction	$\geq nS.C$	$\{x \in \Delta^{\mathcal{I}} \mid \sharp\{y \in \Delta^{\mathcal{I}} \mid (x, y) \in R^{\mathcal{I}} \wedge y \in C^{\mathcal{I}}\} \leq n\}$	$\mathcal{Q}$

Syntax

The OWL 2 syntax is based on $\mathcal{SROIQ}(\mathcal{D}^+)$ which is more expressive than $\mathcal{SHOIN}(\mathcal{D}^+)$ and retain decidability in 2NEXEMP-TIME. Further details on $\mathcal{SROIQ}(\mathcal{D}^+)$ can be found in [99].

Example

All examples from Sects. 3.2.4, 3.2.5, and 3.2.3 are valid OWL 2 examples.

$$\text{department} \sqsubseteq \geq 10 \text{hasMember.faculty} \sqcup \leq 4 \text{hasMember.adminStaff}$$

Department has at least ten faculty members and not more than four members for admin staff.

Table 3.5 OWL 2 DL complexities

Reasoning problems	Complexity			
	Taxonomic	Data	Query	Combined
Ontology consistency, concept satisfiability concept subsumption instance checking	2NP-comp	NP-Hard	N/A	2NP-comp
Conjunctive query answering	Open*	Open*	Open*	Open*

Semantics

The semantics of OWL 2 ($\mathcal{SROIQ}(\mathcal{D}^+)$) is defined in terms of interpretations $\mathcal{I} = (\Delta^{\mathcal{I}}, \cdot^{\mathcal{I}})$. Given concepts C, D, roles R, S, and a non-negative integer n, the extension of complex concepts is defined inductively by the following equations:

$$\top^{\mathcal{I}} = \Delta^{\mathcal{I}} \qquad\qquad \bot^{\mathcal{I}} = \varnothing$$
$$(\neg C)^{\mathcal{I}} = \Delta^{\mathcal{I}}/C^{\mathcal{I}} \qquad\qquad (C_1 \sqcap C_2)^{\mathcal{I}} = C_1^{\mathcal{I}} \cap C_2^{\mathcal{I}}$$
$$(C_1 \sqcup C_2) = C_1^{\mathcal{I}} \cup C_2^{\mathcal{I}} \qquad\qquad U^{\mathcal{I}} = \Delta^{\mathcal{I}} \times \Delta^{\mathcal{I}}$$
$$(R^-)^{\mathcal{I}} = \{(y, x) \mid (x, y) \in R^{\mathcal{I}}\}$$
$$(\exists R.C)^{\mathcal{I}} = \{x \mid \exists y.(x, y) \in R^{\mathcal{I}} \wedge y \in C^{\mathcal{I}}\}$$
$$(\exists R.Self)^{\mathcal{I}} = \{x \mid (x, x) \in R^{\mathcal{I}}\}$$
$$(\forall R.C)^{\mathcal{I}} = \{x \mid (x, y) \in R^{\mathcal{I}}I \rightarrow y \in C^{\mathcal{I}}\}$$
$$(\geq nR.C)^{\mathcal{I}} = \{x \mid \sharp\{y \in \Delta^{\mathcal{I}} \mid (x, y) \in S^{\mathcal{I}} \wedge y \in C^{\mathcal{I}}\} \geq n\}$$
$$(\leq nR.C)^{\mathcal{I}} = \{x \mid \sharp\{y \in \Delta^{\mathcal{I}} \mid (x, y) \in R^{\mathcal{I}} \wedge y \in C^{\mathcal{I}}\} \leq n\}$$

OWL 2 is extended from OWL by adding some new constructors. Table 3.4 summaries the syntax and semantics for these constructors.

Complexity

The complexity in Table 3.5 has been identified for OWL 2 DL [78]:

3.2.2 OWL 2 Profiles

OWL 2 has three important profiles [139]: *OWL 2 EL*, *OWL 2 QL*, and *OWL 2 RL*. An OWL 2 profile is a slim version of OWL 2 that trades some expressive power for the efficiency of reasoning. Each of OWL 2 profiles is designed to achieve efficiency in a different way for different application scenarios.

OWL 2 EL is particularly useful for applications employing ontologies that contain large numbers of classes and properties (TBox). It is equipped with the

Table 3.6 $\mathcal{EL}^{++}$ Summary

$\mathcal{EL}^{++}$	
Language information	
Reference	http://www.w3.org/TR/2008/WD-owl2-profiles-20080411/# EL.2B.2B
Purpose	Geared towards ontologies with large numbers of concepts
Language dependency	
Dependencies	Maximal subset of OWL 2 DL
Language evaluation	
Advantages	Able to capture large-scale ontologies in life science, polynomial time reasoning
Deficiencies	Limited expressivity, cannot describe: - Union, negation, universal property quantification - Cardinality restrictions; inverse, functional properties, etc.

expressive power for most of such ontologies, and, at the same time, the basic reasoning problems can be performed in polynomial time w.r.t. the size of the TBox. $\mathcal{EL}^{++}$ is the core language of *OWL 2 EL*.

OWL 2 QL is particularly useful for applications which need to compute answer sets to queries over very large volumes of instance data (ABox). Relational database systems can be used in computing conjunctive query answering in OWL 2 QL. Theoretically sound and complete conjunctive query answering can be performed in LOGSPACE w.r.t. the size of the ABox. $\mathcal{DL} - \mathcal{L})\sqcup\rceil$ is the core language of *OWL 2 QL*.

OWL 2 RL is aimed at applications that require scalable reasoning without sacrificing too much expressive power. OWL 2 RL reasoning systems can be implemented using rule-based reasoning engines. The ontology consistency, class expression satisfiability, class expression subsumption, instance checking, and conjunctive query answering problems can be solved in polynomial time w.r.t the size of the ontology.

3.2.3 $\mathcal{EL}^{++}$

$\mathcal{EL}^{++}$ is a lightweight description logic that admits tractable reasoning in polynomial time. Primary focus has been on large life-science ontologies, such as Gene Ontology, SNOMED, and GALEN. Please see [10] for details. An overview of $\mathcal{EL}^{++}$ features is given in Table 3.6.

Syntax

$\mathcal{EL}^{++}$ allows conjunction and existential restrictions while remaining tractable.

Example

Example of DL syntax:

GradStudent $\sqsubseteq$ student $\sqcap$ enrolled-in.GradSchool (1)

ungradStudent $\sqsubseteq$ student $\sqcap$ enrolled-in.UngradSchool $\sqcap$ $\exists$takes.Lecture (2)

student $\sqsubseteq$ $\sqcap$ $\exists$student-id.ID$\sqcap$ $\exists$registered-at.University (3)

GradStudent$\equiv$ $\neg$ ungradStudent (4)

enrolled-in $\circ$ registered-at $\sqsubseteq$ registered-at (5)

(1) *GradStudent* is *student* that enrolled in *GradSchool*.(2) *UngradStudent* is *student* that enrolled in *UngradSchool*. (3)*student* has student id and registered at*University*. (4) *GradStudent* is different from *ungradStudent*. (5) Student who enrolled in any school is also registered at University.

$$\text{teaches} \equiv \text{isTaughtBy}^{-} (6)$$

(6) teaches is the inverse relation of isTaughtBy which is not supported by $\mathcal{EL} + +$. However, this statement can be expressed in OWL and OWL2.

Semantics

The extension of $\cdot^{\mathcal{I}}$ to complex concepts is inductively defined as shown in the third column of Table 3.7, where $\sharp$ S denotes the cardinality of the set S. An interpretation $\mathcal{I}$ *satisfies* an equation $A \doteq C$ iff $A^{\mathcal{I}} = C^{\mathcal{I}}$, an inclusion $C \sqsubseteq D$ iff $C^{\mathcal{I}} \subseteq D^{\mathcal{I}}$, an assertion $C(a)$ iff $a^{\mathcal{I}} \in C^{\mathcal{I}}$, and an assertion $r(a, b)$ if $(a^{\mathcal{I}}, b^{\mathcal{I}}) \in r^{\mathcal{I}}$. An interpretation is a model of a TBox $\mathcal{T}$ (ABox $\mathcal{A}$) if it satisfies all equations/inclusions in $\mathcal{T}$ (assertions in $\mathcal{A}$).

Complexity

The complexity of different reasoning tasks is described in Table 3.8 [78].

3.2.4 DL-Lite

DL-Lite provides efficient query answering with only polynomial data complexity. DL-Lite is a fragment of OWL 2 especially tailored for handling large number of facts efficiently. DL-Lite includes most of the main features used in conceptual

Table 3.7 Syntax and semantics of $\mathcal{EL}^{++}$

Name	DL syntax	Semantic
Top	$\top$	$\Delta^{\mathcal{I}}$
Bottom	$\bot$	$\varnothing$
Nominal	$\{a\}$	$\{a\}^{\mathcal{I}}$
Conjunction	$C \sqcap D$	$C^{\mathcal{I}} \cap D^{\mathcal{I}}$
Existential restriction	$\exists r.C$	$\{x \in \Delta^{\mathcal{I}} \mid \exists y \in \Delta^{\mathcal{I}} : (x, y) \in r^{\mathcal{I}} \wedge y \in C^{\mathcal{I}}\}$
Concrete domain	$p(f_1, \ldots, f_k)$ for $p \in \mathcal{P}^{\mathcal{D}_i}$	$\{x \in \Delta^{\mathcal{I}} \mid \exists y_1, \ldots, y_k \in \Delta^{\mathcal{D}_i} : f_i^{\mathcal{I}}(x) = y_i \text{ for } 1 \leq i \leq k \wedge (y_1, \ldots, y_k) \in p^{\mathcal{D}_i}\}$
GCI	$C \sqsubseteq D$	$C^{\mathcal{I}} \subseteq D^{\mathcal{I}}$
RI	$r_1 \circ \ldots \circ r_k \sqsubseteq r$	$r_1^{\mathcal{I}} \circ \ldots \circ r_k^{\mathcal{I}} \subseteq r^{\mathcal{I}}$
Negation	$\neg C$	$\Delta^{\mathcal{I}} \backslash C^{\mathcal{I}}$
Disjunction	$C \sqcup D$	$C^{\mathcal{I}} \cup D^{\mathcal{I}}$
Value restriction	$\forall r.C$	$\{x \mid \forall y : (x, y) \in r^{\mathcal{I}} \rightarrow y \in C^{\mathcal{I}}\}$
At least restriction	$\geq n \, r$	$\{x \mid \sharp\{y \in \Delta^{\mathcal{I}} \mid (x, y) \in r^{\mathcal{I}}\} \geq n\}$
At most restriction	$\leq n \, r$	$\{x \mid \sharp\{y \in \Delta^{\mathcal{I}} \mid (x, y) \in r^{\mathcal{I}}\} \leq n\}$
Inverse roles	$\exists r^-.C$	$\{x \mid \exists y : (y, x) \in r^{\mathcal{I}} \wedge y \in C^{\mathcal{I}}\}$

Table 3.8 $\mathcal{EL}^{++}$ complexities

Reasoning problems	Complexity			
	Taxonomic	Data	Query	Combined
Ontology consistency Concept satisfiability Concept subsumption Instance checking	PTIME-comp.	PTIME-comp.	N/A	PTIME-comp.
Conjunctive query answering	Open	PTIME-hard	Open	Open

models, like UML class diagrams and ER diagrams. An overview of the DL-Lite features is given in Table 3.9.

Syntax

DL-Lite includes some features of OWL DL, such as a constrained form of *someValuesFrom* restrictions, conjunction, concept disjointness, domains, and ranges of properties, inverse properties, and inclusion axioms for object properties. However, DL-Lite disallows property chains in the property inclusion axioms. For more details of the restrictions, see [41].

Table 3.9 DL-Lite summary

DL-Lite	
Information	
Reference	http://www.w3.org/TR/owl2-profiles/#DL-Lite
Purpose	Geared towards ontologies with large numbers of instances
Language dependency	
Dependencies	Intersection between RDFS and OWL 2 DL
Language evaluation	
Advantages	Polynomial time reasoning, use database engine for high performance query answering
Deficiencies	Restricted concept and role inclusion axioms

Table 3.10 Syntax and semantics of DL-Lite

	DL-Lite syntax	Semantics
Atomic concept	A	$A^{\mathcal{I}} \subseteq \Delta$
Exists restriction	$\exists Q$	$\{d \mid \exists e.(d, e) \in Q^{\mathcal{I}}\}$
Atomic concept negation	$\neg A$	$\Delta^{\mathcal{I}} \setminus A^{\mathcal{I}}$
Concept negation	$\neg \exists Q$	$\Delta^{\mathcal{I}} \setminus (\exists Q)^{\mathcal{I}}$
Atomic role	P	$P^{\mathcal{I}} \subseteq \Delta^{\mathcal{I}} \times \Delta^{\mathcal{I}}$
Inverse role	P^-	$(P^-)^{\mathcal{I}} = \{(o, o') \mid (o', o) \in P^{\mathcal{I}}$
Role negation	$\neg Q$	$(\Delta_O^{\mathcal{I}} \times \Delta_o^{\mathcal{I}}) \setminus Q^{\mathcal{I}}$
Concept inclusion	$Cl \sqsubseteq Cr$	$Cl^{\mathcal{I}} \subseteq Cr^{\mathcal{I}}$
Role inclusion	$Q \sqsubseteq R$	$Q^{\mathcal{I}} \subseteq R^{\mathcal{I}}$
Function assertions	(funct Q)	$\forall d, e, e'.(d, e) \in Q^{\mathcal{I}} \wedge (d, e') \in Q^{\mathcal{I}} \rightarrow e = e'$
Membership assertions	$C(a)$	$a^{\mathcal{I}} \in C^{\mathcal{I}}$
	$R(a, b)$	$(a^{\mathcal{I}}, b^{\mathcal{I}}) \in R^{\mathcal{I}}$

Example

Example of DL syntax:

$$associateProfessor \sqsubseteq academicStaffMember \ (1)$$
$$fullProfessor \sqsubseteq academicStaffMember \ (2)$$
$$fullProfessor \sqsubseteq \neg associateProfessor \ (3)$$
$$facultyMember \equiv academicStaffMember \ (4)$$
$$firstYearCourse \sqsubseteq \forall isTaughtBy.fullProfessor \ (5)$$

(1),(2) *associateProfessor* and *fullProfessor* are members of *academicStaffMember*. (3) One person cannot be *associateProfessor* and *fullProfessor* at the same time. (4) *facultyMember* is equivalent to *academicStaffMember*.

(5) All *firstYearCourse* is taught by *fullProfessor*. This is not expressible in DL-Lite because universal quantification to class expression is disallowed in DL-Lite.

Table 3.11 DL-Lite complexities

Reasoning problems	Complexity			
	Taxonomic	Data	Query	Combined
Ontology consistency Concept satisfiability Concept subsumption Instance checking	PTIME	LOGSPACE	N/A	PTIME
Query answering	PTIME	LOGSPACE	NP-comp.	NP-comp.

Semantics

The semantics of DL-Lite is given in terms of interpretations over a fixed infinite domain Δ. An interpretation $\mathcal{I} = \Delta^{\mathcal{I}}, \cdot^{\mathcal{I}}$ consists of a first-order structure over Δ with an interpretation function $\cdot^{\mathcal{I}}$ such that:

$$A^{\mathcal{I}} \subseteq \Delta \qquad\qquad \bot^{\mathcal{I}} = \varnothing$$
$$(\exists R)^{\mathcal{I}} = \{c \mid \exists c'.(c, c') \in R^{\mathcal{I}}\} \qquad (C_1 \sqcap C_2)^{\mathcal{I}} = C_1^{\mathcal{I}} \cap C_2^{\mathcal{I}}$$
$$P^{\mathcal{I}} \subseteq \Delta \times \Delta \qquad\qquad (P^-)^{\mathcal{I}} = \{(c, c') \mid (c', c) \in P^{\mathcal{I}}\}$$

An interpretation $\mathcal{I}$ is a model of an inclusion assertion $C_1 \sqsubseteq C_2$ if and only if $C_1^{\mathcal{I}} \subseteq C_2^{\mathcal{I}}$; $\mathcal{I}$ is a model of a functionality assertion (funct R) if $(c, c') \in R^{\mathcal{I}}$ and $(c, c'') \in R^{\mathcal{I}}$ imply $c' = c''$; $\mathcal{I}$ is a model of a membership assertion $C(a)$ (resp., $R(a; b)$) if $a \in C^{\mathcal{I}}$ (resp., $(a, b) \in R^{\mathcal{I}}$). A model of a KB $\mathcal{K}$ is an interpretation $\mathcal{I}$ that is a model of all assertions in $\mathcal{K}$. A KB is *satisfiable* if it has at least one model. A KB $\mathcal{K}$ logically implies an assertion α if all the models of $\mathcal{K}$ are also models of α.

Table 3.10 summaries the syntax and semantics of DL-Lite.

Complexity

The complexity of different reasoning tasks is described in Table 3.11 [78].

3.2.5 OWL DL

OWL DL provides maximum expressiveness while maintaining decidability in the NEXPTIME-complete complexity class [129]. OWL DL is a standardised formalisation of a DL equivalent to $\mathcal{SHOIN}(\mathcal{D}^+)$. OWL DL supports all OWL language constructs, with some restrictions. For instance, a class cannot be an instance of another class, and users are unable to modify OWL constructors (self-modifying can be done in OWL Full). Furthermore, OWL constructs are defined by an abstract syntax which directly corresponds to the DLs equivalent. For more details, see [98]. An overview of OWL DL features is given in Table 3.12.

Table 3.12 OWL DL summary

OWL DL	
Language information	
Reference	http://www.w3.org/TR/owl-features/
Purpose	Maximum expressiveness while retaining computational completeness
Language dependency	
Dependencies	OWL DL builds on RDF(S) and OWL Lite providing more expressive power
Language evaluation	
Advantages	Maximum expressiveness, computational completeness, supported by most of reasoner
Deficiencies	Disallow user-defined data type

Table 3.13 Syntax and semantics of OWL DL

Construct name	DL syntax	Semantics	
Atomic concept	A	$A^{\mathcal{I}} \subseteq \Delta^{\mathcal{I}}$	
Atomic role	R	$R^{\mathcal{I}} \subseteq \Delta^{\mathcal{I}} \times \Delta^{\mathcal{I}}$	
Transitive role	$R \in \mathbf{R}_+$	$R^{\mathcal{I}} = (R^{\mathcal{I}})^+$	
Top	$\top$	$\top^{\mathcal{I}} = \Delta^{\mathcal{I}}$	
Bottom	$\bot$	$\bot^{\mathcal{I}} = \varnothing$	$\mathcal{S}$
Conjunction	$C_1 \sqcap \ldots \sqcap C_n$	$(C_1 \sqcap C_2)^{\mathcal{I}} = C_1^{\mathcal{I}} \sqcap C_2^{\mathcal{I}}$	
Disjunction	$C_1 \sqcup \ldots \sqcup C_n$	$(C_1 \sqcup C_2) = C_1^{\mathcal{I}} \sqcup C_2^{\mathcal{I}}$	
Negation	$\neg C$	$(\neg C)^{\mathcal{I}} = \Delta^{\mathcal{I}} / C^{\mathcal{I}}$	
Exists restriction	$\forall P.C$	$(\forall P.C)^{\mathcal{I}} = \{x \mid \forall y.(x, y) \in R^{\mathcal{I}} \rightarrow y \in C^{\mathcal{I}}\}$	
Value restriction	$\exists P.C$	$(\exists P.C)^{\mathcal{I}} = \{x \mid \exists y.(x, y) \in R^{\mathcal{I}} I \wedge y \in C^{\mathcal{I}}\}$	
Role hierarchy	$R \sqsubseteq S$	$R^{\mathcal{I}} \subseteq S^{\mathcal{I}}$	$\mathcal{H}$
Inverse role	R^-	$(R^-)^{\mathcal{I}} \subseteq \Delta^{\mathcal{I}} \times \Delta^{\mathcal{I}}$	$\mathcal{I}$
Functional role	$R \in \mathbf{F}$	$\{\{(x, y), (x, z)\} \in R^{\mathcal{I}} \rightarrow y = z\}$	$\mathcal{F}$
Nominals	$\{o_1\} \sqcup \ldots \sqcup \{o_n\}$	$(\{o_1\} \sqcup \{o_2\}) = \{o_1^{\mathcal{I}}, o_2^{\mathcal{I}}\}$	$\mathcal{O}$
At least restriction	$\geq nP$	$(\geq nP)^{\mathcal{I}} = \{x \mid \sharp\{y.(x, y) \in R^{\mathcal{I}}\} \geq n\}$	$\mathcal{N}$
At most restriction	$\leq nP$	$(\leq nP)^{\mathcal{I}} = \{x \mid \sharp\{y.(x, y) \in R^{\mathcal{I}}\} \leq n\}$	

Syntax

OWL DL provides a human-readable abstract syntax as well as a machine-processable RDF/XML syntax.

Table 3.14 OWL axioms and facts

Abstract syntax	DL syntax	Semantics
Class(A partial $C_1 \dots C_n$)	$A \sqsubseteq C_1 \sqcap \dots \sqcap C_n$	$A^{\mathcal{I}} \subseteq C_1^{\mathcal{I}} \cap \dots \cap C_n^{\mathcal{I}}$
Class(A complete $C_1 \dots C_n$)	$A \equiv C_1 \sqcap \dots \sqcap C_n$	$A^{\mathcal{I}} = C_1^{\mathcal{I}} \cap \dots \cap C_n^{\mathcal{I}}$
SubClassOf	$C_1 \sqsubseteq C_2$	$C_1^{\mathcal{I}} \subseteq C_2^{\mathcal{I}}$
EquivalentClass	$C_1 \equiv \dots \equiv C_n$	$C_1^{\mathcal{I}} = \dots = C_n^{\mathcal{I}}$
DisjointClasses	$C_i \sqsubseteq \neg C_j$	$C_1^{\mathcal{I}} \cap C_n^{\mathcal{I}} = \varnothing$
SubPropertyOf	$R_1 \sqsubseteq R_2$	$R_1^{\mathcal{I}} \subseteq R_2^{\mathcal{I}}$
EquivalentProperty	$P_1 \equiv \dots \equiv P_n$	$P_1^{\mathcal{I}} = \dots = P_n^{\mathcal{I}}$
EnumeratedClass($A o_1 \dots o_n$)	$A \equiv \{o_1\} \sqcup \dots \sqcup \{o_n\}$	$A^{\mathcal{I}} = \{o_1^{\mathcal{I}}, \dots, o_n^{\mathcal{I}}\}$
ObjectProperty	$R \sqsubseteq R_i$	$R^{\mathcal{I}} \subseteq R_i^{\mathcal{I}}$
Domain	$\geq 1R \sqsubseteq C_i$	$R^{\mathcal{I}} \subseteq C_i^{\mathcal{I}} \times \Delta^{\mathcal{I}}$
Range	$\top \sqsubseteq \forall R.C_i$	$R^{\mathcal{I}} \subseteq \Delta^{\mathcal{I}} \times C_i^{\mathcal{I}}$
[Transitive]	$R^+ \sqsubseteq R$	$(R^{\mathcal{I}})^+ = R^{\mathcal{I}}$
[Symmetric]	$R \equiv R^-$	$R^{\mathcal{I}} = (R^-)^{\mathcal{I}}$
[Functional]	$\top \sqsubseteq\, \leq 1R$	$\{(x, y) \mid \sharp\{y.(x, y) \in R^{\mathcal{I}}\} \leq 1\}$
[inversFunctional]	$\top \sqsubseteq\, \leq 1R^-$	$\{(x, y) \mid \sharp\{y.(x, y) \in (R^-)^{\mathcal{I}}\} \leq 1\}$
Individual	$o : C_i, 1 \leq i \leq n$	$o^{\mathcal{I}} \in C_n^{\mathcal{I}}, 1 \leq i \leq n$
(o type($C1$) $\dots$ type (C_n))		
SameIndividual	$o_1 = \dots = o_n$	$o_1^{\mathcal{I}} = \dots = o_n^{\mathcal{I}}$
DifferentIndividuals	$o_i \neq o_j$	$o_i^{\mathcal{I}} \neq o_j^{\mathcal{I}}$

Example

Example of OWL DL syntax:

> $mathCourse \sqsubseteq\ \forall\ isTaughtBy.\{123\}$ (1)
> $Course \sqsubseteq\ \geq 10 hasStudent \sqcup\ \leq 30 hasStudent$ (2)
> $peopleAtUni \equiv staffMember \sqcup student$ (3)
> $facultyInCS \equiv faculty \sqcap \exists belongsTo.(CSDepartment)$ (4)
> $adminStaff \equiv staffMember \sqcap \neg(faculty \sqcap techSupportStaff)$ (5)

(1) All *mathCourse* are taught by staffId 123. (2) *Course* has at least 10 students and not more than 30 students. (3) *peopleAtUni* is combination between *staffMember* and *student*. (4) *FacultyInCS* is a *faculty* that belongs to *CSDepartment*. (5) *adminStaff* is *staffMember* that is not in *faculty* and *techSupportStaff*.

> $department \sqsubseteq\ \geq 10 hasMember.faculty \sqcup\ \leq 4 hasMember.adminStaff$ (6)

(6)Department has at least ten faculty members and not more than four members for admin staff. This qualified cardinality is not expressible in OWL DL.

As mentioned, OWL DL corresponds to a description logic. $\mathcal{SHOIN}(\mathcal{D}^+)$ is defined as follows, where A is an atomic concept, R is an abstract role, S is an abstract simple role, T_i are concrete roles, d is a concrete domain predicate, a_i and c_i are abstract and concrete individuals, respectively, and n is a non-negative integer:

Table 3.15 OWL DL complexities

Reasoning problems	Complexity			
	Taxonomic	Data	Query	Combined
Ontology consistency Concept satisfiability Concept subsumption Instance checking	NP-comp.	NP-Hard	N/A	NP-comp.
Conjunctive query answering	Open*	Open*	Open*	Open*

*Open** means the problem is still open

$$C \rightarrow A =| \neg C \mid C_1 \sqcap C_2 \mid C_1 \sqcup C_2 \mid \exists R.C \mid \forall R.C \mid \geq nS \mid \leq nS \mid$$

$$\{a_1, \ldots, a_n\} \mid \mid \geq nT \mid \leq nT \mid \exists T_1, \ldots, T_n.D \mid \forall T_1, \ldots, T_n.D$$

$$D \rightarrow d \mid \{c_1, \ldots, c_n\}$$

Semantics

Table 3.13 summaries the simple syntax and semantics of OWL DL. Since OWL DL is an representative profile of OWL, and OWL ontology is always wrote in the abstract syntax, we summary the abstract syntax, the corresponding DL syntax, and the semantics in Table 3.14, for OWL axioms and facts based on SHOIN(D+)

Complexity

The complexity of different reasoning tasks is described in Table 3.15 [78]:

3.3 Conclusion

In this chapter, we mainly illuminate the big picture of the state of the art of ontology languages and their underpinnings —description logics—the distinguished features of which include decidability and tractability. The key well-known trade-off in KR is between the expressive power and the computational properties of a KR language. The decidability and tractability results of ontology languages/description logics, together with practical tools and system of such languages, make ontology one of the foundations of the Semantic Web.

In the next chapter, we will present some industrial use cases of *ODSD* and the potential benefits ontology could bring. Some advanced ontology services which focus on various scalable reasoning optimisations will be continued in Chap. 5.

Chapter 4
Case Studies for Marrying Ontology and Software Technologies

Krzysztof Miksa, Pawel Sabina, Andreas Friesen, Tirdad Rahmani, Jens Lemcke, Christian Wende, Srdjan Zivkovic, Uwe Aßmann, and Andreas Bartho

Abstract In this chapter, we conclude Part I with several industrial case studies for motivating consistency-preserving software development. Many of these case studies will be revisited in later chapters, in particular Chaps. 9 and 10. Many of the solutions are based on the scalable reasoning technologies to be introduced in Chap. 5.

The rest of this chapter is organised as follows. Section. 4.1 shows which problems companies meet when they want to specify correct and consistent domain models of telecommunication device configurations. Another case study (Sect. 4.2) treats consistency preservation for behavioural models (process models). In business process refinement, the more concrete, refined processes have to conform to the abstract business processes the consultant specified. Showing this form of consistency of refinement is not easy for the process architect, as it turns out. Section 4.3 presents the problem of consistency of product lines, their correct modelling of their variant spaces and the consistent selection of their variants.

4.1 Case Studies on Domain Engineering

Model-driven technologies play an important role in domain engineering today. *Domain-specific language (DSL)*, which alleviates the complexity of the software systems, allows for expressing domain concepts effectively [70]. DSLs provide a simplified description of a specific domain. Maintaining models using small but clearly defined concepts and syntaxes increases productivity, resistance to mistakes and readability of the designed models. The models are typically used to generate code, possibly through a chain of transformations, or interpreted directly.

However, although DSLs constitute a significant step forwards in software development, there are still a number of challenges. The infrastructure of a DSL comprises several artefacts. This obviously includes elements such as the abstract and concrete syntax specifications, the well-formed rules, etc. Additionally, in order to enable the application and to increase productivity, various additional tooling is

J.Z. Pan et al. (eds.), *Ontology-Driven Software Development*,
DOI 10.1007/978-3-642-31226-7_4, © Springer-Verlag Berlin Heidelberg 2013

also provided. Typically, these tools are highly dependent on the semantics of the language constructs. However, current metamodelling technologies lack the means to specify semantics. Thus, in order to provide a tool infrastructure and to guide the developer in modelling, the semantics of the language is hard-coded in the tools. Therefore, there is a clear need for formalisms and techniques to provide an advanced support in order to help the users to make correct decisions. This can be provided by the tools based on knowledge and semantics, able to reason and bring meaningful guidance and answers for the user questions.

Furthermore, DSLs should be expressive enough to represent a broad range of possible cases found in the domain. Thus, a trade-off exists between productivity and expressiveness. A complicated DSL leads to lower productivity, while limiting expressive power may lead to the oversimplification and, in consequence, limited use of the DSL, since complicated cases need to be solved with other measures—typically in code.

In this section, we exemplify the problem and its solution with a case study based on one of the DSLs used in Comarch[1]: *physical devices DSL (PDDSL)*.

4.1.1   Problem Description

One of the challenges faced in the domain of next-generation operation support systems [69] is the increasing need for the consistent management of physical network equipment. However, the state-of-the-art solutions are unable to provide any consistent support to the user by answering questions that involve sophisticated, configuration-related constraints. Myriads of device types and their configurations can make users' everyday work a nightmare.

Let us take an example of a usual situation in telecommunication companies when one of the physical device cards is broken and requires replacement. The process of finding a valid replacement requires deep knowledge about every sub-component of the physical device (what kind of cards can be used as a replacement for a broken card, what kind of constraints a particular card has, etc.). In the state-of-the-art solutions, this problem is either completely ignored, leaving it to the expertise of the user, or the rules are hard-coded in the solution.

PDDSL

At Comarch, people use a DSL that describes the structure of the physical device and stores the information about the possible connections between the physical devices as well as the representation of the concrete instances of the devices: the PDDSL.

---

[1] http://www.comarch.com/

For exemplification, let us consider the simplest type of device found in the Cisco 7600 family, the Cisco 7603 router (Listing 4.1), which contains three slots. The first slot is reserved for a supervisor card, which is required. The second slot can optionally contain a backup supervisor or a `Catalyst_6500_Module`. The third slot is also optional and can contain only a `Catalyst_6500_Module`.

```
DeviceType "Cisco_7603" longName : "CISCO 7603 CHASSIS"
  allowed : {
  PossibleConfiguration "Cisco_7603_Configuration" {
    SlotType "1" allowed : "Supervisor_Engine_2" "Supervisor_Engine_720" required : true
    SlotType "2" allowed : "Supervisor_Engine_2" "Supervisor_Engine_720"
        "Catalyst_6500_Module" required : false
    SlotType "3" allowed : "Catalyst_6500_Module" required : false
  }
}
```

Listing 4.1 Cisco 7603 type model

As an example of instance model , let us consider an instance of the device type `Cisco_7603` (Listing 4.2). The model is invalid since the slot "1" contains a card which is disallowed in this slot.

```
Device serialNumber : "cisco_7603" hasType : "Cisco_7603"
  configuration : {
    Slot id : "1" :
      Card serialNumber : "sip−400" hasType : "7600−SIP−400"
    Slot id : "2" :
    Slot id : "3" :
  }
```

Listing 4.2 Sample incorrect instance model of Cisco 7603

To exemplify the problems faced by the PDDSL users we have selected the concrete use cases (UC), representing typical activities in the modelling process.

UC-1: Detect Errors in Physical Device-Type Definition

The definition of the device types may contain errors. Simple, syntactical errors can be detected by checking if the model conforms to the definition of the metamodel. The errors that break the semantics of the language are more difficult to detect. Such errors need to be reported to the user. The error message should include the reason why the model is incorrect and the model elements which are invalid.

As an example, let us consider the Cisco 7603 router model (Listing 4.1) and assume that an additional constraint requires it to contain a card of type `Cisco_7600_SIP`. Then this constraint is contradictory to the PDDSL specification (Listing 4.1) which does not allow the `Cisco_7600_SIP` in any of the slots.

UC-2: Find Wrongly Configured Instances of Devices and Explain Errors

Another typical situation in the process of modelling with PDDSL is when the user
wants to check if the instances of devices are consistent with the restrictions defined
in the type model. If an error is detected, the user needs to be informed about the
reason for the inconsistency.

Let us consider the instance of the device type `Cisco_7603` from Listing 4.2
and the respective type model presented in Listing 4.1. The inconsistency is related
to the slot "1", which contains a card of a card category which is not allowed
in this type of slot. Thus, the error message should report the invalid slot and
inform about the reason, for instance, by presenting the following error message:
"Slot requires card from the following card categories: Supervisor_Engine_2,
Supervisor_Engine_720".

UC-3: Suggest Card Categories Which Are Allowed in a Slot

The user should also be supported by providing suggestions about the possible
configurations. The suggestion should enumerate the card categories that can be
plugged into a slot in a given configuration instance.

One of the scenarios where the service is used is the model repair process after
the detection of an inconsistency. For instance, if we consider the model from
Listing 4.2, the next step after the inconsistency is detected is to ask for the card
categories which are allowed in slot "1". The user should get the following set of
card categories: `Supervisor_Engine_2`, `Supervisor_Engine_720` as the
result.

4.1.2 Implementation

A prototype implementation of the physical devices modelling tool was developed
using the Eclipse Modelling Framework [39]. The goal of the tool is to enable
modelling physical devices in the DSL and, at the same time, take advantage of
the formal semantics and the expressivity of OWL2. The conceptual architecture
of the prototype is depicted in Fig. 4.1. The user interacts with the `Integrated`
`modelling` component which enables creating structural models of the network
devices (`PD Modelling`) annotated with the additional configuration constraints
expressed in the web ontology language (`OWL Modelling`). This is achieved
through the integration of the DSLs with ontologies and thus opens the new spaces
for modelling the structure and the semantics together. The integrated models
remain easy to edit, process and be reasoned about using the existing tools and
approaches, being a structural and semantic model at the same time. To achieve
these goals, we follow the idea of integration of the models and ontologies [210].
More details on the language integration are provided in Sect. 9.3.

The integrated models are then transformed into the pure semantic descriptions
(the `Ontology`) which can be accepted by the `Semantic Reasoner`. The

Table 4.1 Mapping of the use cases to reasoning services

Use case	Ontology service(s)
UC-1: Detect errors in physical device type definition	• Satisfiability checking • Axiom explanation
UC-2: Find wrongly configured instances of devices and explain errors	• Consistency checking • Inconsistency explanation
UC-3: Suggest card categories which are allowed in a slot	• Subsumption checking

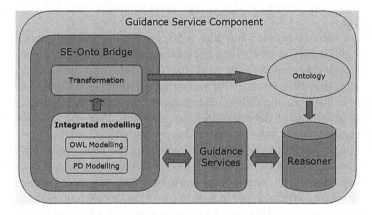

Fig. 4.1 Physical devices guidance service component

prototype was tested to work with two reasoners: Pellet[2] and TrOWL[3]. TrOWL is in fact a reasoning infrastructure that delegates the reasoning services to the other reasoners. Additionally, it can approximate the ontology into a language which offers the lower computational cost of reasoning. We have successfully experimented with the approximation to OWL2-EL [224].

Then, it is possible to invoke the Guidance Services which implement the PDDSL UC. These services can then benefit from the reasoning services provided by the Reasoner, such as the consistency checking, the satisfiability checking and classification. The reasoning results need to be interpreted and returned back to the Integrated modelling environment where they are presented to the user. The interpretation procedure relies on the reasoning explanations.

---

[2]http://clarkparsia.com/pellet/

[3]http://trowl.eu

Table 4.1 shows how we map the use cases to various ontology service(s). The summary of the reasoning services which are used to implement the UC is given in Sect. 8.1. More details on the implementation are provided in Chap. 9.

4.1.3 Results

Our prototypical approach enables the formalisation of the semantics of modelling languages, using a combination of the metamodel integration and model transformation technologies. The resulting ontology can then be reused for various purposes (validation of the type model, validation of the instances against their types and providing suggestions given the current state of the model). The implementation of such UC would require hard-coding the semantics within the tools that interact with the language.

With our case study, we show that it is possible to combine metamodelling and ontologies to handle such cases. The metamodelling (linguistic) aspect defines the domain-specific language for both the type layer and the instance layer. The language definition includes the metaproperty which represents instantiation (hasType). Then, having defined the bridge to the ontology, the semantics of such relationships can be defined as the class assertion. Thus, the validation of the instances against types can be performed, as well as many other UC.

Furthermore, the prototype allows for combining the DSL constructs with the OWL2 axioms in the PDDSL models. We have evaluated this approach in a scenario of representation of the compatibility constraints between the categories of the cards. Without the integrated approach, such constraints would require the extension of the PDDSL language definition. Our observation is that the language concepts should be able to express the typical cases found in the domain, while the rare cases can be expressed by the OWL2 axioms. This way, the DSL is kept simple, while not being limited with regard to its expressiveness.

4.2 Case Studies on Process Modelling and Refinement

In this section, the focus lies on case studies from SAP[4]. As one of the consortium members of the MOST project[5], SAP was responsible for introducing two industry-approaching case studies in the model-driven software development field. The technology providers in the MOST project could then find appropriate solutions and techniques to address the case study challenges. The overall goal of the case studies is thereby to increase the productivity of software developers and the quality

---

[4]http://www.sap.com

[5]http://project.odsd.eu/most/

Fig. 4.2 Development
lifecycle for realising
SOA-based SaaS software
solutions

of the designed artefacts in the main modelling phase of the addressed software
development life cycle.

4.2.1   Introduction

Observing software systems today, one of the ongoing trends in the market is the
Software as a Service (SaaS) business model. The idea behind SaaS is to offer an
application over the internet as a service against a monthly payment for usage by
customers. That means the customer is not the owner of the software but rents a
solution for a period of time during which he can access it remotely. In this model
the *independent software vendor (ISV)* is responsible for the implementation, the
operation and the management of the IT infrastructure.

A big challenge for SaaS solutions today is to guarantee a sufficient interoperability between SaaS offerings delivered by different software vendors. The prerequisite
for doing so is the *service-oriented architecture (SOA)* paradigm. The basic idea of
SOA is to divide software into loosely coupled components that interact via well-
defined service interfaces. This allows the composition of new applications and
missing functionality from existing software components. This is especially relevant
for large organisations with high functionality demands, since their demands can
only be covered by combining several SaaS offerings.

The end-to-end development process in an SOA environment needs a tailored
methodology which strongly supports the additional aspects of software engineering
and development. The software development life cycle, resp. the specific methodology to which the case studies will adhere, is depicted in Fig. 4.2.

To benefit as much as possible from the enterprise SOA development life cycle,
one should first clearly define the business requirements together with any other
use-case specific requirements. This includes specifying the actual process you want
to build, the required services and user interfaces, as well as the required security
protection for the SOA environment. Early definition of requirements ensures that
your business issues are the driver for changes in your IT. Once this definition
is complete, you need to check your requirements against the existing services to
identify missing services. To supply missing functionality, the *service provisioning*
development steps have to be performed. These include the following steps: service

modelling, service definition and service implementation. You start with modelling your services to clearly define the business context and business semantics of the services. This includes specification of relationships between the involved services, defining communication patterns, e.g. synchronous vs. asynchronous, etc. Next, you need to derive the exact definitions of the services from the models you created before. Based on the business semantics, you now need to define the service signatures. When doing this, you should reuse globally aligned data types in your landscape. Once your definitions are complete, you need to implement the appropriate functionality. The next step is discovery and description of services which includes adding documentation. Finally, the service consumption phase in which service operations become orchestrated in a process model takes place. The end result is a new process encapsulated as a newly developed service. These newly developed services can be used to fulfil the initially defined business requirements.

The modelling activities in the case studies mainly address the service consumption phase. This is due to the complexity of this stage and the many stakeholders involved in the service consumption phase. The idea is to apply guidance mechanisms and technologies developed in the MOST project in this critical phase of the development phase in order to increase the overall productivity of developers and the quality of the resulting modelling artefacts. The main modelling artefacts in this stage are process models that adhere to the initially given business requirements.

One of the important methodologies in the MDSD domain is the MDA approach proposed by the *object management group (OMG)*. In this methodology for software development, various layers for meta-metamodelling (M3 layer), metamodelling (M2 layer), modelling (M1 layer) and their concrete instances as data or runtime objects representing entities in the real world (M0 layer) are proposed. Furthermore, the methodology proposes that on the M1 layer, the design of a software system should first comprise *computation-independent model (CIM)*, then *platform-independent model (PIM)* and, finally, after several refinement steps on the PIM level, the *platform-specific model (PSM)* which is often an executable software system or software component on a specific platform and hardware infrastructure. More about MDA can be read on the official OMG website[6], where all the specifications are available.

The methodology that will be used in our case study is process model refinement and is strongly related to the MDA's concept of CIM's, PIM's and PSM's. To understand what is meant here we firstly refer to the following OMG quotations and will build up an analogy to the process refinement methodology used in the case studies and specifically in the service consumption phase.

- **PIM to PIM:** This transformation is used when models are enhanced, filtered or specialised during the development life cycle without needing any platform-dependent information. PIM to PIM mappings are generally related to *model refinement*.

---

[6]http://www.omg.org

- **PIM to PSM:** This transformation is used when the PIM is sufficiently refined to be projected to the execution infrastructure.

One of the evident points in the prior statements is the fact that models become refined, enhanced and extended successively in order to control the complexity of models and consequently software systems. The same holds true in the service consumption phase. Therefore, a process refinement methodology can significantly help to manage complexity of models. In this methodology, processes are not developed in one step, by one developer and based on one and the same model. Moreover, multiple models that are refinements of each other will be created by several development staff members with different roles. Developers will refine activities until a certain level of detail and model granularity is reached in which the models are deployable on existing executable software components. These components expose the behavioural patterns of enterprise software components like the *supply chain management* (SCM) component and the *customer relationship management* (CRM) component that are used by many enterprise application customers these days.

So a CIM model in the process refinement methodology is an abstract process model on a very high level of understanding with some process modelling entities concerned with the core business requirements. The abstract model is then refined to a specific process (CIM to PIM) in which additional process entities can be added, alternative paths can be included and the type of execution can be specified, e.g. parallel or exclusive. Here it is important to capture the linkage between the abstract process entities and the specific process entities as the result of a refinement step. We refer to this kind of information as the *refinement information* between two processes.

Generally, there can exist an arbitrary number of refinement steps (PIM to PIM) until a level of detail is reached where process activities can be mapped to service operations of software components (PIM to PSM). We refer to this mapping as the *grounding information* of a process model. Each software component has a component model which is also described as a process model where activities are concrete service operations that are already bound to a server which is able to execute service operation requests.

The refinement and grounding information have the following usage scenarios that will be addressed in more detail in the case study problem descriptions. Both kinds of information together make up the refinement specifications.

- Consistency checking of control flows between abstract and specific processes
- Tracing of refinement decisions and errors through a refinement hierarchy of processes
- Managing of outstanding development tasks in the service consumption phase

In Fig. 4.3, the reader can see the correspondence of the process refinement methodology with the modelling steps proposed by MDA. Furthermore, arrows marked with an S+V mark the necessary positions where specification and validation

Fig. 4.3 Analogy to MDA
modelling categories

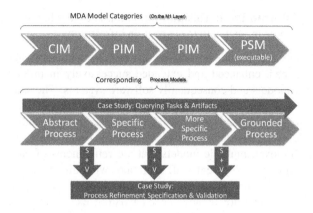

techniques are of high relevance to the case studies, especially for consistency checking of control flows between abstract and specific processes.

4.2.2   Case Study: Process Refinement

One of the increasingly important techniques to reduce the complexity of process modelling in the service consumption phase is modelling on different interrelated levels of abstraction. For this purpose we will focus on *refinement* as a special way of dealing with modelling levels in one and the same modelling language like BPMN. Refinement can be generally seen as a technique which allows to add more information to a model on a certain abstraction level while preserving the original information and constraints on the neighbouring level, either above or below or more concrete or more abstract. This technique is especially useful when several people with different expertise and responsibilities work on the same business process.

In the case of business processes there are generally two major categories of constraints which have to be considered and preserved on any abstraction layer:

- **Behavioural constraints:** Behavioural constraints are represented by the control flow of a process and are necessary to describe which possible execution flows are allowed in a process or will be undertaken in the default or the exceptional cases.
- **Data constraints:** Data constraints are concerned with the compatibility of input and output data of the process activities as well as the data flow of the processes.

In the MOST project all refinement techniques are primarily concerned with behavioural constraints by considering the control flow of processes. For this purpose our focus is on modelling approaches where specification and verification of control flow constraints can be accomplished adequately. Data-related constraints are not considered in our work due to the lack of time and resources for such

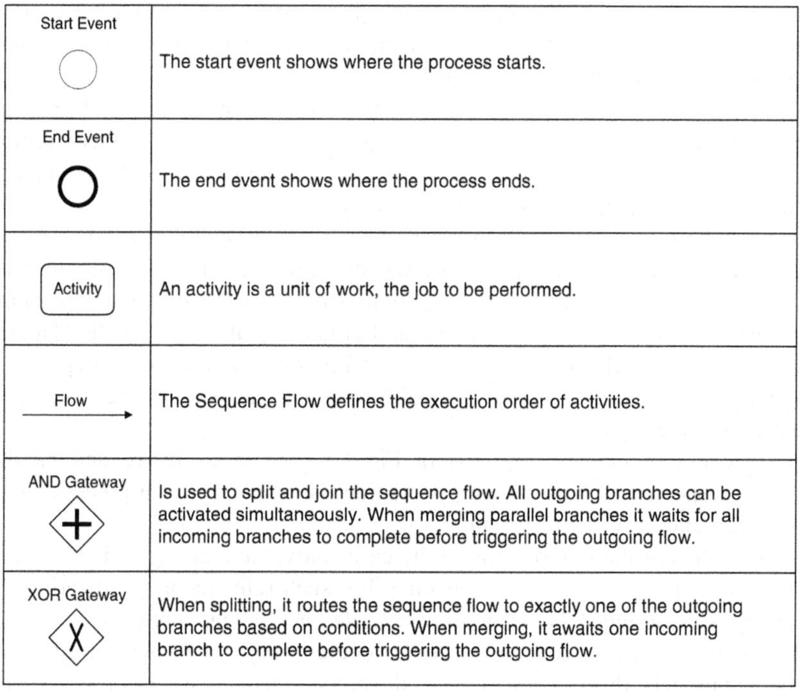

Start Event	The start event shows where the process starts.
End Event	The end event shows where the process ends.
Activity	An activity is a unit of work, the job to be performed.
Flow	The Sequence Flow defines the execution order of activities.
AND Gateway	Is used to split and join the sequence flow. All outgoing branches can be activated simultaneously. When merging parallel branches it waits for all incoming branches to complete before triggering the outgoing flow.
XOR Gateway	When splitting, it routes the sequence flow to exactly one of the outgoing branches based on conditions. When merging, it awaits one incoming branch to complete before triggering the outgoing flow.

Fig. 4.4 Core elements of the business process management and notation (BPMN) standard

a broad scientific area. But in the future we hope to be able to also check data-related constraints of business processes and to combine them with our approaches developed within the MOST project.

All process models in this chapter are based on core modelling elements of BPMN[7], which is a well-known and community-wide accepted OMG standard in the business process management field. Many studies have shown that most people use only the core elements, which are depicted in Fig. 4.4, in almost 80% of the cases where a business process has to be modelled by using BPMN.

Originally, activities and tasks are defined as follows within the BPMN 1.1 specification:

- An activity is work that is performed within a business process. An activity can be atomic or non-atomic (compound). The types of activities that are a part of a business process diagram are process, sub-process and task.
- A task is an atomic activity that is included within a process. A task is used when the work in the process is not broken down to a finer level of process model detail.

---

[7]http://www.bpmn.org/

For simplification reasons, from now on, we talk about activities whenever we refer to atomic and compound activities and mention explicitly whether they are atomic or non-atomic (further decomposable).

A process model in BPMN is a non-simple directed graph, in which multiple edges between any two vertices are not permitted. However, we consider a normal form of process models for the sake of simplicity as opposed to the full set of partly redundant constructs in BPMN.

In our definition, vertices fall into *activities, gateways* and the specific vertices *start event* and *end event*. Figure 4.5 shows several BPMN diagrams of which the bottom left process (a) consists of two activities between the start and end events. A gateway is either opening or closing and either exclusive (i.e. XOR Gateway in Fig. 4.4) or parallel (i.e. AND Gateway in Fig. 4.4). Gateways are depicted as diamonds containing either a plus symbol for parallel gateways or a cross symbol for exclusive gateways.

The process models (c) and (d) in Fig. 4.5 contain exclusive and parallel gateways, respectively. Furthermore, we define the semantics of a process model using the execution set semantics in [222].

As described in the introduction of the case study, the major goal is to support the automatic process refinement checking. For such refinement specification and validation, we distinguish between *process models* and *component models*.

Process models can be refined to a certain degree where they can be grounded on component models. Process refinement is the procedure of creating a process model (the specific model) and mapping that process model to an existing, more abstract process model. During this procedure, abstract activities can be decomposed to more specific activities.

On the other hand, component models cannot be refined but used for grounding. Grounding means to assign a task in a process model to a service operation, i.e. a Web service operation, which will be invoked during run time as the implementation of a activity or task. In our case studies, the Web service operations are embedded in a component model which constrains the allowed invocation sequences of the Web service operations. The component model acts as a contract of a component in that the behaviour of the component at run time is assumed to not go beyond the component model. When a process model is refined and grounded on component models correctly, it will be executable since all the component models are executable.

Here we distinguish between two types of cross-process violation checks to which we refer as the *refinement check* and the *grounding check*.

In a refinement check, violations between the abstract and the specific process will be detected. Based on the found violations, either the abstract process has to be changed or the more specific process needs to be corrected.

The grounding check has to account for which constraints in which used component models are violated. Based on the violations the process must be remodelled and adjusted until all constraints are satisfied. The component models will not be affected by the violation check since they are assumed to be correct and executable.

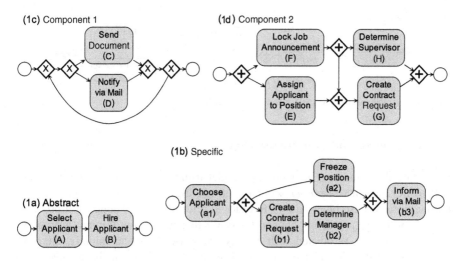

Fig. 4.5 Wrong process refinement

In Fig. 4.5, two component models (c) and (d) at the top and two process models (a) and (b) at the bottom of the figure are depicted. In this example, process (a) is an abstract process that will be refined to the specific process (b) which then will be grounded on the component models (c) and (d). For simplification, we used capital letters as an alias for tasks of the abstract process and the component models which can be seen enclosed in parenthesis at the bottom of each task shape. For tasks of the specific process we used indexed small letters where the small letter inclusively means that these tasks are refinements or groundings of the tasks aliased with corresponding capital letters. This notation in process diagrams will be used constantly through this book.

Now, we will have a deeper look to the refinement validation checks considering the abstract and specific process in Fig. 4.5. By analysing the specific process together with the refinement information, one will find out that task a2 might be interleaved with tasks b1 and b2. According to the abstract process, this is an invalid sequencing of tasks. On the contrary, the specific process depicted in Fig. 4.6 satisfies all constraints given by the abstract process (a) in Fig. 4.5.

The refinement step can be continued until a certain level where one can ground the tasks to tasks within the component models. For instance, by assuming the process in Fig. 4.6 to be refined enough to be grounded, a correct grounding would be {(a1, E), (a2,F), (b1,G), (b2,H), (b3,D)}. Exactly like the refinement step the grounding step needs validation of constraints given by the component models. Only if all these constraints are maintained, processes will be correctly deployable on an execution engine.

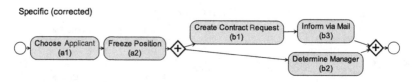

Fig. 4.6 Adapted specific process for correct refinement

Execution Set Semantics of Process Models

We define the semantics of a process model using the execution set semantics [84]. An execution is a *proper* sequence of activities ($a_i \in$ A): $[a_1, a_2, \ldots, a_n]$. Furthermore, we use binary tuples in order to refer to directed edges of a process flow. A proper sequence is obtained by simulating token flow through a process model. A token is associated with exactly one vertex or edge. Initially, there is exactly one token, associated with the start event. Tokens can be created and consumed following the rules below. Whenever a token is created in an activity, the activity is appended to the sequence. Exactly one of the following actions is performed at a time:

- For creating a token in an activity or in the end event, exactly one token must be consumed from the incoming edge (v_2, v_1).
- For creating one token in the leaving edge (v_1, v_2), exactly one token must be removed from an activity or from the start event.

- For creating a token in a parallel close gateway, exactly one token must be consumed from every incoming edge (v, g).
- For creating a token in an exclusive close gateway, exactly one token must be consumed from exactly one incoming edge (v, g).
- For creating one token in the leaving edge (g, v), exactly one token must be removed from a close gateway g.

- For creating a token in an open gateway g, exactly one token must be consumed from the incoming edge (v, g).
- For creating one token in each leaving edge (g, v), exactly one token must be removed from a parallel open gateway g.
- For creating one token in exactly one leaving edge (g, v), exactly one token must be removed from an exclusive open gateway g.

Generally, a simulation of a process ends if none of the actions can be performed. The result then is a proper sequence of activities—an execution. It is to be noted that each execution is finite. However, there may be an infinite number of executions for a process model. The execution set of a process model P, denoted by ES_P, is the (possibly infinite) set of all proper sequences of the process model.

For example, ES_a for process (1a) in Fig. 4.5 is $\{[A, B]\}$: first A, then B (for brevity, we refer to an activity by its short name, which appears in the diagrams in parentheses). Process (1b) contains parallel gateways to express that some activities can be performed in any order: $ES_b = \{[a_1, a_2, b_1, b_2, b_3,]$ $[a_1, b_1, a_2, b_2, b_3], [a_1, b_1, b_2, a_2, b_3]\}$. Exclusive gateways are used in process (1c) to choose from the two activities and to form a loop: $ES_c = \{[C], [D, D], [C, C],$ $[C, D], [D, C], [D, D], \ldots\}$. Process (1d) shows that gateways can also occur in a non-blockwise manner: $[ES]_d = \{[E, F, G, H], [E, F, H, G], [F, H, E, G],$ $[F, E, G, H], [F, E, H, G]\}$.

Categories of Refinement Violations

In order to understand the challenges and solutions behind process refinement specification and validation, a set of inconsistent refinement specification examples between processes are required. These examples will help to build up a proper specification of consistent process refinement based on the requirements that the modellers decide to adhere. Therefore, in the following, a first categorisation of possible inconsistencies will be explained based on comprehensive examples:

1. Incorrect Direct Predecessor and Successor Relation
2. Incorrect Indirect Predecessor and Successor Relation
3. Missing Activities
4. Violation of Exclusivity Constraints

Incorrect Direct Predecessor and Successor Relation

Activities within a process are ordered according to the process flow. During an execution, only some execution sequences are allowed, given by the predecessor and successor relation of activities. Often, it could happen that during a refinement to a specific process the direct ordering of activities becomes violated. In such scenarios, the specific process would not comply with the constraints of the more abstract process which is violating one of our first intuitive principles of refinement.

In Fig. 4.7, a simple direct ordering violation is depicted with the refinement information $\text{orig}(a_1)=\text{orig}(a_2) = a$, $\text{orig}(b_1) = b$ and $\text{orig}(c_1) = c$. According to the abstract process flow activity, a_1 is not allowed to be the predecessor of activity c_1, and activity c_1 is not allowed to be the successor of activity a_1. The same holds also true for activity c_1 and activity a_2.

By taking the incorrect refinement example 1 in Fig. 4.8, an incorrect ordering of activities is depicted. The activity c_2 with $\text{orig}(c_2) = c$ is not allowed to be executed before the end event. In the second example, the activity d_1 with $\text{orig}(d_1) = d$ is not allowed to be the successor of the activity c_1 with $\text{orig}(c_1) = c$.

Process To Refine:

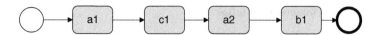

Incorrect Refinement:

Fig. 4.7 A simple direct ordering violation

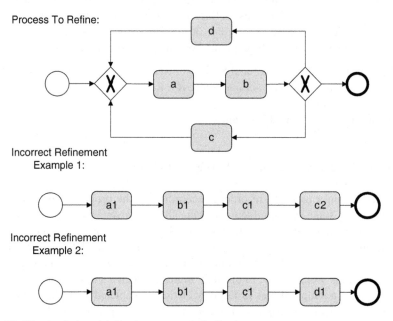

Fig. 4.8 Direct ordering violation in processes including loops

Incorrect Indirect Predecessor and Successor Relation

In parallel execution blocks often independent branches according to the ordering of activities exist. Consequently these activities can be ordered arbitrarily in a refining process and lead to indirect ordering violations on some branches of the process flow.

An example is given in Fig. 4.9 where an incorrect refinement is given because the execution of the activity b_1 with $orig(b_1) = b$ before a_1 with $orig(a1) = a$, although all direct predecessor and successor relations are correct. By exchanging the positions of the activity a_1 and b_1, this violation can be resolved.

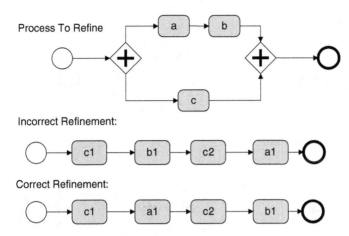

Fig. 4.9 Example of an indirect ordering violation

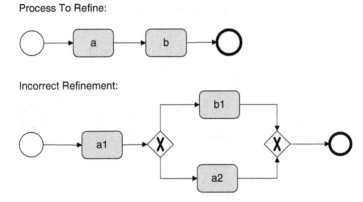

Fig. 4.10 Omission of tasks caused by including exclusive process branches through refinement

Missing Activities

Another type of violation is given when during an execution of the specific process some activities would be missing. Although in some cases such an error would lead to an incorrect direct ordering of activities, there are also cases in parallel execution blocks where the ordering of tasks is absolutely correct but still some activities are missing.

In the first example depicted in Fig. 4.10, a process refinement is given in which an exclusive gateway is included which leads to two execution flows. The execution flow $[start, a_1, a_2, end]$ is erroneous since the abstract process does not permit omission of task b.

Within the second example shown in Fig. 4.11, a parallel execution block is refined, and in the resulting more specific process, the task d has been omitted.

Process To Refine:

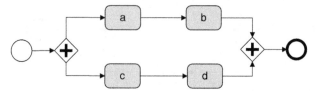

Incorrect Refinement:

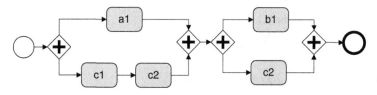

Fig. 4.11 Missing tasks caused by refining a parallel execution block

Process To Refine:

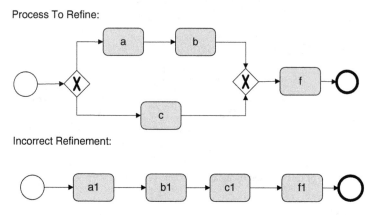

Incorrect Refinement:

Fig. 4.12 Violation of exclusivity constraints in refinements

Violation of Exclusivity Constraints

Some process flow branches include exclusive gateways that split the execution exclusively to several branches. Activities on different branches of such a splitting are not allowed to be executed during the same execution especially when the exclusive gateway does not occur in a looping segment of the process.

For example, in Fig. 4.12 based on the abstract process, either the activities a and b or the activity c has to be executed. But in the specific process refining the abstract process, the sequence of activities $[a_1, b_1, c_1]$ with $\mathrm{ref}(a1) = a, \mathrm{ref}(b1) = b$

and ref($c1$) $=$ c is inconsistent with the abstract process flow since these activities are not allowed to be executed all together.

Remark About Process Refinement Validation

Any validation technology or algorithm to be applied for refinement violation detection should be at least *sound* and in the best case also *complete*. Soundness means that every detected violation is truly a violation based on the refinement specification. Completeness on the other hand means that the validation technique will detect an error whenever a true error based on the specification is existing, but it makes no statement about other cases. Soundness is obviously the more critical property to be ensured, since without soundness any answer of the validation engine would not be trustworthy.

4.2.3   Case Study: Querying Tasks and Artefacts

Besides the specification and verification of correct process refinements, an additional aid for developers, which is highly needed, is tool support for managing the development tasks related to process refinement in the service consumption phase. In this case study we are not looking for a solution which enables a manual management of tasks through editable task lists. Instead, we are looking for a solution which automatically updates the task list of a developer based on the given development status. That means that tasks need not be generated, deleted or assigned manually, as they rather become available as soon as the development process requires them to be executed and will be deleted as soon as they are performed correctly. For such task management scenarios, the following questions have to be answered:

1. What are the modelling artefacts in the service consumption phase?
2. Which type of tasks can be performed on which modelling artefacts?
3. When are tasks applicable on modelling artefacts?
4. What is the effect of performing a certain task on an artefact?
5. Which statuses are possible for an artefact in an development phase?

Methodology

For the task management aspects in this case study it is necessary to follow a methodology to capture all relevant requirements to answer the above questions. Therefore, the following methodology depicted in Fig. 4.13 is proposed which will

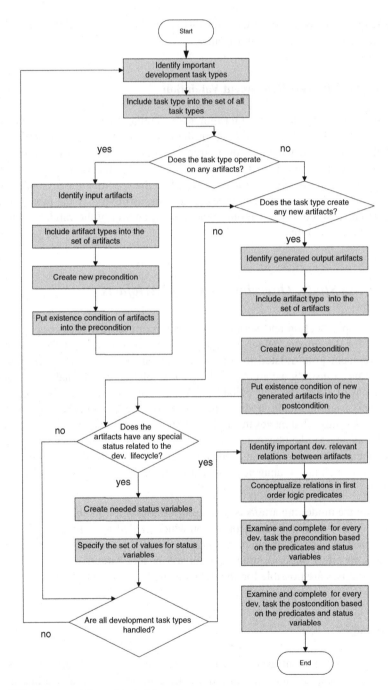

Fig. 4.13 Refinement flaws detected through reasoning

help later on in Sect. 13.4 to develop a guidance ontology for querying tasks and artefacts for task management purposes.

The methodology is independent of any special representation as a data model as long as a certain level of expressiveness, reasoning services and query mechanisms can be guaranteed. The goal of the methodology is a logic-based description of all task types and artefacts together with their interplays. Consequently, it can be used as a pre-stage of conceptual modelling, independent of a specific technology.

1. The most crucial entities in a development phase are the development task types that can be performed. Therefore, the methodology starts with identifying the development tasks firstly. Each development task type will then be included then in a set called *DT* which represents the set of all task types.
2. In order to characterise task types in our methodology depicted as a flow chart in Fig. 4.13, input artefacts on which the development tasks operate and output artefacts which they generate have to be identified. In that way, by starting from the development tasks, also the crucial set of important development artefacts *DA* for the considered development stage can be detected.
3. Development artefacts go through the development stage and undergo changes and modifications. Some of these changes are very crucial to the development life cycle because of their influence on the overall development progress. For instance, the validation of a model before code generation is an important development task, whose outcome decides whether code generation can be started or not. For this kind of changes that have a strong effect on the development process, status variables are considered in our methodology. These variables are used to capture crucial changes and can be referred later on in preconditions and postconditions of task types.
4. The precondition of a task type exactly specifies when a task type is applicable. On the other hand, the postcondition specifies the effects of performing a task type. Generally, performing a development task has an influence on its environment which will be specified as a postcondition in our methodology. But it might be the case that this impact is not crucial for artefacts and the execution of other task types so that it can be left out.
5. Before starting with the completion of the pre- and postconditions, the following items have to be captured and documented completely:

   - The set of all development task types DT
   - The set of all development artefacts AT
   - The set of all development status variables with possible values
   - The possible relations between artefacts

   Based on these items, in the final step, one has to go over every task type of DT with a fine-toothed comb and add the required pre- and postconditions. Thereby, input resp. output artefacts of AT cause additional preconditions resp. postconditions for the application of development tasks. The procedure ends when every task type is handled appropriately.

4.2.4   Process Refinement Validation: Implementation and Results

The ontological service used for process refinement validation is the satisfiability reasoning service, whose characteristics are depicted in Table 8.4. The main idea used for process refinement validation is the transformation of a process model to an ontology TBox which represents all constraints necessary for process refinement. Inconsistent concepts found by the reasoner through satisfiability checking would then indicate all inconsistent tasks and could be marked and highlighted appropriately in the modelling environment.

The prototypes have shown that it is possible to validate process refinements through reasoning. The proofs can be read in Sect. 10.3. Furthermore, one has to think about appropriate error explanation in case of inconsistent refinements. Investigations in that direction are ongoing and would even more lead to a better quality and productivity of developers daily work.

4.2.5   Querying Tasks and Artefacts: Implementation and Results

The ontological services used for querying tasks and artefacts are the querying reasoning services, whose characteristics are depicted in Table 8.9. In this case study the ontology solution consists of a Tbox that includes all generic and case study-specific concepts needed for guidance through task management. For example, there are concepts existing for artefacts and different task types occurring in the development processes. A concrete development project that is in a specific development status where a number of artefacts are created and certain tasks are obligatory or optionally performable are represented by the ABox of the ontology. The task lists of the development staff are filled by applying a query on the ontology. More details on the ontology and the queries can be found in Sect. 10.4.

The result of this case study is a guidance ontology tailored to the case study requirements. This ontology is used as a data model representing developer task lists within the prototypes. On the UI level, a developer who follows the process refinement methodology is supported by a special UI view linked to the guidance ontology, which enables him to see the mandatory and optional outstanding development tasks. The benefit here is that the task lists will be filled automatically based on artefact creation, modification and consistency checking without any user intervention due to appropriate automated query mechanisms.

4.3   Case Study on Software Product Line Engineering

In general, software systems for a particular application domain often not only share some similar functionality, but also vary on some parts. This insight has led software engineers to move from development of single software systems to the development of Software Product Lines (SPLs). A SPL describes a set of related software systems that share a set of common feature. A systematic sharing of such commonalities and the development of software systems in families increases reuse and is, thus, more cost effective [165].

A SPL is typically specified within two specification spaces: *problem space* and *solution space* [51]. In the problem space, *feature models* [114] are typically used to specify features of the members of the SPL, as well as their interdependencies. Therefore, feature models provide a variety of means to express feature relations [18, 52, 53, 114]. The problem space specification provided by feature models is of particular importance for the customisation of concrete product variants from the product line. The set of features selected for a concrete product variant is called *variant model*. Each variant model has to conform to the feature constraints imposed by the according feature model.

Solution space models are comprehensive models that specify the realisation of the complete SPL. From the solution space models, a particular product can be derived automatically by removing parts of it. Therefore, *mapping models* define mappings between features and elements of solution space models. These mappings determine which elements contribute to a variant-specific solution space model: To derive a variant-specific solution space model all elements are removed that are mapped to features not contained in the variant model.

4.3.1   Problem Description

Industrial SPLs can grow very large and contain several thousand features. Accordingly, the feature models describing their problem space can also grow large and complex. In such huge models, it is very time consuming, costly and error prone to manually verify that the feature dependencies are consistent and that each variant model conforms to the corresponding feature model. As product variants shall be instantiated automatically from variant models their validity is of great importance.

For these reasons, and due to the large variety of relations that can be used for problem space modelling, there is a need for a general specification of feature model semantics and an automated approach for feature model analysis of each variant model. Furthermore, in order to facilitate easier repair, there is also a need for explaining the causes of found constraint violations.

The case study described in this section will be used to exemplify and demonstrate the application of ontology technology for that purpose.

4.3.2   Case Study Implementation

One main objective of the MOST project is to demonstrate the benefits and evaluate the limitations of ontology-driven software development (ODSD) by making MDSD tools ontology-enabled. In addition to the standard modelling features such as graphical and textual editors, model and metamodel management or model transformation, such ontology-enabled modelling environments build on an ontological foundation to provide sophisticated means for semantic model validation [72, 73, 115, 131], for transitive tracing among various heterogeneous artefacts [182, 183] and for software process guidance [16, 17, 226]. Building these complex environments is not a trivial task. Various heterogeneous tools need to be integrated into a uniform infrastructure, in order to provide the end user the uniform access to the environment services.

To provide such an infrastructure, previous project deliverables [226] introduced a *Generic MOST Workbench Architecture*—a blueprint for ontology-enabled MDSD tool environments. The manifold applications of MDSD mean a specific challenge for the realisation and practical adoption of such tool environments. Aiming for a more systematic understanding of commonalities and variability among them we applied techniques introduced in Software Product Line Engineering [165] and introduced a feature-based customisation process for ontology-enabled MDSD tools [217, 226].

A Feature-Based Development Process for the MOST TOPF

To enable the development of MOST products in a product line, we require a specific development process. Feature modelling and feature-based development [165] provides means to identify, realise and share common assets of product line members. Figure 4.14 depicts this feature-based process for the realisation and customisation of MOST products from the *MOST tool product family (W3C)*. The process consists of two main phases. The first phase is concerned with realising the MOST TOPF product line. It consists of three basic steps. Step (1) is concerned with the identification of common and variable features of all tools in the MOST TOPF. It results in a feature model [114] that captures both variability and dependencies of workbench functions from the perspective of a MOST product developer. Step (2) involves the implementation of these features in components of the generic workbench and the design of a generic workbench integrating these components. Note that not all components of the MOST TOPF will be part of every MOST product. This variability needs to be supported by an extensible and adaptive component architecture. The third and last step of the TOPF engineering phase is the mapping between features and realisation components. This mapping connects features from the feature model with components in the MOST TOPF architecture. This mapping is stored in the so-called mapping model that is used to allow for an automatic derivation of a concrete workbench instance during the following phase of workbench instantiation.

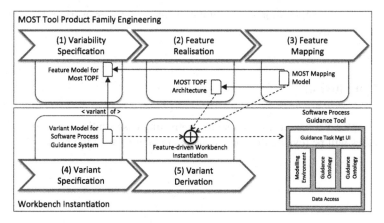

Fig. 4.14 The feature-based development process for the MOST TOPF and the instantiation of the OSGS

Figure 4.14 illustrates how this second phase is used for the derivation of a typical MOST TOPF workbench instance, in particular of the *ontology-driven software guidance system (OSGS)*. In step (4), a concrete variant of the feature model from step (1) is defined. It consists of the features that are required for a particular MOST TOPF instance. The resulting variant model can then be checked against the feature model, to ensure that all feature constraints and feature dependencies are satisfied. Finally, in step (5), the variant model is evaluated together with the specification of the MOST component architecture from step (2) and the mapping model from step (3). In this automatic derivation step all components that are mapped to features not contained in the variant model are removed from the component architecture to generate a refined and customised MOST TOPF product.

4.3.3   Results

The relationship between the MOST TOPF and ontology technology can be considered in two directions. First, the MOST TOPF is an attempt to contribute an infrastructure for ODSD tools that provide means to customise the combination of MDSD and ontology technology for use-case-specific requirements. This direction will be discussed in Chap. 12.

Second, as the development of the MOST TOPF is realised as a model-driven process, it itself is a case study of ODSD. It will be used throughout this book to demonstrate how ontology technology can be used to address current challenges of feature-modelling in *software product line engineering (SPLE)* by ontology technology. In Sect. 2.2.6, we already discussed the foundations of feature-modelling and derived questions important for feature model analysis. Section 9.2

will elaborate the application of reasoning technology for answering these feature analysis questions.

4.4 Conclusion

In this chapter, we have presented some motivating case studies for *ODSD*. These case studies will be revisited in some chapters in later parts of the book.

Part II
Foundational Technologies for
Ontology-Driven Software Development

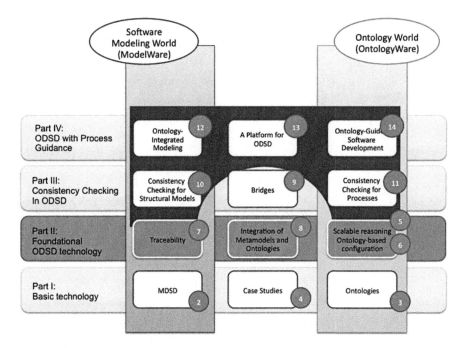

Fig. RoadMap.2 The roadmap of Part II

This part introduces the enabling technologies for ontology-driven software development. First of all, reasoning must be made scalable, so that developers do not need to wait for the answers of the reasoner (Chap. 5). Secondly, traceability has to be extended over models and ontologies (Chap. 6). Based on this, a first integration technology for metamodels and ontologies is introduced, so that integrated languages can be engineered (Chap. 7). All the enabling technologies involve tools that can be made ontology-aware.

Part II contains following chapters:

Chapter 5   Scalable Ontology Reasoning Services
Chapter 6   Traceability
Chapter 7   Metamodelling and Ontologies

Chapter 5
Scalable Ontology Reasoning Services

Edward Thomas, Yuan Ren, Jeff Z. Pan, Yuting Zhao, and Nophadol Jekjantuk

Abstract This chapter presents scalable ontology reasoning technology, one of the enabling technologies for ODSD. For basic definitions about ontology and reasoning, we refer readers to Chap. 3. As to be illustrated in Chaps. 9 and 10, reasoning services will be required to perform consistency checking and to derive implicit knowledge from the ontologies. Given the large number and volume of models, their complexity and the diversities of required reasoning tasks, reasoning technologies must be scalable and efficient and support as much expressive power as possible to minimise user restrictions in modelling. Furthermore, software engineers are usually not ontology experts or logicians. In order to present reasoning results in a user-friendly manner, it is required to not only deliver the answers of queries but also provide explanations of such answers.

In this chapter, we present the scalable ontology reasoning and explanation technologies with the TrOWL infrastructure [203]. In Sect. 5.1 we introduce the TrOWL system and its applications, in particular its technologies and optimisations. In Sect. 5.2 we show how to use the reasoning facilities of TrOWL to generate explanations for reasoning answers.

5.1 TrOWL: Tractable Reasoning Infrastructure for OWL 2

The approach of TrOWL is to offer support for all the expressive power of OWL 2 while maintaining tractability, by using language transformations. In particular, we utilise a semantic approximation [156] to transform OWL 2 DL ontologies into OWL 2 QL for conjunctive query answering and a syntactic approximation [172] from OWL 2 to OWL 2 EL for TBox and ABox reasoning. With such transformation technologies, reasoning with local closed world assumption can also be supported [171]. In addition, TrOWL contains a profile checker to detect

J.Z. Pan et al. (eds.), *Ontology-Driven Software Development*,
DOI 10.1007/978-3-642-31226-7_5, © Springer-Verlag Berlin Heidelberg 2013

which profile an ontology may already fit into, and it has support for heavyweight reasoning using a plug-in reasoner such as Fact++, Pellet, Hermit or Racer.

5.1.1 Applications

Before we go into details of the reasoning techniques in TrOWL, we illuminate the big picture by briefly introducing how reasonings are used in real-world applications.

Validating Process Refinements During software development, processes are modelled in the standard language *business process management notation (BPMN)*; these process models are then refined to produce progressively more detailed models (Sect. 4.2). Several metrics exist to validate these refinements as being consistent with the earlier models, but no tools are available which can validate these refinements automatically across multiple refinements on large models. Our approach has been to translate this process model into an ontology and use ontology reasoning services to validate the model (see Sect. 10.3 for the ontological solution). With this approach, we can check if the refinements are valid or highlight the processes which are causing the problem.

The process refinement case study generates ontologies with *general concept inclusion (GCI)* of particular patterns. At the time of developing REL [172], mainstream reasoners such as Pellet and FaCT++ failed to efficiently provide complete classification results on the generated ontologies. Via the syntactic approximation of TrOWL, the GCIs in these ontologies can be efficiently resolved, and the reasoning results can be proved to be complete (see Sect. 10.3.8 for more details about approximation in this use case).

Software Engineering Guidance Ontology The case study of physical device configuration (Sect. 4.1) uses ontologies to validate the consistency of the configuration of a network device. These devices are configured with several cards, and this configuration must be validated against a model which describes correct configurations.

The case study generates ontologies describing the configuration of network devices. These ontologies can sometimes be inconsistent, reflecting an invalid configuration of a physical device. To understand how this is manifested in the physical device and provide guidance on how it may be resolved, it is necessary to find justifications for the inconsistency and isolate each axiom set which may be causing the inconsistency. Traditional tableaux reasoners usually terminate when an inconsistency is detected, making it difficult to obtain all justifications. In this case, TrOWL can provide a more efficient and reliable service when used as a reasoning back end. Furthermore, in order to provide suggestions to engineers, some of the concepts or properties in the ontology need to be closed (see Sects. 7.3.1 and 9.3 for details). Traditional ontology reasoning imposes the open world assumption (OWA) and does not support such services. In TrOWL we use an NBox (negation as failure box) to allow users to specify the concepts and properties they want to close and provide reasoning support.

Linked Open Data We have also investigated using TrOWL for linked open data repositories. RDF-DL [77] is the overlapping part of linked open data language RDF and ontology language OWL DL and is also a sublanguage of the OWL 2 QL profile. We used the RDF-DL reasoning component of TrOWL in the Billion Triple Challenge in ISWC 2009. We managed to successfully load and reason over the billion triple RDF data set, with full RDFS reasoning over class and property subsumption. The benefit of using TrOWL for linked open data is that it supports reasoning in all profiles of OWL, as well as using RDF-DL reasoning over RDFS data. Since conjunctive query answering is always reduced to OWL 2 QL query answering, this allows queries to be run over large heterogeneous ontologies with its characteristic LogSpace data complexity.

5.1.2 Technology

TrOWL is based around two primary technologies: language transformations and lightweight reasoners. The most important of these are outlined briefly here. More technical details will be presented in the next two subsections.

Language Transformations

TrOWL is the common interface to a number of reasoners. Quill provides reasoning services over RDF-DL and OWL 2 QL; REL provides reasoning over OWL 2 EL; and TrOWL can support full DL reasoning using a plug-in reasoner such as Pellet or Fact++. These reasoners and the languages which they support are optimised for certain applications, for example, OWL 2 QL has excellent ABox query answering performance, but it lacks many constructors present in the more expressive flavours of OWL 2.

The transformation from OWL 2 to OWL 2 QL is based around semantic approximation from OWL DL to DL-Lite which is described in [156]. Semantic approximation uses a heavyweight reasoner to guarantee that every axiom in the approximated ontology is valid with respect to the source ontology. Because the semantics of OWL 2 QL are a subset of, and are hence compatible with, the direct semantics OWL 2, this means that for all reasoning results against the approximated ontology are sound. In fact, it has been shown that for conjunctive query answering, which is the strength of the QL language, results against the semantic approximation are also complete for a very large class of queries (those with no non-distinguished variables or with non-distinguished variables in leaf nodes of the query).

The transformation from OWL 2 to OWL 2 EL is based on the soundness-preserving approximate reasoning approach presented in [175]. This is achieved by representing non-OWL 2 EL concept expressions with fresh named concepts and maintaining non-OWL 2 EL information, such as complementary relations, in separate data structures. In the reasoning stage, additional completion rules are plugged into the inference engine to restore the semantics of these information. The approximation is syntax-based and can be performed in linear time. The additional completion rules retain the tractability of OWL 2 EL. Thus the overall complexity for OWL 2 DL ontologies can be reduced to PTIME. Although known to be incomplete, our evaluation shows that such transformation can classify existing benchmarks very efficiently with high recall (over 95%) [175].

Except for the improved performance of standard reasoning services, the language transformations also enable many other non-standard reasoning services. For example, the support of local closed world reasoning can be reduced to incremental reasoning, which can be further realised more efficiently by transformation to OWL 2 EL as OWL 2 EL has PTIME incremental reasoning capacity.

Lightweight Reasoners

Quill

The Quill reasoner has been implemented in Java using a novel and unique database schema for storing normalised representations of OWL 2 QL ontologies. This allows us to rewrite any conjunctive query into a single, simple SQL query over the underlying database, using the database itself to perform the transitive completion of class and property subsumption with an innovative exploitation of the way database indices work. To support this we have developed new algorithms for query rewriting and ontology normalisation. Initial testing across large knowledge bases with deep concept hierarchies, such as the DBPedia dataset and the Yago ontology, shows a significant performance improvement over other DL-Lite query engines. Using the standard query rewriting algorithm PerfectRef over a deep class or property hierarchy can result in a set of hundreds or thousands of conjunctive queries, where our method will only ever result in a single query. Quill supports all reasoning tasks for OWL 2 QL, including consistency and satisfiability checking, and query answering, and by using an OWL DL reasoner, it can perform semantic approximation of more expressive ontologies.

REL

The REL reasoner [172] is a Java implementation of an OWL 2 EL reasoner, in which an optimisation of the EL+ algorithm [12] has been extended with the completion rules for OWL 2 EL [10]. This allows REL to provide tractable reasoning for OWL 2 EL ontologies and make up the core component of the soundness-preserving syntactic approximation. In this way REL can provide soundness-guaranteed tractable TBox and ABox reasoning services for OWL 2 DL ontologies. In additional, REL also consists of an OWL 2 EL conjunctive query engine [225], which allows queries over OWL 2 EL ontologies to be answered more efficiently without semantic approximation. Non-standard reasoning services such as local closed world reasoning are also supported by REL.

5.1.3   Query Answering Using Semantic Approximation[*]

In this section, we introduce the concept of semantic approximation. Query answering over OWL 2 DL (also as OWL DL) is a hard problem. It has been shown that the complexity of ontology entailment in $\mathcal{SHOIN}(\mathbf{D}^+)$, i.e., OWL DL, is NEXPTIME . This indicates query answering over OWL DL ontologies is at least NEXPTIME . Approximation has been identified as a potential way to reduce the complexity of reasoning over OWL DL ontologies.

Existing approaches [83, 94, 102, 201, 208] are mainly based on naive syntactic approximation of ontological axioms and queries. All these approaches could introduce unsound answers. For example, the authors of [201] proposed to approximate the target query Q with a list of queries $Q_1, \ldots, Q_n$, where $Q_n = Q$ and Q_i is more general than Q_j for all $1 \leq i < j \leq n$. This suggests answers of $Q_1, \ldots, Q_{n-1}$ could contain unsound answers w.r.t. Q. Secondly, some syntactic-based approaches, such as [208], could change the semantics of the original ontology by replacing class description C with $C^\top$ or $C^\perp$ in ontological axioms. In fact, naive syntactic approximation that directly translates an ontology in a richer language into a less rich language can easily introduce unsoundness. Suppose we want to approximate the OWL DL ontology $\mathcal{O}_1 = \{\geq 2R \sqsubseteq \mathsf{C}, R \sqsubseteq S, R(\mathsf{a}, \mathsf{b})\}$ with an $\mathcal{ALC}$ ontology. Using syntactic approximations, one can approximate $\mathcal{O}_1$ with $\mathcal{O}_2 = \{\exists R \sqsubseteq \mathsf{C}, R(a, b)\}$, in which the number restriction $\geq 2R$ is syntactically approximated as $\exists R$ and $R \sqsubseteq S$ is ignored as it is not expressible in $\mathcal{ALC}$. One drawback of this approximation is that $\mathcal{O}_2$ entails $\mathsf{C}(a)$, which is not entailed by the source ontology $\mathcal{O}_1$. Furthermore, there is little literature (such as those provided by Hitzler and Vrandečić [94]) showing that syntactic-based approximations could significantly improve scalability of ontology reasoning. These techniques have focussed on the RDF syntax of OWL and lose much of the richness of the description logic underpinning OWL.

In this section, we recast the idea of knowledge compilation [188] into *semantic approximation* of OWL DL ontologies. The idea of knowledge compilation is simple: users can write statements in an expressive representation language, and these statements can be complied into a restricted language that allows efficient inference. In this way, users do not have to use a less expressive language which might be too limited for practical applications. In [188], Selman and Kautz showed how propositional logical theories can be compiled into Horn theories that approximate the original information; they also applied this idea on subsumption reasoning for the description logic $\mathcal{FL}$. In this section, we investigate applying knowledge compilation on query answering over OWL DL ontologies. We propose approximating OWL DL ontologies (or source ontologies) with corresponding DL-Lite [42, 43] ontologies (or target ontologies), against which query answering has only polynomial data complexity.

One major advantage of our approach is that SQL query engines are sufficient to answer disjunctive queries over the target DL-Lite ontologies since all entailments of a source OWL DL ontology that are expressible in DL-Lite are kept in the target ontology. Furthermore, we identify an important category of queries for which our approach guarantees both soundness and completeness.

Our experiments show that the optimisations significantly reduce the time for computing target ontologies. Our evaluation with the Lehigh University Benchmark [1] shows that query answering over semantic approximations outperforms a number of contemporary ontology reasoning systems.

The syntax and semantics of DL-Lite have been introduced in Sect. 3.2.4. It has been designed to express most features in UML class diagrams but still has a low reasoning overhead [43] (worst case polynomial time, compared to worst case exponential time in the case of most common description logics).

A conjunctive query (CQ) q is of the form $q(\mathbf{X}) \leftarrow \exists \mathbf{Y}.conj(\mathbf{X}, \mathbf{Y}, \mathbf{Z})$ or simply $q(\mathbf{X}) \leftarrow conj(\mathbf{X}, \mathbf{Y}, \mathbf{Z})$, where $q(\mathbf{X})$ is called the head, $conj(\mathbf{X}, \mathbf{Y}, \mathbf{Z})$ is called the body, $\mathbf{X}$ are called the distinguished variables, $\mathbf{Y}$ are existentially quantified variables called the non-distinguished variables, $\mathbf{Z}$ are individual names, and $conj(\mathbf{X}, \mathbf{Y}, \mathbf{Z})$ is a conjunction of atoms of the form $\mathsf{A}(v)$, $R(v_1, v_2)$, where A, R are, respectively, *named* classes and *named* properties and v, v_1 and v_2 are *individual variables* in $\mathbf{X}$ and $\mathbf{Y}$ or *individual names* in $\mathbf{Z}$.

As usual, an interpretation $\mathcal{I}$ satisfies an ontology $\mathcal{O}$ if it satisfies all the axioms in $\mathcal{O}$; in this case, we say $\mathcal{I}$ is a model of $\mathcal{O}$. Given an evaluation $[\mathbf{X} \mapsto \mathbf{S}]$, if every model $\mathcal{I}$ of $\mathcal{O}$ satisfies $q_{[\mathbf{X} \mapsto \mathbf{S}]}$, we say $\mathcal{O}$ entails $q_{[\mathbf{X} \mapsto \mathbf{S}]}$; in this case, $\mathbf{S}$ is called a *solution* of q.

A disjunctive query (DQ) is a set of conjunctive queries sharing the same head. Theoretically, allowing only named classes and properties as atoms is not a restriction, as we can always define such named classes and properties in ontologies. Practically, this should not be an issue as querying against *named* relations is a usual practice when people query over relational databases.

After some careful query rewriting by DL-Lite reasoners [42], query answering over DL-Lite ontologies can be carried out by an SQL engine, so it can take advantage of existing query optimisation strategies and algorithms provided by modern database management systems.

Semantic Approximations of OWL DL Ontologies

In this section, we apply the idea of knowledge compilation on semantically approximating a source ontology $\mathcal{O}_1$ in Description Logics $\mathcal{L}_1$ (source language) with $\mathcal{O}_2$ in $\mathcal{L}_2$ (target language), where $\mathcal{L}_1$ is more expressive than $\mathcal{L}_2$.

We use $\mathbf{N}_C$, $\mathbf{N}_P$ and $\mathbf{N}_I$ to denote the set of named classes, named properties and named individuals, respectively, used in $\mathcal{O}_1$. We always assume $\mathbf{N}_C$, $\mathbf{N}_P$ and $\mathbf{N}_I$ are finite, as $\mathcal{O}_1$ is a finite set of axioms.

The following definition characterises the axioms to compile in our setting; i.e., we consider all $\mathcal{L}_2$ axioms that are entailed by $\mathcal{O}_1$.

Definition 1 (Entailment Set). The *entailment set* of $\mathcal{O}_1$ w.r.t. $\mathcal{L}_2$, denoted as $\mathbf{ES}(\mathcal{O}_1, \mathcal{L}_2)$, is the set which contains *all* $\mathcal{L}_2$ axioms (constructed by using only vocabulary in $\mathbf{N}_C$, $\mathbf{N}_P$ and $\mathbf{N}_I$) that are entailed by $\mathcal{O}_1$.

It should be noted that $\mathbf{ES}(\mathcal{O}_1, \mathcal{L}_2)$ could be infinite. For example, given $\mathcal{O}_1 = \{\top \sqsubseteq \forall R.(\exists R.\top), \mathrm{Trans}(R), R(a, b)\}$, there exist infinitely many axioms (such as $\exists R.\top(a)$, $\exists R.(\exists R.\top)(a)$, $\exists R.(\exists R.(\exists R.\top))(a)$, ...) in $\mathbf{ES}(\mathcal{O}_1, \mathcal{ALC})$. Whether $\mathbf{ES}(\mathcal{O}_1, \mathcal{L}_2)$ is finite depends on the target language $\mathcal{L}_2$. If $\mathbf{ES}(\mathcal{O}_1, \mathcal{L}_2)$ is finite, then $\mathcal{L}_2$ is a suitable target language for semantic approximation of $\mathcal{O}_2$.

One obvious choice for semantic approximation is to approximate $\mathcal{O}_1$ with $\mathbf{ES}(\mathcal{O}_1, \mathcal{L}_2)$. On the one hand, the semantics of the original ontology $\mathcal{O}_1$ are well taken into account since $\mathbf{ES}(\mathcal{O}_1, \mathcal{L}_2)$ contains only axioms which are entailed by $\mathcal{O}_1$. On the other hand, the expressive power of the language $\mathcal{L}_2$ is exploited maximally. $\mathbf{ES}(\mathcal{O}_1, \mathcal{L}_2)$ contains all possible $\mathcal{L}_2$ class axioms, property axioms and individual axioms which are entailed by $\mathcal{O}_1$.

We can construct entailment sets from the corresponding axiom sets.

Definition 2 (Axiom Set). The *axiom set* of $\mathcal{L}_2$ w.r.t. $\mathbf{N}_C$, $\mathbf{N}_P$ and $\mathbf{N}_I$, denoted as $\mathbf{AS}(\mathcal{L}_2, \mathbf{N}_C, \mathbf{N}_P, \mathbf{N}_I)$, is the set which contains all $\mathcal{L}_2$ axioms that are constructed by using only vocabulary in $\mathbf{N}_C$, $\mathbf{N}_P$ and $\mathbf{N}_I$.

It can be shown that $\mathbf{AS}(\text{DL-Lite}, \mathbf{N}_C, \mathbf{N}_P, \mathbf{N}_I)$ is finite [156].

Due to the finite nature of $\mathbf{AS}(\text{DL-Lite}, \mathbf{N}_C, \mathbf{N}_P, \mathbf{N}_I)$, one can compute $\mathbf{ES}(\mathcal{O}_1, \text{DL-Lite})$ in a very straightforward manner for a given $\mathcal{O}_1$:

1. Initialising $\mathbf{ES}(\mathcal{O}_1, \text{DL-Lite})$ as $\varnothing$
2. Enumerating all axiom in $\mathbf{AS}(\text{DL-Lite}, \mathbf{N}_C, \mathbf{N}_P, \mathbf{N}_I)$
3. For each axiom $\alpha \in \mathbf{AS}(\text{DL-Lite}, \mathbf{N}_C, \mathbf{N}_P, \mathbf{N}_I)$, if $\mathcal{O}_1 \models \alpha$, then $\mathbf{ES}(\mathcal{O}_1, \text{DL-Lite}) := \mathbf{ES}(\mathcal{O}_1, \text{DL-Lite}) \cup \{\alpha\}$

It can also be shown that such $\mathbf{ES}(\mathcal{O}_1, \text{DL-Lite})$ can be computed in polynomial time and space w.r.t. the size of $\mathcal{O}_1$.

Query Answering over Entailment Sets

Now we investigate query answering over entailment sets. In order to evaluate from the theoretical point of view query answering based on semantic approximation, we are mostly interested in the soundness and completeness of the solutions. Given an OWL DL ontology $\mathcal{O}_1$ and an arbitrary query q, we denote the set of solutions of q over $\mathcal{O}_1$ as $\mathbf{S}_{q, \mathcal{O}_1}$ and the set of solutions of q over $\mathbf{ES}(\mathcal{O}_1, \text{DL-Lite})$ as $\mathbf{S}_{q, \mathbf{ES}(\mathcal{O}_1, \text{DL-Lite})}$. We say $\mathbf{S}_{q, \mathbf{ES}(\mathcal{O}_1, \text{DL-Lite})}$ is sound if $\mathbf{S}_{q, \mathbf{ES}(\mathcal{O}_1, \text{DL-Lite})} \subseteq \mathbf{S}_{q, \mathcal{O}_1}$.

We say $\mathbf{S}_{q,\mathbf{ES}(\mathcal{O}_1,\text{DL-Lite})}$ is complete if $\mathbf{S}_{q,\mathcal{O}_1} \subseteq \mathbf{S}_{q,\mathbf{ES}(\mathcal{O}_1,\text{DL-Lite})}$. We say $\mathbf{S}_{q,\mathbf{ES}(\mathcal{O}_1,\text{DL-Lite})}$ is sound and complete if $\mathbf{S}_{q,\mathbf{ES}(\mathcal{O}_1,\text{DL-Lite})} = \mathbf{S}_{q,\mathcal{O}_1}$.

Since (1) every axiom in $\mathbf{ES}(\mathcal{O}_1, \text{DL-Lite})$ is entailed by $\mathcal{O}_1$ (see Definition (1)) and (2) OWL DL is monotonic, for any arbitrary query q over $\mathcal{O}_1$, $\mathbf{S}_{q,\mathbf{ES}(\mathcal{O}_1,\text{DL-Lite})}$ is sound.

It remains to investigate how complete $\mathbf{S}_{q,\mathbf{ES}(\mathcal{O}_1,\text{DL-Lite})}$ is. In general, it is possibly incomplete (see the following example) as the complexity of query answering in DL-Lite is obviously lower than that of OWL DL.

Example 1. Let us consider a query $q(x) \leftarrow R(x, y) \wedge C(y)$ over an OWL DL ontology $\mathcal{O}_1 = \{\exists R.C(a)\}$. Since $\mathcal{O}_1 \models q_{[x \mapsto a]}$, we have $\mathbf{S}_{q,\mathcal{O}_1} = \{x \mapsto a\}$.

As the entailment set $\mathbf{ES}(\mathcal{O}_1, \text{DL-Lite}) = \{\exists R(a)\}$ does not entail $q_{[x \mapsto a]}$, we have $\mathbf{S}_{q,\mathbf{ES}(\mathcal{O}_1,\text{DL-Lite})} = \varnothing$.

In what follows, we will identify some categories of important queries for which our semantic approximation guarantees also completeness.

The first category of such query is that with no non-distinguished variables. As described earlier, non-distinguished variables are the variables that appear in the head but not in the body of a query. For example, if we transform $q(x) \leftarrow R(x, y) \wedge C(y)$ in Example 1 into one without non-distinguished variables, we can simply add y into the head: $q'(x, y) \leftarrow R(x, y) \wedge C(y)$. Now we have $\mathbf{S}_{q',\mathcal{O}_1} = \varnothing$ because, given $\mathcal{O}_1$, it is not possible to evaluate the variable y to any named individuals. It has been shown that given intuitively, this is a consistent OWL DL ontology $\mathcal{O}_1$ and an arbitrary conjunctive query q over $\mathcal{O}_1$ that has no non-distinguished variables, $\mathbf{S}_{q,\mathbf{ES}(\mathcal{O}_1,\text{DL-Lite})} = \mathbf{S}_{q,\mathcal{O}_1}$. This completeness guarantee is because all atoms of the form $A(e)$ and $R(e, f)$, where e and f are named individuals, that are entailed by $\mathcal{O}_1$ are stored in $\mathbf{ES}(\mathcal{O}_1, \text{DL-Lite})$.

As disjunctive queries are simply a set of conjunctive queries sharing the same head, we have similar completeness guarantee such that given a consistent OWL DL ontology $\mathcal{O}_1$ and an arbitrary disjunctive query q over $\mathcal{O}_1$ that has no non-distinguished variables, $\mathbf{S}_{q,\mathbf{ES}(\mathcal{O}_1,\text{DL-Lite})} = \mathbf{S}_{q,\mathcal{O}_1}$.

It is important to point out that the restriction of disallowing non-distinguished variables is not really unusual: (1) the well-known traditional DL reasoner Racer (supporting both TBox and ABox) does not allow them in its query language nRQL [85]; (2) the KAON2 DL reasoner [103], which is mainly designed to provide efficient ABox reasoning and query answering, does not support non-distinguished variables either. To the best of our knowledge, this restriction is the price we should pay for scalable query answering over ontologies.

We conclude this subsection by pointing out another kind of query for which our semantic approximation can guarantee soundness and completeness—subsumption queries between named classes $A_1 \sqsubseteq A_2$. Subsumption queries between named classes are useful in Semantic Web tools such as TrOWL, which allows users to search ontologies in which, for example, Professor is a subclass of Client. Specifically, given a consistent OWL DL ontology $\mathcal{O}_1$, the set $\mathbf{N}_C$ of named classes used in $\mathcal{O}_1$ and two arbitrary named classes A_1 and A_2 in $\mathbf{N}_C$, $\mathcal{O}_1 \models A_1 \sqsubseteq A_2$ iff $\mathbf{ES}(\mathcal{O}_1, \text{DL-Lite}) \models A_1 \sqsubseteq A_2$.

Clearly the method of querying over a semantic approximation of an ontology offers large theoretical performance improvements over using a reasoner based on a tableaux algorithm (**PTIME** rather than **NEXPTIME** relative to the size of the ontology). Furthermore, because of the nature of DL-Lite, it is possible to pre-calculate the approximations for a large number of ontologies and hold these in a database, to query against at will. Realising a similar system using a reasoner would incur either a large time overhead as they are loaded and classified each time a different ontology is queried or a huge memory overhead to keep an instance of the reasoner running for each ontology in the repository. Because we only query against entailments which are valid with respect to the original ontology, we guarantee sound results for all queries. This gives an advantage over other approximate reasoners which do not offer this guarantee.

5.1.4 Scalable Reasoning Using Syntactic Approximation[*]

In this section, we present syntactic approximation, a fundamental approach on which many advanced reasoning services are developed and provided to the use cases. Syntactic approximation is first designed to support efficient reasoning in complex TBox, for which we refer readers to [172] for more details. Later this approach is extended to support ABox approximation reasoning [173] with optimisations for nominals (see technical report [174] for more details). Due to the limited space we will go through the major definitions and reasoning rules and refer our readers to the aforementioned articles for more details.

The general idea of syntactic approximation is to replace concept sub-expressions (role expressions) that are not in the target DL, for example, $\mathcal{EL}^{++}$, with atomic concepts (atomic roles) and rewrite axioms accordingly. Then, additional data structures and completion rules are used to maintain and restore some semantic relations among basic concepts, respectively. Different from early days naive syntactic-based approximations, all these approaches are tractable and soundness-guaranteed [172]. Furthermore, syntactic approximation has the following two advantages compared to the semantic approximation presented in the last section:

1. Syntactic approximation does not require pre-computation by a complete and sound heavyweight reasoner.
2. Syntactic approximation has a relatively richer target language whose axiom set is infinite.

In approximation, we only consider concepts corresponding to the particular ontology in question. We use the notion *term* to refer to these "interesting" concept expressions. More precisely, a term is:

1. A concept expression on the LHS or RHS of any GCI or
2. The singleton of any individual in the ontology or
3. The syntactic sub-expression of a term or
4. The complement of a term

In order to represent all these terms and role expressions that will be used in $\mathcal{EL}^{++}$ reasoning, we first assign names to them. Basic concept here includes atomic concepts, top concept, bottom concept and singleton nominal concepts.

Definition 3 (Name Assignment). Given S a set of concept expressions, E a set of role expressions, a *name assignment fn* is a function where each $C \in S$ ($R \in E$), $fn(C) = C$ ($fn(R) = R$) if C is a basic concept (R is atomic); otherwise, $fn(C)$ ($fn(R)$) is a fresh name.

Now we recast the definitions from [172, 173] with extensions regarding disjoint, symmetric or functional roles. It approximates an $\mathcal{SROIQ}$ ontology to $\mathcal{EL}^{++}$ plus a complement table (CT), a cardinality table (QT) and an inverse table (IT). Elements of CT are pairs of names of complementary terms or complementary roles. Elements of QT are triples (A, r, n) where A is a term name, r a role name and n an integer number. Elements of IT are pairs of (r, s) where r and s are names assigned to a role expression and its inverse. The basic idea is to represent (non-$\mathcal{EL}^{++}$) expressions with their name assignments.

Definition 4 ($\mathcal{EL}^{++}_{\mathcal{CQI}}$ Approximation). Given an Ontology $\mathcal{O}$ and a name assignment fn, its $\mathcal{EL}^{++}_{\mathcal{CQI}}$ approximation $A_{fn,\mathcal{EL}^{++}_{\mathcal{CQI}}}(\mathcal{O})$ is a five-tuple $(\mathcal{T}, \mathcal{A}, CT, QT, IT)$ constructed as follows:

1. $\mathcal{T}, \mathcal{A}, CT, QT$ and IT are all initialised to $\varnothing$.
2. For each $C \sqsubseteq D$ ($C \equiv D$) in $\mathcal{O}$, $\mathcal{T} = \mathcal{T} \cup \{fn(C) \sqsubseteq fn(D)\}$ ($\mathcal{T} = \mathcal{T} \cup \{fn(C) \equiv fn(D)\}$).
3. For each RI axiom $\beta \in \mathcal{O}$, $\mathcal{T} = \mathcal{T} \cup \{\beta_{[R/fn(R)]}\}$.
4. For each axiom $inverseRole(R, S) \in \mathcal{O}$, $\mathcal{T} = \mathcal{T} \cup \{fn(R) \equiv fn(Inv(S))\}$.
5. For each axiom $disjointRole(R, S) \in \mathcal{O}$, $\mathcal{T} = \mathcal{T} \cup \{fn(R) \sqsubseteq fn(\neg S)\}$.
6. For each symmetric role R, $\mathcal{T} = \mathcal{T} \cup \{fn(R) \equiv fn(Inv(R))\}$.
7. For each functional role R, $\mathcal{T} = \mathcal{T} \cup \{\top \sqsubseteq fc(\leq 1.R.\top)\}$.
8. For each $a : C \in \mathcal{O}$, $\mathcal{A} = \mathcal{A} \cup \{a : fn(C)\}$.
9. For each $(a, b) : R \in \mathcal{O}$, $\mathcal{A} = \mathcal{A} \cup \{(a, b) : fn(R)\}$.
10. For each axiom $a \not\doteq b \in \mathcal{O}$, $\mathcal{A} = \mathcal{A} \cup \{a \not\doteq b\}$.
11. For each axiom $a \doteq b \in \mathcal{O}$, $\mathcal{A} = \mathcal{A} \cup \{\{a \doteq b\}$.
12. For each term C in $\mathcal{O}$, $CT = CT \cup \{(fn(C), fn(\sim C))\}$, and if C is the form:

    (a) $C_1 \sqcap \cdots \sqcap C_n$, then $\mathcal{T} = \mathcal{T} \cup \{fn(C) \equiv fn(C_1) \sqcap \cdots \sqcap fn(C_n)\}$.
    (b) $\exists r.D$, then $\mathcal{T} = \mathcal{T} \cup \{fn(C) \equiv \exists r.fn(D)\}$.
    (c) $\geq nR.D$, then

        i. If $n = 0$, $\mathcal{T} = \mathcal{T} \cup \{\top \sqsubseteq fn(C)\}$.
        ii. If $n = 1$, $\mathcal{T} = \mathcal{T} \cup \{fn(C) \equiv \exists fn(R).fn(D)\}$.
        iii. Otherwise, $\mathcal{T} = \mathcal{T} \cup \{fn(C) \equiv fn(D)^{fn(R),n}\}$, and $QT = QT \cup \{(fn(C), fn(R), n)\}$,

        otherwise $\mathcal{T} = \mathcal{T} \cup \{fn(C) \sqsubseteq \top\}$.

13. For each pair of names A and r, if there exist $(A, r, i_1), \ldots, (A, r, i_n) \in QT$ with $i_1 < \cdots < i_n$, $\mathcal{T} = \mathcal{T} \cup \{A^{r,i_n} \sqsubseteq A^{r,i_{n-1}}, \ldots, A^{r,i_2} \sqsubseteq A^{r,i_1}, A^{r,i_1} \sqsubseteq \exists\, r.A\}$.

14. For each $r \in RN_{\mathcal{O}}$, $CT = CT \cup \{(fn(r), fn(\neg r)), (fn(\neg r), fn(r)), (fn(Inv(r)), fn(\neg(Inv(r)))), (fn(\neg(Inv(r))), fn(Inv(r)))\}$.

15. For each $r \in RN_{\mathcal{O}}$, $IT = IT \cup \{(fn(r), fn(Inv(r))), (fn(Inv(r)), fn(r)), (fn(\neg r), fn(\neg(Inv(r)))), (fn(\neg(Inv(r))), fn(\neg r))\}$.

Step 2 rewrites all the GCIs; Step 3 rewrites all the RIs; Step 4 defines the equivalence between asserted and approximated inverse roles; Step 5 defines the relations between disjoint roles; Step 6 defines the equivalence between a symmetric role and its inverse; Step 7 rewrites functionality of roles. Steps 8–11 rewrite all the ABox axioms; Step 12 approximates terms and constructs the complement table CT. This step also approximates cardinality expressions into atomic names and constructs the cardinality table QT. Non-$\mathcal{EL}^{++}$ terms such as disjunctions will be approximated via their complements. Step 13 constructs subsumption relations among approximated cardinality expressions. Step 14 maintains the complementary relations for roles; Step 15 maintains the inverse relations.

It can be shown that the $\mathcal{EL}^{++}_{\mathcal{CQI}}$ approximation approximates, in linear time, an $\mathcal{SROIQ}$ ontology into an $\mathcal{EL}^{++}$ ontology with these addition tables.

Given $A_{fn,\mathcal{EL}^{++}_{\mathcal{CQI}}}(\mathcal{O}) = (\mathcal{T}, \mathcal{A}, CT, QT, IT)$, TBox reasoning can be performed without ABox by using the original $\mathcal{EL}^{++}$ completion rules (**R1–8** in Table 5.1) and syntactic approximate reasoning rules. These rules (**R9–16** in Table 5.1) utilise the complementary relations in CT, the cardinality information in QT and the inverse relation in IT. In the table, fc is a function that returns the complement of a concept from CT.

R9 realises tautology $A \sqcap \sim A \sqsubseteq \bot$. **R10** realises $A \sqsubseteq B \rightarrow \sim A \sqsubseteq \sim B$. **R11** builds up the relations between conjuncts of a conjunction, for example, $A \sqcap B \sqsubseteq \bot$ implies $A \sqsubseteq \sim B$. **R12** realises inference $A \sqsubseteq B, R \sqsubseteq S, i \geq j \rightarrow \geq iR.A \sqsubseteq \geq jS.B$. **R13** is the extension of **R4** and **R14–16** are extensions of **R8**.

It can be shown that TBox reasoning with the above rules is tractable and soundness-guaranteed.

Syntactic approximation can be extended to support ABox reasoning. A most naive approach is to internalise all ABox axioms into TBox as follows:

1. $a : A \rightarrow \{a\} \sqsubseteq A$
2. $(a, b) : R \rightarrow \{a\} \sqsubseteq \exists R.\{b\}$
3. $(a, b) : R \rightarrow \{b\} \sqsubseteq \exists fi(R).\{a\}$

where fi is a function that returns the inverse property of a given property from IT.

However, it is obvious that such a naive solution will introduce a lot of singletons. When the number of individuals is large, these singletons can reduce the performance of the reasoner.

In [173] a separate TBox-ABox approximate reasoning was proposed to improve reasoning without nominals. It can be shown that such a separate approach is as

Table 5.1 $\mathcal{EL}^{++}_{\mathcal{CQI}}$ TBox completion rules

R1	If $X \sqsubseteq A$, $A \sqsubseteq B$ then $X \sqsubseteq B$
R2	If $X \sqsubseteq A_1, \ldots, A_n$, $A_1 \sqcap \cdots \sqcap A_n \sqsubseteq B$ then $X \sqsubseteq B$
R3	If $X \sqsubseteq A$, $A \sqsubseteq \exists r.B$ then $X \sqsubseteq \exists r.B$
R4	If $X \sqsubseteq \exists r.A$, $A \sqsubseteq A'$, $\exists r.A' \sqsubseteq B$ then $X \sqsubseteq B$
R5	If $X \sqsubseteq \exists r.A$, $A \sqsubseteq \bot$ then $X \sqsubseteq \bot$
R6	If X, $A \sqsubseteq \{a\}$, $X \rightsquigarrow_R A$ then $X \sqsubseteq A$
R7	If $X \sqsubseteq \exists r.A$, $r \sqsubseteq s$ then $X \sqsubseteq \exists s.A$
R8	If $X \sqsubseteq \exists r_1.A$, $A \sqsubseteq \exists r_2.B$, $r_1 \circ r_2 \sqsubseteq r_3$, then $X \sqsubseteq \exists r_3.B$
R9	If $X \sqsubseteq A$, B, $A = fc(B)$ then $X \sqsubseteq \bot$
R10	If $B \sqsubseteq A$ then $fc(A) \sqsubseteq fc(B)$
R11	If $A_1 \sqcap \cdots \sqcap A_n \sqsubseteq \bot$, $X \sqsubseteq A_j$ $(1 \le j \le n, j \ne i)$, then $X \sqsubseteq fc(A_i)$
R12	If $A \sqsubseteq B$, (A, r, i), $(B, s, j) \in QT$, $r \sqsubseteq s$, $i \ge j$, then $A^{r,i} \sqsubseteq B^{s,j}$
R13	If $X \sqsubseteq A^{r,i}$, $A \sqsubseteq A'$, $\exists r.A' \sqsubseteq B$, then $X \sqsubseteq B$
R14	If $X \sqsubseteq A^{r_1,i}$, $A \sqsubseteq \exists r_2.B$, $r_1 \circ r_2 \sqsubseteq r_3$, then $X \sqsubseteq \exists r_3.B$
R15	If $X \sqsubseteq \exists r_1.A$, $A \sqsubseteq B^{r_2,i}$, $r_1 \circ r_2 \sqsubseteq r_3$, then $X \sqsubseteq \exists r_3.B$
R16	If $X \sqsubseteq A^{r_1,i}$, $A \sqsubseteq B^{r_2,j}$, $r_1 \circ r_2 \sqsubseteq r_3$, then $X \sqsubseteq \exists r_3.B$

complete as but much faster than an internalisation approach when there is no nominal in the ontology.

When nominals are present, an internalisation on-the-fly (see technical report [174] for more details) can be applied to substantially reduce the number of introduced singletons without affecting the degree of completeness of the system.

5.1.5   Local Closed World Reasoning with NBox$^{(*)}$

In this section we introduce NBox reasoning technology, which is developed to support local closed world reasoning in OWL 2. We present the most important notions and claims in this section and refer our readers to [171] for more technical details.

Classical DL reasoning imposes the OWA, which means the truth value of a statement is unknown if its value varies in different interpretations of the ontology. According to the definition of entailment in DL, the truth value of an entailment is true *iff* the entailment holds in all interpretations of the ontology. It is false *iff* the entailment does not hold in any interpretation; otherwise, it is unknown. For example, in ontology $\{a : A, b : B\}$ whether $a : B$ is unknown, so is $b : A$. However, in certain applications, as we will see in Sect. 9.3, it is required to partially or completely close the world or domain. In this case, the truth value of a statement that is not known to be true is false. Thus in the above example $\{a : A, b : B\}$, if A, B are closed, then $a : \neg B$ and $b : \neg A$ can be entailed. The CWA has been widely applied in relational database and logic programming and is a common practice in software engineering.

CWA can be realised in different ways. In [189] the DBox approach is presented. In addition to the TBox $\mathcal{T}$ and ABox $\mathcal{A}$, a DBox $\mathcal{D}$ is specified to close the domain. $\mathcal{D}$ is syntactically similar to $\mathcal{A}$, except that in $\mathcal{D}$ only named concepts and named roles are allowed. Furthermore, the interpretations of predicates appearing in $\mathcal{D}$ is fixed by $\mathcal{D}$. That is to say, in any model of the ontology $\mathcal{I}$, if $A \in CN_D$, then $A^{\mathcal{I}} = \{a^{\mathcal{I}} \mid a : A \in \mathcal{D}\}$. If $r \in RN_D$, then $r^{\mathcal{I}} = \{(a^{\mathcal{I}}, b^{\mathcal{I}}) \mid (a, b) : r \in \mathcal{D}\}$. For predicates not appearing in $\mathcal{D}$, their interpretations are the same as classical DL concepts or roles.

The DBox approach strongly corresponds to relational database. Actually, the data tables in a relation database can be regarded as a DBox. This resemblance makes it easy to reduce query answering with ontologies over DBox to relational database query answering [189].

The use of DBox is based on the assumption that a user has complete knowledge about the predicates he or she wants to close. In this case, a user can confidently encode such knowledge with the DBox. However, the DBox actually prohibits inferences on predicates appearing in it. In certain cases, this can be inconvenient and unscalable. For example, given an ontology $\mathcal{T} = \{PhDStudent \sqsubseteq Student\}, \mathcal{A} = \{Emily : Student, David : PhDStudent, Emily \neq David\}$, one should infer $David : Student$. This kind of inferences is also witnessed by deductive database and DataLog. However, if we close $Student$ by putting only $Emily : Student$ into $\mathcal{D}$, this ontology becomes inconsistent because $David$, which is inferred to be a $Student$, is different from the only instance of $Student$.

From this example, we can see that the DBox approach does not only require a user to have complete knowledge about certain domain, but also require him or her to explicitly assert this knowledge. This will introduce a lot of redundancies and undermines DL's advantages of reasoning.

In what follows, we present our approach to closing certain predicates while still allowing inferences of implicit knowledge about them.

Negation as Failure Box (NBox)

We start from the notion of Negation As Failure (NAF). Then we present the syntax and semantics of an ontology with a NBox.

As we mentioned earlier, the idea of CWA is that the truth value of a statement that is not known to be true is false. However, the meaning of "known" here is unclear. In knowledge representation, people tend to distinguish the **Explicit Knowledge** and **Implicit Knowledge**. Formally speaking, given a knowledge base $\mathcal{O}$, a proposition P is explicit knowledge *iff* $P \in \mathcal{O}$. A proposition P is implicit knowledge *iff* $P \notin \mathcal{O}$ and $\mathcal{O} \models P$.

Obviously, the DBox approach closes the domain w.r.t. the explicit knowledge encoded in $\mathcal{D}$, leaving no space for implicit knowledge of predicates in the DBox.

If we want to close the domain w.r.t. both the explicit and implicit knowledge, it should be done by the following non-monotonic inference rule:

Definition 5 (Negation As Failure (NAF)). For a knowledge base $\mathcal{O}$ and a proposition P, $\mathcal{O} \models \bar{P}$ *iff* $\mathcal{O} \not\models P$, where $\mathcal{O} \models \bar{P}$ means $\mathcal{O}$ entails that P is not true.

Particularly, when $P = a : C$, $\mathcal{O} \models \bar{P}$ *iff* $\mathcal{O} \models a : \neg C$. When $P = (a, b) : r$, $\mathcal{O} \models \bar{P}$ *iff* $\mathcal{O} \models (a, b) : \neg r$.

In ontology reasoning, not all the predicates need to be closed. Therefore, NAF should be applied on a pre-specified set of predicates. We call this set of predicates the *NBox*.

The syntax of NBox and NBox-closed Ontology is defined as follows:

Definition 6 (NBox-closed Ontology). An NBox-closed Ontology (N-Ontology for short) $\mathcal{O}$ is a triple $(\mathcal{T}, \mathcal{A}, \mathcal{N})$, in which $\mathcal{T}$ is a TBox, $\mathcal{A}$ is an ABox and $\mathcal{N}$ is a subset of the set containing $\mathcal{T}$, all the named concepts and named roles in $\mathcal{T}$ and $\mathcal{A}$.

In order to distinguish the classical ontology and N-Ontology, in what follows, we use $\mathcal{O}$ to denote a classical ontology and $\mathcal{O}^{\mathcal{N}}$ to denote an N-Ontology.

The semantics of an N-Ontology can be extended by the NBox as follows:

Definition 7 (N-Ontology Semantics). Given an N-Ontology $\mathcal{O}^{\mathcal{N}} = (\mathcal{T}, \mathcal{A}, \mathcal{N})$, let $\mathcal{O} = (\mathcal{T}, \mathcal{A})$, an *interpretation* $\mathcal{I}$ of $\mathcal{O}^{\mathcal{N}}$ is a pair $\langle \Delta^{\mathcal{I}}, \cdot^{\mathcal{I}} \rangle$ following the classical notion of interpretation except that:

1. If a concept $A \in \mathcal{N}$, then $A^{\mathcal{I}} = \{a^{\mathcal{I}} \mid \mathcal{O} \models a : A\}$.
2. If a role $r \in \mathcal{N}$, then $r^{\mathcal{I}} = \{(a^{\mathcal{I}}, b^{\mathcal{I}}) \mid \mathcal{O} \models (a, b) : A\}$.

In other words, the interpretation of a predicate in $\mathcal{N}$ is restricted to the maximal common subset of its interpretations over $\mathcal{O}$.

With the above semantics, we have the similar definition for entailment checking as in classical ontology: an axiom α is entailed by an N-Ontology $\mathcal{O}^{\mathcal{N}}$ *iff* it is entailed by all interpretations of $\mathcal{O}^{\mathcal{N}}$, denoted by $\mathcal{O}^{\mathbb{N}} \models \alpha$. It can be shown that NBox predicates satisfy the NAF inference in Definition 5 [171], in a sense that for any N-Ontology $\mathcal{O}^{\mathcal{N}} = (\mathcal{T}, \mathcal{A}, \mathcal{N})$, the following holds:

1. If concept $A \in \mathcal{N}$, then $\mathcal{O}^{\mathcal{N}} \models a : \neg A$ *iff* $(\mathcal{T}, \mathcal{A}) \not\models a : A$.
2. If role $r \in \mathcal{N}$, then $\mathcal{O}^{\mathbb{N}} \models (a, b) : \neg r$ *iff* $(\mathcal{T}, \mathcal{A}) \not\models (a, b) : r$.

Closed World Reasoning with N-Ontology

We first show that N-Ontology reasoning can be reduced to classical ontology reasoning.

Definition 8 (NBox Internalisation). Given an N-Ontology $\mathcal{O}^{\mathcal{N}} = (\mathcal{T}, \mathcal{A}, \mathcal{N})$, its *NBox Internalisation* $NI(\mathcal{O}^{\mathcal{N}})$ is an ontology $\mathcal{O} = (\mathcal{T}', \mathcal{A}')$ constructed as follows:

1. $\mathcal{A}' = \mathcal{A}, \mathcal{T}' = \mathcal{T}$
2. $\mathcal{T}' = \mathcal{T}' \cup \{A \equiv \{a \mid (\mathcal{T}, \mathcal{A}) \models a : A\} \mid A \in \mathcal{N}\}$
3. $\mathcal{T}' = \mathcal{T}' \cup \{\exists r.\top \sqsubseteq \{a \mid \exists b, (\mathcal{T}, \mathcal{A}) \models (a, b) : r\} \mid r \in \mathcal{N}\}$
4. $\mathcal{T}' = \mathcal{T}' \cup \{\exists r^-.\top \sqsubseteq \{b \mid \exists a, (\mathcal{T}, \mathcal{A}) \models (a, b) : r\} \mid r \in \mathcal{N}\}$
5. $\mathcal{T}' = \mathcal{T}' \cup \{\{a\} \sqsubseteq \forall r.\{b \mid (\mathcal{T}, \mathcal{A}) \models (a, b) : r\} \mid r \in \mathcal{N}\}$
6. $\mathcal{T}' = \mathcal{T}' \cup \{\{b\} \sqsubseteq \forall r^-.\{a \mid (\mathcal{T}, \mathcal{A}) \models (a, b) : r\} \mid r \in \mathcal{N}\}$

The above Step 2 closes the concepts in $\mathcal{N}$. Steps 3 and 4 close the global domains and ranges of roles in $\mathcal{N}$. Steps 5 and 6 close the local domains and ranges of roles in $\mathcal{N}$. Reasoning on an N-Ontology can be reduced to reasoning on its NBox internalisation [171]. Particularly, for any N-Ontology $\mathcal{O}^{\mathcal{N}} = (\mathcal{T}, \mathcal{A}, \mathcal{N})$ and its NBox internalisation $NI(\mathcal{O}^{\mathcal{N}}) = \mathcal{O} = (\mathcal{T}', \mathcal{A}')$, let α an axiom, then we have $\mathcal{O}^{\mathbb{N}} \models \alpha$ iff $\mathcal{O} \models \alpha$.

According to Definition 8, the NBox reasoning by NBox internalisation requires the following steps:

1. Retrieving the instances of the NBox predicates
2. Internalising the NBox with the materialisation from Step 1
3. Reasoning over the NBox internalisation from Step 2

This procedure actually forms an incremental reasoning over the TBox and ABox in the original N-Ontology with two phases. This is usually difficult in expressive DLs such as $\mathcal{SROIQ}$ because the results in the first phase, i.e., the above Step 1, cannot be reused in the second phase, i.e., the above Step 3. Alternatively, we can approximate this to $\mathcal{EL}^{++}$, which has tractable incremental reasoning service [202]. Such approximation can be realised by the syntactic approximation introduced in Sect. 5.1.4.

5.2 Justification of Reasoning Results

Justification service allows a user of ontology services to find the cause of certain reasoning result. This is generally the minimal set of axioms in the input ontology that imply the result.

5.2.1 Justification in General

In traditional ontology developing environments (e.g. Protégé[120]), users are typically able to model ontologies and use reasoners (e.g. Pellet [195]) to compute unsatisfiable classes, subsumption hierarchies and types for individuals.

However, since in the context of the MOST project ontologies are used in software modelling, it has become evident that there is a significant demand for software modelling environments which provide more sophisticated services. In particular, the generation of explanations, or justifications, for inferences computed by a reasoner is now recognised as highly desirable functionality for both ontology development and software modelling.

A user browsing an ontology or model recognises an entailment and wants to get an explanation for the entailment in order to get reason why the entailment holds (understanding entailments). If the entailment leads to some inconsistency or unsatisfiable classes, the user wants to get debugging relevant facts and the information how to repair the ontology (debugging).

The way for getting explanations and debugging relevant facts leads to the computation of justifications. In the following we want to give some terminology as foundation and afterwards present two methods for computing justifications.

Terminology

In the following the terminology that is related to the field of explanation and debugging is depicted.

Unsatisfiable Class

A class is unsatisfiable (with regard to one ontology) if it cannot possibly have any instances in any model of the ontology. In description logics notation, $C \sqsubseteq \perp$ means that C is not satisfiable. If an ontology $\mathcal{O}$ contains at least one unsatisfiable class, it is called *incoherent*.

Inconsistent Ontology

An ontology $\mathcal{O}$ is inconsistent if and only if it does not have any model. In description logics an ontology $\mathcal{O}$ entails $\top \sqsubseteq \perp$.

Entailment

For an ontology $\mathcal{O}$ and an axiom η, $\mathcal{O} \models \eta$ holds if all models of $\mathcal{O}$ satisfy η.

Justification

Justifications are explanations of entailments in ontologies. Let $\mathcal{O}$ be an ontology with entailment $\mathcal{O} \models \eta$. Then $\mathcal{J}$ is a justification for η if $\mathcal{J} \subseteq \mathcal{O}$ with $\mathcal{J} \models \eta$ and for any $\mathcal{J}' \subset \mathcal{J}$ holds: $\mathcal{J}' \not\models \eta$.

Computing Justifications

In the following we present the ideas of a simple black-box method for computing one single justification and two further methods for computing more than one possible justification.

Simple Black-Box Method

The approach of a simple black-box technique to compute justifications was presented in [111]. Given a concept C which is unsatisfiable with regard to an ontology $\mathcal{O}$, in a first step of the computation, axioms of $\mathcal{O}$ are added to a newly created ontology $\mathcal{O}'$ until C gets unsatisfiable with regard to $\mathcal{O}'$. In a second step extraneous axioms in $\mathcal{O}'$ will be deleted to get a single minimal justification. The deletion of axioms stops when concept C gets satisfiable.

Glass Box Method

In [113] a glass box technique for computing one single justification is presented. The technique is used for presenting the root cause of a contradiction and to determine the minimal set of axioms in the ontology which lead to a semantic clash. In glass box techniques, the internals of a description logic tableaux reasoner are modified to extract and reveal the cause for inconsistency of a concept definition. An advantage of such approaches is that by tightly integrating the debugging with the reasoning procedure, precise results can be obtained. On the other hand, the reasoner needs to maintain extra data structures to track the source and its dependencies, and this introduces additional memory and computation consumption. We refer to [113] where the complete algorithms and methodologies are explained in detail.

Computing All Justifications

If an initial justification is given (e.g. computed by some black-box technique), other techniques are used to compute the remaining ones. In [111], a variation of the classical hitting set tree (HST) algorithm[169] is presented. This technique is also reasoner independent (black-box). The idea is, in the first step we find one justification by an exsiting algorithm (like the above black-box method), and set this justification as the root node of the so called Hitting Set Tree (HST). In the next steps, each of the axioms in the justification is removed individually, thereby creating new branches of the HST, and finds new justifications along these branches on the fly in the modified ontology. This process needs to be exhaustively done in order to compute all justifications. The algorithm repeats this process until the concept turns satisfiable.

5.2.2 Justification on OWL 2 EL$^{(*)}$

OWL 2 EL is a tractable ontology language dedicated for reasoning over large TBoxes. It is based on the description logic $\mathcal{EL}^{++}$. The syntax, semantics and usage of OWL 2 EL have been introduced in Chap. 3 .

Due to the tractability of $\mathcal{EL}^{++}$, finding a single justification in an $\mathcal{EL}^{++}$ ontology is tractable.

In [13], an intuitive algorithm was presented to compute a single justification. It is presented as in Fig. 5.1.

Given an ontology $\mathcal{O}$ and an axiom α, this algorithm starts from the set J of all axioms in $\mathcal{O}$ and shrinks J when J can entail α. If no more axioms can be removed from J while keeping α entailed, J is a justification of α w.r.t. $\mathcal{O}$. Given an ontology and an entailed axiom, this algorithm requires linear (polynomial) entailment checkings.

In [9], this algorithm is optimised to reduce the number of entailment checkings. The optimised algorithm is illustrated in Fig. 5.2.

In Algorithm log-Justification-r-EL$(S, \mathcal{O}, \alpha)$, S is a support set of axioms which is initially an empty set. Given a support set S, a target set $\mathcal{O}$ and an entailed axiom α, this algorithm computes a minimal subset $S' \subseteq \mathcal{O}$ such that $S \cup S' \models \alpha$. When $\mathcal{O}$ contains only one axiom, this axiom is obviously responsible. Otherwise, the algorithm first partitions $\mathcal{O}$ into $S_1 \cup S_2 = \mathcal{O}$ with $||\ S_1\ | - |\ S_2\ || \leq 1$. If $S \cup S_1 \models \alpha$, $S \subseteq S_1$; if $S \cup S_2 \models \alpha$, $S \subseteq S_2$. Otherwise, there exists a partition $S_1' \cup S_2' = S$ s.t. $S_1' \cap S_2' = \varnothing$, $S_1' \subseteq S_1$ and $S_2' \subseteq S_2$. This algorithm recursively computes such S_1' and S_2' and return their union. Obviously, log-Justification-r-EL$(\varnothing, \mathcal{O}, \alpha)$ is a justification of α w.r.t. $\mathcal{O}$.

Different from algorithm lin-Justification-EL$(\mathcal{O}, \alpha)$, the optimised removes half of the ontology axioms when possible. Note that this algorithm can also be adapted to compute a single justification for other DLs.

In [9] the authors also present a modularization-based justification approach, which applies the above two algorithms on a subset of $\mathcal{O}$ that is related to α instead of the entire $\mathcal{O}$. This can also help reducing the number of entailment checks when the ontology is loosely coupled.

Similar to other DL profiles, finding all justifications in $\mathcal{EL}^{++}$ and OWL 2 EL is NP-Hard.

5.2.3 Justification on OWL 2 QL$^{(*)}$

Since OWL 2 QL reasoning first requires that the ontology is transformed into a normalised form, justification of reasoning results in OWL 2 QL relies on two steps. The first is to find those axioms from the normalised form which have contributed to a particular result, then to further justify each axiom using the original (pre-normalised) axiom set in the ontology to give a set of axioms that are present in

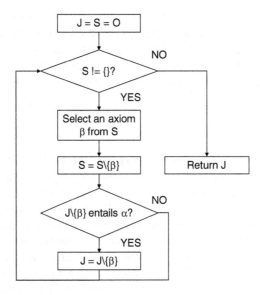

Fig. 5.1 An algorithm lin-Justification-EL($\mathcal{O}$, α): input is an OWL 2 EL ontology $\mathcal{O}$ and an OWL 2 EL axiom α s.t. $\mathcal{O} \models \alpha$. Output is a set of justification axioms J

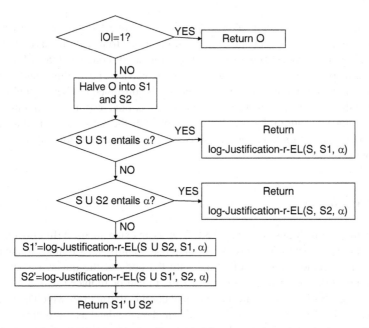

Fig. 5.2 An optimised algorithm log-Justification-r-EL(S, $\mathcal{O}$, α): input is a support set of axioms S, an OWL 2 EL ontology $\mathcal{O}$ and an OWL 2 EL axiom α s.t. $S \cup \mathcal{O} \models \alpha$. Output is a minimal subset $J \sqsubseteq \mathcal{O}$ s.t. $S \cup J \models \alpha$

the original. In this section, we will first investigate OWL 2 QL justification for TBox axioms in general, unsatisfiability and inconsistency results, then look at justification of TBox axioms, then ABox axioms, then finally for query answering. We will then give the general procedure for expanding these justifications with respect to the original ontology before normalisation.

TBox Results

Because of the form that normalised axioms take in OWL 2 QL, all TBox entailments take the form $B_1 \sqsubseteq B_2$, $B_1 \sqsubseteq \neg B_2$ or $R_1 \sqsubseteq R_2$ where B_1 and B_2 are both DL-Lite basic concepts and R_1 and R_2 are atomic roles. In general, the complete set of justifications can be computed by looking at the concept hierarchy and finding every chain of subsumption between the two concepts in question. If only a single justification is required, then only one path between the two concepts needs to be investigated. For example, in the concept hierarchy the complete set of justifications for the axiom $Student \sqsubseteq Mammal$ is found by examining the path $Student \rightarrow Person \rightarrow Mammal$. Thus the set of axioms in the justification is $\{Student \sqsubseteq Person, Person \sqsubseteq Mammal\}$.

ABox Results

In general, an ABox axiom in OWL 2 QL is in the format $C(x)$ or $R(x, y)$ where C is a DL-Lite general concept and R is an atomic role. To justify this axiom, we use the classification service to get the most specific set of concepts that x belongs to or the most specific set of roles that (x, y) participates in. From this result, we then check each candidate concept of role to see if it is subsumed by the original C or R named in the original axiom. The complete set of axioms responsible for entailment can be found by combining the ABox axiom with the set of axioms that justify the TBox subsumption between the successful candidate concept and the original concept or role.

Query Answering

Justification of query answering in OWL 2 QL is an extension of ABox justification. During the query rewriting process, one step is to identify all variables in the query which can be removed and "rolled up" into the body of the query. For example, in the query $Q(x) \leftarrow R(x, y)$, the atom $R(x, y)$ can be replaced with a new atom $\exists R(x)$. Once this has been done, the union of conjunctive queries which is the result of applying the PerfectRef algorithm is executed on the database, and the combined result set is returned to the user. In order to perform a justification for any result in this set, we have to look at every variable which remained in the input query.

In every result, each variable which remained in the query will be bound to some value in the ontology. These are normally not returned as part of the results, as only those variables which appear in the head of the query are of interest to the end user. However, in order to perform justification, every bound variable must be found. In the rewriting process, simply replacing the select clause in the SQL statement with "SELECT *" is usually sufficient. This will give us a set of bindings, which can be referred back to the original rewritten query and placed in the query atom where that variable was found. We can then reduce justification over QL query answering to simple ABox justification, by retrieving the justification for each atom, when the value found in the result is substituted back into the original query.

For example, a query $Q(x, z) \leftarrow A(x) \sqcap B(x, y) \sqcap C(y, z) \sqcap D(z)$ is found in the union of conjunctive queries given by PerfectRef for some input query. When this is executed over the database, one of the result bindings gives us $x = val1$, $y = val2$, $z = val3$. By substituting these values back into the query we are given $A(val1) \sqcap B(val1, val2) \sqcap C(val2, val3) \sqcap D(val3)$. The full justification for this query is the union of the justifications of each of these atoms, using the method described under ABox justification.

Unsatisfiability and Inconsistency Results

Any unsatisfiable concept in OWL 2 QL will be caused by the reasoner entailing $C \sqsubseteq \neg C$. Therefore, the justification for any unsatisfiable concept can be reduced to TBox subsumption justification of this axiom. Furthermore, in QL, an inconsistency result can only be caused by the instantiation of an unsatisfiable concept, so in the case of an inconsistent ontology, the set of axioms which caused it can be found by identifying all unsatisfiable concepts, finding any concepts which are instantiated, and then finding the full set of axioms which cause those instantiations. Therefore, we can say that justification of inconsistency results in QL can be reduced to ABox and TBox justification.

Pre and Post-normalised Ontologies

Because a QL ontology must always be normalised before any reasoning can be performed on it, the procedures above will result in axioms which appear in the normalised version of the ontology. In many cases, an axiom found in a justification will appear in the pre-normalised ontology; however, sometimes this has been transformed from some ground axiom. To relate these post-normalisation axioms back to the original ontology, we simply add some annotation to each normalised axiom which is not in the ground ontology. This allows us to identify which axiom or axioms are responsible for its entailment, and the reasoner can follow these annotations to expand any justification into the original axioms trivially.

5.3 Conclusion

In this chapter, we have presented TrOWL, the tractable reasoning infrastructure for OWL 2. TrOWL is one of the major enabler of the MOST Workbench to be introduced in Chap. 13, which is the first platform for ontology-driven software development (ODSD).

Chapter 6
Traceability

Hannes Schwarz and Jürgen Ebert

Abstract In this chapter, we introduce traceability, which can be defined as the ability to help stakeholders understand the associations and dependencies that exist among entities created or used during a software development process. Typically, these associations and dependencies are represented as traceability relationships between the artefacts or models to be traced. Today, traceability is recognised as being essential for various tasks related to software engineering, such as project management, quality assurance, and maintenance. This chapter will present a comprehensive and generic approach to traceability, supporting all relevant traceability-related activities and allowing for the custom definition of semantically rich traceability relationship types. An interesting feature of the approach is technology-independent, i.e., adaptable to model-driven software development (MDSD)—as well as ontology-based technologies, making it usable for ontology-driven software development. Taking these three attributes together, the traceability approach is referred to as being universal.

This chapter is organised as follows. Section 6.1 presents some fields of application of traceability in software development. Section 6.2 introduces six traceability-related activities associated with traceability. Section 6.3 presents a universal approach to supporting traceability. The following sections show how this approach is implemented using specific technologies from the MDSD and ontology technological spaces. Finally, Sect. 6.7 offers some discussions of the gained insights.

6.1 Fields of Application

The availability of traceability information is necessary for a wide range of tasks related to software development. In this section, we introduce a selection of possible fields of application [5, 32, 54, 205, 219].

J.Z. Pan et al. (eds.), *Ontology-Driven Software Development*,   121
DOI 10.1007/978-3-642-31226-7_6, © Springer-Verlag Berlin Heidelberg 2013

6.1.1   Change Management

In change management, traceability is used for performing impact analysis, i.e., the determination of the effects of changing a particular artefact or model element. For instance, changing a requirement or a model part requires that its implementing code fragments are determined in order to properly adapt them. Conversely, a modified code fragment has to be traced back to the requirement or model part it implements in order to ensure it is still properly implemented [186]. Another example is the propagation of model changes to their documentation [15].

6.1.2   Maintenance

The maintenance of a software system requires the understanding of connections and dependencies between the different parts of that system. These parts do not only comprise the source code, but also include requirements, test cases, documentation, or, especially in an MDSD context, all kinds of models on different levels of abstraction. If the connections and dependencies are represented in the form of traceability relationships, software engineers are able to follow them in order to better comprehend the system's structure and behaviour.

6.1.3   Project Management

Traceability information helps to track the progress of a software development project. If traceability relationships are thoroughly and accurately recorded, a project manager can determine, for example, which requirements are already realised and which ones are still to be implemented. Using traceability information for performing impact analyses, the costs of intended changes may be assessed. Furthermore, the tracing of software artefacts to the authors or other responsible persons facilitates accountability.

6.1.4   Quality Assurance

In quality assurance, traceability relationships can aid in the validation of a system. For example, if a requirement can be traced to source code artefacts, it can be concluded that the system possesses the required functionality. By checking whether there are parts of the implementation which cannot be traced to some requirement, gold plating, i.e., the development of non-required system features, can be avoided [104]. Furthermore, by providing traceability between system components and test cases, test coverage can be determined, and metrics depending on traceability information can be calculated.

6.1.5   Requirements Management

Historically, research on traceability has its origins in requirements engineering. Consequently, a variety of relationship types between requirements has been identified (see [164] or [168], for instance), allowing to maintain a coherent requirements specification. Traceability relationships can also be used to keep track of responsible stakeholders. Furthermore, impact analysis based on the analysis of traceability information allows to assess the effect of changing a requirement on other requirements.

6.1.6   Reuse

In [164] an approach for facilitating reuse of software artefacts in an MDSD context is suggested. The approach makes use of traceability relationships to interconnect the requirements of a software system with the models and source code fulfilling the requirements. Some of the relationships are generated automatically by model transformations that convert parts of the requirements specification to architecture and design models and finally to source code. If the requirements of that software system are similar to the requirements elicited in a later software development project, the traceability relationships can be traversed to find and reuse artefacts which are likely to be reusable for the new system to be developed.

A similar approach was also pursued by the ReDSeeDS project[1] [196], where the reuse approach was embedded in a model-driven context.

6.1.7   Reverse Engineering

Similar to the usage of traceability information in maintenance, it can also be employed in reverse engineering to understand the relationships of source code fragments to entities on higher abstraction levels, such as design models or requirements. Furthermore, tracing the interdependencies between source code artefacts helps developers in understanding and recovering a system's architecture.

---

[1]http://www.redseeds.eu

6.2 Traceability-Related Activities

In this section, we investigate the six traceability-related activities *definition, identification, recording, retrieval, utilisation,* and *maintenance* [163]. For each activity, a short overview of selected related work is given. Note, that although the activities are logically ordered from the definition of models for traceability information to the maintenance of existing traceability relationships, this ordering does not intend to prescribe some kind of process of how to introduce or work with traceability information.

6.2.1 Definition

The traceability-related activity of *definition* is concerned with specifying the structure for traceability information, including the identification of types of entities which are traceable and the types of traceability relationships between them. In many traceability approaches, the result of this activity is some kind of metamodel capturing this structure. *Traceability models* capturing the structure of traced entities and traceability relationships conform to this metamodel.

Literature on the activity of definition falls into one of three categories. The first category introduces collections of traceability relationship types without putting them in the greater context of a full-blown metamodel. For example, various relationship types for interconnecting requirements are introduced in [44, 54]. Relationship types between entities of different types, including requirements, design elements, source code, test cases, and documentation, are proposed in [204].

The second category deals with the metamodelling of traceability information. Some of these publications suggest concrete *metamodels* prescribing entity and relationship types, however, with varying focuses, for example, requirements [164, 168], product line engineering [105, 137], or source code and documentation [221]. The UML [150] also provides constructs for modelling traceability relationships. Other authors proclaim more generic approaches, such as the *traceability meta-type* [66], the *traceability metamodelling language* (*TML*) [59], or the solution described in [209]. These approaches allow for the definition of customised metamodels suiting specific applications.

Publications in the third category have a closer look on the traceability relationship types and try to define their *semantics* in a more formal way than simply providing a natural language description of their meaning. The employed techniques range from simple mathematical expressions [57] and so-called cost/value interdependencies denoting the influence of requirements on one another [54], to integrity constraints [59, 164] and logic formulae [76], to event-condition-action (ECA) rules [3].

Most approaches view traceability relationships as being *binary*, i.e., interconnecting exactly two entities or an entity with itself. Only few approaches, for example, the UML and [127], regard relationships as potentially being *n-ary*.

6.2.2 Identification

Identification refers to the discovery or generation of previously unknown traceability relationships, i.e., instances of the relationship types determined by the *definition* activity.

With respect to the identification of traceability relationships, it can be distinguished between *manual* and *automatic* identification, with several degrees of semi-automation in between. Purely manual identification, conducted by having humans to inspect entities to be traced and look for relationships to other entities, is considered as being very costly and error prone [2].

Semi-automatic approaches such as proposed in [76, 190] derive new traceability relationships from the analysis of specific patterns of already existing relationships. A tool described in [79] suggests candidate relationships to the users and, considering the users' choices, makes use of machine learning techniques to improve its suggestions. Another semi-automatic technique is the integration of the software development tools with the employed process model, resulting in traceability relationships to be automatically created between artefacts used as input and output of specific actions performed by the developers [164].

Most fully automated identification approaches rely on either *information retrieval* or *model transformation* techniques. Basically, information retrieval-based approaches, for example, [5, 56, 101], determine similarities between text-intensive entities such as source code together with comments and documentation. In the course of model transformations, traceability relationships can be created between source and target entities of the transformation [106, 146, 223]. An automatic identification approach based on rules is pursued in [50].

6.2.3 Recording

Recording involves the physical representation of identified traceability relationships as data structures, possibly with the goal of making them persistent. Depending on the employed technology, the form of representation varies.

Traceability relationships can be recorded either *within* traced entities as textual references [218] or hyperlinks [109] or *externally* using various technologies.

The simplest external recording approach makes use of a spreadsheet where rows and columns represent the various entities to be traced and an entry in a table cell represents a traceability relationship between the respective entities. More sophisticated approaches rely on *fact repositories* which make use of suitable data structures to store traceability information. Possible technologies for implementing fact repositories are relational databases [198], deductive database systems [164], the early object-oriented knowledge representation language *Telos* [49], open hypermedia [190], graph-based repositories [26], XML technology [126], or ontologies [221].

The choice of a recording technology is strongly related to the employed approach for the definition of traceability information. For example, ontology technology provides means for both the definition and the recording of traceability information. If heterogeneous technologies are used, suitable mapping approaches are required, for example, an object-relational mapping is needed for storing traceability information represented as a MOF-based model in a relational database.

6.2.4   Retrieval

Given a set of traced entities and recorded interconnecting traceability relationships, *retrieval* deals with determining pieces of this traceability information which are required for specific applications.

Publications concerned with the retrieval of traceability information mainly describe how various languages can be employed for this activity. Evidently, the language chosen for retrieval is highly dependent on the employed technology for recording traceability information. Example languages are SQL for relational database systems, GReQL for TGraph-based repositories [186], or ontology query languages for ontologies [221]. A special *trace query language (TQL)* for querying traceability information recorded in an XML-based repository is specified in [125].

The retrieval of traced entities and interconnecting relationships by specifying patterns with regular expressions is pursued in [162]. In [164], a tool suite supporting retrieval is presented. It allows for a textual search for traceability information as well as for selecting traced entities in a graphical interface which then displays related entities.

6.2.5   Utilisation

Utilisation takes a special role among the six traceability-related activities. It refers to the usage of retrieved traceability information, for example, for the applications described in Sect. 6.1. Although utilisation is part of the "lifecycle" of traceability information, it is not a subject of traceability research in the narrower sense.

Due to the special role of this activity, an overview of related work is out of scope here. However, an important facet of utilisation is the *visualisation* of retrieved traceability information. Often, matrices corresponding to the spreadsheet-based recording approach mentioned in Sect. 6.2.3 and the textual representation as hyperlinks [109,142] are used. Graph-based visualisation, with vertices representing traced entities and edges denoting traceability relationships, is employed by various prototypical research tools [47, 164] as well as commercial tools. Examples for the latter are the requirements management tool IBM Rational DOORS[2] or the modelling tool *Enterprise Architect*[3].

6.2.6 Maintenance

Maintenance of traceability relationships prevents them from deteriorating by adapting them to changes of traced entities and other relationships. Maintenance involves the update or even deletions of existing recorded relationships.

Similar to identification, it is also possible to distinguish between *manual* maintenance, *semi-automatic*, and *automatic* maintenance. Purely manual maintenance of traceability relationships is considered to be costly and error prone [60]. Semi-automatic approaches usually rely on the specification of constraints imposed on the traceability model [59, 75, 164]. Violations of these constraints are reported to the users so that they can take proper reactions.

However, most maintenance approaches are based on the ECA paradigm. In [48], traced entities are registered at a so-called event server which monitors them for changes and updates incident traceability relationships accordingly. The traceability tool *traceMaintainer* [124] is closely coupled with a UML modelling tool and receives change events such as the update of a model element. Specific sequences of such events trigger the execution of actions which modify affected traceability relationships. In [3] traceability relationships in UML are complemented by ECA rules.

6.3 An Universal Traceability Concept

In the following, a universal approach for supporting traceability is presented. The approach is applicable to any development project with its individual landscape of artefacts. Furthermore, it can be implemented by any technology or language that allows to represent entities and connections between these entities, such as Ecore, the TGraph approach, or OWL ontologies. Consequently, the approach is to be considered as *generic* and *technology-independent*.

The approach's main constituent is the so-called *traceability relationship type template (TRTT)*, a generic, technology-independent template for the *definition* of semantically rich traceability relationship types. Relationship types conforming to the TRTT may also possess features supporting the activities of *identification* and *maintenance*. As further contribution besides the TRTT, three *retrieval patterns* describe and categorise common problems of traceability *retrieval*.

---

[2]http://www-01.ibm.com/software/awdtools/doors/

[3]http://www.sparxsystems.com/products/ea/8/index.html

Although *recording* and *utilisation* are not explicitly taken into account by the universal approach, it can be regarded as being *comprehensive*: *recording* of traceability information is highly dependent on the technology chosen for implementing a traceability scheme and is discussed in later sections that describe concrete implementations. As *utilisation* is more application- than technology-oriented, it is also not considered here.

6.3.1   The Traceability Relationship Type Template

In principle, the TRTT can be regarded as a collection of guidelines for the custom definition of traceability relationship types. It is not to be understood as some kind of language itself but can be implemented by specific technologies. The TRTT allows for various properties for relationship types in order to facilitate rich, formalised semantics going beyond a mere description in natural language. The two properties *constraints* and *impact designators* serve identification or maintenance purposes. If required due to limitations of the expressiveness of implementing technologies, some properties may be omitted. Furthermore, it is not needed for a relationship type to implement all properties.

Table 6.1 gives a concise overview of the TRTT. It specifies the following properties:

Name

The Name property refers to the name of the relationship type. It has to be unique so that the relationship type can be unambiguously distinguished from other types.

Description

The Description property refers to a natural language description of the semantics of the relationship type. The description shall precisely explain the meaning and purpose of the type so that developers can distinguish it from other types.

Supertypes

The Supertypes property refers to other relationship types which generalise the relationship type at hand. The exact semantics of generalisation is dependent on the underlying technology. Typically, in languages such as Ecore or grUML, a type can be used anywhere one of its supertypes is requested [123]. This results in a subtype to inherit its supertypes' attributes and in constraints and impact designators defined for a supertype also to refer to instances of the type at hand.

Table 6.1 Overview of the TRTT

Property	Multiplicity	Description
Name	1	The traceability relationship type's unique identifier
Description	1	An accurate description of the meaning and purpose of the traceability relationship type
Supertypes	0..*	Any number of other traceability relationship types being generalisations of the traceability relationship type at hand
Schema fragment	1	A schema excerpt specifying how instances of the traceability relationship type connect traceable entities to each other
Attributes	0..*	Any number of *identifier-domain* pairs that describe attributes of the traceability relationship type
Relational properties (for binary traceability relationship types only)	0..*	Any feasible combination of relational properties such as *reflexivity*, *symmetry*, or *transitivity*
Constraints	0..*	Any number of constraints which must all hold true for an instance of the traceability relationship type to be valid
Impact designators	0..*	Any number of rules specifying how changes to recorded relationships or entities affect other relationships or entities
Examples	0..*	Some examples illustrating the usage of the traceability relationship type

Schema Fragment

The Schema Fragment property refers to an excerpt of the traceability schema or metamodel which specifies the traced entity types and the interconnecting relationship types. The excerpt only includes the relationship types at hand, the entity types it connects, and other relationship and entity types referred to by some *constraint* or *impact designator*. Relationship types do not necessarily have to be modelled as binary links, but may be represented by more complex constructs.

Attributes

The Attributes property refers to any number of *identifier-domain* pairs. Instances of the relationship types assign a value of the domain to the identifier.

Relational Properties

The Relational Properties refers to a combination of relational properties such as *reflexivity*, *irreflexivity*, *symmetry*, *antisymmetry*, or *transitivity*. The combination of relational properties must be feasible, for example, an instance relationship type cannot be reflexive as well as irreflexive. Furthermore, relational properties can only be defined for *binary* relationship types, i.e., which connect exactly two entity types or an entity type with itself. If the relationship type connects two different entity types, only suitable relational properties such as *injectivity* are possible.

Constraints

The Constraints property refers to a set of invariants which have to hold true during the lifetime of an instance of the relationship type. Since constraints capture the conditions which must be met for an instance to be valid, they can be used for maintenance purposes. Instances whose constraints are violated can be dealt with automatically in a suitable way or be reported to the users who can then modify them accordingly or even delete them.

Impact Designators

The Impact Designators property refers to a set of rules specifying how a change to an instance of the relationship type or to an instance of the entity type incident to the relationship type *impacts*, i.e., affects, other instances. By automatically creating or updating relationships, impact designators can fulfil identification and maintenance purposes, respectively. Depending on the technology used for implementing the TRTT, impact designators can be realised as ECA or condition-action rules.

Examples

The Examples property refers to a selection of applications of the relationship type that clarify its usage. The examples should originate from the environment the relationship type is used in as well as from other more general contexts.

6.3.2   Traceability Retrieval Patterns

The analysis of the various traceability problems implied by the case studies described in Chap. 4 and other traceability applications that can be found in literature resulted in the derivation of three *retrieval patterns*: *existence*, *reachable entities*, and *slice*. They describe the majority of retrieval problems in an abstract form. In other words, most retrieval problems correspond to one of these three patterns. For the implementation of a traceability approach, it is therefore recommended to choose a technology which supports retrieval according to the patterns. In the following, the three patterns are explained in greater detail.

Existence Pattern

The existence pattern is concerned with the question whether any two traced entities out of two sets of entities are related. More formally, given two sets of traced entities E_1 and E_2, it is to be checked whether there exist any two traced entities $e_1 \in E_1$ and $e_2 \in E_2$ which are directly connected by a traceability relationship or indirectly connected by a path of traceability relationships. In many cases it is required that only specific relationship types, relationships with specific properties, or paths of a specific structure are considered.

Applications for this pattern can be found in quality assurance, where it is to be checked whether there exists a test case for each system component, for instance. Strictly adhering to the pattern, a series of retrieval operations corresponding to the number of components has to be performed, so that for each operation, E_1 includes all test cases and E_2 contains a single component. The path structure has to reflect the (sequence of) traceability relationships representing that a test case is assigned to that specific component. Modern query languages allow to resolve such a retrieval problem in a single query. Another potential application area is project management. For example, it can be checked which requirements are already implemented and which ones are not.

Reachable Entities Pattern

The reachable entities pattern serves to determine the set of traced entities related to any entity out of a given set of entities. That means, given a set of traced entities E_1, the sought-for set E_2 contains all entities which are reachable by a path of traceability relationships (possibly consisting of only one relationship) from some entity $e_1 \in E_1$. Again, the possible structures of the path must often be restricted. If a specific path structure is given, only the entities at the *end* of paths conforming to that structure are to be included in the set of returned entities.

For example, this pattern can be used in change management for determining traced entities impacted by a change to another entity or to a set of other entities. If source code fragments such as a set of classes are modified, it is needed to identify the requirements implemented by those classes. Then, it can be checked whether these implementation relationships are still valid. Here, E_1 corresponds to the set of changed classes. Furthermore, the eligible paths to be traversed have to be restricted to those expressing the implementation relationship. Possibly, the classes in the source code are only indirectly connected to the requirements via some design or architecture models. Considering requirements engineering, reachable entities can be used to find the stakeholders who authored a given set of requirements, for example, to clarify open questions.

Slice Pattern

The slice pattern is similar to the reachable entities pattern in that given a set of entities E_1, the set of traced entities E_2 reachable from any entity $e_1 \in E_1$ is to be determined. But here, in addition, the interconnecting traceability relationships are also to be reported to the users. If a specific structure for the eligible paths of traceability relationships is given, not only the entities at the end of conforming paths, but also all intermediate entities and the entities in E_1 are to be included in E_2.

The slice pattern can be applied to implement the reuse scenario described in Sect. 6.1.6. Given some requirements from a current development project, they can be compared to the requirements specification of an already accomplished project. Starting from requirements of the old project which are identified to be similar, slicing could make use of existing traceability relationships connecting to architecture components, design models, and further on to source code in order to yield all entities realising these requirements. Furthermore, slices are always useful if users are not only interested in the entities situated at the end of specific paths of traceability relationships, but also need an explanation of how they are connected to understand the nature of the relationship, such as in maintenance or reverse engineering contexts.

6.4   Implementation Based on Ecore(*)

In practice, the universal concepts presented in Sect. 6.3 for facilitating the definition, identification and maintenance, as well as the retrieval of traceability information have to be applied to specific technological spaces. Taking Ecore together with ATL and OCL, which form an important technological space in MDE, the mapping of TRTT properties to language properties, the identification of traceability relationships, their recording on the basis of the *eclipse modelling framework (EMF)*, and the realisation of queries conforming to the retrieval patterns is conducted as follows.

As an example, the BPMN process refinement case study presented in Sect. 4.2 is drawn on, assuming that BPMN process models together with *refinement* and *grounding* relationships between tasks of different models are represented in Ecore.

6.4.1   Mapping of TRTT Properties

With the exception of impact designators, Ecore and OCL constructs are able to represent all TRTT properties. Figure 6.1 shows the instantiated TRTT for the Refinement relationship type between tasks in a BPMN refinement chain. The modelling of relationship types with Ecore is heavily influenced by the fact that

Property	Value
Name	Refinement
Description	A Refinement relationship maps a refining Task to the refined Task.
Supertypes	None
Metamodel fragment	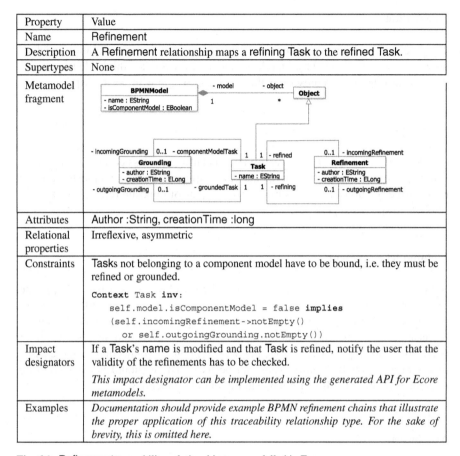
Attributes	Author :String, creationTime :long
Relational properties	Irreflexive, asymmetric

Constraints	Tasks not belonging to a component model have to be bound, i.e. they must be refined or grounded.
	
	`Context Task inv:`
	    `self.model.isComponentModel = false implies`
	    `(self.incomingRefinement->notEmpty()`
	       `or self.outgoingGrounding.notEmpty())`

Impact designators	If a Task's name is modified and that Task is refined, notify the user that the validity of the refinements has to be checked. *This impact designator can be implemented using the generated API for Ecore metamodels.*
Examples	*Documentation should provide example BPMN refinement chains that illustrate the proper application of this traceability relationship type. For the sake of brevity, this is omitted here.*

Fig. 6.1 Refinement traceability relationship type modelled in Ecore

references between classes are navigable in one direction only and do not exhibit an own identity.

In the following, the general implementation of the individual TRTT properties with Ecore is discussed.

Name

A relationship type's name corresponds to the name of the class which represents the type. If the relationship type is modelled as a pair of opposite references, the name can only be part of the documentation, as the names of the references correspond to role names (see *Metamodel fragment*).

Description

The description of the relationship type is usually part of its documentation and does not need to be represented by a model element. However, it is thinkable to annotate the class or references representing the relationship type with the description.

Supertypes

The definition of a supertype is realised by declaring the class corresponding to the supertype to be a generalisation of the class representing the relationship type at hand. If the relationship type is modelled as a pair of opposite references, it is not possible to specify supertypes.

Metamodel Fragment

A binary relationship type can be modelled as a class or as a pair of opposite references. However, if the second option is chosen, it is not possible to specify supertypes and attributes. A representation as a single reference is not recommended because such traceability relationships would be traversable in one direction only. For *n*-ary types, a class together with references connecting to the classes representing the traced entity types can be used. These should possess opposite references in order to allow for navigability in both directions.

Attributes

Attributes are realised as attributes of the class which represents the relationship type. If the type is represented and is modelled as pair of opposite references, it is not possible to specify attributes.

Relational Properties

It is possible to represent all relational properties by OCL constraints. However, this is only recommended for properties ensuring the *non-existence* of particular relationships, such as *irreflexivity*, *antisymmetry*, or *intransitivity*. Concerning *reflexivity* and *symmetry*, which ensure the *existence* of relationships, the specification of such constraints would require the population of the model holding the traceability information with additional relationships. Alternatively, these properties can also be considered during retrieval by accordingly formulated OCL queries. *Transitivity* of a relationship, which also asserts the existence of relationships, is a special case because although OCL does not directly provide a function to compute transitive closure, it is possible to emulate this behaviour by the recursive definition of attributes. However, this only works for paths of references not including cycles [14].

Constraints

Constraints can be specified by using OCL *invariants*, returning a boolean value. With respect to the specification of constraints involving transitive closure of potentially cyclic paths of references, the same restrictions apply as explained in the *relational properties* paragraph.

Impact Designators

Since there is no common ECA rule language in the Ecore technological space, impact designators have to be realised programmatically, i.e., by manually implementing the desired behaviour using the generated APIs for Ecore metamodels.

6.4.2   Transformation-Based Identification

Although ATL maintains traceability relationships between source and target elements, they are exclusively meant for internal usage, i.e., standard ATL does not provide the possibility to make the relationships persistent. Consequently, the generation of traceability relationships has to be encoded in the ATL transformation manually. Since ATL transformations can be treated as models themselves, it is also possible to transform the transformation itself in order to automatically include the traceability relationship generation [106].

The EMF [199], which is based on Ecore as metametamodel, allows for references to span model boundaries, meaning that it is possible for an instance to possess a reference to an instance which is contained by another model. Therefore, source and target models of the transformation do not have to be kept as submodels in a single model in order to maintain traceability relationships between their elements.

6.4.3   Technologies for Recording

Ecore-based models can be created and handled using the EMF providing a Java API. While persistence is usually achieved by serialising the models to an XML representation, the *Teneo* project[4] allows for the storage of models using relational database systems, thus facilitating improved scalability.

For all software development artefacts which are not natively represented as Ecore models, for example, documentation or source code, the relevant information to be traced must be extracted using tools such as parsers and be stored as Ecore model.

6.4.4　Querying Conforming to the Retrieval Patterns

The three retrieval patterns *existence*, *reachable entities*, and *slice* can all be implemented as OCL queries. However, the expression of traceability relationship path structures going beyond mere sequences of relationships can become very complex. Furthermore, as discussed in Sect. 6.4, the computation of transitive closure is not straightforward and only possible by using complex constructions. These are not considered by the examples below.

Another possibility to circumvent the restriction of OCL is to programmatically implement required retrieval operations using Ecore's Java API. However, such a solution is not applicable if ad hoc queries are to be formulated by end users of some Ecore-based traceability tool.

Existence Pattern

One possibility to realise the existence pattern is to use two `let` expressions to define variables bound to the two sets of traced entities whose interconnection is to be tested. The `exists` operation then checks if any entity of the second set is reachable from any entity in the first set via a specific path of references.

In the following example, it is tested if the Task with the name Hire Applicant refines the Hiring Task.

```
let hireApplicant : Set(Task) = Task.allInstances()
      ->select(name = 'Hire_Applicant') in
   let hiring : Set(Task) = Task.allInstances()
         ->select(name = 'Hiring') in
      hireApplicant->exists(outgoingRefinement.refined = hiring)
```

Reachable Entities Pattern

The reachable entities pattern can be implemented by employing a `let` expression to assign a variable to the set of traced entities which serve as starting points for

---

[4]http://wiki.eclipse.org/Teneo

retrieving entities related to them. In the `let` expression's `in` part, the `collect()` operation is called, returning all entities reachable from any entity in the set by a given path of references.

The query below retrieves all Tasks directly refining the `Hiring` Task.

```
let hiring : Set(Task) = Task.allInstances()->select(name = 'Hiring') in
    hiring->collect(incomingRefinement.refining)
```

Slice Pattern

OCL does not provide a concept to directly pose a query according to the slice pattern. A laborious but possible workaround is to take the union of the results of multiple reachable entities queries. Based on the original description of the required path structure for a slice query, each of these queries computes the entities reachable via a fraction of this description. The inclusion of the traceability relationships in the slice is only possible if their types are represented as classes.

The following example returns a set including the Task with the name `Hiring`, all Tasks indirectly refining that Task with a single intermediate Task, the intermediate Tasks, and all involved instances of Refines.

```
let hiring : Set(Task) = Task.allInstances()->select(name = 'Hiring') in
    hiring->
        union(hiring->collect(incomingRefinement))->
        union(hiring.incomingRefinement->collect(refining))->
        union(hiring.incomingRefinement.refining->collect(incomingRefinement))->
        union(hiring.incomingRefinement.refining.incomingRefinement->
            collect(refining))
```

6.5 Implementation Based on the TGraph Approach[*]

With grUML, GReTL, and GReQL, the TGraph approach (see Chap. 2) provides suitable technologies for realising the TRTT properties, identifying relationships with transformations, recording using the TGraph-based *JGralab* tool suite, and formulating queries which conform to the retrieval patterns. Compared to OCL, GReQL with its regular path expressions allows to describe the structure of paths of traceability relationships much more concisely. In addition, the computation of transitive closure over relationships is supported by iterated path expressions.

Analogously to the description of the Ecore-based implementation of the TRTT, the BPMN process refinement case study is used as example here.

6.5.1 Mapping of TRTT Properties

All TRTT properties except for impact designators can be mapped to grUML and
GReQL concepts. For representing impact designators, an approach for specifying
ECA rules is employed. Figure 6.2 shows the instantiated TRTT for the Refines
relationship type between tasks in a BPMN refinement chain. Note, that to conform
with grUML modelling guidelines, a verb is used as identifier here, instead of a
noun as used for the similar relationship type modelled as Ecore class (see Fig. 6.1).
Furthermore, there is an additional constraint based on the computation of transitive
closure in order to test for cyclic refinements. This cannot be expressed in OCL.

In the following, the general implementation of the TRTT properties using the
TGraph approach is shown.

Name

A relationship type's name corresponds to the name of the edge class or vertex class
which represents the type (see *Metamodel fragment*).

Description

The description of the relationship type is usually part of its documentation and does
not need to be represented in a graph. However, it is thinkable to *comment* the class
or references representing the relationship type with the description.

Supertypes

The definition of a supertype is realised by declaring the edge class or vertex class
corresponding to the supertype to be a generalisation of the edge or vertex class
representing the relationship type at hand.

Metamodel Fragment

A binary relationship type can be modelled as edge class. For *n*-ary types, a vertex
class together with edge classes connecting to the vertex classes representing the
traced entity types can be used.

Property	Value
Name	Refines
Description	A Refines relationship maps a refining Task to the refined Task.
Supertypes	None
Metamodel fragment	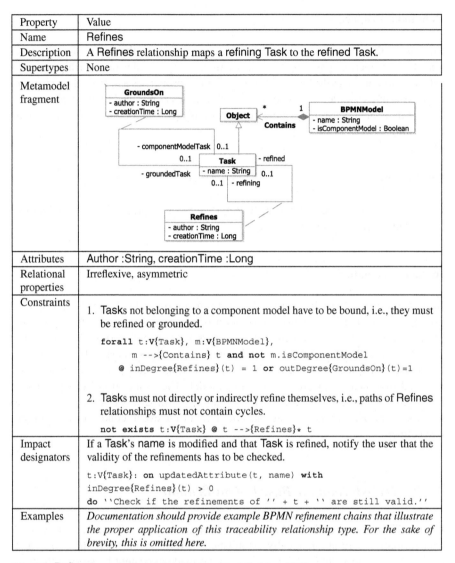
Attributes	Author :String, creationTime :Long
Relational properties	Irreflexive, asymmetric

Constraints	1. Tasks not belonging to a component model have to be bound, i.e., they must be refined or grounded.
	
	`forall t:V{Task}, m:V{BPMNModel},`
	`    m -->{Contains} t and not m.isComponentModel`
	`    @ inDegree{Refines}(t) = 1 or outDegree{GroundsOn}(t)=1`
	
	2. Tasks must not directly or indirectly refine themselves, i.e., paths of Refines relationships must not contain cycles.
	
	`not exists t:V{Task} @ t -->{Refines}* t`

Impact designators	If a Task's name is modified and that Task is refined, notify the user that the validity of the refinements has to be checked.
	
	`t:V{Task}: on updatedAttribute(t, name) with`
	`inDegree{Refines}(t) > 0`
	`do ''Check if the refinements of '' + t + '' are still valid.''`

Examples	*Documentation should provide example BPMN refinement chains that illustrate the proper application of this traceability relationship type. For the sake of brevity, this is omitted here.*

Fig. 6.2 Refines traceability relationship type modelled in grUML

Attributes

Attributes are realised as attributes of the edge class or vertex class which represents the relationship type.

Relational Properties

Similar to the representation of relational properties on the basis of OCL (see Sect. 6.4), properties ensuring the *non-existence* of particular relationships can be safely formulated as GReQL constraints, whereas properties asserting the *existence* of relationships should be treated by GReQL queries at retrieval time. In contrast to OCL, this is also possible for transitive relationships which potentially form paths containing cycles.

Constraints

Constraints can be specified using GReQL boolean expressions. In most cases, quantified expressions are employed.

Impact Designators

Impact designators can be realised by an ECA approach based on TGraphs. The possible events are the creation or deletion of a vertex or an edge, the update of an attribute value, or the change of an edge's start or end vertex. As condition, anybBoolean GReQL expressions can be used. The actions can specify suggestions to the users or can even call a GReTL transformation to automatically perform the required modifications to the traceability model. The syntax used for ECA rules conforms to the on E with C do A pattern, with on, with, and do being keywords and E, C, and A being placeholders for the event, condition, and action, respectively.

6.5.2   Transformation-Based Identification

Using GReTL, traceability relationships between source and target elements of transformations are automatically established in form of the mappings img_T and $arch_T$. As described in Sect. 2.4.2, they can be made persistent by storing them to an XML file. However, these relationships cannot be queried with GReQL queries, for they are not represented as a TGraph.

To create relationships which can be queried using GReQL, transformations can be modified so that the target graph contains the source graph and the original target graph as subgraphs. The transformation also generates traceability relationships between corresponding elements of the two subgraphs. Obviously, only vertices can be interconnected in this way. To automate this approach, GReTL provides a predefined generic copy transformation which copies the source schema and graph. When writing their transformations, users can first call the copy transformation and then further extend the schema, create the target subgraph, and connect it to the source subgraph.

An example for relationship identification using GReTL transformations has been given in Sect. 2.4.2, where Refines edges are generated between tasks with the same name.

6.5.3   Technologies for Recording

With JGraLab[5], short for *Java Graph Laboratory*, there exists an implementation of the TGraph approach providing means to create, manipulate, and traverse TGraphs as well as their schemas. Both can be made persistent using the dedicated TG file format.

Similar to the implementation of a traceability approach based on Ecore and EMF, information to be traced included in development artefacts which are not TGraphs must be extracted and stored in a TGraph-based fact repository. In order to facilitate efficient querying with GReQL, multiple TGraphs, i.e., models natively represented as TGraph as well as TGraphs resulting from fact extraction, must eventually be integrated to a single graph representing the entire traceability model.

6.5.4   Querying Conforming to the Retrieval Patterns

The three retrieval patterns *existence*, *reachable entities*, and *slice* can all be implemented as GReQL queries. Compared to OCL, GReQL's regular path expressions allow for the convenient specification of complex descriptions of the desired structure of relationships between traced entities. Since GReQL allows for the user-friendly and efficient computation of transitive closure over paths in a graph, it is also easily possible to consider path structures of arbitrary length.

Existence Pattern

The existence pattern can be realised using GReQL *existentially quantified expressions* or, provided that variables are already bound, stand-alone *path existence expressions*.

In the following example, a quantified expression is used. Assuming that Task names are unique, the two sets of traced entities whose interconnection is to be checked consist of a single Task each. It is tested whether the Task with the name Interview Approval refines the Hiring Task.

---

[5]http://jgralab.uni-koblenz.de

```
exists s:V{Task}, s.name "Interview Approval",
       t:V{Task}, t.name = "Hiring"
  @ s -->{Refines} t
```

Assuming that variables have already been bound to specific vertices externally, i.e., outside the GReQL query using the API of the GReQL evaluator, the following path existence expressions perform the same check:

```
interviewApproval -->{Refines} hiring
```

Reachable Entities Pattern

Queries conforming to the reachable entities pattern employ GReQL *FWR expressions* or, if the starting set of traced entities consists of a single vertex for which a variable has already been bound externally, stand-alone *forward vertex set expressions* .

The following FWR expression yields all Tasks directly refining the Hiring Task.

```
from s:V{Task}
with s.name "Hiring"
reportSet s <--{Refines}
end
```

Provided that the Hiring Process Task has already been bound to a variable externally, a single *forward vertex set expressions* could be employed:

```
hiring <--{Refines}
```

To obtain all Tasks which indirectly refine the Hiring Process, the above query only has to be slightly modified by adding the Kleene plus to the path description.

```
hiring <--{Refines}+
```

Slice Pattern

For realising the slice pattern, GReQL provides the slice function. As parameters, it takes a set of vertices acting as starting points for the slice computation and regular path expressions specifying the structure of paths to be considered.

The application of the slice function below uses a nested FWR expression to determine a set consisting of the Hiring Task. The result of the function call is the set of Tasks which indirectly by a single intermediate Task refine the Hiring Task. The intermediate Tasks, the Hiring Task, and the Refines edges are also included in the slice.

```
slice(from s:V{Task} with s.name "Hiring" reportSet s end,
      <--{Refines}<--{Refines}
)
```

Again, the Hiring Task could have been bound to a variable externally. The appropriate GReQL expression then looks as follows:

```
slice(hiring, <--{Refines}<--{Refines})
```

6.6 Implementation Based on OWL[(*)]

Conforming with the view on ontology technology adopted in this book, the W3C family of ontology languages is chosen for implementing traceability in the ontology technological space. Besides OWL, this includes the *SPARQL protocol and RDF query language (SPARQL)*, a query language for *RDF* documents. Since OWL can be serialised to RDF [160], SPARQL is commonly used for querying OWL ontologies.

Based on these languages, it is first shown how traceability relationship types conforming to the TRTT can be defined, with impact designators serving identification and maintenance purposes. Subsequently, the recording of traceability information in the ontology technological space is shortly discussed. Finally, the usage of SPARQL for retrieval is described. Since currently, there is no technology or language especially tailored to the transformation of OWL ontologies, identification by transformation is not covered here.

6.6.1 Mapping of TRTT Properties

The application of the TRTT to ontologies makes use of OWL and SPARQL concepts. Figure 6.3 shows the instantiated TRTT for the Refinement relationship type between tasks in a BPMN refinement chain (see Sect. 4.2).

In the following, the general implementation of the TRTT properties using OWL and SPARQL is described.

Name

A traceability relationship type's name corresponds to the name of the OWL object property or class which represents the type (see *Metamodel fragment*).

Property	Value
Name	Refinement
Description	A Refinement individual specifies that the Task connected by the refining property is a refinement of the Task connected by the refined property. With refines, these traceability relationships can be treated as a single object property.
Supertypes	None

Metamodel fragment	Declaration(Class(Refinement))
	
	Declaration(DataProperty(author))
	DataPropertyDomain(author Refinement) DataPropertyRange(author xsd:string)
	Declaration(DataProperty(creationTime))
	DataPropertyDomain(author Refinement) DataPropertyRange(author xsd:dateTime)
	
	Declaration(ObjectProperty(refining))
	ObjectPropertyDomain(refining Refines)
	ObjectPropertyRange(refining Task)
	Declaration(ObjectProperty(refined))
	ObjectPropertyDomain(refined Refines) ObjectPropertyRange(refined Task)
	
	SubPropertyOf(
	    ObjectPropertyChain(ObjectInverseOf(refining) refined)
	    Refines)

Attributes	Author, creationTime (modelled as data properties)
Relational properties	Irreflexive, asymmetric

Constraints	1. Tasks not belonging to a component behaviour model have to be bound, i.e., they must be refined or grounded.
	
	    SubClassOf(Task ObjectUnionOf(
	        ObjectSomeValuesFrom(InverseObjectProperty(refines))
	        ObjectSomeValuesFrom(groundsOn))
	    )
	2. Tasks must not directly or indirectly refine themselves, i.e., paths of Refines relationships must not contain cycles.
	
	    SubPropertyOf(ObjectPropertyChain(refines refines)
	    refines)
	    SubClassOf(Task ObjectComplementOf(ObjectHasSelf(refines)))

Impact designators	If a Task's name is modified and that Task is refined, notify the user that the validity of the refinements has to be checked. *This impact designator can be implemented using an ontology API.*
Examples	*Documentation should provide example BPMN refinement chains that illustrate the proper application of this traceability relationship type. For the sake of brevity, this is omitted here.*

Fig. 6.3 Refinement traceability relationship type modelled in OWL

Description

The description of the relationship type is usually part of its documentation and does not necessarily need to be represented in an ontology. However, it is thinkable to *annotate* the OWL object property or class representing the relationship type with the description.

Supertypes

The definition of a supertype is realised by declaring the object property or class corresponding to the supertype to be a superproperty or superclass, respectively, of the property or class representing the relationship type at hand.

Metamodel Fragment

A relationship type can be modelled as object property or as class. The decision on which concept is to be employed depends on two aspects: whether the relationship type shall be binary or n-ary (with $n > 2$), and to which extent the relationship type shall feature attributes.

While a binary relationship type can be modelled as object property or as class together with dedicated object properties connecting to the classes representing the traced entity types, an n-ary relationship type requires the latter kind of modelling.

If a relationship type is modelled by an object property, attributes have to be mapped to annotations to the object property assertions which interrelate two individuals representing the traced entities. However, since annotations do not have any formal semantics in OWL, it is not possible to refer to them in constraints, impact designators, or anywhere else where reasoning services are involved. If an OWL class is chosen to model a relationship type, data properties having that class as domain can be used as representation of attributes.

Using an object property chain, a binary relationship type modelled as class together with two object properties can be treated as a single object property.

Attributes

If the relationship type is modelled as object property, the object property assertions may contain annotation axioms representing simple attributes such as a comment or rationale. However, annotations do not possess formal semantics. If the type is modelled as class, data properties or annotation assertions can be used to assign data values to the instances of these classes.

Relational Properties

It is possible to directly represent the following relational properties with OWL axioms: *reflexive, irreflexive, symmetric, asymmetric, transitive,* and *functional.* These axioms can be applied to the object property or the object property chain representing the TR type. Analogous to *constraints*, other relational properties can be specified by OWL expressions.

Constraints

There are two possibilities for the specification of constraints using ontology technology. First, SPARQL ASK queries may be used. They correspond to existential quantification, testing whether there is at least one individual, property, or combination thereof which adheres to a given restriction. Universal quantification or negation is not possible with SPARQL.

An alternative is to use OWL *expressions.* They are used to describe special classes representing constraints. Classes of individuals which are supposed to fulfil a constraint are declared to be subclasses of the respective special class. Testing the consistency of the ontology checks whether all individuals being instance of a class are also valid instances of its superclasses. Thus, it is tested whether the constraints are fulfilled.

Impact Designators

To realise impact designators in ontologies, OWL itself can be employed. Using entailment, the addition of new axioms representing impact designators to the ontology can result in the inference of facts. For example, by specifying that an object property chain is a subproperty of some single object property, traceability relationships being a "shortcut" of a path of several other relationships can be inferred. Alternatively, rule languages such as RIF [30] or SWRL [100] could be used to formulate suitable rules.

However, neither the OWL-based nor the rule-based approaches correspond to the original idea of impact designators as ECA rules. The point in time at which the inference is conducted depends on the usage of reasoners and is not an inherent characteristic of the rules. In contrast, an ECA rule is to be executed immediately after the occurrence of the event. Furthermore, it is not possible to retract knowledge from an ontology, for example, to delete entities or to modify data values.

Another option for the realisation of impact designators is to implement them using a programming language. With APIs such as Jena[6], it is possible to mimic ECA rules by reacting to changes to the ontology, i.e., events, posing queries

---

[6]http://jena.sourceforge.net

representing the conditions, and finally by modifying the ontology according to the specified actions. Using this approach, actions may also refer to the deletion of entities, the modification of data values, or the display of messages for users, for instance.

6.6.2 Technologies for Recording

To make traceability information recorded in OWL persistent, these ontologies are typically serialised to RDF and then stored in text files using an XML-based syntax [20]. For storing large ontologies, it is possible to use frameworks such as *Sesame* [35] or *Jena* [45]. By offering an abstraction layer for persistence, they allow to rely on relational database systems, for instance, thus facilitating more efficient retrieval and maintenance. Sesame and Jena both provide a Java API which supports querying and reasoning.

Large ontologies may be partitioned into several smaller ones capturing specific parts of the traceability information, consequently improving comprehensibility. For example, each sub-ontology could contain the traceability information for a single subsystem. Using the *import* concept of OWL, the sub-ontologies are imported into an integrating ontology. This ontology also has to establish the traceability relationships which cross subsystem boundaries.

6.6.3 Querying Conforming to the Retrieval Patterns

All three retrieval patterns—*existence*, *reachable entities*, and *slice*—only require the retrieval of explicitly specified information. Since SPARQL in its currently recommended version 1.0 only returns knowledge which is explicitly specified in ontologies, it is a suitable language for specifying queries conforming to the three patterns. However, SPARQL 1.0 is not able to directly compute the transitive closure over object properties, requiring the specification of additional OWL expressions that infer the closure. In the following, the structure of suitable SPARQL queries is briefly explained.

Existence Pattern

Existence queries check if a path traceability relationship conforming to a specific structure exists between any two traced entities out of two sets of entities. Such queries can be realised using the SPARQL ASK query form. The query's where clause can be divided into three parts. While the first two specify the two sets of individuals whose interconnection is to be tested, the third part describes the structure of the traceability relationship path between them.

In the following example query, it is asked whether the Task with the name Interview Approval refines the Hiring Process Task.

```
ASK
WHERE {
    # Description of first set of traced entities
    ?s rdf:type Task .
    ?s name "Interview_Approval" .

    # Description of second set of traced entities
    ?t rdf:type Task.
    ?t name "Hiring_Process" .

    # Description of required path structure
    ?s refines ?t .
}
```

Reachable Entities Pattern

Starting from any traced entity out of a given set of entities, queries conforming to the reachable entities pattern yield all traced entities reachable via a sequence of traceability relationships adhering to a specific path structure. Since individuals have to be returned, SPARQL SELECT queries are used here. The where clause consists of two parts: the first one for specifying the set of individuals serving as starting points for the reachability analysis and the second one for describing the path structure.

The following SPARQL query returns all Tasks directly refining the Hiring Process Task.

```
SELECT ?t
WHERE {
    # Description of traced entities set
    ?s rdf:type Task .
    ?s name "Hiring_Process" .

    # Description of required path structure
    ?t refines ?s .
}
```

Slice Pattern

The slice pattern is an extension of the reachable entities pattern in that not only the traced entities at the end of paths conforming to the specified structure have to be returned but also intermediate entities and the traceability relationships themselves. Therefore, compared to SPARQL queries implementing the reachable entities pattern, the where clause not only features two parts for specifying the set of start individuals and the path structure, respectively, but also a third part for assigning additional variables to the object properties representing the traceability relationships, so that they can be returned by the query.

The following example query returns all tuples `?t2 ?ref ?t1 ?ref ?s` where `?ref` denotes the `refines` property and `?t2` is a `Task` refining `Task` `?t1` which in turn refines `Task ?s`—the `Hiring Process Task`.

```
SELECT ?t2 ?ref ?t1 ?ref ?s
WHERE {
    # Description of traced entities set
    ?s rdf:type Task .
    ?s name "Hiring_Process" .

    # Binding of traceability relationship variables
    ?ref rdf:type refines .

    # Description of required path structure
    ?t2 ?ref ?t1 .
    ?t1 ?ref ?s .
}
```

6.7 Discussions

Before concluding this chapter, we discuss its contributions and their insights. The main constituent of the approach is the TRTT, which describes desirable properties of semantically rich traceability relationship types. The TRTT can be regarded as a kind of guideline for defining custom, project-specific relationship types. Some of its properties, *constraints* and *impact designators* (which are essentially ECA rules), serve to identify new and maintain already existing traceability relationships.

Another contribution of the universal approach is the description of three *traceability retrieval patterns*. These patterns, called *Existence*, *Reachable Entities*, and *Slice* characterise common problems concerning the retrieval of traceability information. Implementation should therefore be able to cope with queries according to the three patterns.

As ontology-driven software development requires the representation and handling of traceability information in both the MDSD and the ontology world, it is further investigated how the TRTT and the retrieval patterns can be implemented using respective technologies. In addition, the identification of new traceability relationships by model transformation and issues concerning the recording of traceability information are discussed. On the MDSD side, the considered technologies are Ecore together with ATL and OCL as well as the TGraph approach including grUML, GReTL, and GReQL. On the ontology side, OWL and the query language SPARQL are used for implementation.

In general, all three technologies are able to implement a comprehensive traceability approach with semantically rich relationships. However, there are some specific characteristics of the single technologies that lead to individual deficiencies. For example, the description of complex structures of paths of traceability relationships is rather difficult and cumbersome using OCL or SPARQL, whereas it is more concise in GReQL. The same applies to the computation of transitive closure, which is even not possible in SPARQL (1.0) without using additional OWL constructs as workaround. With respect to transformation-based identification of new traceability relationships, generated Ecore references may connect instances in different models. In contrast, GReTL is only able to generate TGraph edges between source and target elements of transformations if they are all included in the same graph. Concerning OWL-based approach, there is room for further investigation.

6.8   Conclusion

In this chapter we have introduced a universal traceability approach that tackles all relevant traceability activities, can be customised to the individual artefact landscapes of different software development projects, and is adaptable to various technologies.

The notion of traceability will be revisited in a few follow-up chapters. For example, Sect. 10.3 will investigate traceability issues related to business process refinements; Sect. 12.5 will address how to ease developers' work for handling traceability information represented using different technologies.

Chapter 7
Metamodelling and Ontologies(*)

Gerd Gröner, Nophadol Jekjantuk, Tobias Walter, Fernando Silva Parreiras, and Jeff Z. Pan

Abstract Metamodelling plays an interesting role in MDSD. Following the discussions on metamodelling in Sect. 2.2.2, this chapter presents technologies on integrating metamodelling and ontologies. On the one hand, there are metamodels for standard ontology languages, such as OWL 2. On the other hand, there have been efforts enriching standard ontology languages with metamodelling capabilities. Chapter 11 will provide further discussions on metamodelling on how it can be useful for ontology-integrated modelling.

This chapter is organised as follows. In the first part (Sect. 7.1), we present the three most dominant state of the art (linguistic) metamodels for OWL, namely the *OMG ODM* [150], the *Neon OWL Metamodel* [34] and the *OWL 2 Metamodel* [140]. In Section 7.2, We present OWL FA [157], a metamodelling extension of OWL. Section 7.3 discusses an important aspect of metamodelling, i.e. open world and closed world assumption. The discussions on OWL FA and the open world/closed world assumption are related to earlier discussions on ontology reasoning (cf. Chaps. 3 and 5).

7.1 Metamodelling for Ontologies

The notion of metamodelling is well established and commonly used in the realm of model-driven engineering. There are standards which describe the model-driven architecture [149] and provide language and modelling specifications as UML [151]. However, *metamodelling* is only weakly considered in the realm of ontologies and ontology engineering.

This might be a weakness in two dimensions. Firstly, from an ontology engineering point of view, the modelling and design principles of model-driven engineering,

J.Z. Pan et al. (eds.), *Ontology-Driven Software Development*,
DOI 10.1007/978-3-642-31226-7_7, © Springer-Verlag Berlin Heidelberg 2013

including metamodelling, benefit from abstraction of a concrete system. These principles are only weakly exploited in ontology engineering. Secondly, if we consider metamodelling more generally as modelling with metadata, this becomes a relevant issue in various domains, and this has been considered as a challenging issue in OWL (cf. [138, 157]). Moreover, metamodelling is already supported by the OWL 2 language [160]).

A key issue of metamodelling is that there is no clear-cut distinction between classes and individuals. Let us take the knowledge base about animals as an example [216] "Ted is an Eagle" and "Eagles are an endangered species". The first statement can be represented in OWL by asserting the individual Ted to be an instance of the class Eagle. The second statement cannot be modelled in OWL, because it does not allow one symbol to refer both, to a class as well as to an individual. One may model the class Eagle as a subclass of the class EndangeredSpecies. However, an Eagle is a species and not a set of all living eagles. Thus, this could lead to consequence that is doubtful (Ted is an endangered species) or out-right unwanted. Therefore, it should be modelled by stating the individual Eagle to be an instance of the class EndangeredSpecies. Hence, the symbol Eagle should be used to refer both to a class as well as to an individual. This style of modelling is often called metamodelling.

The rest of this section presents a short description of the three most prominent states of the art OWL metamodels, namely the *OMG ODM* [150], the *Neon OWL Metamodel* [34] and the *OWL 2 Metamodel* [140]. The contribution of this section is the comparison of these metamodels.

7.1.1 Ontology Definition Metamodel

The *OMG OWL metamodel* is part of the *ontology definition metamodel (ODM)* OMG Adopted Specification. The ODM [150] includes six metamodels that are grouped together according to their representation formalism like (1) logic formalism (DL and FOL), (2) structural or descriptive representation and (3) conceptual or object-oriented modelling style. The OMG *OWL metamodel* and the OMG *RDF metamodel* belong to the group of structural or descriptive representations. ODM provides relationships between the RDF and OWL packages.

ODM offers a high number of classes due to the import of the *OMG RDF metamodel*. Accordingly, some relations between classes are described in the RDFS metamodel and are reused in the OWL metamodel. It was one of the motivation of ODM, to provide metamodels that capture W3C standardised languages, including OWL, RDF and RDFS, but also ISO languages like Topic Maps.

The justification for defining a new metamodel for ontologies instead of extending the UML metamodel is based on the origin of OWL (especially OWL DL). OWL as well as UML class diagrams are based on set semantics,

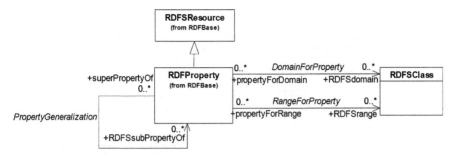

Fig. 7.1 The properties diagram of the RDFS package [150]

The *RDF metamodel* is composed of three metamodels packages: (1) The RDF-Base package defines the core concepts of RDF that are specified in the abstract syntax of RDF, like Node, RDFSResource and URIReference. (2) The RDFS package extends the RDFBase package with additional RDFS language constructs. (3) Finally, the RDFWeb package is also an extension of the RDFBase package, but these constructs are not available in the RDFS package.

The RDFS packages provide further definitions like the package for classes that defines, for instance, sub- and superclass relations between classes as well as the package on properties that are defined as relations between pairs of resources. Moreover, it contains specifications on domain and range of properties and sub- and super-property relations. The property package is depicted in Fig. 7.1.

The *OWL metamodel* extends the RDF metamodel. The OWL metamodel consists of a base package that describes common parts for OWL DL and OWL Full and two sub-packages that are specific for the OWL DL and OWL Full dialects. (OWL Lite is covered by the base package and parts of the OWL DL package.) The base package provides various descriptions like for OWL classes and properties. The Class Description Diagram of the base package is depicted in Fig. 7.2.

There are three class constructors, representing intersection, union and complement of class(es). They are adopted from description logics. Moreover, a class can be defined as an enumeration of individuals (EnumeratedClass). OWLRestriction allows the definition of a class as a restriction of a particular property (datatype and object properties) in combination with a value or cardinality.

Another package of the OWL metamodel is the property package, which is displayed in Fig. 7.3. It is a refinement of the RDF property. Compared to the RDF property, there are further means to specify property, like in case of an object property, we can define subclasses like InverseFunctionalProperty, SymmetricProperty or TransitiveProperty. Moreover, properties can be defined as inverse of other properties.

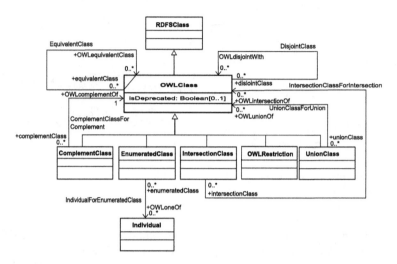

Fig. 7.2 The OWL class descriptions diagram of the OMG OWL metamodel[150]

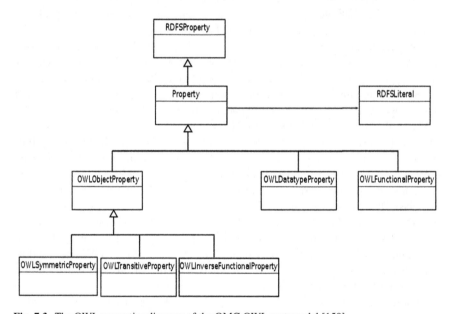

Fig. 7.3 The OWL properties diagram of the OMG OWL metamodel [150]

7.1.2 NeOn OWL Metamodel

The *NeOn Metamodel* [33, 34] is a concise metamodel which is able to cover the OWL DL functional syntax. The NeOn OWL Metamodel is based on MOF.

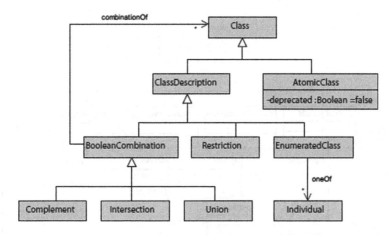

Fig. 7.4 The OWL class descriptions diagram of the NeOn metamodel

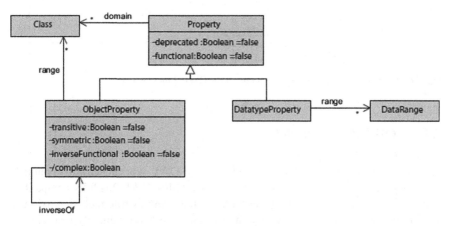

Fig. 7.5 The OWL properties diagram of the NeOn metamodel

The motivation of this work was the ability to use UML-like notations and tools in ontology engineering. Compared to the ODM, the NeOn OWL Metamodel supports the specification of networked ontologies, where networked ontologies are distributed ontologies that are connected and related to each other.

Figure 7.4 and 7.5 depict the OWL class hierarchy and the property diagram of NeOn, respectively [33]. The relationship between Class and Property is direct, since the NeOn OWL Metamodel does not provide support for RDFS like ODM.

According to the intention of the NeOn OWL Metamodel as a metamodel for networked ontologies, it offers further modelling constructs like Mapping classes that allow the definition of mappings between two ontologies.

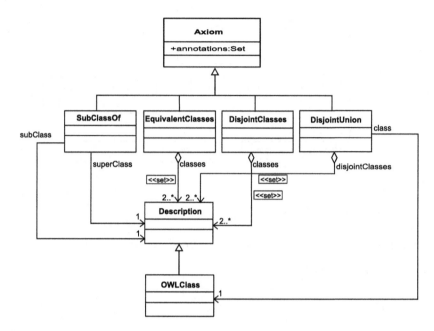

Fig. 7.6 The OWL class descriptions diagram of the OWL 2 metamodel

7.1.3 OWL 2 Metamodel

Improvements on the OWL language led the W3C OWL Working Group to publish working drafts of a new version of OWL: *OWL 2* [140]. OWL 2 is fully compatible with OWL DL and extends the latter with limited complex role inclusion axioms, reflexivity and irreflexivity, role disjointness and qualified cardinality restrictions. Moreover, OWL 2 uses a new XML serialisation and provides a set of profiles with different levels of expressiveness.

As one may note, the OWL 2 metamodel is considerably different from the available metamodels for OWL. Constructs like axiom and OWLEntity play central roles, and associations between classes and properties are done by axioms. There are different kinds of axioms provided like class or description axioms for describing class relations like equivalence and disjointness, object property axioms, data property axioms and axioms for facts. Facts express statements on individuals like same and different individual expressions and class assertions.

Figure 7.6 depicts the OWL class description diagram and the usage of axioms to describe class expressions like expressing the equivalence of classes.

In Fig. 7.7 the OWL properties diagram is depicted. It exemplifies the usage of the construct OWLEntity as a central building block.

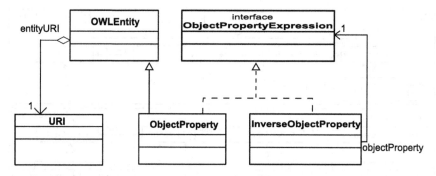

Fig. 7.7 The OWL properties diagram of the OWL 2 metamodel

7.2 Ontologies for Metamodelling: OWL FA

We already motivated metamodelling in the beginning of this chapter. We come back to this issue in this section and provide deeper investigations in metamodelling in OWL. Besides a motivating illustration of metamodelling in OWL, we present OWL FA[157], a metamodelling enabled ontology language. OWL FA is an extension of OWL DL, which has the description logics expressivity $\mathcal{SHOIN}(\mathcal{D})$. Ontologies in OWL FA are represented in a layered architecture. This architecture is mainly based on the architecture of RDFS(FA) [155].

7.2.1 Motivating Example

The running example in this section aims at clarifying the problem that is tackled by OWL FA and is used throughout this section for demonstrating how the example model is represented in OWL FA. Models are depicted in UML-like notations [153]. Metamodels are more than a syntactic language description of a modelling language; a metamodel is a description of the concepts of a modelling language specifying the structure and the kind of information that can be handled [144]. Models and metamodels are commonly used in model-driven software engineering (MDSE). In order to improve software development processes, new technologies, which provide reasoning support like consistency checking of models and meta-models, are beneficial. In MDSE, each model layer can contain both class and object definitions (cf. [8]). In ontology engineering, ontologies for metamodelling like OWL FA separate classes and objects into different layers in order to maintain the decidability of the language. In the rest we use ontologies for metamodelling to improve software development processes by validating, consistency checking and classifications of models with respect to their metamodels.

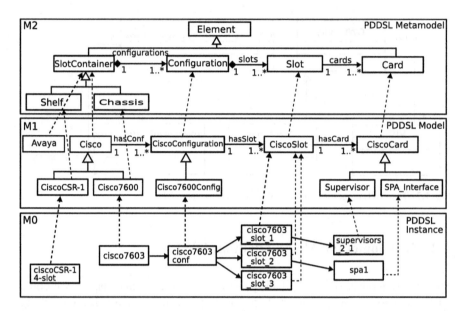

Fig. 7.8 Layered architecture for a physical device model

In order to use these benefits, a transformation of software models and metamodels, which are mainly graphical models to OWL DL ontologies, is not sufficient, since OWL DL does not support reasoning in a layered modelling architecture. This may introduce incomplete meaning of the model or it does not provide a valid semantic base at all. OWL FA provides more expressive power for metamodelling, and the semantics of OWL FA are well defined.

Example 1. In Fig. 7.8, a layered modelling architecture is demonstrated for physical device modelling (an application of configuration management). A physical device domain-specific language (PDDSL) is a domain-specific language (DSL) for physical devices which is used in business IT system modelling. The figure depicts three layers M_0, M_1 and M_2. M_3 is a meta-metamodelling layer, which is not included in the example. The arrows between the layers demonstrate instance relationships; the arrows within a layer are relations between concepts (like object properties and subclass hierarchies).

Cisco, CiscoConfiguarion, CiscoSlot and CiscoCard are instances of some classes from the M_2 layer. At the same time, these artefacts are concepts in the layer M_1 and each of these concepts can contain some instances from layer M_0. The rest of the relationships in a layer like concept subsumption and object properties are represented by arrows.

There are additional modelling constraints imposed on different layers. In layer M_2, a model designer requires that each SlotContainer has a Configuration, expressing that the ObjectProperty configurations. Each Configuration may contain Slot, which is expressed by the ObjectProperty slots as a functional property. And each Slot may contain Card, this is also expressed as an ObjectProperty cards. Moreover, the modeller requires the disjointness of the two classesChassis and Shelf. There are also three ObjectProperty assertions from the layer M_2 to M_1: configuration(Cisco, CiscoConfiguration), slots(CiscoConfiguration, CiscoSlot) and cards(CiscoSlot, CiscoCard).

In layer M_1 a model designer requires that each Cisco has at least one Configuration. Each CisoConfiguration may contain one or more CiscoSlot and each Slot may contain one or more CiscoCard. hasConfig, hasSlot and hasCard are expressed as ObjectProperty.

Additionally, assume the modeller requires the disjointness of the classes Supervisor and SPA_interface. Moreover, Cisco7600Config. can have only three CiscoSlot and Cisco7600_Slot_1 can contain only card from Supervisor class.

A crucial task in model-driven engineering is the validation of models and metamodels. A valid model refers to its metamodel and satisfies all the restrictions and constraints. However, the validation of multiple layers may lead to inconsistency even if the consistency is satisfied between all adjacent layers.

For instance, in the previously described scenario, the model on layer M_1 and also the corresponding metamodel on layer M_2 are consistent. The inconsistency occurs when they are combined, i.e. consider the modelling restrictions like equivalence or disjointness for the whole model, covering multiple layers simultaneously instead of only two adjacent layers. If one would like to add, Avaya is a Shelf and Avaya is equivalent to concept Cisco7600 in M_1 and then Avaya and Cisco7600 are concepts in layer M_1. This equivalence condition does not cause any inconsistency of the modelling layer (M_1 and M_0 for instances).

However, combined with the constraints on the metamodel layer M_2 which requires the disjointness of Shelf and Chassis, this leads to a contradiction and therefore to an inconsistent ontology. Without capturing multiple layers in combination, this inconsistency is not detected since the adjacent layers M_1, M_0 and M_2, M_1 are consistent on its own.

7.2.2 OWL FA Syntax and Semantics

OWL FA specifies a layer number in class constructors and axioms to indicate the strata they belong to. Let $i \geq 0$ be an integer. OWL FA consists of an alphabet of distinct class names $\mathbf{V}_{C_i}$ (for layer i), datatype names $\mathbf{V}_D$, abstract property names $\mathbf{V}_{AP_i}$ (for layer i), datatype property names $\mathbf{V}_{DP}$ and individual (object) names ($\mathbf{I}$), together with a set of constructors (with subscriptions) to construct class and property descriptions (also called *OWL FA-classes* and *OWL FA-properties*, respectively).

The semantics of OWL FA are a model-theoretic semantics, which is defined in terms of interpretations. Given an OWL FA alphabet $\mathbf{V}$, a set of built-in datatype names $\mathbf{B} \subseteq \mathbf{V_D}$ and an integer k $\geq$ 1, an *OWL FA interpretation* is a pair $\mathcal{J} = (\Delta^{\mathcal{J}}, \cdot^{\mathcal{J}})$, where $\Delta^{\mathcal{J}}$ is the domain (a non-empty set) and $\cdot^{\mathcal{J}}$ is the interpretation function, which satisfy the following conditions below (where $0 \leq i \leq k$):

1. $\Delta^{\mathcal{J}} = \bigcup_{0 \leq i \leq k-1} \Delta_A{}^{\mathcal{J}}_i \cup \Delta_\mathbf{D}$, where $\Delta_A{}^{\mathcal{J}}_i$ is the domain for layer i and $\Delta_\mathbf{D}$ is the datatype domain.
2. $\Delta_A{}^{\mathcal{J}}_{i+1} = 2^{\Delta_A{}^{\mathcal{J}}_i} \cup 2^{\Delta_A{}^{\mathcal{J}}_i \times \Delta_A{}^{\mathcal{J}}_i}$ and $\Delta_\mathbf{D} \cap \Delta_A{}^{\mathcal{J}}_i = \varnothing$.
3. $\forall\, a \in \mathbf{V_I}: a^{\mathcal{J}} \in \Delta_A{}^{\mathcal{J}}_0$ and $\forall\, C \in \mathbf{V}_{C_{i+1}}: C^{\mathcal{J}} \subseteq \Delta_A{}^{\mathcal{J}}_i$.
4. $\forall\, R \in \mathbf{V}_{AP_{i+1}}: R^{\mathcal{J}} \subseteq \Delta_A{}^{\mathcal{J}}_i \times \Delta_A{}^{\mathcal{J}}_i$ and $\forall\, T \in \mathbf{V}_{DP}: T^{\mathcal{J}} \subseteq \Delta_A{}^{\mathcal{J}}_0 \times \Delta_\mathbf{D}$.
5. $\bigcup_{\forall\, d \in \mathbf{B}} V(d) \subseteq \Delta_\mathbf{D}$, where $V(d)$ is the value space of d.
6. $\forall\, d \in \mathbf{V_D}$, if $d \in \mathbf{B}$, then[1]

   (a) $d^{\mathcal{J}} = V(d)$, where $V(d)$ is the value space of d.
   (b) if $v \in L(d)$, then $(``v"{}^{\wedge\wedge\wedge}d)^{\mathcal{J}} = L2V(d)(v)$, where $L(d)$ is lexical space of d and $L2V(d)$ is the lexical-to-value mapping of d.
   (c) if $v \notin L(d)$, then $(``v"{}^{\wedge\wedge\wedge}d)^{\mathcal{J}}$
       is undefined;

   otherwise, $d^{\mathcal{J}} \subseteq \Delta_\mathbf{D}$ and $``v"{}^{\wedge\wedge\wedge}d \in \Delta_\mathbf{D}$.

In the rest, we assume that i is an integer such that $1 \leq i \leq k$. The interpretation function can be extended to give semantics to OWL FA-properties and OWL FA-classes. Let $RN \in \mathbf{V}_{AP_i}$ be an abstract property name in layer i and R an abstract property in layer i. Valid OWL FA abstract properties are defined by the abstract syntax: $R ::= RN \mid R^-$, where for some $x, y \in \Delta_A{}^{\mathcal{J}}_{i-1}$, $\langle x, y \rangle \in R^{\mathcal{J}}$ iff $\langle y, x \rangle \in R^{-\mathcal{I}}$. Valid OWL FA datatype properties are datatype property names.

Let $CN \in \mathbf{V}_{C_i}$ be an atomic class name in layer i, R an OWL FA-property in layer i, $o \in \mathbf{I}$ an individual, $T \in \mathbf{V}_{DP}$ a datatype property name and C, D OWL FA-classes in layer i. Valid OWL FA-classes are defined by the abstract syntax:

$$C ::= \top_i \mid \bot \mid CN \mid \neg_i C \mid C \sqcap_i D \mid C \sqcup_i D \mid \{o\} \mid \exists_i R.C$$
$$\forall_i R.C \mid \leq_i nR \mid \geq_i nR$$
$$(\text{if } i = 1)\, \exists_1 T.d \mid \forall_1 T.d \mid \leq_1 nT \mid \geq_1 nT$$

The semantics of OWL FA-classes are presented in Table 7.1.

A class C is *satisfiable* iff there exist an interpretation $\mathcal{I}$ s.t. $C^{\mathcal{J}} \neq \varnothing$; C subsumes D iff for every interpretation $\mathcal{I}$ we have $C^{\mathcal{J}} \subseteq D^{\mathcal{J}}$.

An OWL FA ontology $\mathcal{O}$ consists of $\mathcal{O}_1, \ldots, \mathcal{O}_k$. Each $\mathcal{O}_i$ consists of a TBox $\mathcal{T}_i$, an RBox $\mathcal{R}_i$ and an ABox $\mathcal{A}_i$. An OWL FA *TBox* $\mathcal{T}_i$ is a finite set of class inclusion axioms of the form $C \sqsubseteq_i D$, where C, D are OWL FA-classes in layer i. An interpretation $\mathcal{I}$ satisfies $C \sqsubseteq_i D$ if $C^{\mathcal{J}} \subseteq D^{\mathcal{J}}$. Let R, S be OWL FA abstract properties in layer i. An OWL FA *RBox* $\mathcal{R}_i$ is a finite set of property axioms, namely property inclusion axioms ($R \sqsubseteq_i S$), functional property axioms ($\mathsf{Func}_i(R)$) and

---

[1] To simplify the presentation, we do not distinguish datatype names and datatype URIrefs here.

Table 7.1 OWL FA-classes

Constructor	DL syntax	Semantics
Top	$\top_i$	$\Delta_{A_{i-1}}^{\mathcal{J}}$
Bottom	$\perp$	$\varnothing$
Concept name	CN	$\mathsf{CN}^{\mathcal{J}} \subseteq \Delta_{A_{i-1}^{\mathcal{J}}}$
General negation	$\neg_i C$	$\Delta_{A_{i-1}}^{\mathcal{J}} \setminus C^{\mathcal{J}}$
Conjunction	$C \sqcap_i D$	$C^{\mathcal{J}} \cap D^{\mathcal{J}}$
Disjunction	$C \sqcup_i D$	$C^{\mathcal{J}} \cup D^{\mathcal{J}}$
Nominals	$\{o\}$	$\{o\}^{\mathcal{J}} = \{o^{\mathcal{J}}\}$
Exists restriction	$\exists_i R.C$	$\{x \in \Delta_{A_{i-1}}^{\mathcal{J}} \mid \exists y. \langle x, y \rangle \in R^{\mathcal{J}} \wedge y \in C^{\mathcal{J}}\}$
Value restriction	$\forall_i R.C$	$\{x \in \Delta_{A_{i-1}}^{\mathcal{J}} \mid \forall y. \langle x, y \rangle \in R^{\mathcal{J}} \rightarrow y \in C^{\mathcal{J}}\}$
Atleast restriction	$\geq_i mR$	$\{x \in \Delta_{A_{i-1}}^{\mathcal{J}} \mid \sharp\{y \mid \langle x, y \rangle \in R^{\mathcal{J}}\} \geq m\}$
Atmost restriction	$\leq_i mR$	$\{x \in \Delta_{A_{i-1}}^{\mathcal{J}} \mid \sharp\{y \mid \langle x, y \rangle \in R^{\mathcal{J}}\} \leq m\}$
Datatype exists restriction	$\exists_1 T.d$	$\{x \in \Delta_{A_0}^{\mathcal{J}} \mid \exists t. \langle x, t \rangle \in T^{\mathcal{J}} \wedge t \in d^{\mathcal{J}}\}$
Datatype value restriction	$\forall_1 T.d$	$\{x \in \Delta_{A_0}^{\mathcal{J}} \mid \forall t. \langle x, t \rangle \in T^{\mathcal{J}} \rightarrow t \in d^{\mathcal{J}}\}$
Datatype atleast restriction	$\geq_1 mT$	$\{x \in \Delta_{A_0}^{\mathcal{J}} \mid \sharp\{t \mid \langle x, t \rangle \in T^{\mathcal{J}}\} \geq m\}$
Datatype atmost restriction	$\leq_1 mT$	$\{x \in \Delta_{A_0}^{\mathcal{J}} \mid \sharp\{t \mid \langle x, t \rangle \in T^{\mathcal{J}}\} \leq m\}$

transitive property axioms ($\mathsf{Trans}_i(R)$). An interpretation $\mathcal{I}$ satisfies $R \sqsubseteq_i S$ if $R^{\mathcal{J}} \subseteq S^{\mathcal{J}}$; $\mathcal{I}$ satisfies $\mathsf{Func}_i(R)$ if, for all $x \in \Delta_{A_{i-1}}^{\mathcal{J}}$, $\sharp\{y \in \Delta_{A_{i-1}}^{\mathcal{J}} \mid \langle x, y \rangle \in R^{\mathcal{J}}\} \leq 1$ ($\sharp$ denotes cardinality); $\mathcal{I}$ satisfies $\mathsf{Trans}_i(R)$ if, for all $x, y, z \in \Delta^{\mathcal{J}} i - 1$, $\{\langle x, y \rangle, \langle y, z \rangle\} \subseteq R^{\mathcal{J}} \rightarrow \langle x, z \rangle \in R^{\mathcal{J}}$. The semantics for datatype property inclusion axioms and functional axioms can be defined in the same way as those in OWL DL. Like in OWL DL, there is no transitive datatype property axioms.

Let $a, b \in \mathbf{I}$ be individuals, C_1 a class in layer 1, R_1 an abstract property in layer 1, l a literal, $T \in \mathbf{V}_D$ a datatype property, X, Y classes or abstract properties in layer i;, E a class in layer $i + 1$ and S an abstract property in layer $i+1$. An OWL FA *ABox* $\mathcal{A}_1$ is a finite set of individual axioms of the following forms: $a :_1 C_1$ called *class assertions*, $\langle a, b \rangle :_1 R_1$ called *abstract property assertions*, $\langle a, l \rangle :_1 T$ called *datatype property assertions*, $a = b$ called *individual equality axioms* and $a \neq b$ called *individual inequality axioms*.

An interpretation $\mathcal{I}$ satisfies $a :_1 C_1$ if $a^{\mathcal{J}} \in C_1^{\mathcal{J}}$; it satisfies $\langle a, b \rangle :_1 R_1$ if $\langle a^{\mathcal{J}}, b^{\mathcal{J}} \rangle \in R_1^{\mathcal{J}}$; it satisfies $\langle a, l \rangle :_1 T$ if $\langle a^{\mathcal{J}}, l^{\mathcal{J}} \rangle \in T^{\mathcal{J}}$; it satisfies $a = b$ if $a^{\mathcal{J}} = b^{\mathcal{J}}$; it satisfies $a \neq b$ if $a^{\mathcal{J}} \neq b^{\mathcal{J}}$.

An OWL FA *ABox* $\mathcal{A}_i$ is a finite set of axioms of the following forms: $X : E$ called *meta-class assertions*, $\langle X, Y \rangle : R$ called *meta-property assertions* and $X =_{i-1} Y$ called *meta-individual equality axioms*. An interpretation $\mathcal{I}$ satisfies $X : E$ if $X^{\mathcal{J}} \in E^{\mathcal{J}}$; it satisfies $\langle X, Y \rangle : R$ if $\langle X^{\mathcal{J}}, Y^{\mathcal{J}} \rangle \in R^{\mathcal{J}}$; it satisfies $X =_{i-1} Y$ if $X^{\mathcal{J}} = Y^{\mathcal{J}}$.

An interpretation $\mathcal{I}$ satisfies an ontology $\mathcal{O}$ if it satisfies all the axioms in $\mathcal{O}$. $\mathcal{O}$ is *satisfiable* (*unsatisfiable*) iff there exists (does not exist) such an interpretation $\mathcal{I}$ that satisfies $\mathcal{O}$. Let C, D be OWL FA-classes in layer i, C is *satisfiable* w.r.t. $\mathcal{O}$ iff there exist an interpretation $\mathcal{I}$ of $\mathcal{O}$ s.t. $C^{\mathcal{J}} \neq \varnothing_i$; C subsumes D w.r.t. $\mathcal{O}$ iff for every interpretation $\mathcal{I}$ of $\mathcal{O}$ we have $C^{\mathcal{J}} \subseteq D^{\mathcal{J}}$.

7.2.3   Metamodelling with OWL FA

In this section, we present the way of expressing metamodelling with OWL FA. Although the layer numbers can/should be encapsulated by tools, there are two rules of thumb to help users to get the number right. Firstly, the subscript numbers are only used to indicate a sub-ontology (e.g. $\mathcal{O}_2$), a constructor (e.g. $\exists_2$) or axiom symbols (e.g. $\sqsubseteq_2$, $:_2$) in a sub-ontology. Secondly, subscript numbers for constructors and axiom symbols indicate the sub-ontology that the class descriptions constructed by these constructors and axioms belong to.

The following example shows how to model a physical device ontology with OWL FA notation. The main reason for the functional syntax is that it is obvious to see which layer or layer they belong to. Below, we show how to express a multilevel model with an OWL FA notation.

According to the PDDSL modelling architecture from Sect. 4.1, we can represent the class, property and instance relations in the M_2 layer. Example 2 shows how to describe class constructs by using OWL FA. Examples 3 and 4 show how to describe constraint, class and property assertions from the layer M_2 to M_1, respectively.

Example 2.   Class construct in M_2 layer:

$$\text{SlotContainer} \sqsubseteq_2 \text{Element} \tag{7.1}$$

$$\text{Shelf} \sqsubseteq_2 \text{SlotContainer} \tag{7.2}$$

$$\text{Chassis} \sqsubseteq_2 \text{SlotContainer} \tag{7.3}$$

$$\text{Configuration} \sqsubseteq_2 \text{Element} \tag{7.4}$$

$$\text{Slot} \sqsubseteq_2 \text{Element} \tag{7.5}$$

$$\text{Card} \sqsubseteq_2 \text{Element} \tag{7.6}$$

Example 3.   Constraint in M_2 layer:

$$\text{SlotContainer} \sqsubseteq_2 \exists_2 \text{ configurations.Configuration} \tag{7.7}$$

$$\text{Configuration} \sqsubseteq_2 \exists_2 \text{ slots.Slot} \tag{7.8}$$

$$\text{Slot} \sqsubseteq_2 \exists_2 \text{ cards.Card} \tag{7.9}$$

Example 4.   Classes and properties assertion from the layer M_2 to M_1:

$$(\text{Cisco, CiscoConfiguration}) :_2 \text{configurations} \tag{7.10}$$

$$(\text{CiscoConfiguration, CiscoSlot}) :_2 \text{slots} \tag{7.11}$$

$$(\text{CiscoSlot, CiscoCard}) :_2 \text{cards} \tag{7.12}$$

$$\text{CiscoConfiguration} :_2 \text{Configuration} \tag{7.13}$$

$$\text{CiscoCard} :_2 \text{Card} \tag{7.14}$$

$$\text{CiscoSlot} :_2 \text{Slot} \tag{7.15}$$

$$\text{Cisco7600} :_2 \text{Chassis} \tag{7.16}$$

$$\text{Avaya} :_2 \text{SlotContainer} \tag{7.17}$$

$$\text{CiscoCSR} - 1 :_2 \text{Shelf} \tag{7.18}$$

This layered representation, i.e. representing the OWL FA knowledge base in sub-ontologies allows to represent entities that are classes and instances at the same time. Due to limitations of space, we could not show the complete OWL FA ontology in this chapter. However, the class, property and instance relations in M_1 layer can be described in the same manner.

7.2.4 Reasoning in OWL FA

Now, we briefly discuss some reasoning tasks in OWL FA. According to the layered architecture, the knowledge base $\mathcal{O}$ in OWL FA is divided into a sequence of knowledge bases $\mathcal{O} = \mathcal{O}_1, \ldots \mathcal{O}_k$, whereas k is the number of layers. Since individuals in layer $i + 1$ can be classes and properties in layer i, this also affects the axioms of the layer below. Hence, individual axioms in the knowledge base $\mathcal{O}_{i+1}$ can be considered as class axioms in the knowledge base $\mathcal{O}_i$.

In an OWL FA knowledge base $\mathcal{O}$, $\mathcal{O}_2, \ldots, \mathcal{O}_k$ are $\mathcal{SHIQ}$ knowledge bases, i.e. nominals are not allowed. A nominal in a higher layer can lead to unsatisfiability of the knowledge bases. An interesting feature of $\mathcal{O}$ is that there could be interactions between $\mathcal{O}_i$ and $\mathcal{O}_{i+1}$.

7.2.5 Preprocessing

In this section, we discuss how to reduce the reasoning problem in OWL FA into a reasoning problem in OWL DL.

Definition 1. Let $\mathcal{O} = \langle \mathcal{O}_1, \ldots, \mathcal{O}_k \rangle$ be an OWL FA knowledge base, where each of $\mathcal{O}_1, \ldots, \mathcal{O}_k$ is consistent. $\mathcal{O}^* = \langle \mathcal{O}_1^*, \ldots, \mathcal{O}_k^* \rangle$, called the *explicit knowledge base*, is constructed by making all the implicit atomic class axioms, atomic property axioms and individual equality axioms explicit.

As we have a finite set of vocabulary, we have the following lemma:

Lemma 1. *Given an OWL FA knowledge base $\mathcal{O} = \langle \mathcal{O}_1, \ldots, \mathcal{O}_k \rangle$. The explicit knowledge base $\mathcal{O}^*$ (OWL DL knowledge base) can be calculated from $\mathcal{O}$ in finite number of steps.*

Fig. 7.9 Reduce algorithm

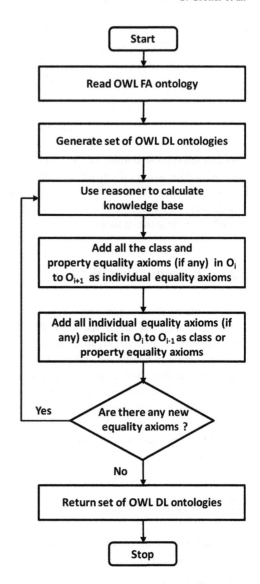

We now present the algorithm Reduce that will reduce an OWL FA knowledge base $\mathcal{O}$ into a set of OWL DL knowledge bases $\langle \mathcal{O}_1^*, \ldots, \mathcal{O}_k^* \rangle$. This algorithm is based on Definition 1 and Lemma 1. The algorithm takes an OWL FA KB $\mathcal{O}$ as input and returns a set of OWL DL KB $\langle \mathcal{O}_1, \ldots, \mathcal{O}_k \rangle$. The Algorithm Reduce is shown in Fig. 7.9.

The following theorem shows the termination of the algorithm Reduce, applied to an OWL FA KB $\mathcal{O}$:

Theorem 1. *Given an OWL FA knowledge base* $\mathcal{O} = \langle \mathcal{O}_1, \ldots, \mathcal{O}_k \rangle$, *then* *Reduce($\mathcal{O}$) terminates.*

Fig. 7.10 Consistent
algorithm

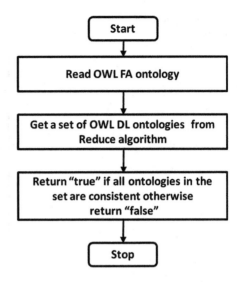

7.2.6 Consistency Checking

In this section, we present the algorithm `Consistent` that checks the consistency
of an OWL FA knowledge base $\mathcal{O}$. We can reduce an OWL FA knowledge base
to a collection of OWL DL knowledge bases; therefore, existing DL reasoner
capabilities can be used. Consistency checking for OWL FA is done in two steps:
First, we check the syntax of OWL FA. For example, $\Sigma = \{C \sqsubseteq_2 D, C \sqsubseteq_3 E\}$ is
not well formed in OWL FA, because we do not allow OWL class construct between
layers except an instance-of relation. Secondly, we check the consistency of each
OWL DL knowledge base that is computed from the OWL FA knowledge base with
an existing DL reasoner. The Algorithm `Consistent` is shown in Fig. 7.10.

We invite the reader to note that *check-dl-consistent* is a function call to a DL
Reasoner.

Theorem 2. *Given an OWL FA knowledge base $\mathcal{O} = \langle \mathcal{O}_1, \dots, \mathcal{O}_k \rangle$. $\mathcal{O}$ is consistent
iff each $\mathcal{O}_i^*$ ($1 \leq i \leq k$) is consistent.*

Theorem 2 shows we can reduce the OWL FA knowledge base consistency
problem to the OWL DL knowledge base consistency problem.

7.2.7 Instance Retrieval

Instance retrieval in OWL FA is trivial because after the reduction process, we get a
set of OWL 2 DL ontologies. Then, we could perform instance retrieval against
those ontologies. However, without specifying a target ontology, it is not efficient
since we have to go through all ontologies in a set. Therefore, we need a smart
algorithm for instance retrieval for OWL FA in order to select the right ontology

Fig. 7.11 InstanceOf
algorithm

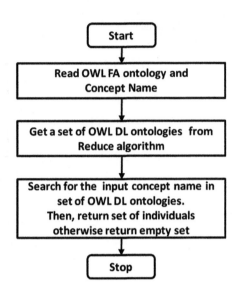

that contains a target concept. Firstly, we need to search for a target concept in each ontology of the set. This step does not require any DL reasoner. Then, we could perform instance retrieval against a selected ontology with a DL reasoner. A formal definition of instance retrieval for OWL FA is given in Definition 2.

Definition 2. Given an $ABox$ $\mathcal{A}_i$ and a query Q, i.e. a concept expression, find all individuals a such that a is an instance of Q, i.e. $\{a \mid \forall a \in \mathcal{A}_i, a : Q\}$.

We present the instance retrieval for OWL FA in Fig. 7.11. The algorithm *instanceOf* will take an OWL FA ontology $\mathcal{O}$ and a concept C as input. The algorithm returns a set containing the instances of concept C.

7.2.8 Justification on OWL FA

A justification for an entailment in an OWL FA ontology can be extended from justification for an entailment in an OWL DL ontology because we can reduce the reasoning problem in OWL FA to a reasoning problem in OWL DL. However, in the reduction process, a new axiom can be added to an OWL DL ontology. Therefore, if a justification for an entailment axiom in $\mathcal{O}_i$ contains those new axioms which have been added during the reduction process, we need to store an information for that axiom from another ontology in the lookup table. Concerning the ontology at the next higher modelling layer, if the new axiom has been added as class or property equality axioms, we can map those axioms from class or property equality axioms to individual equality axioms in the $\mathcal{O}_{i+1}$. Hence, we can retrieve the further justification from the upper ontology if needed. From a lower ontology, if a justification contains object equality axioms, we can map those object equality axioms to class or property equality axioms in the $\mathcal{O}_{i-1}$ and then we can retrieve the further justification from the upper ontology if needed.

Definition 3. For an OWL FA ontology $\mathcal{O} = \langle \mathcal{O}_1, \ldots, \mathcal{O}_k \rangle$ and an entailment η_i where i is a layer number, a set of axioms $\mathcal{J}_i$ is a justification for η_i in $\mathcal{O}$ i. $\mathcal{J}_i$ may contain further justifications from $\mathcal{O}_{i+1}$ and/or $\mathcal{O}_{i-1}$ if the ontology $\mathcal{O}$ has added class or property equality axioms and/or added object equality axioms, respectively. The further justification can be retrieved from the information stored in the lookup table.

In order to keep trace of the new axioms that have been added in the reduction process, we extend the algorithm Reduce from Sect. 7.2.4. The algorithm takes an OWL FA knowledge base $\mathcal{O}$ as input and returns a set of OWL DL knowledge bases $\langle \mathcal{O}_1, \ldots, \mathcal{O}_k \rangle$ and a lookup table between new axioms and its correspond axiom. The lookup table is indexed by the layer, i.e. the axioms in the table refer to the layer which contains additional axioms after the reduction. These additional axioms affect also the justifications for this layer. Hence, we will later exploit the information from the lookup table about added axioms to compute the justification.

We now present the algorithm Justification that will retrieve a justification for an entailment in an OWL FA ontology. The algorithm takes an OWL FA KB $\mathcal{O}$ and an entailment η_i as input and returns a set of justification axioms $\mathcal{J}$. The algorithm Justification is shown in Fig. 7.12.

We invite the reader to note that *compute-dl-justification* is a function call to a DL Reasoner. The mapping table MP_i indicates added axioms to the ontology by the reduction. In this case, the adjacent ontology $\mathcal{O}_{i+1}^*$ or $\mathcal{O}_{i-1}^*$ is also relevant for the justifications of the ontology $\mathcal{O}_i^*$.

7.3 Metamodelling in Ontologies and Metamodelling in MOF

In this section, we lead to different possible interpretations. In contrast, in MDA this is realised by having multiple modelling layers according to the layered structure in MOF. Both are different methodologies to handle interpretations of individuals. Hence, in OWL DL (and DL), there are different properties on how instances are interpreted compared to the semantics of instances of a class in MDA.

In order to bridge the gap from OWL DL instance interpretations compared to MDA instance modelling, there are different approaches applied for OWL DL knowledge bases. The basic idea is to use different interpretations for different modelling layers or different universes of discourse [138, 216]. In Sect. 7.2, we already discussed the language OWL FA that provides a comprehensive solution for handling the layered modelling problem by still remaining decidable and using DL reasoning services for the metamodelling knowledge base.

While the previous section already discussed means for handling these different interpretations in order to support MOF-based metamodelling in OWL (DL), we continue in the next chapter with a further crucial difference in ontology modelling

Fig. 7.12 The algorithm for
computing a single
justification for OWL FA

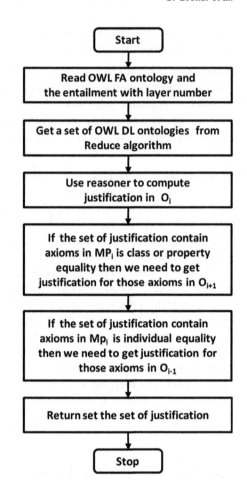

compared to MOF-based modelling. There are two different assumptions about
instance relations or more precisely on missing instance relations. This problem
is discussed in the next subsection (Sect. 7.3.1).

7.3.1   Open and Closed World Assumptions

We start this section with the *closed world assumption (CWA)* which is realised
in database systems (including deductive database systems) and object-oriented
models. The basic assumption is to consider the knowledge base as a closed world,
i.e. we consider all statements in the knowledge base as true statements and
everything that is not stated in or entailed by the knowledge base is considered
as false. Everything that is unknown is considered as false.

A key property that is given by the CWA is the negative results in case of
missing statements in the knowledge base. In order to understand the closed world

assumption, an intuitive example is a database query that asks for a certain fact (i.e. individual or instance) in a database. The query returns all statements that are contained in the database. However, if a fact is not in the database, we know that this fact does not hold. Here, the world is closed to those facts that are explicitly mentioned in the database and/or entailed by the knowledge base.

In OWL, the *open world assumption (OWA)* is realised which considers a given knowledge base as an incomplete part of an open world. The intuition behind this assumption is that a knowledge base can be extended by further statements and combined with other knowledge bases. The open world assumption of OWL is monotonic, i.e. adding new statements will never falsify previously inferred statements.

We demonstrate the difference between both assumptions on an axiom that is related to the running example from Fig. 7.8. The following axiom in the knowledge base (ABox) describes that an instance cisco7603 of the class Cisco has a configuration cisco7603conf which is an instance of the class CiscoConfiguration:

$$(cisco6703, cisco7603conf) \in hasConf \qquad (7.19)$$

We assume there is no further axiom that describes cisco6703 has another configuration. Hence, in the CWA, it can be inferred that the instance cisco6703 has exactly one configuration, i.e. $cisco6703 \in \exists_{=1} hasConf.CiscoConfiguration$. Obviously, such a result would be also expected for a database query. However, in the OWA, this cannot be inferred since given knowledge base is considered as incomplete, i.e. there could be further configurations of $cisco6703$ that are asserted in another (unknown) knowledge base.

In various applications, it is known that the knowledge base is complete but due to the OWA of an OWL knowledge base, the inference does not take this completeness into account. One argument in favour of closed word reasoning in OWL is integrity constraints that cannot be enforced in the OWA. For instance, according to the running example from Fig. 7.8, each instance of Cisco is either an instance of CiscoCSR-1 or an instance of Cisco7600. This could be described by the following TBox axiom:

$$Cisco \sqsubseteq CiscoCSR - 1 \sqcup Cisco7600 \qquad (7.20)$$

However, given this TBox axiom in the OWA, we cannot guarantee that each instance of Cisco is an instance of either CiscoCSR-1 or Cisco7600. For the CWA, each instance of Cisco has to satisfy this condition.

In order to solve this problem, there are different approaches that allow closed world reasoning in OWL. Epistemic operators for OWL are described in [58, 81]. These additional operators allow to describe that a certain statement is known or asserted. For instance, using epistemic operators in the previous axiom allows the description of an integrity constraint, e.g. by using the K (known) and A (asserted) operator (cf. [81]):

$$\mathbf{K} Cisco \sqsubseteq \mathbf{A} CiscoCSR - 1 \sqcup \mathbf{A} Cisco7600 \qquad (7.21)$$

This axiom requires for each known instance of Cisco, i.e. there is assertion in the knowledge base; it is asserted that this instance is also an instance of the class CiscoCSR-1 or Cisco7600. If there is no such assertion in the knowledge base, this would be an inconsistent knowledge base. Obviously, this is not the case without epistemic operators.

Besides epistemic operators, there is another methodology in order to infer certain statements that cannot be derived in case of the OWA. In contrast to the CWA, it is not assumed that the knowledge base is complete. Instead, the domains of classes and object properties are closed. In the *closed domain assumption (CDA)*, the domain is restricted to an enumeration of individuals. This can be realised by progressively adding axioms defining that a class equivalent to an enumeration of individuals and likewise the domain or range of an object property equivalent to an enumeration of individuals. A special case of CDA can be realised by NBox as introduced in Sect. 5.1.5, where the domain of a concept or an object property is restricted to be their inferrable instances.

7.3.2   Ensuring Integrity Constraints in a Closed Domain

Although the OWA has many advantages, we have to ensure that validation of integrity constraints is still possible. In the following, we consider three basic integrity constraints and show how to define a closed domain to ensure the constraints.

We first start with explaining the unique name assumption (UNA) because it is part of the closed domain and a requirement for ensuring the integrity constraints.

Ensuring UNA

The *UNA* requires that instances have different names they are understood as different. The UNA is mainly considered in the CWA and CDA. In OWA the UNA is not considered, since two instances are not declared as different. Two instances i_1 and i_2 are different from each other ($i_1 \neq i_2$) if the nominal concept (provided by description logic $\mathcal{O}$) $\{o_1\}$ is disjoint with the nominal concept $\{o_2\}$ ($\{o_1\} \sqsubseteq \neg\{o_2\}$).

Ensuring Types of Instances

To ensure that a given instance *device*1 only has the asserted type *Device* all other concepts must be declared as disjoint with *Device* (e.g. *Device* $\sqsubseteq \neg(Slot \sqcup Configuration)$). Hence, instances of *Device* cannot have the types *Slot* or *Configuration*.

Ensuring Role Start and End Types

The following axiom in the TBox of a knowledge base restricts the instances of *Configuration* to be connected with some instance of type *Slot*.

$$Configuration \sqsubseteq \exists\, hasSlot.Slot$$

To ensure that the type of instances connected via *hasSlot* to slots is *Configuration* we have to add the following axiom to the TBox:

$$\exists\, hasSlot.\top \sqsubseteq Configuration$$

Furthermore, all concepts must be declared as disjoint with *Configuration* (*Configuration* $\sqsubseteq \neg(Device \sqcup Slot)$).

To ensure that configuration instances are only connected with slot instances via the *hasSlot* role we have to introduce the following axiom:

$$Configuration \sqsubseteq \forall\, hasSlot.Slot$$

In addition, all concepts in the TBox must be disjoint with the end type *Slot*. For example, *Slot* is declared as disjoint with *Configuration* and *Device* (*Slot* $\sqsubseteq \neg(Device \sqcup Configuration)$).

Ensuring Cardinalities

The following axiom in the TBox of a knowledge base describes the instances of *Configuration* to be connected with exactly two slots.

$$Configuration \sqsubseteq= 2hasSlot.Slot$$

As we have seen in the previous section the knowledge base with the TBox above and the following ABox is consistent, although the number of slots is too low (for *conf*1) or too high (for *conf*2).

$$conf1 \in Configuration \qquad\qquad conf2 \in Configuration$$

$$slot1 \in Slot \qquad\qquad slot2, slot3, slot4 \in Slot$$

$$(conf1, slot1) \in hasSlot \qquad\qquad (conf2, slot2) \in hasSlot$$

$$(conf2, slot3) \in hasSlot$$

$$(conf2, slot4) \in hasSlot$$

To ensure cardinality constraints first we have to apply the UNA on all instances in the ABox as described above.

To avoid the assumption of further instances which are not logically inferrable from the current knowledge base, all concepts should be equivalent to the set of instances they are describing. Thus, we can include concepts *Configuration* and *Slot* into the NBox. Semantically, this is equivalent to adding the following definitions into the knowledge base:

$$Configuration \equiv \{conf1, conf2\}$$

$$Slot \equiv \{slot1, slot2, slot3, slot4\}$$

Consequently, *Configuration* and *Slot* will be inferred as disjoint (*Configuration* $\sqsubseteq$ $\neg Slot$) given the UNA of individuals.

To get an inconsistency checking the number of slots for the two configurations (*conf1* and *conf2*) in the knowledge base given above, we have to declare which instances of *Slot* are *not* connected with *conf1* and *conf2*, respectively. This can also be realised by putting *hasSlot* into the NBox. Semantically, it is equivalent to explicitly asserting that each pair of individuals that are not inferred to have *hasSlot* relation does not have such a relation. For example, *conf1* does not *haveSlot slot2* ($\{conf1\} \sqsubseteq \neg hasSlot.\{slot2\}$). With NBox, this and similar assertions for other pairs will be automatically included into the original knowledge base.

In general, it is possible to check the validity of integrity constraints. There are two disadvantages of checking constraints. At first, the number of additional axioms in the knowledge base increases and thus reduces the performance of reasoning tools. Secondly, if the ABox is modified (e.g. by adding, updating or deleting instances and role assertions), all the additional axioms must be rebuild.

Relations Between Models and Metamodels

Model-driven engineering has already been comprehensively discussed in Chap. 2. This section aims at clarifying some terms and definitions concerning models, metamodels and transformations and how they are related to each other in model-driven engineering.

The meaning of models and metamodels is informally described by Seidewitz [187] by describing what models and their relationships are and what their meaning is. Informally, a model is a set of statements describing a certain system. A model is interpreted according to a model theory to that the model belongs to. An interpretation is mainly a mapping of the modelled elements to the elements of the concrete system.

Seidewitz [187] defined a metamodel as a specification model where the considered system (system under study) is a model. According to this definition, a metamodel on what can be expressed in valid models of this metamodel. Metamodels are interpreted like models according to the underlying model theory.

This notion of metamodels, models and the corresponding interpretation is generalised to relations and interpretations between arbitrary adjacent modelling layers in a layered modelling architecture in order to capture the well-established four-layered metamodelling architecture as it is realised in MOF models. In this case, an element in the modelling layer M_i is interpreted as an instance of an element of the corresponding metamodel above.

Atkinson and Kühne [7] extended the four-layer modelling architecture by adding a further modelling dimension. This two-dimensional modelling architecture allows linguistic and ontological metamodelling. The reasons for this extension are further requirements that occur in metamodelling like the support for deployment platforms where platform-specific artefacts are obtained from platform-independent by describing mappings between them. Another requirement is a high interoperability by allowing different representations of artefacts.

A more detailed consideration of metamodelling requirements in [7] indicates the advantages of more discrimination possibilities than the instance-of relation between layers or using metalevel descriptions to describe predefined concepts. In [7], linguistic and ontological metamodelling is demonstrated as two possible two-dimensional metamodelling techniques.

In linguistic metamodelling, the relation between entities crossing the modelling layers (M_i) is described as linguistic instance-of relations, i.e. the element in the model in layer, M_i is a linguistic instance of the corresponding class in layer M_{i+1}. The second dimension describes the ontological instance-of relation within one layer M_i and is used to define a (logical) type-of relation between entities. These relations are also called an intra-level instantiation between the (ontological) models O_1 and O_0 in layer M_i.

While the described linguistic metamodelling extends the four-layered architecture by these two ontological layers, the ontological metamodelling extends the notion of type-of relations (ontological instance-of relation) by meta-type relations, i.e. the ontological modelling architecture has more than the two layers O_1 and O_0. Traditional metamodelling architecture and techniques do not distinguish between ontological and linguistic instantiations.

Finally, we consider the work of Favre on representing and modelling of MDE in [67] which emphasises models, metamodels and transformation as basic concepts of MDE and gives an overall model of how they are related to each other. This representation of the MDE artefacts and the evolution process is called megamodel.

The proposed megamodel is an abstraction of models, metamodels and languages and their relations. The term **system** represents a certain element that is modelled in the MDE process. There are four relations between these elements: (1) The **decomposedIn** relation specifies whether a system is decomposed into subsystems or parts of the system. (2) The relation **representationOf** describes whether a model represents a certain system (system under study). (3) According to the set theory, the relation **elementOf** is used to define a set of systems like a language can be defined as a set of sentences. (4) Finally, the **conformsTo** relation describes whether a model conforms to its metamodel.

7.4 Conclusion

In this chapter, we have considered metamodelling and ontologies from two viewpoints. Firstly, we have presented snippets of common OWL metamodels in order to outline the usage of metamodels in ontology engineering. Moreover, the last part of this chapter has depicted argumentation and comparisons between metamodelling in OWL DL ontologies compared to metamodelling in MOF.

Secondly, OWL FA as a metamodelling enabled extension of OWL DL was introduced. OWL FA extends OWL DL with a multi-layered modelling architecture that allows reasoning across multiple modelling layers, where elements in a particular modelling layer might be considered as classes with respect to the next layer below, but at the same time, they serve as individuals regarding the next higher layer.

At the same time, this chapter concludes Part II. In the next part, we will discuss how to apply scalable reasoning services to provide consistency checking in ODSD.

Part III
Consistency Checking in Ontology-Driven Software Development (ODSD)

Part III
Consistency Checking in Ontology-Driven
Software Development (ODSD)

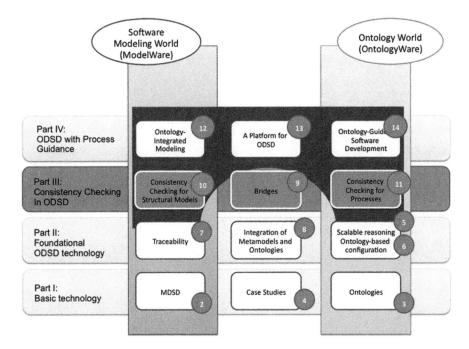

Fig. RoadMap.3 The roadmap of Part III

Having survived the enabling technologies, you are now prepared to dig deeper into ontology-driven software development (ODSD). The chapters in Part III cover many major aspects of consistency checking in ODSD. We show how the bridging of the ModelWare technical space and the ontology ware technical space works (Chap. 8). This bridging technology allows for invisible use of ontologies in the modelling of software artefacts, in particular for the consistency checking of structural (Chap. 9) and behavioural models (Chap. 10).

Part III contains following chapters:

Chapter 8 Ontology and Bridging Technologies
Chapter 9 Ontology Reasoning for Consistency-Preserving Structural Modelling
Chapter 10 Ontology Reasoning for Process Models

Chapter 8
Ontology and Bridging Technologies

Uwe Aßmann, Jürgen Ebert, Tobias Walter, and Christian Wende

Abstract In this chapter, we present two kinds of bridges in the ODSD infrastructure, namely the transformation bridge and the integration bridge. We revisit the ontology reasoning services introduced in Chaps. 3 and 5. We show how they can be used, as key-enabling technologies, to support bridging technologies for combining ModelWare technological spaces and OntologyWare technological spaces. ModelWare technological spaces provide modelling languages, which are used for representing models or metamodels. The OntologyWare technological space provides the ontology language OWL 2 to design ontologies.

Chapter 11 will show how an integration bridge presented in this chapter can be used to develop DSL editors for the domain engineering case studies discussed in Chap. 4.

The rest of this chapter is organised as follows. Section 8.1 will provide some tables (together with explanations) to summarise ontology reasoning services for software developers. Sections 8.2 and 8.3 will provide detailed discussions for transformation bridges and integration bridges, respectively.

8.1 Ontology Services

To better understand the differences that ontologies make, how they can be applied and what their potential for MDSD is, this section provides an overview of the services ontology technology offers. In Sect. 8.1.1 we introduce a generic pattern to precisely and unambiguously define individual ontology services and their interface. In Sect. 8.1.2 we apply this pattern to provide a specification of all ontology services used in the ODSD infrastructure of the MOST project.

J.Z. Pan et al. (eds.), *Ontology-Driven Software Development*,
DOI 10.1007/978-3-642-31226-7_8, © Springer-Verlag Berlin Heidelberg 2013

Table 8.1 Template for the specification of reasoning services

Characteristic	Explanation	Example
Name	The identifier of the service	*Consistency*
Signature	The formal interface of the service, represented in the form *returnType serviceName (inputType inputIdentifier, inputType inputIdentifier, …)*	boolean isConsistent(Ontology o)
Pattern	The call pattern of the service, given in the form *returnIdentifier class.serviceName(inputIdentifier, inputIdentifier, …)*	b=Ontoware.isConsistent(o)
Description	A natural language explanation of the service	"Returns b=true, if the ABox $\mathcal{A}$ of o is consistent with regard to its TBox $\mathcal{T}$"

8.1.1 Pattern for Specification of Ontology Services

In order to allow for MDSD vendors, researchers and users to employ ontology reasoning technology, even when they are not very proficient in doing so, it is essential to precisely and unambiguously specify the individual ontology services. The specifications should be high level, i.e., they should describe the ontology services at a level of abstraction that (i) is precise enough to be understandable by MDSD vendors and (ii) does not dive too much into the notational depth of a programming language.

A template for such specifications is given in Table 8.1.

The results of applying this specification methodology for existing ontology technology and the consequences of using ontology services in MDSD tools are presented in Chap. 12.

8.1.2 Specification of Ontology Services

In this chapter, an *ontology* is a formal description of the structure of concepts and relationships in a knowledge domain, for the purpose of enabling knowledge sharing, reuse and derivation. An ontology language is a formal language used to encode the ontology. There are a number of such languages for ontologies, both proprietary and standard based. The web ontology language (OWL) defines a family of knowledge representation languages for authoring ontologies and is endorsed by the World Wide Web Consortium. This family of languagesis based on description logics, which enables *ontology representation* and *reasoning*.

Description logics [11] are a family of knowledge representation languages that have been studied extensively in artificial intelligence over the last two decades. They can be used to represent the concept definitions of an application domain

Table 8.2 Reasoning service: consistency checking

Name	Consistency checking
Signature	boolean isConsistent(Ontology o)
Pattern	b=Ontoware.isConsistent(o)
Description	Returns true, if the ABox $\mathcal{A}$ of o is consistent with regard to its TBox $\mathcal{T}$. $\mathcal{A}$ is consistent with regard to the TBox $\mathcal{T}$, if it has a model $\mathcal{I}$, which is also a model of $\mathcal{T}$

Table 8.3 Reasoning service: satisfiability checking

Name	Satisfiability checking
Signature	boolean isSatisfiable(Ontology o, ClassExpression c)
Pattern	b=Ontoware.isSatisfiable(o, c)
Description	Returns true if the class expression c in o is satisfiable. c is satisfiable if $(c)^{\mathcal{I}} \neq \varnothing$ for some model $\mathcal{I}$ of $\mathcal{T}$

Table 8.4 Reasoning service: find unsatisfiability

Name	Find unsatisfiability
Signature	Set<Concept> GetUnsatisfiable (Ontology O)
Pattern	b = Ontoware.GetUnsatisfiable (O)
Description	Find all unsatisfiable concepts in given ontology O. A concept in an ontology is unsatisfiable if it is an empty set. Return NULL if there is not any unsatisfiable concept
Input	An Ontology O
Output	b = NULL iff there is no unsatisfiable concept b = a set of unsatisfiable concepts otherwise

(known as terminological knowledge) in a structured and formally well-understood way. Nowadays, description logics are considered the most important knowledge representation formalisms unifying and giving a logical basis to the well-known traditions of frame-based systems, semantic networks and KL-ONE-like languages, object-oriented representations, semantic data models and type systems.

In this section, we describe basic services provided by ontology technology following the template in Table 8.1. All services used to reason on ontologies and to query ontologies are implemented as static operation and are part of the Ontoware API.

Ontology Reasoning Services

Ontology reasoning services provide means to trigger the derivation and retrieval of implicit knowledge based on the logical foundation of ontologies. Based on basic reasoning tasks presented in Sect. 3.1.3, here we list the most typical and widely used functional services. Their specifications are illustrated in Tables 8.2–8.8, respectively.

Table 8.5 Reasoning service: subsumption checking

Name	*Subsumption checking*
Signature	boolean subsume(Ontology o, ClassExpression c_{sup}, ClassExpression c_{sub})
Pattern	b=Ontoware.subsume(o, c_{sup}, c_{sub})
Description	Returns true if c_{sub} is subsumed by c_{sup}. c_{sub} is subsumed by c_{sup} if $(c_{sub})^{\mathcal{I}} \subseteq (c_{sup})^{\mathcal{I}}$ for all models $\mathcal{I}$ of $\mathcal{T}$

Table 8.6 Reasoning service: classification

Name	*Classification*
Signature	boolean classify(Ontology o, ClassExpression c, Individual i)
Pattern	b=Ontoware.classify(o, c, i)
Description	Returns true if i in o is an instance of the class expression c. i is an instance of c if $(i)^{\mathcal{I}} \in (c)^{\mathcal{I}}$ for all models $\mathcal{I}$ of $\mathcal{T}$ and $\mathcal{A}$

Table 8.7 Reasoning service: axiom explanation

Name	*Axiom explanation*
Signature	Set<Set<Axiom>> explainAxiom(Ontology o, Axiom a)
Pattern	S=Ontoware.explainAxiom(o, a)
Description	Returns a set S of sets of axioms, where each set $s_i \in$ S of axioms is minimal and entails the axiom a. a is entailed by s_i if all models of s_i also satisfy a

Table 8.8 Reasoning service: inconsistency explanation

Name	*Inconsistency explanation*
Signature	Set<Set<Axiom>> explainInconsistency(Ontology o)
Pattern	S=Ontoware.explainInconsistency(o)
Description	Returns a set S of minimal sets of axioms for each inconsistency. If at least one axiom of each set $s_i \in$ S is removed from o, o becomes consistent

Table 8.9 Query service: query answering

Name	*Query answering*
Signature	Set answering (Ontology o, query q)
Pattern	res = Ontoware.answering (o, q)
Description	Returns the answer sets res for a query q to ontology o. res = NULL if there is not any answer

Query Reasoning Services

Query services allow flexible querying of explicit and implicit knowledge stored in ontologies. In order to keep the ontology technologies as a black box, special patterns of queries are designed by the ontology engineers and stored in the query database. So a MDSD developer can simply ask for specific answer sets by indicating the ontology name O and the query name Q. The specification of query answering service is illustrated in Table 8.9.

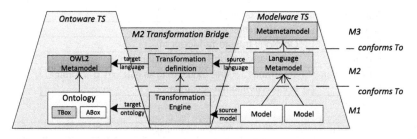

Fig. 8.1 M2 Transformation bridge

8.2   Transformation Bridges[(*)]

A *transformation bridge* creates for an input model a respective output model according to a transformation definition. The transformation definition established describes which types of elements in the input model are considered to build an element in the target model.

For example, a UML class diagram may be used as a lightweight ontology in some OntologyWare environment by generating a corresponding OWL ontology from it. With respect to the scenarios presented in Chap. 10, a process model like a UML activity diagram is transformed to an ontology. The transformation rules or patterns are defined by the bridge. Thus, having a process model as an ontology, we can provide services for reasoning on the semantics of process models.

A transformation bridge usually implies some loss of information; since both worlds have different properties, not all of which are transformable into the other world.

Figure 8.1 depicts the conceptual schema of the transformation-translating software models conforming to language metamodels to OWL ontologies.

8.2.1   Transformation Services

A *transformation bridge* may be realised as a service.

The transformation service specified in Table 8.10 transforms a Model according to a transformation definition which is based on a mapping to an Ontology. A simple mapping between the UML class diagram language and the ontology language OWL is depicted in Fig. 8.2.

In this case, the transformation service creates for each class in a model a concept in the ontology. All associations and attributes are transformed to corresponding roles. Because UML class diagrams and ontologies contain instances of classes and concepts, respectively, objects of a model are transformed to individuals of an ontology. The transformation builds for each domain definition in a model a datatype

Table 8.10 Transformation service

Name	*Transformation service*
Signature	Ontology transform(Model m)
Pattern	o=TransformationBridge.transform(m)
Description	Transforms a source model m to an ontology o according to a *transformation definition*

UML class diagram	Ontology language
Class	Atomic concept
Association	Concept role
Attribute	Datatype role
Object	Individual
Domain	Datatype
Subclassing	Subclass axiom

Fig. 8.2 Mapping between UML class diagrams and ontologies

Table 8.11 Ecore and OWL: comparable constructs

Ecore	OWL
Package	Ontology
Class	Class
Instance and literals	Individual and literals
Reference, attribute	Object property, data property
Data types	Data types
Enumeration	Enumeration
Multiplicity	Cardinality

in the ontology. For the subclassing relations in models, the transformation builds a subclass axiom in the ontology.

8.2.2 Example: OWLizer

An M3 transformation bridge called OWLizer allows language designers and language users to achieve representations of software languages (metamodel/model) in OWL. It provides the transformation of software language constructs like classes and properties into corresponding OWL constructs.

As one might notice, Ecore and OWL have a lot of similar constructs like classes, attributes and references. Table 8.11 presents a complete list of similar constructs.

Based on these mappings, we develop a generic transformation service to transform any Ecore metamodel and model into OWL TBox/ABox - *OWLizer*. The OWLizer transformation service is depicted in Table 8.12.

Table 8.12 Multi-layer transformation service (OWLizer)

Name	*Multi-layer transformation service (OWLizer)*
Signature	Ontology transform(Metamodel mm, Model m)
Pattern	o=TransformationBridge.transform(mm, m)
Description	Transforms a metamodel mm to the TBox of an ontology o and a model m to the ABox of an ontology o. The transformation definition relies on the mapping in Table 8.11

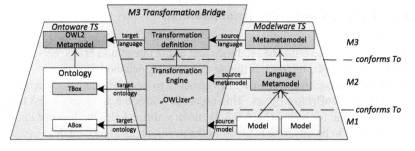

Fig. 8.3 OWLizer

Figure 8.3 depicts the conceptual schema of transforming Ecore into OWL. Figure 8.3 shows three modelling levels according to the OMG metamodel architecture: the metametamodel level (M3), the metamodel level (M2) and the model level (M1). Vertical arrows denote instantiation, whereas the horizontal arrows are transformations.

Having a transformation service established, language users are able to build models with the modelling language (e.g. UML) and concrete syntaxes they are familiar with. The users are restricted to the expressiveness (e.g. different syntactic constructs) of the modelling language they are working with. The transformation services between query and constraint languages increase the expressiveness of models to be transformed by the bridge, since they consider the models as well as annotated constraints or queries.

The tools and modelling environments for creating and processing models and ontologies remain the same. The transformation bridge establishes interoperability between modelling environments and different ontology tools (like reasoners).

8.3 Integration Bridge(*)

The strongest form of bridging is the integration of both technological spaces into one single integrated one. Based on a mapping of modelling language concepts, it is possible in principle to integrate the *metamodels* of both worlds (assuming they are written in a common language like MOF) by identifying (or subclassing) the respective notions. Then, the additional notions from both worlds may be added leading to a hybrid modelling language which may use the best of both worlds.

A hybrid model conforms to a hybrid modelling language and is built by constructs of both languages being integrated.

8.3.1 Integration Bridge Establishment

In this section, we describe the establishment of the integration bridge between two different metamodels. Its result is the new integrated metamodel.

Each integration bridge for two metamodels to be integrated is encapsulated in one IntegrationBridge object. This object provides the services for the bridge establishment and for its use (Sect. 8.3.2) and in addition holds the two metamodels mm_1 and mm_2 to be integrated as well as the new integrated metamodel.

Construction of Integrated Metamodels

The integration of the metamodels of two modelling languages consists of two steps: (1) mapping of language concepts and (2) application of integration services. These two steps are explained in the following.

1. Mapping of Concepts

Before an integration bridge is established, a mapping between the concepts of both languages must be performed. Based on the intensional knowledge about the languages to be integrated, correspondences between the modelling languages must be identified, and concepts of the languages to be integrated are related. A mapping of concepts in the second step of the integration establishment suggests which elements of two metamodels should be considered by integration services to be integrated.

These mappings of language concepts may be similar to the ones set up for the transformation bridge design. For example, we can use the mappings set up for the OWLizer relating language concepts of Ecore and OWL2 (Table 8.11).

Sometimes, concepts in the metamodels to be integrated are realised by different constructs. Hence, in the mapping step, adaptations of the metamodels may have to be performed. These adaptations, which are not explained in detail in this chapter, are needed, for example, to relate an association to a class. In this case, the association is replaced in the metamodels by a new class. This new class is associated by two new associations with the two classes the origin association was

Table 8.13 Integration services

Name	*Merge class service*
Signature	Class mergeClasses(Class c_1, Class c_2, String s)
Pattern	c_i=b.mergeClasses(c_1, c_2, s)
Description	Merges the two classes c_1 and c_2 by replacing them by a new class with name s. All incidences with associations and specialisation relations and all nested attributes are moved to the new class c_i
Name	*Specialisation service*
Signature	void specializeClasses(Classifier c_{sub}, Classifier c_{sup})
Pattern	b.specializeClasses(c_{sub}, c_{sup})
Description	Creates a specialisation relationship between two given classes or associations c_{sub} and c_{sup}, respectively
Name	*Associate service*
Signature	Association associateClasses(Class c_s, Property p_s, Class c_t, Property p_t, String $name$)
Pattern	a=b.associateClasses(c_s, p_s, c_t, p_t, $name$)
Description	Associates two classes c_s and c_t by a newly created association a with name n which has the two properties p_s (for class c_s) and p_t (for class c_t)
Name	*Merge associations service*
Signature	Associations mergeAssociations(Associations a_1, Associations a_2, String s)
Pattern	a_m=b.mergeAssociations(a_1, a_2, s)
Description	Merges two associations a_1 and a_2 by replacing them by a new association a_m with name s. All specialisation relations and all nested attributes are moved to the new association. The service only merges a_1 and a_2, if the multiplicities at the incidences of a_2 are the same or more specific than the multiplicities at the incidences of a_1, and if the classes at the incidences of a_2 are the same or specialisations of the classes at the incidences of a_1
Name	*Merge attributes service*
Signature	Attribute mergeAttributes(Attribute a_1, Attribute a_2, String s)
Pattern	a_m=b.mergeAttributes(a_1, a_2, s)
Description	Merges two attributes by replacing them by a new attribute a_m with name s. The service is executed, if the domains of a_1 and a_2 are the same or the one of a_2 describes a subset of the domain of a_2, and if both attributes are in the same class or association or a_2 is in a specialisation of the one of a_1

incident with. Thus, we keep the relation between two classes, where the relation after the adaption is established by a separate class.

2. Application of Integration Services

In Table 8.13 we present a set of integration services. All integration services are implemented in the IntegrationBridge class and are provided by a corresponding object to language designers.

The integration services work in place on the metamodel mm_{Int}, which is encapsulated by the integration bridge. Before any integration service is applied, mm_{Int} represents the disjoint union of the metamodels to be integrated.

The integration services directly consider elements of the metamodel mm_{Int} and either merge them or relate them by a specialisation relationship or an association. The result of applying a set of integration services is an integrated metamodel.

The mergeClasses service is used if the intensional meaning of two classes in a metamodel is the same. The specializeClasses service is used if two classes or two associations in a metamodel are related, where one of them intensionally specialises the other one. The associateClasses service is used if two classes in a metamodel should be related by an association. The mergeAssociations service is used if two associations are intensionally identified to represent the same relations between classes. The mergeAttributes service is used if one class or association contains two attributes that are identified to be merged.

8.3.2 Integration Bridge Use

The use of the integration bridge provides integrated modelling and supports the projection of integrated models to models conforming to one of the respective metamodels. The IntegrationBridge object encapsulating the integrated metamodel and the integration information provides such services.

Given the integrated metamodel, which is result of the integration bridge, language users are able to build integrated models. Elements (instances, links and attribute assignments) in this model either conform to concepts defined in only one of the metamodels to be integrated or conform to concepts lying in the intersection of the two merged metamodels. The projection of integrated models is a model which consists only of those elements which conform to concepts of one given metamodel to be integrated or of merged concepts of the integrated metamodel.

Creation of Integrated Models

One part of using the integration bridge is the creation of hybrid models. A hybrid model is an instance model which conforms to the integrated metamodel mm_{Int}. Listing 8.1 depicts an excerpt of an integrated Ecore-based metamodel using the extended KM3 textual syntax [107]. It conforms to the integrated metametamodel which is depicted below in Fig. 8.4. It shows that a *Configuration* model has at least 1 *Slot*. And a *Configuration*7603 model extends *Configuration* to have exactly 3 *Slots*.

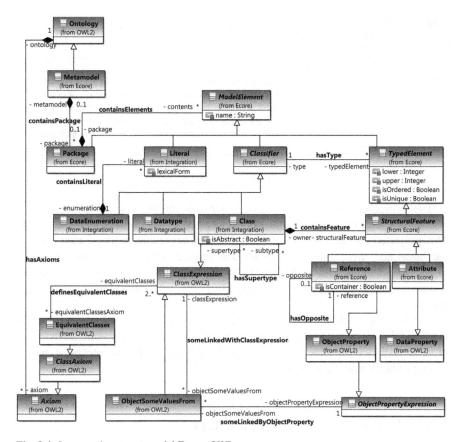

Fig. 8.4 Integrated metametamodel Ecore+OWL

Listing 8.1 Example of a hybrid model

```
class Configuration extends hasSlot min 1 Slot {
  reference hasSlot [1−*]: Slot;
}
class Configuration7603 extends Configuration equivalentTo hasSlot exactly 3 Slot {
}
```

Projection of Integrated Models

An important service on an integrated model is its projection to a model conforming purely to one of the respective original metamodels (e.g. to the OWL 2 metamodel mm_{OWL}). Language users require projection services because they need interoperability with tools they used before the integration; for example, ontology reasoners only allow ontology models as input, while Ecore tools only work with Ecore-based models.

Table 8.14 Projection service

Name	*Projection service*
Signature	Model project$_{mm_i}$(Model m_h)
Pattern	$m = \text{project}_{mm_i}(m_h)$
Description	Returns a model m which conforms to mm_i. m consists of those instances and links in m_h which conform to classes or associations in mm_i or conform to merged or specialised elements in mm_{Int} which can be traced back to constructs of mm_i. All attribute assignments in m conform to attributes nested in classes or associations in mm_i or conform to merged attributes which can be traced back to attributes in mm_i

The projection of integrated models depends on the integration. A projection service creates a model conforming to a metamodel which was integrated. The projected model contains elements which are projections of elements in the integrated metamodel. The projection service selects only those elements in the integrated model which conform to integrated constructs (e.g. merged classes or classes integrated by specialisation) or which conform to pure language constructs.

The IntegrationBridge object provides such projection services, one for each metamodel mm_1 or mm_2 to be integrated. Table 8.14 depicts the specification of the projection service for mm_i (where $i \in \{1, 2\}$) getting as input an integrated model and returning a model conforming to mm_i.

8.3.3 Example: M3 Integration Bridge

The design of an M3 integration bridge at first consists of the identification of concepts of a metametamodel (Ecore) and the OWL metamodel.

Figure 8.5 depicts the conceptual schema of an M3 integration bridge allowing for hybrid metamodelling.

An integrated metamodelling language provides all classes of the Ecore metametamodel and OWL metamodel. It merges, for example, OWL Class with Ecore EClass, OWL ObjectProperty with Ecore References or OWL DataProperty with Ecore Attribute. Thus, a strong connection between the two languages is built. Since a language designer creates a class, he is in the scope of both OWL class and ECore class. Hence, a language designer can use the designed class within OWL class axioms and simultaneously use features of the Ecore metamodelling language, like the definition of simple references between two classes.

The following listing depicts the initialisation of the integration bridge object. Here, the two metamodels for Ecore and OWL are loaded. Afterwards, several integration services are applied.

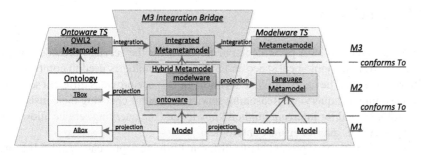

Fig. 8.5 M3 Integration bridge

```
// Integration bridge initialisation
b = new IntegrationBridge(mm_{Ecore}, mm_{OWL});

// Use of integration services
b.specializeClasses(Package, Ontology);
Class=b.mergeClasses(Class, EClass, "Class");
b.specializeClasses(Reference, ObjectProperty);
b.specializeClasses(Attribute, DataProperty);
Datatype=b.mergeClasses(Datatype, Datatype, "Datatype");
```

After all integration steps are successfully applied, the integration bridge object may return the integrated metametamodel Ecore+OWL.

The integration bridge itself is used at the M2 layer by a language designer. He is now able to define hybrid language metamodels with integrated OWL annotations to restrict the use of concepts he modelled and to extend the expressiveness of the language.

For language designers and users, the interoperability with other tools is important. In particular, language users having created a hybrid model want to project it to a pure ontology which serves as input for several reasoning tools. For example, to provide reasoning services to language users and language designers, the integrated metamodel is projected into an OWL ontology TBox. The models created by the language users are projected into a corresponding OWL ontology ABox. Based on the knowledge base consisting of a TBox and ABox, we can provide standard reasoning services and provide specific modelling to both language user and designer.

From the perspective of language users, the integration bridge provides a common view together on ModelWare and OntologyWare conceptual models, namely hybrid models. The modelling of hybrid models requires an understanding of both integrated languages. A language user has to be familiar with different concrete syntaxes (at least one for each modelling language) and how they are used in combination. To provide interoperability between different tools, projection services must be given by the integration bridge. Projection services extract all relevant information from hybrid models and translate them to models understandable by given tools. For example, hybrid models are projected to ontologies to be readable by reasoners.

8.4 Conclusion

In this chapter, we have presented specifications for the services provided by an OntologyWare technological space and bridging technologies used to combine two different spaces. The OntologyWare technological space provides different services for reasoning and querying. Reasoning services allow for checking the consistency of ontologies and for inferring implicit knowledge. The querying service allows for asking SPARQL queries against ontologies.

In addition, we have presented two different bridging approaches. All bridges are used to combining different modelling languages. The transformation bridge is used to translate ModelWare models into ontologies according to some transformation definition. We suggest the use of the integration bridge if language users are not familiar with ontology languages and its constructs and purely want to use the language they are familiar with. The integration bridge supports language designers to combine different modelling languages. Language users are able to use both languages simultaneously and to create hybrid models. The use of the integration bridge is proposed if language users want to design models with the language they are familiar with but in addition want to simply annotate model elements with ontology constructs.

In the following two chapters, we will discuss how to use scalable ontology reasoning services to support consistency checking for structure models (Chap. 9) and dynamic models (Chap. 10).

Chapter 9
Ontology Reasoning for Consistency-Preserving Structural Modelling

Christian Wende, Katja Siegemund, Edward Thomas, Yuting Zhao, Jeff Z. Pan, Fernando Silva Parreiras, Tobias Walter, Krzysztof Miksa, Pawel Sabina, and Uwe Aßmann

Abstract In this chapter, we discuss and demonstrate concrete applications of ontology reasoning for the analysis and validation of structural models in the ODSD infrastructure. We illustrate how the ontology services (see Chaps. 3 and 5 for details) summarised in Chap. 8 are employed to enable consistency-preserving structural modelling by providing means for the specification of consistency constraints, static semantics, or the derivation of suggestions for modellers.

Structural modelling is of importance in various phases of software development. Its applications range from *descriptive* models used to capture the requirements for software systems to *prescriptive models* used for their design and implementation. The examples presented in this chapter relate to our examples and case studies introduced in Chaps. 1, 2, and 4. They demonstrate different styles for employing ontology services to leverage structural modelling in software development: Firstly, ontologies can be used as first class entities during software development; see the example given in Sect. 9.1. Secondly, a prescriptive model-based representation of structural information can be bridged with ontology-based specifications of consistency rules for particular domains. Ontology services can then be used to check the consistency of structural models and to derive additional knowledge.

The rest of this chapter is organised as follows. In Sect. 9.2 we describe the application of ontology technology for feature model analysis in SPLE. Section 9.3 illustrates how ontologies aid in structural modelling in the domain of physical devices with the example of the Comarch case study from Sect. 4.1. In Sect. 9.4 we introduce the reasoning services for unified modelling language (UML) class diagrams by presenting the TwoUse approach that combines UML models and OWL ontologies. We conclude this chapter with Sect. 9.5.

J.Z. Pan et al. (eds.), *Ontology-Driven Software Development*,
DOI 10.1007/978-3-642-31226-7_9, © Springer-Verlag Berlin Heidelberg 2013

9.1 Reasoning for Requirement Engineering

Usually, requirements engineering (RE)—i.e. the identification, specification, and documentation of requirements—is the first task of a software development process. It results in some kind of requirement specification which is often treated as a *contract between* software developers and customers. An important challenge for requirements engineering is to cope with inconsistencies or incompleteness in requirements specifications. Such inconsistencies result from the acquisition, specification, and evolution of goals and requirements from multiple stakeholders and sources [207]. Inconsistent and incomplete requirements have crucial influences on all following tasks of software development. In this section, we will introduce *ontology-driven requirements engineering (ODRE)*, an ontology-based approach for the specification and validation of requirements for completeness and consistency.

9.1.1 The ODRE Approach

In Fig. 9.1 we present the architecture of ODRE. A so-called Requirement Metamodel is generated from the knowledge of the requirements analysis and builds the TBox of the Requirement Ontology. It formalises the RE concepts as well as relationships between requirement artefacts. This domain independent ontology TBox can be instantiated with the requirement artefacts (goals, requirements, obstacles, etc.) for a particular project. This way, the ABox is generated from the results of requirement analysis of an application project. It builds the requirement Specification Base. Once the Requirement Elicitation has been completed and the Requirements Ontology is filled with all information, we execute consistency and completeness queries, generated from consistency checking rules (cf. Section 9.1.2) and completeness checking rules (cf. Section 9.1.3), respectively. These rules are used to enable the validation of the Requirements Specification Base of the project. The following sections present the rules for completeness and consistency checking and exemplarily explain how they have been implemented so far.

9.1.2 Rules for Consistency Checking

The notions of consistency and completeness are based on the violation of consistency and completeness rules. Therefore, we have predefined two set of rules in natural language and realised the appropriate checks by querying techniques. We will have a brief look at the concrete realisation of these rules separately for consistency and completeness (cf. Sect. 9.1.3). The consistency rules check for valid relations between the requirement artefacts, e.g. whether a goal is indeed connected

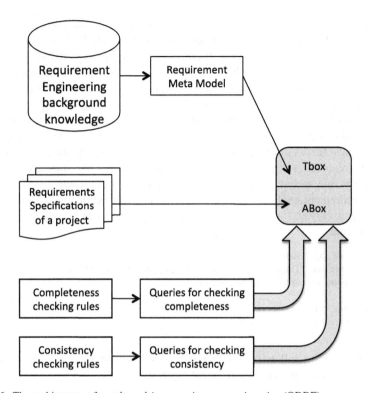

Fig. 9.1 The architecture of *ontology-driven requirement engineering* (ODRE)

with at least one requirement. Moreover, requirement relationships are verified in order to prevent competing requirement, conflicts, and so on. We predefined six consistency rules that have to be met for a requirements specification to be valid.

To realise these rules in the Requirements Ontology, we have encoded them as a set of DL axioms. If these rules (axioms) are fulfilled, the ontology will be logically consistent. Any violation of the rules will result in an inconsistent ontology. One such rule is modelled by the following axiom:

$ChosenRequirement \sqsubseteq \neg\exists isExclusionOf.ChosenRequirement$
This means that a chosen requirement should not be specified to be excluded by some other chose requirement.

It is worth noting that whether a certain requirement belongs to the *Chosen-Requirement* or whether two chosen requirements have a *isExclusionOf* relation are not always explicitly asserted in the requirement specification. For example, a requirement r_1 may depend on another requirement r_2, which further depends on requirement r_3. Thus when choosing r_1, r_2, and r_3 should also be implicitly chosen. Similarly, if some requirement r_4 excludes R_3, it should also implicitly exclude r_2 and r_1. With appropriately devised requirement ontologies, such implicit knowledge can be inferred and exploited in consistency checking.

Other consistency rules are specified in a similar way. The mapping between the axioms in the ontology and the rules is given in the ontology using annotation properties on the particular axioms. If one of these axioms is violated, we can use an explanation service to find which axioms caused this violation. The reasoner can determine the axioms in the inconsistency justification that represent a consistency rule. The additional axioms are used to find which individuals had caused the error. This allows us to explicitly mention the invalid requirements in the error message that is displayed to the user. For inconsistencies we distinguish errors and warnings. Errors must be resolved by the requirements engineer and warnings should be resolved. A template is used to define generic error messages for each consistency rule and suggestions to resolve found inconsistencies. For example, if one requirement excludes another, they cannot both be included in the set of requirements chosen for the final model. This constraint can be described by the following rule:

IF excluding requirements
THEN print error: "The following requirements exclude others [R_n]."
"Please choose one of the following options:

Exclude the following requirements: [R_n], find alternatives for [R_n] or revise the requirement relationships of [R_n]."

We assume the following individuals and relationships as an extract of the ontology resulting from the Requirement Analysis:

$isExclusionOf(Functional\_Requirement5, Functional\_Requirement7)$
$ChosenRequirement(Functional\_Requirement5)$
$ChosenRequirement(Functional\_Requirement7)$

This set of axioms results in an inconsistency with regard to the previously defined consistency rule. We use the approach described above to derive errors and warnings displayed to the user. To support the requirements engineer in error elimination, the system suggests a list of possible solutions. The concrete error message and the suggestion to resolve our inconsistency is shown below:

Excluding requirements can not be included in the same chosen requirement subset.

Error.
"The following requirements exclude others: Functional Requirement5."
"Please choose one of the following options:"

Suggestion.
Exclude the following requirements from the chosen requirement set: Functional Requirement5
Find alternatives for: Functional_Requirement5 or
Revise the requirement relationships of (Functional_Requirement5, Functional_Requirement7).

After the RE has done the appropriate actions to remove errors and warnings, the requirement subset has to be checked for consistency once more. In case the set is now consistent, all requirements will be automatically asserted "Checked" and "Valid" in the ontology. If not, another revision and check becomes necessary until the Requirement Specification Base is consistent or the analyst refuses to do any further action. In the latter case, all the requirements will be asserted "Checked" as well, but all invalid requirements will be asserted "Invalid". This way it is possible to display all invalid requirements and change them manually or check for options without being forced to run too many consistency checks. However, it is always possible to have another consistency check.

9.1.3 Rules for Completeness Checking

We have defined 43 completeness rules to check the completeness of the requirement artefacts, e.g. whether goals, requirements, use-case descriptions, and so on have been specified and if all required attributes and relations have been specified. According to Firesmith [68] the most important metadata to capture is:

- Project-unique identifier (PUID)
- Prioritisation
- Rationale
- Source
- Status (may include more than one kind of status)
- Verification method

This metadata has been integrated into our completeness rule set and extended by further completeness criteria regarding the existence of requirement artefacts and their relationships to each other. An extract of these rules is shown below:

Every Functional Requirement (FR) must define whether it is mandatory or optional.
IF FR is not mandatory AND not optional
THEN print error: "You did not specify whether the following FRs are mandatory or optional"
"Please specify whether the following FRs are mandatory or optional: [FR_n]."

Every FR must specify AT LEAST ONE property hasRequirementRelationship.
IF FR has NOT specified a property "hasRequirementRelationship"
THEN print error: "You did not specify any requirement relationship for the Functional Requirements [FR_n].
Please check the relationships for the following Functional Requirements: [FR_n]."

Example

We assume an extract of the following individuals and relationships:

isRelatedTo(Goal2, UseCase7)
NonFunctionalRequirement(NonFunctionalRequirement1)
isOptional(NonFunctionalRequirement1, true)
FunctionalRequirement(FunctionalRequirement1)

This raises the following error messages and suggestions for our completeness rules:

Every Requirement must state whether it is mandatory or optional.
Error.
"You did not specify whether the following FR are mandatory or optional: FunctionalRequirement1."
"Please specify this attribute for the FR: FunctionalRequirement1."

Every FR must specify AT LEAST ONE requirement relationship.
Warning.
"You did not specify any requirement relationship for the following FR: FunctionalRequirement1."
"Please check whether there exists any relationship to another requirement for the FR FunctionalRequirement1."

The completeness rules have been realised as SPARQL queries. If the patterns encoded in the rule match the entailed ontology, then the particular completeness rule being tested failed, and the requirements model is deemed incomplete. The results of the query identify those parts of the ontology which are incomplete. Since we are looking for incomplete requirements, we had to allow the query to work in a closed world environment. This requires the use of negation as failure in the query, which is available in the draft SPARQL 1.1 specification using the "NOT EXISTS" keyword and functionality. This can be realised by putting corresponding requirement types and requirement relations into the negation as failure box (NBox) (Sect. 5.1.5) and use reasoning to derive the incomplete results. Another implementation of these database style constraints is also described by Sirin and Tao in [194].

9.1.4 Verification of the Requirement Specification Base

We have implemented the ontology using Protege 4.0, and created completeness constraints as queries in SPARQL, using the SPARQL 1.1 OWL profile and support for negation as failure against OWL knowledge bases. The reasoner and query engine used is the TrOWL tractable reasoning infrastructure[1]. This is particularly well suited to this application, as once a consistent and complete set of requirements is loaded, it is possible to make a SPARQL endpoint available permanently to allow traceability links to be established between the artefacts in the Requirements

---

[1] Available at http://trowl.eu/

Ontology and the rest of the software engineering life cycle. The TrOWL reasoner also supports explanation of consistency checks for OWL DL ontologies and supports justification of query answers. The additional functionality for rewriting the reasoning explanations and justifications into English has been implemented into the RELib package.

9.1.5   Results

In this section, we have introduced the ODRE approach for requirements engineering. ODRE exemplifies an approach for the direct application of ontology technology in MDSD. It demonstrates the benefits and applicability of ontology technology for requirements engineering. Compared to structural modelling, the application of ontology technology contributes a formal and easily extensible way to avoid inconsistency and to ensure the completeness of requirements specifications.

9.2   Reasoning for Feature Model Analysis[(*)]

In Sect. 2.2.6 we have introduced the structural modelling language of feature models and motivated the need for an automatic way to feature analysis. We also introduced a case study for feature-based software product line engineering and discussed the potential of applying ontology technology for feature analysis in Sect. 4.3. The general idea of applying ontology technology for feature analysis and validation was proposed by Wang et al. [215]. In this section, we will introduce an extended approach to support efficient and domain-specific inconsistency reporting, inconsistency repairing, and variant model completion for feature models. The realisation of our approach can be split into two basic steps:

1. Translation of feature models and their explicit and implicit constraints to an ontology-based formalisation.
2. Application of the ontology-based formalisation to answer the feature analysis questions defined in Sect. 2.2.6.

In the following, we will report on each step individually (cf. Sects. 9.2.1 and 9.2.2) and finally conclude the contributions of ontology technology for feature model analysis (cf. Sect. 9.2.3).

9.2.1   Ontology-Based Formalisation of Feature Models

To prepare a precise specification for the mapping between feature models and ontology concepts, we first provide a set-based representation of the feature models and feature relationships introduced in Sect. 2.2.6. Each feature model (FM) is completely described by:

- F: A set of features contained in the feature model.
- $F_p \subset F \times F$: A set of pairs of child features and their respective parents.
- $F_m \subset F_p$: A set of pairs of mandatory features and their respective parent. All other features are implicitly considered optional.
- $F_{or} \subset \wp(F) \times F$: A set of pairs of a set of features (from the powerset of F) that are related by an or relationship and their respective parent.
- $F_{xor} \subset \wp(F) \times F$: A set of pairs of a set of features (from the powerset of F) that are related by an alternative relationship and their respective parent.
- $F_{prop} \subset F \times T$: A set of pairs of a feature f and a logical term T of features that is implied by f, where T can be build using $f \in F$, $\sqcap$, $\sqcup$, and $\neg$. This set can be used to describe basic relationships like conflicts, requires, and more complex propositional cross-tree relationships [18].

Given this set-based representation the following mappings are applied to translate feature models and their implicit semantics to an ontology-based formalisation. They correspond to the propositional logic semantics for feature relations introduced in Table 2.1:

Feature Model First all features of the feature model are mapped to ontology classes. To be able to express the presence and absence of a concrete feature in a feature relationship or a variant specification, we include the following axioms for all features $f \in F$ to our OWL ontology:

$Feature\_f \sqsubseteq \top$ (expresses presence of feature)
$not\_Feature\_f \sqsubseteq \neg\ Feature\_f$ (expresses absence of feature)

To reflect all implicit and explicit constraints implied by the feature model we extend the ontology with a number of constraint classes ca collected in the set Ω. These constraint classes subsume all violations of constraints.

Parent Features For each parent feature fp with child feature fc $((fp, fc) \in F_p)$ we add a constraint class following the pattern:

$fc\_NeedsParent\_fp \sqsubseteq Feature\_fp \sqcup \neg\ Feature\_fc$

Mandatory Features For each mandatory feature fm with parent feature fp $((fm, fp) \in F_m)$ we add a constraint class following the pattern:

$fp\_Needs\_fm \sqsubseteq Feature\_fm \sqcup \neg\ Feature\_fp$

Alternative Features For each parent feature fp with n child features Fx within an alternative group $((fp, Fx) \in F_{xor})$ we add a constraint class following the pattern:

$$fp\_NeedsExactlyOneOf\_Fx \sqsubseteq (\bigsqcup_{1 \leq i \leq n} (Feature\_fx_i) \sqcap$$
$$\bigsqcap_{1 \leq i \leq j \leq n} (\neg\ (Feature\_fx_i \sqcap Feature\_fx_j))) \sqcup \neg\ Feature\_fp$$

Or Features For each parent feature fp with n child features Fo within an OR group $((fp, Fo) \in F_{or})$ we add a constraint class following the pattern:

$$fp\_NeedsAtLeastOneOf\_Fo \sqsubseteq \bigsqcup_{1 \leq i \leq n} (Feature\_fo_i) \sqcup \neg \, Feature\_fp$$

Propositional Feature Terms For each logical feature term T implied by feature fd $((fd, T) \in F_{prop})$ we add a constraint class following the pattern:

$$fd\_Requires\_T \sqsubseteq T_{translated} \sqcup \neg \, Feature\_fd$$

where $T_{translated}$ is derived from T by applying the translation Δ:

$$\Delta(f) \Rightarrow Feature\_f$$
$$\Delta(T_i \sqcap T_j) \Rightarrow \Delta(T_i) \sqcap \Delta(T_j)$$
$$\Delta(T_i \sqcup T_j) \Rightarrow \Delta(T_i) \sqcup \Delta(T_j)$$
$$\Delta(\neg \, T_i) \Rightarrow \neg \, \Delta(T_i)$$

Variant Models A variant specification consists of:

- $I \subseteq F$: A set of features explicitly included for a variant
- $E \subseteq F$: A set of features explicitly excluded for a variant

Given this set-based representation of variant models, a variant specification VS is translated to a class in our ontology-based representation:

$$VS \sqsubseteq \bigsqcap_{1 \leq i \leq n} (Feature\_i_i) \sqcap \bigsqcap_{1 \leq j \leq m} (\neg \, Feature\_e_j)$$

where $i_i \in I$, $e_j \in E$, $\mid I \mid = n$ and $\mid E \mid = m$. A variant specification is complete *iff* all features in the feature model are either explicitly included or excluded ($I \sqcup E \equiv F$ and $I \sqcap F \equiv \varnothing$).

9.2.2 Application of Ontology Services for Feature Analysis

Feature Model Validation, Debugging, and Repair

To validate a feature model for consistency we derive a check class that is a subclass of all constraint classes $ca \in \Omega$:

$$FeatureModel\_Consistency \sqsubseteq \bigsqcap_{1 \leq i \leq n} (ca_i)$$

If this class is asserted unsatisfiable by the reasoner, we know that the feature model is inconsistent.

Finding the constraints that cause an inconsistency and repairing the feature model is—especially for large feature models with many constraints—not an easy task. We argue that the best situation to assist developers in this regard is during the introduction of the inconsistency. Every propositional constraint nca that is newly added to the feature model is checked for consistency w.r.t. the existing feature model. Therefore, we introduce a check class as subclass of nca and all existing constraint classes $ca \in \Omega$:

$$nca\_Validity \sqsubseteq \prod_{1 \leq i \leq n} (ca_i) \sqcap nca$$

If the reasoners report this check class as unsatisfiable, we know that the newly introduced constraint is inconsistent and should be repaired.

Variant Model Validation, Debugging, and Repairing

To validate a variant model, we derive an individual check class that validates a variant specification VS for each constraint class $ca \in \Omega$. All such check classes are collected in Θ:

$$VS\_Check\_ca \sqsubseteq VS \sqcap ca$$

Given this ontological representation of the feature model, of the relationship semantics, and of the variant specification, we apply reasoning to find all unsatisfiable constraint classes in our ontology. If unsatisfiable classes are found the variant is invalid. This answers Q4 (cf. Sect. 2.2.6). Due to the one-to-one translation, these classes can be directly related to a specific feature model relationship and the involved features. Table 9.1 summarises the errors and repair suggestions derived for each constraint type. These domain-specific errors and suggestions provide answers to the questions Q5 and Q6 (cf. Sect. 2.2.6).

Partial Variant Completion

Another useful service ontology technology that can provide for variant specifications is partial completion for incomplete variant specifications. Partial variant completion means the suggestion of an inclusion or exclusion of features whose inclusion or exclusion status can be automatically derived for a given incomplete variant configuration. Consider for instance a feature f_i that requires the feature f_j. For an incomplete variant specification IVS that includes f_i, variant completion would automatically suggest the inclusion of f_j. Ontology classification can be used to derive completion suggestions for such simple but also more complex cases. We apply the same transformation to validate the consistency of an incomplete variant specification as to validate variant specifications. In addition, we introduce helper class $IVS\_Completion$ to collect all super-class assertions automatically derived by classification. It is modelled as subclass of all constraint classes $ca \in \Omega$ and the incomplete variant specification IVS:

$$IVS\_Completion \sqsubseteq \prod_{ca \in \Omega} (ca) \sqcap IVS$$

Table 9.1 Errors and suggestions for guided variant configuration

Constraint	Reported error	Repair suggestion
Mandatory feature		
$((fm, fp) \in F_m)$	Feature fp requires the inclusion of fm	Add fm to variant
		Remove fp from variant
OR group		
$((fp, \{f_1..f_n\}) \in F_{or})$	Feature fp requires the inclusion of f_1 or .. or f_n	Add f_1 or .. or f_n to variant
		Remove fp from variant
XOR group		
$((fp, \{f_1..f_n\})) \in F_{xor})$	Feature fp requires the inclusion of either f_1 or .. or f_n	Add either f_1 or .. or f_n to variant
		Remove fp from variant
Required term		
$((fd, T) \in F_{req})$	Feature fd requires the inclusion of T	Add T to variant
		Remove fd from variant
Conflicting term		
$((fd, T) \in F_{confl})$	Feature fd conflicts with the inclusion of T	Remove T from variant
		Remove fd from variant

After classification by the reasoner, we query *IVS_Completion* for all asserted super-classes. Matching this super-class against the classes included to represent present features (*Feature_f*) and absent features (*not_Feature_f*) results in the desired completion suggestions for feature include and exclude, respectively. This provides answers to question Q7 (cf. Sect. 2.2.6). This approach will only provide completion proposals that can be deterministically derived. If such assertions are not possible, the variant would be reported invalid, and inconsistencies would have to be handled manually using the above described variant model debugging and repair procedure.

9.2.3 Results

In this section, we proposed a dedicated approach for ontology-based feature analysis. We implemented a M2 transformation bridge (cf. Chap. 8) by providing a set of transformation rules to represent the structure and semantics of feature models in an ontology. Using this ontology-based representation, we suggested the application of ontology services to check feature and variant models for inconsistencies, to guide developers in repairing inconsistencies, and to complete variant models.

Table 9.2 Contributions of ontology-based feature validation for feature analysis

Question	Provided service
Q1: Feature Model Validity	Feature models can be checked for consistency regarding the interplay of all their constraints.
Q2: Feature Model Debugging	To detect constraints that cause invalidity each individual constraint is validated when it is added to the feature model and marked inconsistent if it invalidates the feature model.
Q3: Feature Model Repair	As each constraint is validated during the construction of a feature model, inconsistent constraints are immediately reported and can be repaired.
Q4: Variant Model Validity	All explicit and implicit constraints are represented and checked individually during variant configuration.
Q5: Variant Model Debugging	As each constraint is checked individually, inconsistencies and the features that are involved are also reported individually.
Q6: Variant Model Repair	Given a set of features and the constraint they invalidate, repair suggestions can be computed (cf. Table 9.1).
Q7: Variant Model Completion	For variant specification that are considered incomplete all completions that can be deterministically derived are provided by our variant completion approach.

Table 9.2 concludes the contributions of ontology technology beyond structural modelling by relating our approach to the questions identified as important for feature analysis in Sect. 2.2.6.

9.3 Reasoning for Domain Engineering

Ensuring and preserving the consistency of specifications for structural models is important not only during requirements engineering but also during later phases of software development. In Sect. 4.1 we motivated the need for consistency checking in domain models of physical telecommunication device configurations. In this section, we describe an integration between OWL 2 and PDDSL, which is a DSL for modelling physical devices introduced in the domain engineering case study (Sect. 4.1). The purpose of the integration is to enable semantic reasoning on the PDDSL models, in order to realise the use cases (UC-1, UC-2, UC-3) introduced in the case study description.

9.3.1 Physical Devices Ontology

The physical devices ontology is an OWL 2 ontology that enables semantic modelling of the physical devices. Thus, it constitutes the ontological solution for the case study and is basis for the language integration described in Sect. 9.3.2 and for performing semantic reasoning. However, due to its complexity, the physical devices ontology is not intended to be directly used by the end users.

Ontology TBox

The TBox of the physical ontology consists of two parts. Firstly, the core concepts of the ontology, which are independent of the particular device types being modelled, are defined (Listing 9.1). This includes classes Device, Card, Configuration, and Slot and the object and data properties that refer to these classes.

```
Class: pd:Device
Class: pd:Card
Class: pd:Configuration
Class: pd:Slot
ObjectProperty: pd:hasSlot
  Domain: pd:Configuration
  Range: pd:Slot
  Characteristics: InverseFunctional
  InverseOf: pd:isInConfiguration
ObjectProperty: pd:hasConfiguration
  Domain: pd:Device
  Range: pd:Configuration
  Characteristics: InverseFunctional , Functional
ObjectProperty: pd:hasCard
  Domain: pd:Slot
  Range: pd:Card
  Characteristics: InverseFunctional , Functional
  InverseOf: pd:isInSlot
DataProperty: pd:id
  Domain: pd:Slot
  Characteristics: Functional
```

Listing 9.1 Core concepts of the physical device ontology

Secondly, the TBox contains the definitions of the particular types of devices. This part reflects the (M1, O2) part (see Fig. 2.7) of the PDDSL model and includes the configuration constraints of the devices. An example excerpt of this part of TBox, with basic information about the Cisco 7603 router, is given in Listing 9.2.

```
Class: Cisco_7603
  SubClassOf: pd:Device, pd:hasConfiguration exactly 1
                (Cisco_7603_Configuration)
Class: Cisco_7603_Configuration
  SubClassOf: pd:Configuration , pd:hasSlot exactly 3 pd:Slot
Class: Cisco_7603_Configuration_slot_1
  SubClassOf: pd:Slot ,
        pd:hasCard only ( Supervisor_Engine_2 or
                        Supervisor_Engine_720 ) ,
        pd:hasCard some pd:Card
  EquivalentTo: pd_isInConfiguration some Cisco_7603_Configuration
                and pd:id value 1
```

Listing 9.2 TBox excerpt describing the Cisco 7603 router

The Cisco_7603_Configuration_slot_1 class is an example slot type definition. It is equivalent to the slot with id "1" of the Cisco_7603_

Configuration. It is mandatory to put some card in this kind of slot. Also, the slot type allows only for the following categories of cards: Supervisor_ Engine_2 or Supervisor_Engine_720.

Ontology ABox

The ABox of the ontology describes the instance part of the model (M1, O1 in Fig. 2.7). The instances reflect the real devices, their configurations, slots, cards, and relations among them.

Closing the World

The reasoning tasks performed on models, such as consistency checking, often require the *closed domain assumption (CDA)* or even *closed world assumption (CWA)* [55]. In contrast, OWL 2 adopts the *open world assumption (OWA)*. Therefore, it is necessary to be able to close the knowledge base explicitly. As we have mentioned in earlier sections, this can be done naively by procedurally enriching the given knowledge base by further axioms to simulate a closed world view of the knowledge base. This has to be either hard-coded or performed manually by users. A more convenient realisation is to use NBox to specify the concepts and roles that are required to be closed and leave the reasoning and closure of the reasoner (see Sect. 5.1.5 for more details). We use this approach and the associated services provided by TrOWL in our implementation. Similarly, OWL 2 does not assume the *unique name assumption (UNA)* which is required for the purpose of guidance services. And this can also be realised by explicitly asserting that all named individuals are different.

Our experiments revealed that in the physical devices use case, it cannot be decided in general what should be closed in the ontology. Rather, some of the decisions depend on the use case. Specifically, the use case UC-2 (cf. Sect. 4.1) requires closing the pd:hasCard object property to perform the consistency checking, while the UC-3 (cf. Sect. 4.1) requires the same property to remain open. All aspects of domain closure independent of a particular use case are realised in the transformation. An example is the addition of the disjoint classes axioms. It is assumed that all top-level card categories are disjoint and that the subcategories within the same CardCategory are mutually disjoint. Then, it is enough to close the pd:Card class (the root class of the CardCategory inheritance hierarchy), by putting it into the NBox, in order to ensure the CDA for all of the branches in the hierarchy. In contrast, the pd:hasCard object property has to be closed for the purpose of the consistency checking, while the same property has to remain open for other services. In order to close the property, for each individual that represents a slot without known cards, it is stated that it is of the type pd:hasCard exactly 0 pd:Card. After performing the service, the added axioms should be removed from the ontology. Additionally, we adopt the UNA for all individuals. Listing 9.3

provides a generic model transformation snippet that makes all individuals in an ontology different: an additional frame is added into the ontology, listing all individuals under the `DifferentIndividuals` axiom.

```
model.frames += object DifferentIndividuals{
    individuals += model.allSubobjects() [OWL::Individual];
};
```

Listing 9.3 Unique Name Assumption for all individuals expressed (QVTO transformation snippet)

9.3.2 Integrating PDDSL and OWL 2

The metamodel and textual concrete syntax of PDDSL is introduced in Sect. 4.1. This section describes how OWL 2 can be represented in the metamodelling technical spaces and describe the integration between OWL 2 and PDDSL. The integration takes place at the abstract syntax (metamodel) level and the concrete syntax level.

OWL 2 Manchester Syntax Metamodel

The *OWL 2 Manchester syntax* [97] can be used to represent the OWL 2 ontology. The corresponding metamodel is large and complicated, since it reflects the complete specification of the Manchester syntax. Figure 9.2 shows a small excerpt of the metamodel with some of the core concepts. The ontology in the Manchester syntax consists of the frames representing, among other entities, the classes and the individuals. The definition of a class can contain the descriptions, representing the related class expression. For instance, through `equivalentClassesDescriptions`, it is possible to define the equivalent classes. Similarly, an individual can be related to the class description representing its type, through the `types` reference. The metamodel and the corresponding concrete syntax are available at the EMFText Concrete syntax Zoo[2].

9.3.3 Metamodel Integration

The integration of the OWL 2 and PDDSL metamodels is depicted in Fig. 9.3. Firstly, we state that the `ArtefactType` class from the PDDSL metamodel is a subclass of the `Class` from OWL 2 metamodel. Secondly, we define the `Artefact` from PDDSL metamodel as a subclass of the `Individual` from

---

[2]http://www.reuseware.org/index.php/EMFText_Concrete_Syntax_Zoo

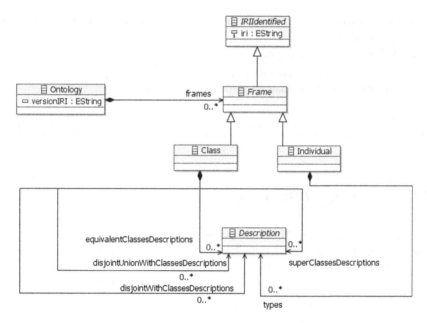

Fig. 9.2 OWL 2 Manchester syntax metamodel excerpt

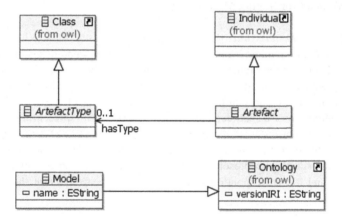

Fig. 9.3 PDDSL-OWL 2 metamodel integration

OWL 2 metamodel. Finally, we state that the Model from the PDDSL metamodel is a subclass of the Ontology from the OWL 2 metamodel.

Concrete Textual Syntax Integration

The textual syntax specifications of PDDSL and OWL 2 were integrated by altering the PDDSL syntax, so that the enrichment of PDDSL constructs with the OWL 2 descriptions is possible. For instance, the PDDSL constructs that are subclasses of the `Class` from the OWL 2 metamodel can be attributed with the OWL 2 descriptions which are allowed for the classes (e.g. the equivalent classes description) as well as the annotations (Listing 9.4 contains an example for the `CardCategory`).

```
CardCategory::= !1 "CardCategory" iri[","]
  (
    (annotations !1)
     | ("SubClassOf:" superClassesDescriptions
        ("," superClassesDescriptions )* !1)
     | ("EquivalentTo:" equivalentClassesDescriptions
        ("," equivalentClassesDescriptions)* !1)
     | ("DisjointWith:" disjointWithClassesDescriptions
        ("," disjointWithClassesDescriptions )* !1)
     | ("DisjointUnionOf:" disjointUnionWithClassesDescriptions
        ("," disjointUnionWithClassesDescriptions)* !1)
  )*
  ("longName" ":" longName[","])? ("description" ":"
description[","])?
            (!1 "cardTypes" ":" "{" cardTypes* !0"}")?
            (!1 "includedCategories" ":" "{"includedCategories* !0"}" )?
;
```

Listing 9.4 Integrated syntax definition for CardCategory (in EMFText concrete syntax specification language)

Transformation

The purpose of the model transformation, specified in the *operational QVT language (QVTO)* [147] language, is to convert an input PDDSL model into a pure OWL 2 ontology. The transformation step is needed despite the fact that the PDDSL is integrated with OWL 2 and can be treated as an ontology metamodel. The reason is that such integrated models cannot be directly fed into the semantic reasoner. First, the transformation reorganises the structure of the model (Listing 9.5). The OWL 2 Manchester syntax is a frame-based language, while the PDDSL uses a custom structure of containment of model elements. The elements corresponding to the OWL 2 classes or individuals have to be moved into the top level collection of frames.

```
// Move all OWL::Class objects
model.frames += model.allSubobjects() [OWL::Class] —> sortedBy(iri);
```

Listing 9.5 QVTO—Example of reorganising PDDSL model elements

Besides moving the objects from one collection to another, the information implicitly defined in the PDDSL has to be explicitly formalised in the ontology. For instance, the class types listed as the value of the `SlotType.allowedCardTypes` property form the ObjectPropertyOnly restriction on the `hasCard` property (Listing 9.6).

```
mapping inout SlotType::updateSlotType() {
   // Define a specific Slot subclass containing
   // only allowed CardTypes, like in example:
   //
   // pd_hasCard only (Supervisor_Engine_2
   //            or Supervisor_Engine_720)
   self.superClassesDescriptions += object ObjectPropertyOnly {
      featureReference := object FeatureReference {
         feature := hasCardProperty;
      };
      primary := object NestedDescription {
         description := object Disjunction {
            self.allowedCardTypes -> forEach (i) {
               conjunctions += object ClassAtomic{
                  clazz := i;
               }
            }
         }
      }
   };
}
```

Listing 9.6 QVTO—Example of processing SlotTypes

As an example, let us consider the transformed model presented in Listing 9.7[3]. After the execution of the mapping for `SlotType` "1", the `SlotType` is enriched with a `SubClassOf` axiom. The axiom is based on a universal restriction on the `pd:hasCard` object property. The card categories listed in the restriction correspond to the card categories specified in the source model (Listing 4.1) for the `SlotType` "1".

```
DeviceType "Cisco_7603"
longName : "CISCO 7603 CHASSIS"
  allowed : {
  PossibleConfiguration "Cisco_7603_Configuration" {
    SlotType "1"
       SubClassOf:
         pd:hasCard only ( Supervisor_Engine_2 or Supervisor_Engine_720 ),
            allowed : "Supervisor_Engine_2" "Supervisor_Engine_720" required :
true
         [...]
    }
  }
```

Listing 9.7 Cisco 7603 type model after execution of mapping (integrated PDDSL-OWL2 syntax)

---

[3]The integrated PDDSL-OWL2 textual concrete syntax is used to present the results. Hence, the result is linguistic instances of the integrated PDDSL-OWL2 metamodel.

Furthermore, the transformation defines the semantics of the *ontological instantiation* relationship: the `hasType` property. The semantics of this relationship is equivalent to the class assertion. Thus, every occurrence of the `hasType` is transformed to an appropriate class assertion axiom.

9.3.4 Reasoning with Integrated PDDSL and OWL 2 Models

In the following, the use cases introduced in the domain engineering case study (Sect. 4.1) are revisited. For each of the use cases, we show how their implementation can be achieved with use of semantic reasoning.

Compute Incorrect Device Types

The validation of the `DeviceTypes` is required by the use case UC-1 (cf. Sect. 4.1). The service is based on the satisfiability checking, which is realised by a direct call to the reasoner. For the OWL 2 classes contained in an unsatisfiable classes set, their counterpart `DeviceTypes` is identified and returned to the user as incorrect. As an example, let us consider the Cisco 7603 router model (Listing 4.1) and let us suppose that the following additional OWL 2 axiom is added to the model: `Cisco_7603_Configuration SubClassOf: pd:hasSlot some (pd:hasCard some Cisco_7600_SIP)`. The axiom requires the only possible configuration of the `Cisco_7600` to contain at least one `Cisco_7600_SIP` card. The constraint is contradictory to the PDDSL specification (Listing 4.1) which does not allow the `Cisco_7600_SIP` in any of the slots. The problem can be detected after the transformation of the integrated PDDSL+OWL 2 model to the pure OWL 2 ontology. The reasoner will infer that the OWL 2 class corresponding to the `Cisco_7603` device type is unsatisfiable. Such result is then interpreted as an error in the type layer of the integrated PDDSL+OWL 2 model and reported back to the user.

Compute and Explain Inconsistencies

The consistency checking and explaining of the inconsistencies is the service required by the use case UC-2 (cf. Sect. 4.1). The service implementation includes three steps:

Consistency checking is realised via a direct call to the reasoner which returns an answer in terms of a Boolean value.

Explanation generation is an algorithm which computes the minimum inconsistency preserving subsets of the ontology [86] (also referred to as the justifications for the inconsistency).

Explanation interpretation   The reasoning explanation is not itself meaningful for the device modeller. Therefore, it is post-processed. The aim of the post-processing is to interpret the explanation in the domain-specific manner. This is done in two steps:

1. The set of individuals that occur in any of the object property assertion axioms involved in the explanation is extracted. These individuals are reported to the user as invalid.
2. In order to report to the user the reason for the inconsistency, we rely on the annotation mechanism of OWL 2. The assumption is that every axiom which is meaningful to the user is annotated with a user friendly description of the error. Such description is then reported to the user if such axiom occurs in the explanation.

Let us consider the instance of the device type Cisco_7603 from Listing 4.2 and the respective type model presented in Listing 4.1. The inconsistency detected by the reasoner is related to the axioms describing the slot "1" (Listing 9.8). Specifically, the only restriction on pd:hasCard property lists the allowed card categories in the slot. This axiom appears in the inconsistency explanation. The OWL 2 definition of the slot, generated from the PDDSL model, contains also the annotation: "Slot requires card from the following card categories: Supervisor_Engine_2, Supervisor_Engine_720." This description is interpreted as the error message presented to the user.

```
Class: Cisco_7603_Configuration_slot_1
Annotations: rdfs:comment
  ' ' Slot requires card from the following card categories:
Supervisor_Engine_2, Supervisor_Engine_720.
        SubClassOf:   pd:Slot ,
                      pd:hasCard only   (Supervisor_Engine_2 or
                      Supervisor_Engine_720 ) ,
                      pd:hasCard some   pd:Card
        EquivalentTo: pd:isInConfiguration some Cisco_7603_
                      Configuration and pd:id value 1
```

Listing 9.8   Slot "1" of Cisco 7603 (integrated PDDSL-OWL2 syntax)

Suggest Allowed Card Categories

Supporting the user by providing suggestions about the allowed card categories that can be plugged into a slot in a given configuration instance is the guidance service required by the use case UC-3 (cf. Sect. 4.1). The service is realised via a direct call to the reasoner.

Ontology pre-processing   is needed when the ontology already contains a card in the slot being queried. If such axiom exists, it is removed from the ontology.

Subsumption checking   is realised via a direct call to the reasoner. Specifically, we look for all descendant classes of the following class: `pd:Card and not (inv(pd:hasCard) value ?slotId)`, where `?slotId` is a placeholder for the slot, which is the parameter of the service. That is, we check for all subclasses of the `pd:Card` for which we can prove that they cannot be inserted into the given slot.

CWA complement computation   phase is responsible for transforming the negative answer returned by the subsumption checking (the disallowed `CardCategories`) into positive answer required by the user (the allowed `CardCategories`). More specifically, in OWA semantics, the fact that a card category not being subsumed by the disallowed `CardCategories` does not necessarily implies that it is subsumed by its complement, i.e. the allowed `CardCategories`. Hence, we need to close the disallowed `CardCategories` with its positive answer returned. This complement computation requires the CWA and can be realised by using NBox as introduced in Sect. 5.1.5.

Result interpretation   involves retrieving the `CardCategories` from the PDDSL model that correspond to the set of classes from the ontology, computed in the previous steps. The set of those `CardCategories` is the result returned to the user.

One of the scenarios where the service is used is the model repair process after the detection of an inconsistency. For instance, if we consider the model from Listing 4.2, the next step after the inconsistency is detected is to ask for the card categories which are allowed in slot "1". For the purpose of this query, the wrong card is removed from the slot and the reasoner is asked for the named subclasses of `pd:Card and not (inv(pd:hasCard) value cisco_7603_slot_1)`. The result of this query is the set of all named classes which are known not to be allowed in the slot. After the complement of this set of classes is computed, the user would get the following set of card categories: `Supervisor_Engine_2`, `Supervisor_Engine_720` as the result of the service.

In this section, we have been talking about the required reasoning services but do not discuss how they can be realised. As we can see from Sect. 9.3.1, the physical device ontology is in a rather complex language (actually $\mathcal{SROIQ}$), and thus its reasoning should have a high complexity. To improve efficiency, it is necessary to employ approximation technologies to reduce reasoning complexity. While on the other hand, the quality of results, namely soundness and completeness, should not be sacrificed. Fortunately, it has been shown that the syntactic approximation technology introduced in Sect. 5.1.4 can be successfully applied in the physical device configuration use case to achieve the above goals [170]. In this solution, ontologies are approximated into $\mathcal{EL}^{++}$ and reasoning is tractable. Another consequence is that the justification technology of $\mathcal{EL}^{++}$ (Sect. 5.2.2) can now be applied on the physical device ontologies.

9.3.5 Results

In this section, we have introduced a domain-specific approach for the integration of DSLs and ontology technology. The integration of PDDSL and OWL 2, using a combination of the integration and transformation bridge, enables the formal specification of consistency rules for physical device types and device configurations. The application of ontology technology enhances structural modelling of physical devices by contributing the formal and technical foundations for checking and preserving the consistency of physical device types, concrete device configurations, and enable the interactive suggestion of configuration options using basic ontology services. To improve efficiency, such services can be realised with approximations.

9.4 Reasoning for UML Class Diagrams

UML class diagram is one of the most important and widely used modelling facilities in software engineering. To provide a formal semantics and associated reasoning services to UML class diagram is an important task of ontology-driven software development. In this section, we present an integration of UML class diagram and ontology models. It provides abstract syntax, concrete syntax, transformation rules, and a combined query language.

9.4.1 TwoUse

TwoUse (Transforming and Weaving Ontologies and UML in Software Engineering [158]) is an approach combining UML class-based models with OWL ontologies to leverage the unique and complementary strengths of the two. TwoUse's building blocks are (a) an integration of the MOF-based metamodels for UML class-based modelling and OWL, (b) the specification of dynamic behaviour referring to OWL reasoning (using SPARQL-like expressions), and (c) the definition of a joint profile for denoting hybrid models as well as other concrete syntaxes. We build the TwoUse approach based on four core ideas

1. As abstract syntax, it provides an integrated *MOF-based metamodel* as a common backbone for UML class-based modelling and OWL modelling.
2. As concrete syntaxes, it uses pure UML, Ecore, an *UML profile* supporting standard UML2 extension mechanisms and a textual concrete syntax to write UML-based class and OWL descriptions.
3. It provides a canonical *set of transformation rules* in order to deal with integration at the semantic level.
4. It provides a novel SPARQL-like language to write queries and constraints over OWL ontologies, SPARQLAS.

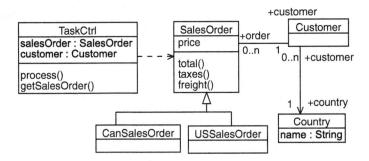

Fig. 9.4 UML class diagram of the problem domain

In order to illustrate the TwoUse approach, we have chosen an existing example from the literature for motivating and studying our approach. We use the case of an international e-commerce system. The characteristics of the system to be designed include:

- It is supposed to be a sales order system for Canada and the United States.
- Calculate freight and taxes based on the country.
- Use Government Sales Tax (GST) and Provincial Sales Tax (PST) for tax in Canada.

A snippet of the corresponding UML class diagram is presented in Fig. 9.4. The class TaskCtrl is responsible for controlling the sales orders. A SalesOrder can be a USSalesOrder or a CanSalesOrder, according to the Country where the Customer lives.

Here, the target behaviour could be denoted by the following OCL expression:

```
context TaskCtrl :: getSalesOrder (): SalesOrder
  body :
    if customer . country . name = 'USA' then
      salesOrder . oclAsType ( USSalesOrder )
    else
      if customer . country . name = 'Canada' then
        salesOrder . oclAsType ( CanSalesOrder )
      endif
    endif
```

However, this way of specifying the operation getSalesOrder() exhibits some shortcomings. The semantics of the subclasses of SalesOrder, i.e. the semantics of USSalesOrder and CanSalesOrder, are embedded in nested conditions in the operation specification of a method of TaskCtrl. Hence, the semantics of USSalesOrder and CanSalesOrder may be difficult to find and understand in larger domains. They may even appear redundantly when the same conditions need to be applied somewhere else in the specification. Furthermore, the description of the classes CanSalesOrder and USSalesOrder is stated at least twice: once in the class declaration and once, implicitly, as an expression

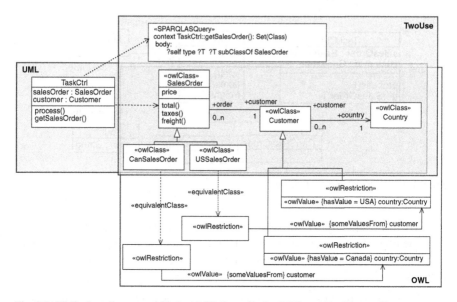

Fig. 9.5 UML class diagram profiled with UML profile for OWL and TwoUse profile

of the operation `TaskCtrl.getSalesOrder()`. To give an idea of the target integration, let us consider our running example. Instead of defining the operation `getSalesOrder()` in the class `TaskCtrl` using complex OCL constructs, a more transparent and maintainable solution will use the expressiveness of the OWL language. Querying an *OWL reasoning service*, an OCL-like query may just ask which OWL subclass of `SalesOrder` a given instance fulfils all the logical requirements of. The body of the `getSalesOrder()` operation will then be specified very simply by:

```
context TaskCtrl
    def getSalesOrder(): Set(Class)
    ?self type ?T
    ?T subClassOf SalesOrder
```

As specified above, to identify which subclasses are applicable, we use the variable ?T to get all types of ?self that are subclasses of SalesOrder. To facilitate such specification, the integration of the UML class diagram and OWL ontology model via TwoUse is depicted in Fig. 9.5.

The usage of the variable self means that at the implementation level, we consistently correlate application class instances with individuals in the ontology. That is, for every object in the application, we generate a corresponding individual in the ontology. As the classification of these individuals depends on structural relationships between objects, we need to use reflection to create the individuals and we update the individual information whenever changes in the object state occur. The advantage of this integrated formulation of `getSalesOrder()` lies in separating two sources of specification complexity. First, the classification of complex classes remains in an OWL model. The classification is easily re-useable for specifying other operations and it may be maintained using diagram visualisations as well as decidable, yet rigorous reasoning models. Second, the specification of the business logic itself remains in an OCL specification. It becomes smaller and, hence, better understandable and easier to maintain.

9.4.2 Results

In this section, we have introduced the ontology reasoning technologies for UML class diagrams. Particularly, the TwoUse approach presented in this section integrates the MOF-based metamodels for UML class-based modelling and OWL and uses SPARQL-like expression to retrieve query results via OWL reasoning. By doing this, the features of UML class diagrams and OWL ontologies can benefit each other, and the concrete technologies remain transparent to users.

9.5 Conclusion

In this chapter we have introduced different approaches for applying scalable ontology technology (cf. Chap. 5) to provide consistency-preserving software development with structural modelling languages. The presented approaches were meant to demonstrate the application of different bridging technologies introduced in Chap. 8 by practical examples. From the implementation of these examples, we conclude the following lessons for applying ontology technology for structural modelling:

Versatility Ontology technology can be applied to various domains of structural modelling (e.g. requirements specification, feature modelling, DSLs, UML). This enables consistency-preserving software development throughout the complete development life cycle (requirements engineering, design, implementation).

Expressiveness Ontology technology provides sufficient expressiveness to represent information commonly found in structural modelling languages. Furthermore, it contributes means to express consistency rules and evaluate such rules to provide suggestions and guidance to repair inconsistencies.

Effort The effort of applying ontology technology varies from domain to domain and strongly depends on the bridging technology employed.

Applicability The applicability of a given approach is related to the applied bridging technology. For example, the ODRE approach directly employed ontology technology which strongly reduced the effort for its implementation. However, ODRE users are required to encode requirements specifications using ontologies directly, which induces some initial learning effort. Other approaches that employ sophisticated bridges can provide a better abstractions for approach users and, thus, enhanced applicability.

In summary, the examples motivate the application of ontology technology to address challenges in structural modelling. Furthermore, we have experienced a trade-off between the effort invested in integrating ontology technology and structural modelling and the applicability and usability of the resulting approach. What bridging technology to employ, thus, depends on the experience and qualification of the expected users and the size of user base addressed.

The individual bridges build in this chapter are strongly coupled to the domain they are built for. However, we have experienced several pattern that were repeatedly used in different examples. These experiences and the correspondences discussed for (meta)modelling languages and ontologies in Chap. 7 suggest potential to generalise means for integrating ontology technology and structural modelling. This would significantly reduce the effort to build individual approaches, while ensuring good applicability. This idea will be continued by introducing ontology integrated modelling (OIM) in Chap. 11.

Chapter 10
Ontology Reasoning for Process Models

Yuan Ren, Gerd Gröner, Tirdad Rahmani, Jens Lemcke, Andreas Friesen,
Srdjan Zivkovic, Yuting Zhao, and Jeff Z. Pan

Abstract Processes in software development generally have two facets. They can
be model objects, as described in Sect. 4.2, and also workflows, as described in
Sect. 4.3. In this chapter, we analyse typical problems in process modelling and
develop ontology reasoning technologies to address them in the ODSD infrastructure. We show how different ontological representation of process models can be
constructed for different purposes and how reasoning can be applied to guarantee
the consistency of models.

We provide ontology support for both process models and process workflows. We
will use *Business Process Management Notation (BPMN)*, the graphic syntax to represent process models. Its introduction and the basic definitions regarding process
models and their operations in refinement can be found in Sect. 4.2. For state-of-
the-art process model technologies, we refer the readers to Sect. 2.5.3. For basic
requirements of using process workflow for guidance, we refer readers to Sect. 4.3.
For application of the technology developed in Sect. 10.4 and its connection to the
MOST-TOPF, we refer readers to Chap. 13. For basic definitions about ontology
and reasoning, we refer readers to Chap. 3. For reasoning technologies utilised in
this chapter, we refer readers to Chap. 5.

To be coherent, we present a running example in Sect. 10.1. Sections 10.2
and 10.3 will focus on processes as models, while Sect. 10.4 will focus on process as
workflows. More specifically, Sect. 10.2 shows how to model and retrieve processes
with ontologies. Section 10.3 shows how to validate the refinement relation between
process models. Section 10.4 shows how to provide guidance information for
engineers working in a workflow, in which they can perform various tasks depending
on their roles.

J.Z. Pan et al. (eds.), *Ontology-Driven Software Development*,
DOI 10.1007/978-3-642-31226-7_10, © Springer-Verlag Berlin Heidelberg 2013

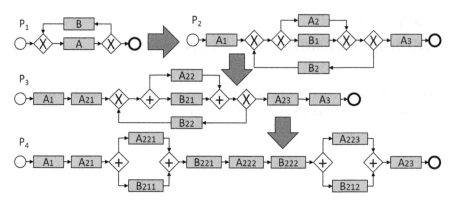

Fig. 10.1 A refinement chain of processes

10.1 A Running Example

When looking at the model facet of processes, engineers should be able to build, retrieve, modify and deploy processes, which are regarded as artefacts. When looking at the workflow facet of processes, engineers should be able to "generate" processes by performing tasks. Interestingly, in one scenario there can be both process models and process workflows. For example, when a group of software engineers are building and refining processes models, their actions of creating process, editing process, deploying process, etc., make up a process workflow. Such a scenario can be demonstrated by the following example.

Example 1. In Fig. 10.1, there are four process models P_1, P_2, P_3 and P_4. They form a refinement chain, in which each process (except P_1) describes the behaviour of the previous process at a more fine-grained level.

For example, P_2 refines P_1 by decomposing activity A into A_1, A_2 and A_3, B into B_1 and B_2. P_2 is further refined by P_3, in which A_2 is further decomposed into A_{21}, A_{22} and A_{23}, B_2 into B_{21} and B_{22} and so on. The ordering relations between activities are also restructured.

It is the mission of our technologies to support engineers building and validating such a refinement chain, discovering sources of potential problems and correcting it if necessary.

We will use the above example in Fig. 10.1 throughout this chapter. Therefore, the activities described in Sects. 10.2 and 10.3 can be regarded as performing tasks in a workflow, e.g., *creating a process* and *validating refinement relation between two process models*, in Sect. 10.4.

Our solutions are based on ontology technologies, such as ontology construction and reasoning. They include two important aspects:

1. Representing the domain as ontologies and reducing the problems to reasoning problems.

2. Providing efficient reasoning and tool support for the reasoning problems.

To show the flexibility of ontology technologies, in each section, we use different ontology representations and apply different ontology reasoning technologies to solve problems.

10.2   Reasoning for Process Modelling and Retrieval

In this section, we introduce modelling principles for process models like BPMN diagrams in OWL. Moreover, we demonstrate how DL reasoning can be used to retrieve process models and instances. In order to use reasoning services for process management tasks in general and for process retrieval in particular, we represent process models in OWL (OWL DL). Based on this representation, standard reasoning services like subsumption checking and concept satisfiability checking can be used to find process models.

10.2.1   Semantic Representation of Process Models

In software engineering, process models are mainly represented by graphical models like BPMN diagrams. A diagram can be considered as a view of the model. They provide flexible means to describe complex processes with various modelling principles like subprocesses, branches and loops. However, it becomes quite hard to analyse the process model and understand the intended meaning of (parts of) the model.

A description in [82] demonstrated the need for an enhanced semantic representation of process models in order to capture at least the following characteristics of process models: (1) An explicit representation of dependencies between activities in a process, i.e., the execution ordering of activities. Examples for such dependency constraints are predecessor and successor relations between activities, i.e., an activity requires a certain activity as predecessor or successor (directly or indirectly). (2) In model-driven engineering, process models might be specialised or refined into a more fine-grained representation. For instance, activities are decomposed into a subprocess or activities are replaced by sub-activities for a more precise process description. (3) Some process properties are expressed using different modalities, for instance, to describe the occurrence of an activity as optional or as necessary in each process instance.

Process models must cover all allowed process runs. We use OWL classes to represent activities and object properties to represent relations between activities. In this section, we represent a process as a complex class expression that contains all activities that may occur in the process flow. We will demonstrate in the next section that this representation of processes by a complex expression is quite beneficial for process retrieval. However, as we will see later, for process refinement, we give

Table 10.1 Transformation to OWL

Construct	BPMN notation	DL notation
1. Start	O	*Start*
2. End	●	*End*
3. Activity	[A]	*A*
4. Edge	→	to_i
5. Process P	O→[A]→●	$P \equiv Start \sqcap \exists_{=1} to_i.$ $(A \sqcap \exists_{=1} to_i.End)$
6. Flow	[A] ⟶▷ [B]	$A \sqcap \exists_{=1} to_i.B$
7. Exclusive decision and merge	[B] ; [A]▷◇▷[C]▷◇▷[D]	$A \sqcap \exists_{=1} to_i.$ $((B \sqcup C)$ $\sqcap \exists_{=1} to_i.D)$
8. Condition	[A] —[Cond]▷ [B]	$A \sqcap \exists_{=1} to_i.$ $(B \sqcap \kappa_{Cond})$
9. Parallel	[B] ; [A]▷◇▷[C]▷◇▷[D]	$A \sqcap \exists to_i.$ $(B \sqcap \exists_{=1} to_i.D)$ $\sqcap \exists to_i.(C \sqcap$ $\exists_{=1} to_i.D) \sqcap = 2 to_i.\top$
10. Loop	[A]▷◇→[B]	$Loop_j \sqcap \exists_{=1} to_i.B,$ $Loop_j \equiv A \sqcap \exists_{=1} to_j.$ $(Loop_j \sqcup End_j)$

an alternative representation that is more appropriate for this particular process management service.

We use the object property *to* and its inverse *from* to describe the successor and predecessor relations of activities. In order to allow nested process descriptions as it is realised in loops and the decomposition of activities, we introduce subproperties to_i of the property *to*. We define *to* as a subproperty of the transitive property *totr* to capture also indirect predecessor and successor connections between activities.

A transformation from BPMN modelling primitives to OWL TBox, classes, properties and axioms is described in Table 10.1. Activities are represented by OWL classes (No. 1–3), and flow connection is represented by the object property to_i which is a subproperty of *to* (No. 4). A complex class expression that defines a process by a TBox axiom is depicted in No. 5. The class definition captures all activities that occur in the control flow of the process. We describe a control flow (No. 6) by a class expression in OWL using an object property restriction on the object property to_i describing the flow relation to the successor activity. We describe that for the activity A, there is exactly one direct successor activity B.

Exclusive decisions are represented using concept union (No. 7). The exclusiveness is represented by additional disjointness conditions, which are represented by disjoint classes in OWL. Inclusive decisions are described without additional disjointness conditions. Conditions are also represented as concepts (No. 8). The flow condition is modelled as a restriction on all instances of the target activity, i.e. instances are instances of B and of the concept κ_{Cond}. Parallel branches are represented in OWL using intersections as depicted in No. 9. The expression requires that there are two successors of A. Loops are special decisions (No. 10). The OWL class $Loop_j$ is introduced in the process description in order to allow the descriptions of multiple occurrences of the activities.

The presented design decisions aims at a representation of BPMN-like process models in OWL in order to support the retrieval of processes and process informations. Therefore, we omit further potential restrictions like the disjointness of activities that occur in parallel or exclusive branches and more restrictive join conditions like for inclusive branches (No. 7).

10.2.2   Reasoning for Process Retrieval

Once the BPMN process models are represented in OWL as described in the previous section, we exploit this representation in combination with DL reasoning in order to retrieve processes from a knowledge base (KB). The knowledge base can either be a local process model repository or distributed models for process, workflow or service descriptions.

If a user is interested in a certain process that satisfies a specified characterisation, then the corresponding query describes this required characterisations. Other process properties are neglected in the query. Likewise, in our retrieval approach, queries are represented by general and incomplete process descriptions that only specify the core functionality of the process. The process query description is like all process descriptions a complex class expression. The result of the query contains all processes that satisfy this description based on DL inference. For instance, a query Q that retrieves all processes that execute the activity A before the activity B with an arbitrary number of activities between them:

$$Q \equiv \exists\, totr.(A \sqcap \exists\, totr.B).$$

In order to demonstrate the benefits and power of the introduced semantic representation of processes, we exemplify how the process retrieval covers three patterns of process structures. (1) The query describes direct and indirect ordering relations between activities in a process flow. (2) Process retrieval takes into account terminological knowledge like hierarchical structuring of activities (3) Queries allow for handling modality, i.e. to express whether a certain activity in a query has to occur in each process or it might occur only in some processes.

Given the process models in an OWL KB and a query Q (which is again a process description), DL reasoning provides different kinds of reasoning or entailment methodologies that can be exploited in process retrieval. We demonstrate process retrieval for two entailment regimes: concept subsumption and concept satisfiability.

The entailment of *concept subsumption* assumes that the query Q is a general process description, just describing the key features of the searched process, while the processes that are defined in the KB are more specific and contain further activities, intersections and (additional) conditions. Hence, all retrieved processes that satisfy the query process description Q are specialisations in OWL of the general query process. They are subsumed by the query process Q.

For instance, we consider a query similar to the example above that looks for all processes that execute the activity A directly before B and the activity A can occur somewhere in the process. The query Q is expressed by the class expression $Q \equiv \exists\, totr.(A \sqcap \exists\, to.B)$. The results using concept subsumption are all processes that are subsumed by Q. This includes a process that consist just of two activities A and B like $P \equiv Start_i \sqcap \exists\, to_i.(A \sqcap \exists\, to_i.(B \sqcap \exists\, to_i End_i))$. More complex process descriptions that consist of further activities and conditions are in the subset as well.

A weaker entailment method that leads to a larger result set is the *satisfiability of concept intersection*. The concept intersection is an intersection of the query process description Q and a process from the knowledge base (KB). The results of a query Q are all process models P of KB that satisfy the intersection of the query process Q, i.e. $Q \sqcap P$ is satisfiable. All processes that are results of the previous entailment method (concept subsumption) are results of this weaker entailment methodology as well.

In order to demonstrate advantages of this weaker inference, we are looking for a process that is not represented in the knowledge base by any process description. For instance, consider the following query:

$$Q \equiv \exists\, totr.(A \sqcap \forall\, to.B).$$

In this case, it is required that the successor of the activity A is restricted to activity B. We assume there is no such restriction for a process in the knowledge base. Obviously, the stronger inference (concept subsumption) would not retrieve any process model. However, using satisfiability of concept, intersection retrieves all processes that do not explicitly contradict the query description like a successor activity of A that is defined as disjoint from B.

10.3 Reasoning for Process Refinement in BPMN (*)

In the last section, we are mainly dealing with the modelling of a single process model and retrieval of process models with certain patterns. But how to model and validate the relationships between two process models and their components? In this section, we apply ontology and reasoning in refinement checking of BPMN processes. As motivated in Sect. 4.2, we first investigate how to define the correctness of a refinement (Sects. 10.3.1 and 10.3.2); then we represent more and more complex process refinement with ontologies and use reasoning to validate them (Sects. 10.3.3–10.3.5). After that, we show that process grounding can be validated in a similar way as refinement (Sect. 10.3.6). In order to support more user-friendly development, we provide not only validation results but also explanation for incorrect refinements (Sect. 10.3.7). At the end (Sect. 10.3.8), we show that the performance of reasoning services we use in refinement checking can be substantially improved by approximation techniques (Sect. 5.1.4).

10.3.1 Defining Valid Process Refinement

In Sect. 4.2.2, we have already introduced two types of process refinement, *refinement* and *grounding*, with examples of violations (see Figs. 4.5 and 4.6 for an example of a wrong refinement and its correction). A *refinement* is a mapping of entities from an abstract to a more specific process which represents the decomposition of activities. For this reason, it is also called decomposition. A *grounding* refinement is a mapping from a concrete process model to a component model, which is also specified in BPMN processes. Refinement specification and validation are concerned with both kinds of mappings. Whenever only grounding information is referred to, we use the term grounding specification explicitly.

Intuitively, a refinement or grounding is a transformation from an abstract to a more specific model which contains the decomposition and/or restructuring of activities in the abstract model. However, this statement does not provide formal criteria for determining the correctness of a refinement.

In the MIT business process handbook [222], a process *superior* subsumes another process *inferior* under maximal execution set semantics *iff* $ES_{inferior} \subseteq ES_{superior}$, where ES is the execution set. This can be regarded as a formal semantics of refinement as the execution sets reflect the behaviours of process models. However, this definition is not sufficient for dealing with real world problems. Taking refinement as an example, on the one hand, abstract process and specific process may use different vocabularies due to introduction of new activities. On the other hand, the specific process usually has more activities due to decomposition of abstract activities. These make it hardly the case that the execution set of an abstract process perfectly subsumes the execution set of a specific process.

Ren et al. [175] addressed the above issues by renaming activities in the specific process with the corresponding activities in the abstract process and further replacing consecutive activities of the same name in an execution with a single one. This recovers the decomposed (and thus renamed) activities in the abstract process so that refinement can be reduced to subsumption checking between (transformed) execution sets. In their later work [176], they further extend this definition with the notion of *decomposable process* to make activities in abstract process interruptible, so that decompositions of parallel activities can also be executed in parallel. We revisit the examples in Fig. 10.2 to illustrate this revised definition of valid process refinement.

For validation of refinement, the process architect has to declare which activities of Fig. 10.2b implement which activity of Fig. 10.2a: $orig(a_1) = orig(a_2) = A$,

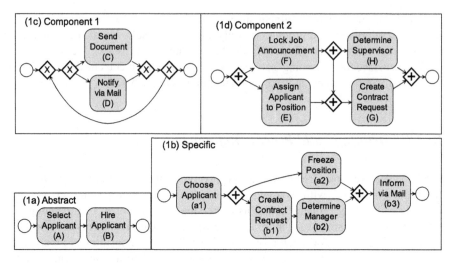

Fig. 10.2 Wrong process refinement

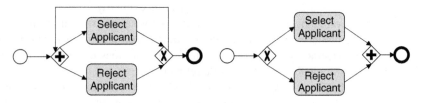

Fig. 10.3 Unsound process examples: left = lack of synchronisation and right = deadlock

$\mathrm{orig}(b_1) = \mathrm{orig}(b_2) = \mathrm{orig}(b_3) = B$. For validation of grounding, the process architect needs to link activities of Fig. 10.2b to service operations (which are already
bound to endpoints) given in Fig. 10.2c and d: $\mathrm{ground}(a_1) = \mathrm{E}$, $\mathrm{ground}(a_2) = \mathrm{F}$,
$\mathrm{ground}(b_1) = \mathrm{G}$, $\mathrm{ground}(b_2) = \mathrm{H}$, $\mathrm{ground}(b_3) = (D)$. One can split ground() to
the separate component specific functions $\mathrm{ground}[C_1]()$ and $\mathrm{ground}[C_2]()$—one for
each component.

Last but not least, we only consider sound processes. According to the BPMN
specification, unsoundness results from either deadlock or lack of synchronisation.
A process has a deadlock whenever no token coming from the start event can
ever reach the end event considering the token flow semantics of BPMN. Lack of
synchronisation is given when a token reaches the end event although other tokens
are still existing somewhere in the process. Examples are given in Fig. 10.3.

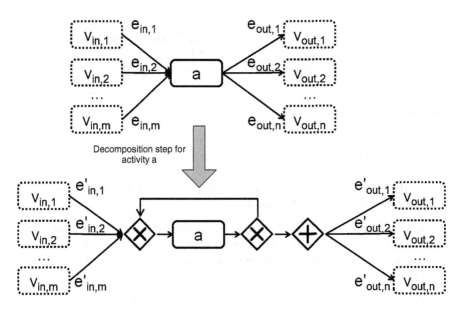

Fig. 10.4 Process decomposition by example

Correct Refinement

We say that a process Q is a *correct* refinement of a process P if $ES_Q \subseteq ES_{P^D}$ after the following transformations.

1. *Decomposition.* First we decompose the abstract process P as follows:

    Definition 1. For an abstract process P, its *decomposable process*, denoted by P^D, is constructed from P by constructing a loop around every activity of P (see Fig. 10.4).

    In a decomposable process, abstract activities might happen repeatedly. For example, in Fig. 10.4, activity a can happen any finite number times in an execution. This allows for multiple refined activities of a in a specific process.

2. *Projection.* Replace all activities in each execution of ES_Q by their originators given by the function orig().

    The execution set $\{[a_1, a_2, b_1, b_2, b_3]$, $[a_1, b_1, a_2, b_2, b_3]$, $[a_1, b_1, b_2, a_2, b_3]\}$ of Fig. 10.2b can be projected on the activities in the abstract process which yields the execution set $\{[A, A, B, B, B], [A, B, A, B, B]$, $[A, B, B, A, B]\}$.

    Since $\{[A, B], [A, B, B], [A, B, \ldots], [A, A, B], [A, \ldots, A, B], \ldots\} \not\supseteq \{[A, A, B, B, B]$, $[A, B, A, B, B]$, $\ldots\}$, the refinement specification in Fig. 10.2b depicts a wrong refinement of Fig. 10.2a. The cause is the potentially inverted order of A, B by b_1, a_2 or b_2, a_2.

Specific (corrected)

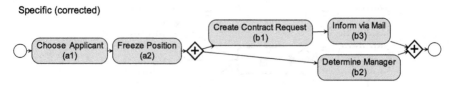

Fig. 10.5 A correct refinement of the abstract process

Correct Grounding

We say that a component model P is a *correct grounding* of a process Q if $\mathrm{ES}_Q \subseteq \mathrm{ES}_P$ after the following transformations.

1. *Projection.* Replace all activities in each execution of ES_Q by their activities in the component model to which they are grounded (function ground()).
2. *Reduction.* Remove all activities in each execution of ES_Q that do not appear in P.

The execution set $\{[a_1, a_2, b_1, b_2, b_3], \ [a_1, b_1, a_2, b_2, b_3], \ [a_1, b_1, b_2, a_2, b_3]\}$ of Fig. 10.2b projected on the component model yields the execution set $\{[E, F, G, H, D], [E, G, F, H, D], [E, G, H, F, D]\}$. For our example, reduction with respect to Fig. 10.2c yields $\{[D]\}$. Reduction with respect to Fig. 10.2d yields $\{[E, F, G, H], [E, G, F, H], \ [E, G, H, F]\}$.

Thus, Fig. 10.2c is a correct grounding of 10.2b because:

$$\{[C], \ [D], \ [C, C], \ [C, D], \ [D, C], \ [D, D], \ldots\} \supseteq \{[D]\}$$

and Fig. 10.2d is a wrong grounding of 10.2b because:

$$\{[E, F, G, H], \ [E, F, H, G], \ [F, H, E, G], \ [F, E, G, H], \ [F, E, H, G]\}$$

$$\nsupseteq \{[E, F, G, H], \ [E, G, F, H], \ [E, G, H, F]\}.$$

The cause for the wrong refinement is the potentially inverted execution of F, G by b_1, a_2 in Fig. 10.2b.

A correct refinement of the abstract process in Fig. 10.2 is illustrated in Fig. 10.5. The refinement is $\mathrm{orig}(a1) = \mathrm{orig}(a2) = A$ and $\mathrm{orig}(b1) = \mathrm{orig}(b2) = \mathrm{orig}(b3) = B$. The grounding specification is $\mathrm{ground}(a_1) = E$, $\mathrm{ground}(a_2) = F$, $\mathrm{ground}(b_1) = G$ and $\mathrm{ground}(b_2) = H$, $\mathrm{ground}(b_3) = D$.

In the remainder of this section, we refer to these two types of refinement relations by refinement and grounding, respectively. That is to say, the word "refinement" would specifically mean the first type of refinement, without further clarification. And the word "grounding" always mean the second type of refinement.

10.3.2   Constraints on Refinement Relations

Generally, refinement can be performed in two ways. The first way is the refinement of an activity by a completely new process with a syntactically well-formed process flow. For instance in Fig. 10.6 on the left hand side, an abstract process with the two consecutive activities A and B can be seen that are refined within a specific process. The activity A is thereby refined through a replacement of process A, and activity B is refined through the replacement of process B process A and Process B are both well-formed processes, and we refer to this kind of refinement as the process-based action refinement. The second way of refining an activity A within an abstract process can be by relating an arbitrary set of activities $orig^{-1}(A) = \{a_1, a_2, \ldots, a_n\}$ occurring in the more specific process with activities in the more abstract process by the functions orig (or ground) defined in Sect. 10.3.1. Therefore, we call this kind of refinement also function-based action refinement. By doing, so the following constraints need to be taken into account:

- *orig* is a partial function
- For every activity A, A and $orig(A)$ belong to different processes.
- If $A \wedge B$ belong to the process P then $orig(A) \wedge orig(B)$ belong also to the same process $P' \neq P$ and vice versa.
- If $A \neq B$ then $orig^{-1}(A) \cap orig^{-1}(B) = \varnothing$.
- for every chain $(A_1 \in orig^{-1}(A_2) \wedge A_2 \in orig^{-1}(A_3) \ldots A_{n-1} \in orig^{-1}(A_n))$ with pairwise distinct activities $\{A_1, \ldots, A_n\}$, it holds true: $A_n \notin orig^{-1}(A_1)$

An example for function-based refinement is given in Fig. 10.6 on the right hand side. Obviously, this kind of refinement allows more flexibility in defining relational dependencies between activities and can handle the first way of refinement as well. With the first way of refinement, one would not be able to handle the second refinement example on the right of Fig. 10.6, since decomposition of the refinement relation in well-formed process flows is not possible. The process refinement validation investigations in this work are considering function-based action refinement.

Additionally to the first and second constraints, which only consider an abstract and a specific process, the third constraint prohibits cycles in the whole refinement hierarchy. Based on this constraint, cases like that depicted in Fig. 10.7 are not allowed.

The grounding takes place at the moment where activities are fine-grained enough to be realisable by a service operation of a component model. Since for the behavioural description of component models we had decided to use the BPMN language as well, service operations are represented by activities in the component models. The following constraints must hold true for a grounding:

- Ground is a partial function
- The set of component models CM and process models PM is disjoint: CM $\cap$ PM $= \varnothing$

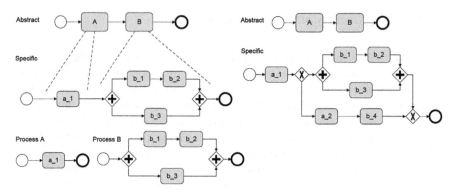

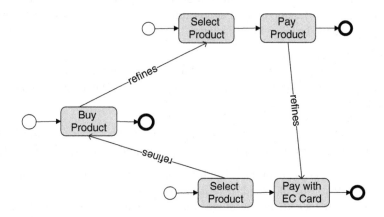

Fig. 10.6 Process-based and function-based action refinement

Fig. 10.7 An incorrect refinement chain

- For all abstract activities, A: $|\text{ground}^{-1}(A)| = 1 \vee |\text{ground}^{-1}(A)| = 0$
- If $\text{ground}(A)$ is defined then $\text{ground}(A)$ is an activity of a component model
- Activities of component models are not allowed to be refined

Partiality of the refinement specifications is an elementary requirement, since developers should be able to validate refinements at any stage in the development process in order to avoid lately detected errors according to emerging deadlines. Consequently, any solution for the refinement problem should be able to deal with partial refinement information.

Additionally to the above constraints, there are also some constraints related to refinements and groundings at the same time:

- If $\text{orig}(A_1) = \text{orig}(A_2) = A$ with $A_1 \neq A_2$, then $\text{ground}(A) = $ undefined.
- If $\text{orig}(A_1) = A$ and $\text{ground}(A_1) = G_1$ and $\text{ground}(A) = G$, then $G = G_1$

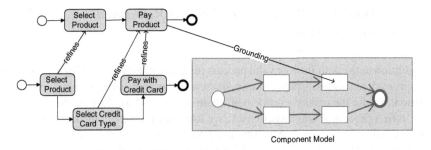

Fig. 10.8 An invalid grounding: grounded activities are not allowed to be further decomposed

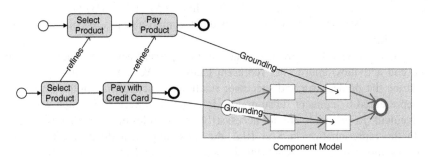

Fig. 10.9 An invalid grounding: identical refinements of grounded activities have to be grounded on the same service operations

The first constraint means that grounded activities are not allowed to be further decomposed. Consideration of (Fig. 10.8) reveals that further decomposition would lead to ambiguity. When a task is grounded, it means that it has been mapped to a concrete realisation through a service operation within a component model. So when it gets further decomposed, it will not be clear what the semantics behind the decomposition should be. Should all refining activities be grounded on the same service operation which leads to several invocations or should multiple executions be omitted?

If an activity is refined by only one identical activity within the specific process, then it has to be ensured that both activities in case of a grounding of the more abstract activities be grounded on the same service operation within the same component model (see Fig. 10.9)

10.3.3 Validating Parallel-Free Process Refinement with Ontology

In addition to the definition of valid process refinement, Ren et al. [176] also present an approach to validating process refinement with ontology and reasoning. From this section, we use the example refinement chain in Fig. 10.1 to illustrate this solution.

Given a process P and an activity a, we use A_P to represent the set of activities in P. Obviously, $a \in A_P$. Also, we use $PS_P(a)$ and $SS_P(a)$ to represent the set of direct predecessor activities and successor activities of a in P, respectively. Note that gateways are not included in the predecessor sets or successor sets. For example, in P_1 of Fig. 10.1, $PS_{P_1}(A) = \{Start, B\}$, $SS_{P_1}(A) = \{B, End\}$. Obviously, for any process P and its activity A, we have $PS_{P^D}(A) = PS_P(A) \cup \{A\}$ and $SS_{P^D}(A) = SS_P(A) \cup \{A\}$, where P^D is the decomposable process of P as defined in Definition 1.

Similar as Sect. 10.2, we use concepts to represent activities (including start and end activities) and do not represent gateways. We use *from* and *to* roles to describe the predecessor and successor relations of activities. Origin of activities is represented by concept subsumption. In contrast to Sect. 10.2, when validating refinement, *from* and *to* are not necessarily inverse roles of each other. Compared with the representation in Sect. 10.2, the most important difference is that the process models are not represented by a complex class expression but a set of axioms. Furthermore, pre-refinement process and post-refinement process use different representations. To facilitate the construction of ontology, four operators are defined to build concept expressions for abstract and specific process:

Definition 2. Let S a predecessors or successors set; we define four operators for translations as follows:

- Pre-refinement-from operator $\mathbf{Pr}_{from}(S) = \forall \, from. \bigsqcup_{x \in S} x.$
- Pre-refinement-to operator $\mathbf{Pr}_{to}(S) = \forall \, to. \bigsqcup_{y \in S} y.$
- Post-refinement-from operator $\mathbf{Ps}_{from}(S) = \bigsqcap_{x \in S} \exists \, from.x.$
- Post-refinement-to operator $\mathbf{Ps}_{to}(S) = \bigsqcap_{y \in S} \exists \, to.y.$

In the pre-refinement operators, constructor $\forall$ are used because they should represent all possible executions that are allowed by the abstract process. In the post-refinement operators, constructor $\exists$ are used because they represent the actual executions that are specified in the specific process.

For a set of concepts $A_1, A_2, \ldots, A_n$, if $A_i \sqcap A_j \sqsubseteq \bot$ for very $1 \leq i, j \leq n$ and $i \neq j$, then we say that they are mutually disjoint with each other, denoted by $Disjoint(A_1, A_2, \ldots, A_n)$.

Now, we can represent refinements by ontologies. For conciseness of presentation, we always have one abstract process P and one specific process Q, and both P and Q are parallel-free. Let Z of P be an activity being refined. Simultaneous refinement of multiple activities can be done in a similar manner of single refinement. Then, we construct an ontology $\mathcal{O}_{P\to Q}$ with the following patterns. Examples w.r.t. the refinement from P_1 to P_2 in Fig. 10.1 are given to explain each pattern:

1. For each $a \in A_Q$ and $orig(a) = Z$, $a \sqsubseteq Z$
   These axioms represent the composition of activities with concept subsumption, which realise **Projection**. For example, $A_1 \sqsubseteq A$ and $B_2 \sqsubseteq B$
2. For each $Y \in \{Start, End\}$. $Y \sqsubseteq \mathbf{Pr}_{from}(PS_P(Y))$, $Y \sqsubseteq \mathbf{Pr}_{to}(SS_P(Y))$.
   These axioms represent the predecessor and successor sets of all the non-decomposable activities in the abstract process. For example, $Start \sqsubseteq \forall to.A$, $End \sqsubseteq \forall from.A$.
3. For $A \in A_P \setminus \{Start, End\}$, $A \sqsubseteq \mathbf{Pr}_{from}(PS_P(A) \cup \{A\})$, $A \sqsubseteq \mathbf{Pr}_{to}(SS_P(A) \cup \{A\})$.
   These axioms represent the predecessor and successor sets of all the decomposable activities in the pre-refinement process. Due to the decomposable process, we add A to its predecessor and successor sets. For example, $A \sqsubseteq \forall from.(Start \sqcup A \sqcup B)$, $A \sqsubseteq \forall to.(End \sqcup B \sqcup A)$, $B \sqsubseteq \forall from.(B \sqcup A)$, $B \sqsubseteq \forall to.(A \sqcup B)$. From the examples, we can see that loops can be easily handled.
4. For each $a \in A_Q$, $a \sqsubseteq \mathbf{Ps}_{from}(PS_Q(a))$, $a \sqsubseteq \mathbf{Ps}_{to}(SS_Q(a))$.
   These axioms represent the predecessor and successor sets of all the activities in the specific process. For example, $A_2 \sqsubseteq \exists from.A_1$, $B_2 \sqsubseteq \exists to.A_2 \sqcap \exists to.B_1$, etc.
5. $Disjoint(a \mid a \in A_Q$ and $orig(a) = Z)$
   These axioms represent the uniqueness of all the sibling activities refined from the same Z. For example, $Disjoint(A_1, A_2)$
6. $Disjoint(a \mid a \in A_P)$.
   This axiom represents the uniqueness of all the activities before refinement. For example, $Disjoint(Start, End, A, B)$.

With the above axioms, ontology $\mathcal{O}_{P\to Q}$ is a representation of the refinement from P to Q by describing the predecessor and successor sets of corresponding activities with axioms. The number of axioms is linear w.r.t. the size of P and Q. The language is $\mathcal{ALC}$.

In ontology $\mathcal{O}_{P\to Q}$, all the activities in Q satisfy the ordering relations in P^D by satisfying the universal restrictions ($\forall$) and satisfy the ordering relations in Q by satisfying existential restrictions ($\exists$). Given the uniqueness of concepts, the inconsistency between P^D and Q will lead particular concepts to be unsatisfiable. Theorem 1 shows that parallel-free refinement from P to Q can be validated by unsatisfiability checking of all the atomic concepts in ontology $\mathcal{O}_{P\to Q}$. For proof, we refer the readers to [176]:

Theorem 1. *Given a parallel-free refinement from P to Q, the refinement is invalid, iff there exists $a \in A_Q$ such that $\mathcal{O}_{P\to Q} \models a \sqsubseteq \bot$.*

For example, in the refinement from P_1 to P_2, no activity is unsatisfiable; thus, we know that it is a valid refinement. In later sections, we will have examples of invalid refinement as well. Thus, the process engineers can modify the refinement accordingly to make it valid.

The above solution has the following restrictions:

1. The type of refinement is restricted to parallel-free.
2. Although the correctness of refinement can be validated, it is not clear why a wrong refinement is incorrect.
3. According to the DL profile, the reasoning complexity for unsatisfiability checking in DL $\mathcal{ALC}$ is EXPTIME-Complete. This is intractable in practice.

In later sections, we will address all these issues with model transformation and reasoning.

10.3.4 Extending Specific Process with Parallel Gateways

In this section, we extend the parallel-free approach to capture parallel branches in the specific process. We still assume that the abstract process has no parallel branches, and we use the refinement from P_2 to P_3 in Fig. 10.1 as an example.

In general, processes with parallel branches implicitly describe different possible executions. For instance, in P_3 of Fig. 10.1, there are two parallel branches and each of them contains one activity (A_{22} and B_{21}). The implicit executions of the parallel sibling activities A_{22} and B_{21} are $[A_{22}B_{21}]$ and $[B_{21}A_{22}]$, i.e. either activity A_{22} is executed before B_{21} or B_{21} before A_{22}. For the refinement validation, we have to take into account all these implicit executions of parallel branches. It is easy to see in the example that activities in parallel sibling branches might occur in an arbitrary order. Therefore, for each activity of a parallel branch, all other activities of sibling branches can be predecessors as well as successors. For instance, A_{22} is the predecessor of B_{21} in one execution and the successor of B_{21} in another execution. It's natural to assume that such property should also be satisfied by their origins if the refinement is valid. In the example of Fig. 10.1, this is actually the case. Particularly, $orig(A_{22}) = A_2$, $orig(B_{21}) = B_2$, $A_2 \in PS_P(B_2) = \{B_1, A_2\}$, $A_2 \in SS_P(B_2) = \{B_1, A_2\}$, $B_2 \in PS_P(A_2) = \{B_1, B_2\}$ and $B_2 \in SS_P(A_2) = \{B_1, B_2\}$.

Based on this observation, we can replace parallel gateways in the specific process by exclusive gateways and edges between all parallel activities. For example, the P_3 in Fig. 10.1 can be replaced by the following process models (Fig. 10.10).

As we can easily see from the figure, the parallel gateway containing A_{22} and B_{21} has been replaced by an exclusive gateway in which A_{22} and B_{21} are both predecessor and successor of each other. We call this process P_3^R. Although structurally different, P_3^R makes all the implicit predecessor and successor relations in P_3 explicit. Thus, it can be used to represent P_3 in refinement validation. That is to say, P_3 is a valid refinement of P_2 iff P_3^R is a valid refinement of P_2. In [176], it has been proved that such a replacement is sound and complete in general case, i.e. a process Q is a valid refinement of a parallel-free process P iff Q^R is a valid refinement of P.

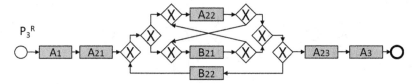

Fig. 10.10 P_3^R: Replaced process P_3

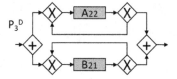

Fig. 10.11 Parallel gateway in decomposed P_3^D

By doing such a replacement, a refinement problem with parallel-gateways in its specific process can be reduced to a parallel-free refinement problem, which can be solved by the solution we proposed in the last section.

10.3.5   Extending Abstract Process with Parallel Gateways

In this section, we further extend the solution to handle more complicated refinement checkings in which the abstract process contains parallel gateways. We use the refinement from P_3 to P_4 in Fig. 10.1 as an example to demonstrate the problem and our solution.

For example, in Fig. 10.1, the activities A_{22} and B_{21} of process P_3 are in parallel. According to the decomposition transformation, P_3^D should contain the following parallel gateway (Fig. 10.11), in which A_{22} and B_{21} are surrounded by their loops.

According to the execution set semantics, one can first execute A_{22}, then before finishing A_{22}, one can turn to execute B_{21} and after finishing B_{21} come back and finish executing A_{22} and so on and so forth. This actually indicates that the ordering relations between components of A_{22} and B_{21}, e.g., A_{221}, B_{211}, etc., in P_4, do not affect the validity of refinement from P_3 to P_4. So the sibling parallel activities A_{22} and B_{21} can be regarded as "transparent" to each other in refinement checking. Therefore, we can reduce the original refinement problem into the two refinement sub-problems in Fig. 10.12.

In the first one, A_{22} is removed from P_3 and its components are removed from P_4 so that the ordering relations between B_{21} components and other activities can be checked. In the second one, B_{21} is removed from P_3, and its components are removed from P_4 so that the ordering relation between A_{22} components and other

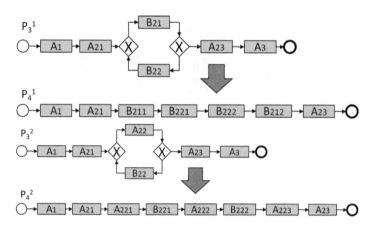

Fig. 10.12 Parallel branch break-down

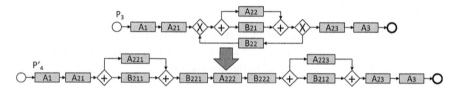

Fig. 10.13 Repaired refinement from P_3 to P_4'

activities can be checked. We call such a transformation a parallel branch break-down.

Obviously, the two sub-problems are both parallel-free. Thus, we can easily check the validity of them. By applying the techniques we developed in earlier sections, we immediately know that both of them are invalid, due to the absence of A_3 in the specific processes. Thus, the original refinement from P_3 to P_4 is also invalid.

By noticing this, an engineer can, e.g. add A_3 back to P_4. And we will have the following repaired refinement (Fig. 10.13).

However, the parallel gateways within a loop are still a problem. Considering the above repaired refinement, applying the parallel branch breaking-down technique will show that sub-problems are all valid refinements. However, the refinement in Fig. 10.13 is still invalid because of the subsequence $[B_{221}, A_{222}, B_{222}]$ in the specific process P_4'. If we compare this execution with the executions given by the abstract process, we observe that between each two executions of the activity B_{22}, there must be execution of both parallel A_{22} and B_{21}, or none of them, but between B_{221} and B_{222}, there is only one execution of A_{222} but not any decomposition of B_{21}.

In order to tackle this problem, we can further break down loop branches and generate a third sub-problem refinement as follows (Fig. 10.14):

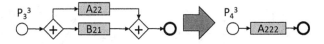

Fig. 10.14 Loop branch break-down

This sub-problem checks whether there is a valid refinement of the parallel A_{22} and B_{21} between the two components of B_{22} in P_4'. It contains a parallel gateway in the abstract process. After applying the parallel branch break-down technique, we can easily discover that this is a invalid refinement. Thus, the refinement from P_3 to the repaired P_4' is still invalid. This reveals another reason for the invalid refinement from P_3 to P_4:

Combining the parallel branch break-down with the described break-down of loops for parallel gateways in abstract processes, the process refinement is valid if and only if the validation of the final parallel-free refinements are valid.

Together with reduction of parallel gateways in specific processes, we can now reduce any refinement problems into parallel-free refinement sub-problems.

10.3.6 Validating Grounding with Ontology

In this section, we show how to use ontology technologies to automatically validate process grounding.

According to the definition of correct grounding (Sect. 10.3.1) we know that a correct grounding implies the subsumption relation between two execution sets after performing projection and reduction. We use $Ground(ES_Q)$ to denote the results of replacing all activities in each execution of ES_Q by their grounding activity in P, and use $ES_Q^{\backslash P}$ to denote the results of removing all activities in each execution of ES_Q that do not appear in P. Then by definition, a process P is a correct grounding of a process Q iff $Ground(ES_Q)^{\backslash P} \subseteq ES_P$. We use $Q^{\backslash P}$ to denote the results of replacing all activities in Q that do not appear in P with a direct edge. It has been shown in [176] that for a process Q grounded to process P, $Ground(ES_Q)^{\backslash P} \subseteq ES_P$ iff $Ground(ES_{Q^{\backslash P}}) \subseteq ES_P$.

This indicates that a grounding validation problem can be reduce to a simpler problem in which the grounded process contains only activities whose grounding are in the component behaviour model (CMP). For example, the grounding from Fig. 10.2b–d can be reduced to the two problems in Fig. 10.15, in which the thicker arrows indicate the ground() relations. The original grounding is valid iff the two groundings in Fig. 10.15 are valid.

After such reduction, we can apply the similar technique of parallel breaking down as we did in refinement validation (Sect. 10.3.5). For example, the grounding between P_{C2} and P_{S2} in Fig. 10.15 can be broken down into the 3 sub-problems illustrated in Fig. 10.16. Obviously, the grounding between P_{C2} and P_{S2} is valid *iff* the above three groundings are valid.

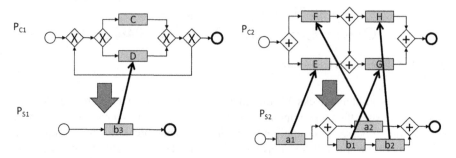

Fig. 10.15 Reduced grounding problems

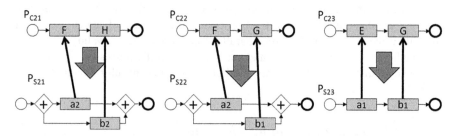

Fig. 10.16 Parallel branch break-down of grounding problem

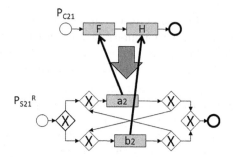

Fig. 10.17 P_{S21}^{R}: Replaced process P_{S21}

After such breaking down, the CMPs become parallel-free but the specific processes P_{S21} and P_{S22} still contain parallel gateway. Again, we can apply the similar technique for refinement validation introduced in Sect. 10.3.4. For example, the P_{S21} in Fig. 10.16 can be replaced by the process illustrated in Fig. 10.17. The grounding between P_{C21} and P_{S21} is valid *iff* the grounding between P_{C21} and P_{S21}^{R} is valid.

Applying the similar technique to P_{S22} we will eventually reduce the original grounding problem into several parallel-free grounding sub-problems. These parallel-free sub-problems can again be solved with similar technique for parallel-free refinement checking, except that no decomposition is needed.

Suppose we have one CMP P and one process Q, both P and Q are parallel-free. Without loss of generality, we can safely assume all activities in Q are grounded to some activity in P. Then, we construct an ontology $\mathcal{O}_{P \leftarrow Q}$ with the following patterns. Examples w.r.t. the grounding from P_{C21} in Fig. 10.16 to P_{S21}^R in Fig. 10.17 are given to explain each pattern:

1. For each $a \in A_Q$ and $ground(a) = Z$, $a \sqsubseteq Z$
   These axioms represent the grounding of activities with concept subsumption, which realise **Projection**. For example, $a_1 \sqsubseteq F$ and $b_2 \sqsubseteq H$.
2. For $A \in A_P$, $A \sqsubseteq \mathbf{Pr}_{from}(PS_P(A))$, $A \sqsubseteq \mathbf{Pr}_{to}(SS_P(A))$.
   These axioms represent the predecessor and successor sets of all the grounded activities in the CMP. Compared to item 3 in parallel-free refinement checking, we don't have A itself in the predecessor and successor sets because decomposition is not needed in grounding validation. For example, $F \sqsubseteq \forall from.Start$, $F \sqsubseteq \forall to.H$, $H \sqsubseteq \forall from.F$, $H \sqsubseteq \forall to.End$.
3. For each $a \in A_Q$, $a \sqsubseteq \mathbf{Ps}_{from}(PS_Q(a))$, $a \sqsubseteq \mathbf{Ps}_{to}(SS_Q(a))$.
   These axioms represent the predecessor and successor sets of all the activities in the grounding process. For example, $a_2 \sqsubseteq \exists from.Start \sqcap \exists from.b_2$, $b_2 \sqsubseteq \exists to.a_2 \sqcap \exists to.End$, etc.
4. $Disjoint(a \mid a \in A_Q$ and $ground(a) = Z)$
   These axioms represent the uniqueness of all the sibling activities grounding to the same Z. In our example, this is not needed as each the grounded activity has only one grounding activity.
5. $Disjoint(a \mid a \in A_P)$.
   This axiom represents the uniqueness of all the activities in the CBM. For example, $Disjoint(Start, End, F, H)$.

With the above axioms, ontology $\mathcal{O}_{P \leftarrow Q}$ is a representation of the grounding between P and Q by describing the predecessor and successor sets of corresponding activities with axioms. The number of axioms is linear w.r.t. the size of P and Q. The language is $\mathcal{ALC}$. The following Theorem 2 implies that parallel-free grounding from Q to P can be validated by unsatisfiability checking of all the named concepts in ontology $\mathcal{O}_{P \leftarrow Q}$. For proof, we refer readers to [176].

Theorem 2. *For any parallel free grounding from Q to P, the grounding is invalid, iff there exists $a \in A_Q$ such that $\mathcal{O}_{P \leftarrow Q} \models a \sqsubseteq \bot$.*

For example, in the grounding from P_{C21} to P_{S21}^R, a_2 is invalid because it can come from b_2 and/or go to End, and b_2 is invalid because it can come from $Start$ and/or go to a_2. Therefore the grounding is invalid. For similar reason, the grounding from P_{C22} to P_{S22} is also invalid. Eventually, we know that the original grounding is invalid.

It is apparent that the solution to grounding validation is quite similar to the solution of refinement validation. It also shares the same limitation of the refinement validation solution: difficult for users to discover the reason of incorrectness; and high worst-case computational complexity. In later sections, we will present our technologies to address these issues. We will only demonstrate with refinement checking. But the techniques can also be used in grounding checking.

10.3.7 Pinpointing and Explaining Sources of Invalidity with Ontology Reasoning

In the previous sections, we showed how to use ontology representation and reasoning technology to support validating process refinement with more and more complex process models. It is more interesting to find out where does invalidity come from and why. This involves two steps: (1) finding the source of invalidity and (2) explaining why the invalidity is derived. However, this is not supported by the solution presented in previous sections.

For example, in the running example in Fig. 10.1, we detected that in Sect. 10.3.5, the refinement from P_3 to P_4 is invalid. Manually checking would reveal that there are two sources of problems:

1. Between B_{221} and B_{222}, a component of B_{21} is missing.
2. After A_{23}, A_3 or its components are missing.

In any case, missing activities causes conflicts between universal restrictions and existential restrictions, leading to unsatisfiability of concepts. Taking the missing A_3 as an example:

Example 2. The absence of A_3 will be revealed by the following axioms:

1. $A_{23} \sqsubseteq \forall to.\{A_3 \sqcup A_{23}\}$ (pre-refinement successor set derived from P_3)
2. $A_{23} \sqsubseteq \exists to.End$ (post-refinement successor set derived from P_4)
3. $Disjoint(A_3, A_{23}, End, \ldots)$ (uniqueness of activities in P_3)

Obviously, from the above axioms, we can infer that $A_{23} \sqsubseteq \bot$.

However, due to other post-refinement successor set and predecessor set axioms, this unsatisfiability will be propagated to other activities. For example, with axiom $A_{223} \sqsubseteq \exists to.A_{23}$, A_{223} will be unsatisfiable although the refinement on A_{223} is correct. This makes it difficult to discover the real sources of invalid refinement. In this section, we extend the representation used in Sect. 10.3.3 to overcome this problem.

Previously in the pre-refinement process, the relations between an activity A, its predecessors $B_1, \ldots, B_n$ and its successors $C_1, \ldots, C_m$ are described by axioms of the following forms. If A is not decomposable:

$$A \sqsubseteq \forall from.(B_1 \sqcup \cdots \sqcup B_n)$$

$$A \sqsubseteq \forall to.(C_1 \sqcup \cdots \sqcup C_m).$$

If A is decomposable:

$$A \sqsubseteq \forall \mathit{from}.(A \sqcup B_1 \sqcup \cdots \sqcup B_n)$$

$$A \sqsubseteq \forall \mathit{to}.(A \sqcup C_1 \sqcup \cdots \sqcup C_m).$$

These are presented by steps 2 and 3 in Sect. 10.3.3.

Now, we introduce a concept *Invalid* to indicate source of invalidity and extend the above axiom into:

$$A \sqsubseteq \mathit{Invalid} \sqcup \forall \mathit{from}.(B_1 \sqcup \cdots \sqcup B_n)$$

$$A \sqsubseteq \mathit{Invalid} \sqcup \forall \mathit{to}.(C_1 \sqcup \cdots \sqcup C_m)$$

and

$$A \sqsubseteq \mathit{Invalid} \sqcup \forall \mathit{from}.(A \sqcup B_1 \sqcup \cdots \sqcup B_n)$$

$$A \sqsubseteq \mathit{Invalid} \sqcup \forall \mathit{to}.(A \sqcup C_1 \sqcup \cdots \sqcup C_m).$$

It's obvious that such extension does not change the expressive power and reasoning complexity of the ontology language.

With the above extension, a concept will be classified as subsumed by *Invalid* iff its predecessors or successors in pre- and post-refinement ontology do not match. They will not be classified as unsatisfiable. Hence, those valid ones will not be classified as unsatisfiable neither *Invalid* even if they are connected to some actually invalid ones:

Theorem 3. *Given a pre-refinement process P and a post-refinement process Q, let the extended refinement ontology be $O_{P \to Q}$, and then any activity a in Q is a wrong refinement w.r.t. its originator in P iff $O_{P \to Q} \models a \sqsubseteq \mathit{Invalid}$.*

This theorem shows that the subclasses of *Invalid* are sources of incorrect refinements. For proof we refer to [176]. Now, we revisit Example 2:

Example 3. With the above extensions, the absence of A_3 now will be revealed by the following axioms:

1. $A_{23} \sqsubseteq \mathit{Invalid} \sqcup \forall \mathit{to}.\{A_3 \sqcup A_{23}\}$ (extended with *Invalid* concept)
2. $A_{23} \sqsubseteq \exists \mathit{to}.End$
3. $\mathit{Disjoint}(A_3, A_{23}, End, \ldots)$

Obviously from the above axioms, we can infer that $A_{23} \sqsubseteq \mathit{Invalid}$.

Similarly, we will have $End \sqsubseteq \mathit{Invalid}$ because End is supposed to follow from A_3, but it directly follows from A_{23} in P_4.

Because $\exists \mathit{to}.\mathit{Invalid} \not\sqsubseteq \mathit{Invalid}$ and $\exists \mathit{from}.\mathit{Invalid} \not\sqsubseteq \mathit{Invalid}$, the invalidity of A_{23} and End will not be propagated to other activities.

Once we detect $A_{23} \sqsubseteq \mathit{Invalid}$, using the justification services (Sect. 5.2.1), we can obtain the minimal set of axioms responsible for this subsumption. Actually, the justification is the axioms in Example 3.

Because every axiom in the refinement ontology is transformed from certain facts in the refinement scenario, we can reverse-transform the justification axioms to provide a user-friendly explanation to the incorrect refinement. For example, one explanation for the incorrect refinement from P_3 to P_4 is that "A_{23} should only go to A_3 or itself, but in P_4 it actually goes to End, which is different from both A_{23} and A_3"..

10.3.8 Efficient Refinement Validation with Approximate Ontology Reasoning

So far, we have reduced the validation of process refinement into subsumption checking in DL $\mathcal{ALC}$. According to Chap. 3, the reasoning complexity of $\mathcal{ALC}$ is EXPTIME-Complete. This is quite expensive when used in real-time applications, e.g. the guidance system, as we will introduce in Chap. 13. In this section, we show that the syntactic approximation introduced in Sect. 5.1.4 can be applied to reduce complexity to PTIME-Complete while preserving the completeness and soundness of solutions.

Because the refinement ontology contains no cardinality restriction, we approximate refinement ontology introduced in Sects. 10.3.3 and 10.3.7 as follows:

Definition 3 (Refinement Ontology Approximation). Given a refinement ontology $\mathcal{T}$ and a name assignment fn, its *Refinement Ontology Approximation* is $A_{fn,\mathcal{EL}_{\mathcal{CQI}}^{++}}(\mathcal{T})$. fn is a name assignment defined in Definition 3 of Sect. 5.1.4. $A_{fn,\mathcal{EL}_{\mathcal{CQI}}^{++}}$ is the $\mathcal{EL}_{\mathcal{CQI}}^{++}$ approximation defined in Definition 4 of Sect. 5.1.4.

Applying the above definition, each type of axioms in a refinement ontology will be approximated as follows:

1. $a \sqsubseteq Z$ will remain the same
2. $Y \sqsubseteq Invalid \sqcup \mathbf{Pr}_{from}(PS_P(Y))$ will be approximated to:

   (a) $Y \sqsubseteq X_1$
   (b) $nX_1 \equiv nInvalid \sqcap X_2$
   (c) $X_2 \equiv \exists from.X_3$
   (d) $X_3 \equiv \displaystyle\prod_{B_i \in PS_P(Y)} nB_i$

   where X_1 is the name assigned to $Invalid \sqcup \mathbf{Pr}_{from}(PS_P(Y))$, nX_1 the name assigned to its complement, $nInvalid$ the name assigned to $\neg Invalid$, X_2 the name assigned to $\exists from. \displaystyle\prod_{B_i \in PS_P(Y)} \neg B_i$, X_3 the name assigned to $\displaystyle\prod_{B_i \in PS_P(Y)} \neg B_i$ and nB_i the name assigned to $\neg B_i$.

   $Y \sqsubseteq Invalid \sqcup \mathbf{Pr}_{to}(SS_P(Y))$ will be approximated in a similar way. Furthermore, the approximations for $Z \sqsubseteq Invlaid \sqcup \mathbf{Pr}_{from}(PS_P(Z) \cup \{Z\})$ and $Z \sqsubseteq Invalid \sqcup \mathbf{Pr}_{to}(SS_P(Z) \cup \{Z\})$ follow a similar pattern.

3. $a \sqsubseteq \mathbf{Ps}_{from}(PS_Q(a))$ will be approximated to $a \sqsubseteq \exists from.x$ for each $x \in PS_Q(a)$. $a \sqsubseteq \mathbf{Ps}_{to}(SS_Q(a))$ will be approximated in a similarly way.
4. $Disjoint(a_1, \ldots, a_n)$ will be approximated to $a_i \sqcap a_j \sqsubseteq \bot$ for each two $1 \leq i, j \leq n, i \neq j$.

Assuming $A_{fn.\mathcal{ELC}_{CQI}^{++}}(T) = (T, CT, QT, IT)$, then T should contain the above axioms, while CT should contain above pairs of complement concepts, i.e. $CT = \{(X_1, nX_1), (nX_1, X_1), (Invalid, nInvalid), (nInvalid, Invalid), (B_1, nB_1), (nB_1, B_1), \ldots\}$.

For example, the axioms in Example 3, which are responsible for the invalidity of A_{23}, will be approximated to the following axioms:

1. $A_{23} \sqsubseteq X_1$
2. $nX_1 \equiv nInvalid \sqcap X_2$
3. $X_2 \equiv \exists to.X_3$
4. $A_{23} \sqsubseteq \exists to.End$
5. $X_3 \equiv nA_3 \sqcap nA_{23}$
6. $A_3 \sqcap A_{23} \sqsubseteq \bot$
7. $A_3 \sqcap End \sqsubseteq \bot$
8. $A_{23} \sqcap End \sqsubseteq \bot$

Reasoning on refinement ontology approximation can be performed by **R1–R11** (Table 5.1) as presented in Sect. 5.1.4. This will not affect the soundness and completeness of refinement checking:

Theorem 4. *Given a refinement ontology T constructed as in Sects. 10.3.3 and 10.3.7, let its approximation $A_{fn.\mathcal{ELC}_{CQI}^{++}}(T) = (T, CT, QT, IT)$, then for each activity a in T, we have $T \models_{\mathcal{ALC}} a \sqsubseteq Invalid$ iff $(T, CT, QT, IT) \models a \sqsubseteq Invalid$. Entailment checking on $A_{fn.\mathcal{ELC}_{CQI}^{++}}(T) = (T, CT, QT, IT)$ is defined in Sect. 5.1.4.*

The proof of this theorem is trivial. For example, in the above approximated ontology, we can do reasoning as follows:

1. Normalising axiom 2, we will have $nInvalid \sqcap X_2 \sqsubseteq nX_1$.
2. Normalising axiom 5, we will have $nA_3 \sqcap nA_{23} \sqsubseteq X_3$.
3. From axiom 7, we know $End \sqsubseteq nA_3$. Similarly from axiom 8, we know $End \sqsubseteq nA_{23}$.
4. Together with $nA_3 \sqcap nA_{23} \sqsubseteq X_3$ we have $End \sqsubseteq X_3$.
5. Together with axioms 3 and 4 we know $A_{23} \sqsubseteq X_2$.
6. Together with axiom 1 and $nInvalid \sqcap X_2 \sqsubseteq nX_1$ we can infer that $A_{23} \sqsubseteq Invalid$.

As mentioned in [172] entailment checking on $\mathcal{ELC}_{CQI}^{++}$ approximation is tractable. Together with the above theorem, the identification of invalid activities in a refinement ontology can be accomplished in PTIME. As a consequence, the explanation of the invalidity can also be performed in PTIME, if we applied the algorithm presented in Sect. 5.2.2.

10.4 Reasoning for Process Guidance

In this section, we consider processes as workflows and show how to use ontology technologies to provide guidance information to engineers who are working in the workflow. To illustrate the idea, we use the process modelling and refinement as an example (Example 1). In this example, we set a scene in which engineers are modelling and refining process models, while our goal is to provide guidance services for such development process with ontologies and reasoning. For this purpose, the ontology representation and reasoning technologies will be different from the ones we used in previous sections.

10.4.1 Concepts and Knowledge Assets of a Modelling Scenario

There are several important notions in modelling procedures, such as artefact, task and role. We will revisit these notions later in Sect. 13.1.2 in which they are combined with the practice of developing a guidance engine. In this section, we investigate the logic aspect of process guidance and are mostly interested in capturing the semantics of the following notions:

1. *Tasks* of different types can be performed in a particular modelling environment, such as creating a model and remodelling a model, refining a model .
2. *Pre- and post- conditions* describe the prerequisites and effects of tasks of certain types. In legacy systems, they are usually described in natural languages. For example, the post-condition of creating a model is that a model is created.
3. *Artefacts* are the various entities that can be operated in the modelling environment. Usually, an artefact can be a model or its component.
4. *Roles* represent the types of logical user profiles of the modelling systems. A user can have multiple roles. A role can be played by multiple users.

The relations between tasks, conditions, artefacts and roles are also interesting. Generally speaking, the status of artefacts satisfies some pre-conditions, thus enables corresponding tasks. A task type can only be performed by certain roles. When a task is performed, its post-conditions will result in changes of artefacts. For example, the refinement relation between P_3 and P_4 invokes the "Validate Refinement" task. As we introduced earlier, this validation yields a negative answer, which calls another task "Remodel Process" and so on.

The guidance functionality should be designed and developed independently from concrete modelling scenarios. For a specific application, except for the above notions, the following knowledge assets have to be considered:

1. *Domain Meta-model* defines the syntax of the models and global constraints that are independent from concrete task types. For example, in process refinement, an activity can only be connected to another activity (including *Start* and *End*) or a gateway. Because in the modelling systems, concrete models are regarded as model instances, the meta-model actually corresponds to TBox in an ontology.
2. *Model Knowledge* is the concrete status of the models under development. Models in the guidance system can also be specified in ADOxx. In contrast to the meta-model, models correspond to the ABox of an ontology. Given the fact that models will be constantly changed during the development procedure, the ABox will also be frequently updated.
3. *Task Knowledge* characterises the pre-/post-conditions of specific task types. For example, a process should be refined or grounded when it contains activity not yet grounded or refined. This knowledge is the interaction between artefacts and task types; therefore, they cannot be solely defined in the meta-model.
4. *Role Knowledge* characterises the authorities of users over artefacts. For example, a grounding activity task can only be performed by the developer role. Similar as the task knowledge, role knowledge can not be solely defined in the meta-model.
5. *Queries* are used to retrieve tasks and artefacts. They should be designed in a way that they are as independent from concrete domains as possible.

The proper interpretation of task knowledge, role knowledge and their integration with meta-model/model is the major challenge of an ontology-guided modelling system.

For an application scenario, the above knowledge assets should be integrated into a generic guidance engine to form an dedicated system. In this section, we use process modelling and refinement as an example to illustrate the above notions in detail. Our focus will be knowledge about various task types.

The artefacts in this example include, among others, *Process*, *Activity*, *Component Model*, etc. The meta-model includes constraints such as "a process contains only activities (including start and end) and gateways". The task types include *Remodel Process*, *Refine Process*, *Ground Process*, etc. Knowledge about some typical tasks, their pre- and post-conditions and respective roles can be described in natural language as follows:

1. *Remodel Process*: an engineer can always remodel an existing process.
   Pre-condition: a process exists.
   Post-condition: the process is remodelled.
   Role: All roles are allowed to remodel their respective processes. These are: business expert, analyst, and developer.
2. *Refine Process*: when a process is neither refined nor grounded, the process needs to be refined by another process.

Pre-condition: a process neither refined nor grounded exists.

Post-condition: another process is created or referred to as the refinement of the current process.

Role: Analysts and developers are responsible for performing process refinements.

3. *Ground Process*: any process that can be refined can also be grounded to a CMP.

Pre-condition: a process neither refined nor grounded exists.

Post-condition: a CMP is created or referred to as the grounding of the current process.

Role: The grounding of processes is performed by a developer.

When a user is modelling processes, the system should automatically tell which task is available for which artefact. When the user performs a task and hence changes the models, task availability will also be updated accordingly.

In later sections, we first introduce the representation and retrieval of tasks w.r.t. their pre-conditions and post-conditions. Then, we extend our solution with knowledge about roles. At the end, we present the generalised solution and discuss its computational property.

10.4.2 Formalising Guidance Knowledge into Ontologies

In the specification of example, the pre- and post- conditions of a task and performing roles are described in natural language. However, a machine-readable specification requires representation in a formal language. In this section, we use an ontology to represent the knowledge.

Domain Ontology: Meta-model and Model

Intuitively, various artefacts can be categorised into concepts such as *Process*, *Activity* and *ComponentBehaviorModel*. These concepts have a common super concept *artefact*. The relations between these concepts are modelled as object properties. We call such an ontology the domain ontology. The domain ontology is usually generated out of a modelling environment. There, the meta-model(the language) defines the basic concepts and relationships used to describe a domain, whereas the model, which conforms to the defined metamodel, describes specific domain. In our case, the meta-model describes the BPMN language for modelling processes, and the model, e.g. "'Hiring Process'" describes the concrete process in the domain. Having said that, the TBox corresponds to the meta-model, whereas the ABox corresponds to the models of the domain. However, as we will show, domain ontology has little influence on the inference mechanism of tasks, so we can regard them as separate.

Task Ontology

Various tasks can be categorised into concepts such as *RefineProcess* and *GroundProcess* . These task types have a common super type *Task*. Once a task is performed, Task ontology ABox will be updated.

The pre-conditions of a task type can be described by axioms. For example, when a process is **NOT** refined or grounded, it should be refined or grounded. This actually implies that **EVERY** process should be refined or grounded, to either an existing process/CMP, or an implicit one. The former implies that a **Refine Process** or **Ground Process** task has already been performed. The latter implies that a **Refine Process** or **Ground Process** tasks has to be performed. Therefore, the existence of a process actually becomes the pre-condition of a **Refine Process** or **Ground Process** task.

However, the disjunction implies that neither **Refine Process** nor **Ground Process** is really **compulsory** for processes, but **Refine or Ground Process** is. We call these two *Alternative Tasks*. If we query for one of a set of alternative tasks, the ontology will not infer its necessity. We have to query for all of them. To solve this problem, we introduce a new task type *RefineOrGroundProcess* as the super-concept of both *RefineProcess* and *GroundProcess*. Of course, *RefineOrGroundProcess* will also be a sub-concept of *Task*. We can model such semantics with an axiom in Manchester syntax [97] as follows:

$$SubClassOf : \ Process, \ preconditionOf \ some \ RefineOrGroundProcess$$

Once a task of *RefineOrGroundProcess* is found to be needed, we shall generate two tasks *RefineProcess* and *GroundProcess* to be displayed for the user. This means *RefineOrGroundProcess* will not have direct instances. Once a *RefineProcess* or *GroundProcess* task is performed on an artefact, a *RefineOrGroundProcess* is regarded as performed because an instance of *RefineProcess* or *GroundProcess* is also an instance of *RefineOrGroundProcess*.

Regarding post-conditions, the effect of the task is the creation of another process or CMP. Thus, the existence of such a process or CMP actually becomes the post-condition of the task that is either performed or to be performed. Because *RefineOrGroundProcess* is an "abstract" task type, we only model the postcondition for *RefineProcess* and *GroundProcess*:

$$SubClassOf : \ RefineProcess, \ hasPostcondition \ some \ Process$$

$$SubClassOf : \ GroundProcess, \ hasPostcondition \ some \ ComponentBehaviorModel$$

Similarly, we will have **Remodel Process:**

$$SubClassOf : \ Process, \ preconditionOf \ some \ RemodelProcess$$

$$SubClassOf : \ RemodelProcess, \ hasPostcondition \ some \ Process$$

Roles in the task ontology can be described in a similar fashion using axioms. For each role, we should specify its role type. And for each role type, we can say which task types can be performed by it. For example, the role **analyst** can perform task types **Remodel Process** and **Refine Process**. Assuming we have two analysts $a1$ and $a2$ in the current development environment, we can model such constraints with axioms in Manchester syntax as follows:

$$Types : \ a1, \ Analyst$$

$$Types : \ a2, \ Analyst$$

$$SubClassOf : \ Analyst, \ perform \ some \ RemodelProcess$$

$$SubClassOf : \ Analyst, \ perform \ some \ RefineProcess$$

From these axioms, we can generalise the formalisation patterns as:

$$SubClassOf : \ [Artefact], \ preconditionOf \ some \ [Task]$$

$$SubClassOf : \ [Task], \ hasPostcondition \ some \ [Artefact]$$

$$SubClassOf : \ [Role], \ performe \ some \ [Task]$$

where $Task$ is a concrete type of task (or the super type of alternatives), $Artefact$ is a concrete type of artefact and $Role$ is a concrete type of role in the development process. Obviously, one artefact type can be pre-condition of multiple task types.

As we can see, these three patterns are independent from concrete task types, concrete role types and even concrete domains. This implies that we can also design generic patterns to retrieve tasks regardless of which type or domain it is.

10.4.3   Retrieving Tasks by Query Answering

Once we generate the domain ontology and task ontology by the axioms presented in the previous section, we can use a reasoner to automatically retrieve the tasks. Intuitively, this can be performed by querying the artefacts on which certain task types should or could be performed. For example, if we propose the following query:

$$?x \leftarrow ?x : Artefact, (?x, ?y) : preconditionOf, ?y : RemodelProcess$$

to a query engine, it will return all artefacts $?x$ such that there exists some instance of $RemodelProcess$ $?y$ of which $?x$ is the pre-condition. This literally presents all the processes that can be remodelled.

However, this query can not yet be generalised to other task types. For example, if we use the similar query for $RefineOrGroundProcess$ task, the results will include the processes that have already been refined or grounded. These redundancies are due to the fact that there are actually two categories of tasks:

1. *Compulsory Task*: a task that must be performed. Once performed, it is not necessary to perform it again. Task types such as **Refine Process** and **Ground Process** belong to this category.
2. *Optional Task*: a task that could be performed. Once performed, it can still be performed again. Task types such as **Remodel Process** belong to this category.

Optional tasks can use the similar query pattern presented above. The presented compulsory tasks should only contain tasks that have not been performed yet, i.e. the **implicit** instances of tasks. They can be obtained by subtracting the performed ones from the whole set. Taking *RefineOrGroundProcess* as an example, we propose the following two queries:

$$?x \leftarrow ?x : Artefact, (?x, ?y) : preconditionOf, ?y : RefineOrGroundProcess$$

$$?x, ?y \leftarrow ?x : Artefact, (?x, ?y) : preconditionOf, ?y : RefineOrGroundProcess$$

in which the first query returns all the processes that should be refined or grounded and the second query returns all the processes that have been refined or grounded, together with the corresponding tasks. The difference of the two will be the processes on which *RefineOrGroundProcess* must be performed. Therefore, the redundancy of compulsory tasks is resolved.

In order to distinguish the compulsory tasks and the optional tasks we introduce two concepts *CompulsoryTask* and *OptionalConcept* as the sub-concepts of *Task* and super-concepts of all the compulsory tasks and optional tasks, respectively. Then, the query can be generalised as follows:

1. For each direct sub-concept T of *OptionalTask*, propose query.

$$?x \leftarrow ?x : Artefact, (?x, ?y) : preconditionOf, ?y : T.$$

The solution will be the artefacts on which task type T could be performed.
2. For each direct sub-concept T of *CompulsoryTask*, propose two queries

$$?x \leftarrow ?x : Artefact, (?x, ?y) : preconditionOf, ?y : T$$

$$?x, ?y \leftarrow ?x : Artefact, (?x, ?y) : preconditionOf, ?y : T.$$

The difference of solution $?x$ will be the artefacts on which task type T should be performed. Note that individual alternative concepts will not be tested, but their common super-concept will be. Due to the introduction of common super-concepts for alternative concepts, T needs to be translated before presented to user.

After obtaining the available task types and corresponding artefacts, we can report these results to users. As we mentioned before, the returned results of task types such as *RefineOrGroundProcess* should be their sub-concepts, i.e. the alternative task types *RefineProcess* and *GroundProcess*.

In order to consider the roles while querying for tasks, we need to extend the generalised queries to get the roles. For each **returned task type** T and each concrete role type R, we generate the following query:

$$?x \leftarrow ?x : R, (?x, ?y) : perform, ?y : T.$$

The solution will be the roles of type R which can perform task type T. It is important to query with the return task type; otherwise, the results could be incorrect. For example, if a user wants to find a role to perform *GroundProcess* but queries for *RefineOrGroundProcess*, the reasoner will return roles of both *Analyst* and *Developer* because roles of *Analyst* can perform *RefineProcess*; thus, they are also capable of *RefineOrGroundProcess*. But they cannot really perform *GroundProcess*.

10.4.4 Generalised Solution for Representation and Retrieval

Now we summarise the above findings to provide a generalised solution:

- Defining the domain ontology.
- For alternative tasks, introducing common super task type.
- Categorising compulsory and optional tasks.
- For each type of compulsory task, posing two queries and getting the difference to retrieve the artefacts to which such type of task is necessary.
- For each type of optional task, posing one query to retrieve the artefacts on which such type of task can be performed.
- Translating the query results to generate the task list.
- For each returned task type and each concrete role type, posing one query to retrieve the roles of the certain type that can perform the task.
- Return all results to users.
- Updating the ABox with the relations of artefacts and tasks such that compulsory tasks will not be repeated.

As we can see, the above solution is independent from the concrete task types and even application scenarios; thus, it can be generalised. Actually, when applied to different domains, the system only needs to load the domain ontology, task ontology and role Ontology, and then generate queries on the available task types.

10.4.5 Computational Properties

We first review the language needed. There are two major types of axioms: one for pre-conditions and the other for post-conditions. They are both within the expressive power of OWL 2 EL, especially considering that disjunction of task types must be resolved.

The reasoning services requested include both TBox classification and conjunctive query answering. In order to present a generic solution for guidance, it is necessary to automatically detect all the concrete compulsory task types and optional task types instead of hard-coding them into queries. This can be easily realised by getting all the direct-subconcepts of *CompulsoryTask* and *OptionalTask*, which is a service provided by TBox classification.

When processing the queries, especially the first query of compulsory task, the query of optional task and query for roles, it is important to notice that the variable $?y$ is not returned. This implies that $?y$ is a non-distinguished variable, which can be bound to either an existing individual, or an implicit individual. In terms of ontology reasoning, this arises the requirement of query answering under open world asssumption (OWA). Query answering with non-distinguished variables is an open issue for expressive DLs. And it is even proved that query answering in arbitrary $\mathcal{EL}^+$ ontology is already undecidable [121]. However, we restrict the task ontology to be regular [121], for which query answering algorithm and implementation has already been developed [225]. Also, in the current example, the query can be rewritten into a instance retrieval of, e.g. *preconditionOf some RemodelProcess*.

10.5 Conclusion

In this chapter, we have shown how to use ontology and reasoning technologies to address the problems of process retrieval, refinement checking and guidance. As the content suggested, for different problems, the ontological representation of the process models can be different and such differences lead to the diversities of reasoning technologies and complexities. Particularly, in process retrieval (Sect. 10.2), we focus on the characterisation of individual process models. We use complex concept expressions to represent process models, and a query is also formalised as a concept definition such that all process models that satisfy the query conditions will be inferred as sub-concepts of the query concept. In process refinement checking (Sect. 10.3), we focus on the relations between two processes and their activities. We use an ontology TBox to represent the refinement from an abstract process to a specific process. Reasoning services can thus be employed to check if the refinement is valid, or even pinpoint the source of problems (Sect. 10.3.7). In process guidance (Sect. 10.4), we focus on the interactive and dynamic nature of workflows. We represent the key questions in process guidance as monitoring queries and use the query results to assist engineers.

These diversities ensure that for a certain problem, more optimised solution can be developed. For example, in process refinement checking, the ontology language used corresponds to description logic $\mathcal{ALC}$. However, its limited forms of axioms enable application of the syntactic approximation technology, reducing the complexity of solution to polynomial time with soundness and completeness guaranteed. While in the process guidance use case, with careful design of the axioms of the guidance models, the generated ontology can be restricted to be in tractable language OWL2 EL.

In the future, it will be interesting to extend the solutions to support more process features, and to investigate a potential unified solution to cover all these problems.

This chapter concludes Part III. In the next part, we will show how to integrate scalable reasoning infrastructure such as TrOWL (cf. Chap. 5) in an ODSD platform, so as to provide guidance services for ODSD.

Part IV
Ontology-Driven Software Development (ODSD) with Process Guidance

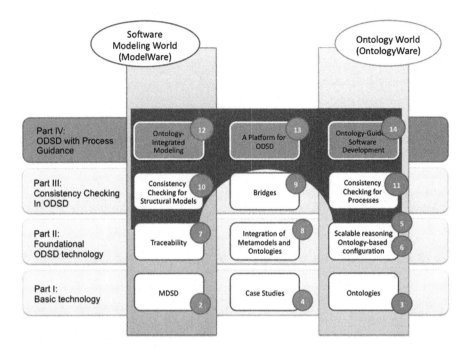

Fig. RoadMap.4 The roadmap of Part IV

We could mess around all day talking about the theory of ODSD, but that won't help us pay the bills. So, let's put our hands onto something concrete.

The final part of this book binds all the previous parts together. Chapter 11 presents an ontology-driven metamodelling approach to incremental, interactive consistency checking for DSL (domain-specific language) editors, applicable to all DSLs. Chapter 12 presents the MOST workbench, the first platform for ODSD, which can be controlled by a process engine based on process guidance ontologies (Chap. 13). The engine presents to a programmer the next task on the agenda, based on ontological knowledge of the software process.

Part IV contains following chapters:

Chapter 11 Ontology-Driven Metamodelling for Ontology-Integrated Modelling
Chapter 12 A Platform for ODSD: The MOST Workbench
Chapter 13 Ontology-Guided Software Engineering in the MOST Workbench

Chapter 11
Ontology-Driven Metamodelling
for Ontology-Integrated Modelling(*)

Uwe Aßmann, Jürgen Ebert, Tobias Walter, and Christian Wende

Abstract In this chapter, we continue the discussion on metamodelling (cf. Chap 7) and on how it can be useful for ontology-integrated modelling (OIM) in the ODSD infrastructure. It shows how an M3 integration bridge (cf. Chap. 8) can be employed to enable ontology-driven metamodelling (ODMM), which is meant to provide a sound base and appropriate tooling to support language engineers in the design phase of ontology-integrated structural modelling languages.

From the perspective of language users, the resulting languages share the qualities and benefits of the languages introduced in Chap. 9. Scalable ontology reasoning (cf. Chap. 5) run silently in the background, but provides consistency and guidance during all editing and modelling steps nevertheless. We call this systematic semantic support for language users *OIM*.

The rest of the chapter is organised as follows. In Sect. 11.1, we not only discuss the design of an M3 ontology integration bridge at M3 to provide ODMM but also show how an exemplary language built with ODMM supports OIM. In Sect. 11.2, we introduce OWLText, a tool that provides means for applying ODMM in the development of textual DSL. It uses a double language bridge between the technical spaces grammar world, metamodelling world, and ontology world.

11.1 Reasoning for Language Engineering and Use

In this section, we discuss how to bridge the ontology world and the modelling world at the M3. In particular, we show how language engineers can restrict the abstract syntax of structural modelling languages by the use of an ODMM approach. The challenge is to formally define language metamodels with integrated ontology-based axioms and expressions that allow for reasoning on the metamodel itself and all conforming models. Furthermore, we discuss how ontology reasoning

J.Z. Pan et al. (eds.), *Ontology-Driven Software Development*,
DOI 10.1007/978-3-642-31226-7_11, © Springer-Verlag Berlin Heidelberg 2013

can then be employed to provide OIM when using the language developed with ODMM to build models.

In recent works (e.g. [213, 214]) we experienced using ontology reasoning for engineering and for structural modelling languages. The approach is mainly enabled by combining a metamodelling language (e.g. Ecore, KM3) with the metamodel of an ontology language. Having an M3 integration bridge with the OWL metamodel, a language engineer is able, for example, to define formal well-formedness constraints based on OWL to restrict the use of concepts provided by the metamodel. The metamodel and conforming models are transformed to an ontology representation for reasoning on the structure of models that is prescribed by the language metamodel (and additional well-formedness constraints).

11.1.1 Defining an M3 Integration Bridge

As a bridge for structural modelling, we propose an M3 integration bridge. The bridge is defined at the M3 layer by an integration of a metamodelling language and ontology language (cf. Fig. 11.1). To integrate different languages, their metamodels are combined by first combining the sets of classes and associations and by subclassing classes or merging two classes.

We designed an M3 integration bridge where the metamodelling language Ecore is combined with the OWL2 metamodel. Thus, we can provide a new metamodelling language which allows for integrated modelling of both KM3-based metamodels and OWL ontologies. The integrated metamodels use KM3 [107] (KernelMetaMetaModel)—an implementation of Ecore that provides a textual concrete syntax to implement metamodels in textual editors. An overview of bridge definition and use is depicted in Fig. 11.1. The bridge itself is used at the M2 layer. Here, the language designer is able to define constraints and expressions within his metamodel to formally define the abstract syntax of a new modelling language. The modelling language itself is used at the M1 layer. The constraints and expressions restrict the creation of domain models which are instances of the metamodel.

In the following, we present some excerpts of the integrated M3 metamodelling language, which defines the abstract syntax for defining metamodels with integrated ontology annotations. Furthermore, we present some parts of the concrete syntax that are used by the language designer to implement metamodels. In this section, we use a textual syntax that is easy to implement, as an extension of the concrete syntax of KM3, and might increase productivity in coding metamodels. Thus, we give the idea of how to define such a syntax using *Extended BNF (EBNF)* grammar rules.

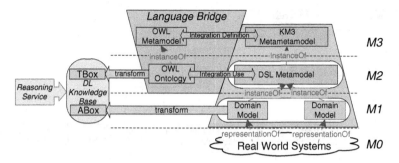

Fig. 11.1 M3 integration bridge between ecore (KM3) and OWL 2

Abstract Syntax

The integrated M3 metamodelling language enables language designers to describe metamodels for structural modelling languages together with OWL annotations. Plain metamodelling languages allow only for specifying structural features of classes. The integration of the OWL metamodel contributes means for the use of OWL primitives to constraint these metamodels and to use sound and complete reasoning for consistency checking and preservation.

Our integration approach integrates corresponding classes of the OWL 2 meta-model and a plain metamodelling language (Ecore, KM3) and combines corresponding classes by creating a so-called TU-class (two uses class) which is a specialisation of both classes and, thus, inherits the properties of both.

Figure 11.2 depicts an excerpt of the integrated metamodelling language. Here, the central concepts are the **TUClass**, the **TUAttribute**, and the **TUReference**. **TUClass** is a specialisation of KM3 **Class** and **OWLClass** and inherits their properties. Using the TU-classes **TUAttribute** and **TUReference**, we connect OWL **DataProperty** with KM3 **Attribute** and OWL **ObjectProperty** with KM3 **Reference**, respectively. Using the TU-classes for references and attributes of KM3, we ensure that all instances have the properties of an OWL Object Property or OWL Data Property, respectively.

The integration between the plain metamodelling language and the OWL 2 metamodels is done by applying the class adapter design pattern [74] (for similarities between OWL and class-based modelling languages, see [192]; for integration methods of (meta-)modelling language and ontology languages, see [210, 211]).

Concrete Syntax

In the following, we present some parts of a concrete syntax which extends the one from KM3 [107]. In this section, we only want to give the idea of how to extend the KM3 syntax by OWL class axioms and object property axioms. Because the KM3

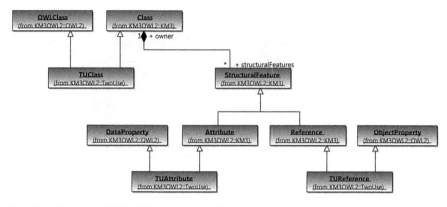

Fig. 11.2 Excerpt of KM3+OWL 2 metamodelling language (M3 layer)

concrete syntax is based on a grammar, in the following, we define rules in EBNF and give an example of how to use them to code metamodels.

OWL Class Axioms

The first line of Listing 11.1 shows rules for the definition of a class. Each class is optionally abstract, is defined by the keyword **class**, has a name and a list of super types. Between the curly brackets, a list of class features are defined such as attributes and references. In our special case, the grammar rule is extended by the new non-terminal **classAxioms** which optionally produces a list of OWL 2 class axioms (see Listing 11.1, line 2). The non-terminal **ClassAxiom** is used and is defined by an OWL 2 textual concrete syntax.

Listing 11.1 Adopting OWL Class Axioms

```
class = ["abstract"] "class" name [supertypes] [classAxioms] " { " features " } ";
classAxioms = ClassAxiom { " , " ClassAxiom};
```

Listing 11.2 presents an example of using OWL class axioms in combination with the declaration of classes in KM3. In line 1, the class **Configuration** is defined having a reference called **hasSlot** to a further class **Slot**. Line 4 depicts the head of the class **Configuration7603** which has the super type **Configuration** and thus inherits the feature **hasSlot**. After declaring the super types, the definition of an OWL class axiom follows. It defines that the class **Configuration7603** is equivalent with the anonymous OWL class **restrictionOn hasSlot with exactly 3 Slot**, the instances which are connected with exactly 3 further instances of type **Slot** using the **hasSlot** reference.

Listing 11.2 Example of using OWL Class Axioms (M2 layer)

```
class Configuration extends restrictionOn hasSlot with min 1 Slot {
  reference hasSlot [1−*]: Slot;
}
class Configuration7603 extends Configuration equivalentTo restrictionOn hasSlot with
```

```
exactly 3 Slot {
  }
```

Object Property Axioms

Listing 11.3 presents the grammar rules that adopt OWL object property axioms on references. A general reference feature in KM3 is declared by the keyword reference, a name, a multiplicity, the optional indication if the reference acts as a container, and a type where the reference points to. In addition to this declaration, we introduce the new non-terminal objectPropertyAxioms which is defined in line 2 of the Listing and produces a list of ObjectPropertyAxiom. Again, this non-terminal is defined in our OWL 2 natural style syntax. Thus, a list of OWL object property axioms can be appended to the declaration of KM3 references.

Listing 11.3 Adopting OWL Object Property Axioms

```
reference = "reference" name multiplicity isContainer " : " typeref "oppositeOf"
name [objectPropertyAxioms] " ; ";
objectPropertyAxioms = ObjectPropertyAxiom { " , " ObjectPropertyAxiom};
```

Listing 11.4 depicts an example of using OWL object property axioms together with the reference features of KM3. Here, the two classes Slot and its subclass Slot7609-2 are defined. Slot contains a reference called hasCard; Slot7609-2 contains a reference called hasInterfaceCard. hasCard points to elements of type Card; hasInterfaceCard points to elements of type CiscoInterface, a subclass of Card. Using OWL object property axioms, we state that hasInterfaceCard is a sub-property of hasCard. Thus, if an instance of CiscoInterface is connected via the reference hasInterface with some interface, we can infer that this instance is also connected via the reference hasCard with the interface instance. Thus, the restriction MinCardinality(1 hasCard) holds.

Listing 11.4 Example of using OWL Object Property Axioms (M2 layer)

```
class Slot equivalentTo restrictionOn hasCard with min 1 Card{
  reference hasCard [1−*]: Card;
}
class Slot7609−2 extends Slot{
  reference hasInterfaceCard [1−*]: CiscoInterface subpropertyOf hasCard;
}
```

11.1.2 Using an M3 Integration Bridge

In the following, we show how to adopt reasoning services on structural modelling languages. In particular, we consider languages for modelling physical devices. In the following, we exemplify the bridging approach which tackles the design and use of the *Physical Devices DSL (PDDSL)*. Further bridging approaches between configuration languages and ontology technologies can be found in [132].

Designing PDDSL

The development of PDDSL provides an example for ODMM that is enabled by the M3 integration bridge introduced previously. Listing 11.5 depicts an example of an integrated PDDSL language. Here, we define constraints and restrictions within the metamodel definition. PDDSL provides classes for modelling devices with configurations, slots and cards. To design the metamodel of PDDSL, we used the combined metamodelling language consisting of KM3+OWL. The metamodel represents the abstract syntax of the PDDSL as well as well-formedness constraints for the *M1 layer*. These additional constraints are useful to define the syntactic structure of the domain model at the M1 layer as well as to indicate constraints that apply at the level of the modelling language itself (M2 layer).

Listing 11.5 Example of defining an integrated metamodel for PDDSL

```
class Device {
  reference hasConfiguration [1−∗]: Configuration;
}
class Cisco7603 extends Device, equivalentWith restrictionOn hasConfiguration
with min 1 Configuration7603 {
}
class Configuration extends IntersectionOf(restrictionOn hasSlot with min 1
Slot, restrictionOn hasSlot with some restrictionOn hasCard with some
SuperVisor720){
  reference hasSlot : Slot;
}
class Configuration7603 extends Configuration, equivalentWith
IntersectionOf restrictionOn hasSlot with exactly 3 Slot, restrictionOn hasSlot
with some restrictionOn hasCard with some UnionOf(HotSwappableOSM,
SPAinterfaceProcessors) { }
class Slot {
  reference hasCard [1−∗]: Card;
}
class Card {
}
class SuperVisor720 extends Card {
}
class SPAinterfaceProcessors extends Card {
}
class HotSwappableOSM extends Card {
}
```

Using PDDSL

Using PDDSL shows how the language implementation resulting from ODMM enables OIM. Having a PDDSL metamodel specified by the language designer, the language user is able to build different domain models. These domain models describe possible configurations of physical devices. Possible domain models are depicted in Fig. 11.3.

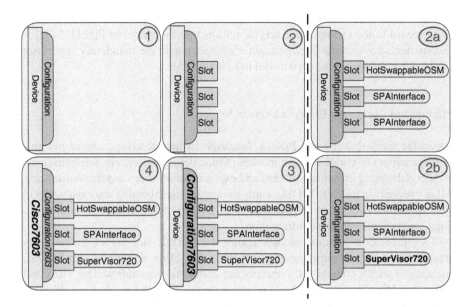

Fig. 11.3 Example domain models of PDDSL

During domain modelling, the language user experiences several benefits, for example, consistency checking, model debugging and repairing. In development environments, these benefits would be implemented by reasoning services (cf. Sect. 8.1) which are automatically invoked. The language user needs no background information on how the reasoning services work and how they are connected with the knowledge base. The reasoning engine returns suggestions and explanations to the DSL user. To allow for such services, the ABox and TBox of an ontology are extracted from the domain model (*M1 layer*) and the integrated metamodel (*M2 layer*), respectively. In the following, we will consider more precisely the services that are provided to the user.

Reasoning Services for Modelling Domain Models

In the following, we present some concrete services that are used by language users.

Detecting Inconsistencies in Domain Models

To detect inconsistencies in domain models, the PDDSL metamodel is transformed into a description logics TBox. All classes in the PDDSL metamodel are transformed to a concept in a description logics TBox. All references in the metamodel are represented by roles (object properties) in the TBox. The domain model itself is transformed to a description logics ABox. To check whether the domain models are consistent, we use the *consistency checking reasoning service*. With regard to the example, the service returns that the model in Fig. 11.3 (2a) is inconsistent, because the configuration does not contain the mandatory supervisor card (as it is defined in the metamodel in Listing 11.5).

Finding and Explaining Errors in Domain Models

Language users that use the PDDSL language (which describes sets of possible configurations) to create domain models (which describe concrete configurations) require debugging of domain models and explanation of errors and inconsistencies. More precisely, a user of PDDSL wants to identify illegal configurations, wants to get explanations why the configuration of a device is inconsistent and wants to get suggestions how to fix the configuration.

To validate configuration models against the PDDSL metamodel, the model is transformed into a description logics ABox. The TBox is built by the PDDSL metamodel which contains all concepts and additional constraints. The TBox and ABox build the description logics' knowledge base. Using the consistency checking reasoning service, we can check if the knowledge base is consistent and, thus, validate the configuration.

If we want to detect invalid cards in a configuration, we need some explanations why the model is inconsistent with regard to its metamodel. Explanations are provided by explanation services specified in Sect. 8.1.

Figure 11.3 (2a) depicts an example of a domain model with an invalid configuration element. It needs the consistency checking reasoning service and requests some explanations which are resulted from the ontology justification service. The reasoner delivers the answer shown in Listing 11.6:

```
CHECK CONSISTENCY

Consistent: No

Explanation:
   Configuration7603 subClassOf Configuration
   config76 type Configuration7603
   card_SPA1 type SPAInterface
   Configuration subClassOf hasSlot min 1 Slot
                 and hasSlot some hasCard some Supervisor720
*********************************************************************
   card_SPA2 type SPAInterface
   card_HS type HotSwappableOSM
   Supervisor720 subClassOf Card
```

Listing 11.6 Explanation for domain model inconsistency

The upper part in Listing 11.6 depicts the TBox axioms which are not fulfilled. The part below depicts the parts of the domain model which are involved in the inconsistency. The reason for the inconsistency in the example is the missing supervisor card, which must be part of every configuration. Since config76 has as type Configuration7603 which is a subclass of Configuration, it must be connected via a slot with some card of type Supervisor720. This is not fulfilled because all cards

(card_SPA1, card_SPA2, card_HS) plugged into the configuration are either of
type HotSwappableOSM or type SPAInterface.

Classification of Domain Model Elements

Language users often start modelling with general concepts, for example, with
model elements of type Device or Configuration, depicted in Fig. 11.3 (1).
To classify a device or configuration element, we have to again transform the
instances together with its links into a description logics ABox. The TBox is built by
the PDDSL metamodel. Since description logics allow for simultaneous reasoning
on the model (TBox) and instance layer (ABox), we are able to use the *classification
reasoning service* (introduced in Sect. 8.1) to compute all possible types of the
individual config76 with regard to all other individuals and relations in the ABox.
The result is the more specific type Configuration7603 of the individual
config76. Again the individual device76 can be classified. The most specific
type here is Cisco7603.

11.2   OWLText

In this section, we introduce OWLText—a tool that provides means for applying
ODMM in the development of textual modelling languages (textual DSLs). It results
from an evolution and extension of the ideas presented for ODMM in the previous
section. The section is structured as follows. Section 11.2.1 gives an overview
of the ODMM approach implemented in OWLText. Section 11.2.2 discusses the
design and implementation of OWLText, and Sect. 11.2.3 shows an example of using
OWLText in the design and application of a textual modelling language.

11.2.1   ODMM with OWLText

To provide a comprehensive approach for the development of textual,
ontology-integrated modelling languages, OWLText combines three technical
spaces:

Metamodelling World.   The metamodelling world addresses the specification
   of abstract syntax (syntactic representation) for modelling languages using
   formalisms like metamodels and metamodelling languages like Ecore.
   It provides meta-tools (e.g., EMF) to generate implementations for metamodels
   that enable the model-based representation of specifications conforming to a
   given metamodel (language).
Grammar World.   The grammar world addresses the specification of textual
   syntax for modelling languages using grammar formalisms like context-free

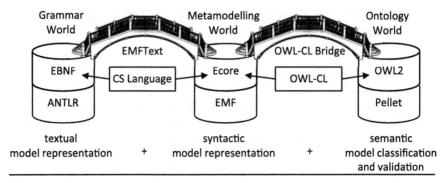

Fig. 11.4 Architecture of the OWLText technology bridges

grammars and metamodelling languages like EBNF. It provides meta-tools like parser (e.g., ANTLR[1]) and printer generators to convert textual specification written in a particular modelling language to a model-based representation and vice versa.

Ontology World. The ontology world addresses the structural and semantic representation and validation of data using formalisms like ontologies and languages like OWL2. It provides tools like reasoners (e.g., Pellet) to validate and explain the structural and semantic consistency of ontologies at type and instance level.

As depicted in Fig. 11.4, OWLText contributes two technology space bridges to combine the benefits of these technical spaces. Both bridges are based on an M3 integration bridges between the metamodelling languages of the respective technical space. The EMFText bridge contributes the CS language to integrate EBNF-based textual syntax specifications and Ecore-based metamodelling. The OWLCL Bridge contributes *OWL Constraint Language (OWLCL)* to integrate Ecore-based metamodelling and OWL-based validation of modelling languages.

Given these integrations, OWLText enables the ODMM approach presented in Fig. 11.5. It involves three roles for language engineers:

Metamodelling Expert. The metamodelling expert specifies the language metamodel using Ecore. This metamodel is fed to the EMF that generates a metamodel implementation.

Textual Syntax Expert. The textual syntax expert specifies the languages concrete textual syntax in relation to the metamodel. He uses the CS language provided by EMFText. Using the language metamodel and the concrete syntax specification, EMFText generates a parser, printer and advanced textual editor.

---

[1]http://www.antlr.org/

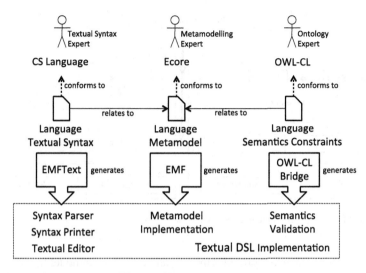

Fig. 11.5 Roles and steps in the OWLText ODMM approach

Ontology Expert.   The ontology expert specifies semantic constraints in relation to the metamodel. He uses the language OWLCL to annotate constraints and error messages. Given the language metamodel and the semantic constraints, the OWLCL Bridge generates a component that enables the transformation of language models to an ontology representation and the application of ontology technology to validate and preserve the consistency of language models.

The combination of all generation results is considered the language implementation. Based on a seamless integration of parser, printer, editor, metamodel implementation and semantic validation, the suggested approach contributes a generative way to develop DSLs that allow for OIM.

11.2.2   Realisation and Application of the M3 Bridges and M2 Bridges in OWLText

This section documents the realisation of the introduced technology space bridges. As OWLText covers both the development and application of languages for OIM, it introduces and uses various bridges at several meta-levels.

Bridging in EMFText

For the integration of the grammar world and the metamodelling world, OWLText integrates EMFText—a tool for generating parsers, printers and editors for EMF-based modelling languages. For the specification of concrete

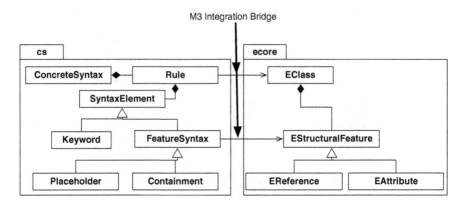

Fig. 11.6 M3 integration bridge used in EMFText

textual syntaxes, EMFText provides the CS language. A metamodel for CS is given in Fig. 11.6. It establishes an M3 integration bridge by referencing elements of the Ecore metamodel. Each syntax `Rule` is associated with an `EClass` it defines a textual representation for. In the rule body, `SyntaxElements` specify individual syntactic elements of a textual representation (e.g. `Keywords`). A particular kind of `SyntaxElement` is `FeatureSyntax`. Each `FeatureSyntax` refers to a specific `EStructuralFeature` in the metamodel to define its textual representation. For containment `EReferences` in the metamodel, a `Containment` element defines a syntax non-terminal. At this point, the parser would descend to the syntax rules defined for `EClasses` that match the type of the corresponding `EReference`. For non-containment `EReferences` and `EAttributes`, a `Placeholder` element needs to be given, which specifies a grammar terminal to represent reference or attribute values.

The M3 integration bridge (cf. Fig. 11.7) realised by the integrated metamodelling languages is applied at M2 to specify textual syntax for language metamodels. Based on the coupling between syntax specification and metamodel, EMFText can automatically generate M2 transformation bridges (parser and printer) that are then applied at M1 to synchronise textual and model-based representations of language expressions.

Bridging for OWLCL

For the integration of the ontology world and the metamodelling world, OWLText provides the OWLCL Bridge. The language OWLCL is used to specify semantic constraints against a given metamodel. The metamodel for OWLCL is depicted in Fig. 11.7. OWLCL uses a combination of two M3 integration and two M3 transformation bridges. One M3 integration bridge connects each OWLCL `Constraint` to a constrained `EClass`. To enable the definition of constraints, each `Constraint` contains to OWL2 to class `Descriptions` in

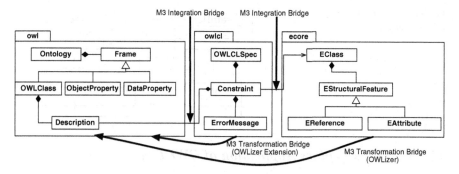

Fig. 11.7 M3 integration and transformation bridges for OWLCL

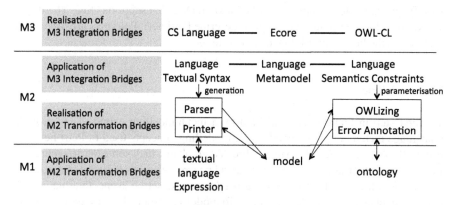

Fig. 11.8 Realisation and application of OWLText M2 and M3 bridges

OWL2 Manchester syntax. As these class descriptions are meant to be defined against the ontology that corresponds to the language metamodel, the OWLizer (cf. Sect. 8.2) is used as M3 transformation bridge. OWLizer transparently translates the language to an ontology TBox, and OWLCL constraints are defined against the OWLClasses, ObjectProperties and DataProperties of this TBox. A second M3 transformation bridge is used to incorporate the consistency constraints defined with OWLCL as consistency classes to the ontology TBox. This bridge is implemented as extension to OWLizer.

As depicted in Fig. 11.8, the M3 bridges implemented with OWLCL can be applied at M2 to specify language semantic constraints. Given such OWLCL-based constraint definition, the OWLCL Bridge parameterises an M2 transformation bridge that is applied at M1 for semantic validation. The M2 bridge transforms model-based representations of language expressions, the language metamodel and the language constraints to an integrated ontology. Finally, a generated semantic validation component uses reasoning services to find constraint violations in this ontology and to propagate errors back to the corresponding model elements.

Fig. 11.9 Metamodel for
Petri net language

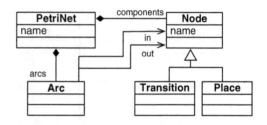

11.2.3   An Exemplary Application of OWLText

In this section, we will discuss how the OWLText ODMM approach is used to specify and generate a simple exemplary textual DSL that supports OIM. Therefore, we will develop a structural language to describe Petri nets. Petri nets are often used to describe the behaviour of concurrent systems.

Metamodelling

The first step in ODMM is conducted by a metamodelling expert. They provide a language metamodel that specifies the modelling concepts used in Petri nets (cf. Fig. 11.9). A `PetriNet` describes a directed graph in which some `Nodes` represent `Places` and other nodes represent `Transitions`. `Places` describe states in the `PetriNet`; they can hold tokens. `Transitions` describe events that may occur and lead to changes of the Petrinet state. To model such state changes, they consume or produce tokens at places they are connected to. Connections between `Places` and `Transistions` are specified using `Arcs`.

Textual Syntax Specification

After the specification of the metamodel a textual syntax expert specifies the language concrete syntax. He applies the metamodelling language CS and the tools provided by the EMFText bridge to generate a parser, a printer and an advanced syntax-aware editor. The syntax specification for the Petri net language is shown in Fig. 11.10. In the TOKENS section, it defines a set of tokens used for lexical analysis of language expressions. The section TOKENSTYLES customises the syntax colouring in the generated language editor. The syntax rules for the previously introduced metaclasses are defined in the RULES section. A `PetriNet` element is indicated by the keyword ``petrinet`` followed by its name (corresponding to the `IDENTIFIER` token), its `arcs` and its `components` (`Places` or `Transitions`) enclosed in curly brackets. `Transistions` and `Places` are represented by the respective keyword (``transition`` or ``place``) and their name. `Arcs` are specified by the name of their in `Node`,

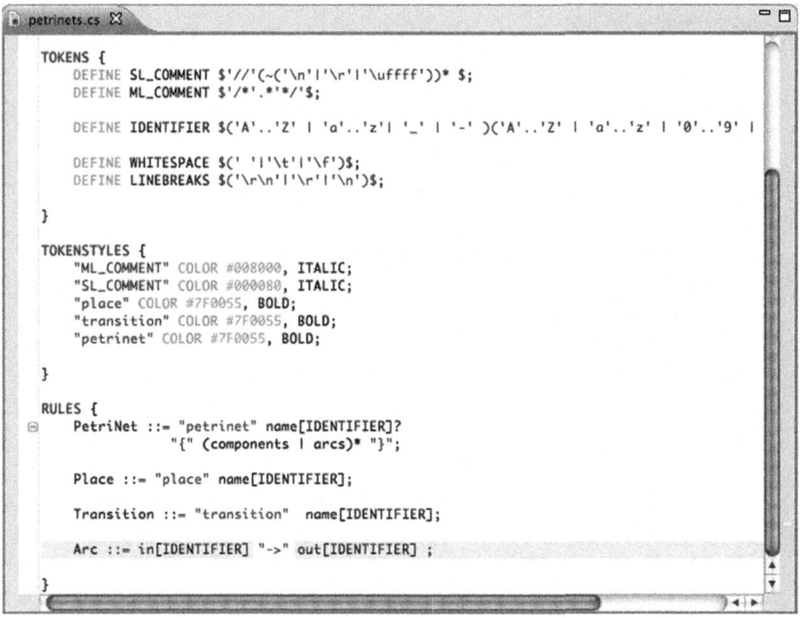

```
 petrinets.cs  ⊠                                                      ⊟ ⊡

  TOKENS {
      DEFINE SL_COMMENT $'//'(~('\n'|'\r'|'\uffff'))* $;
      DEFINE ML_COMMENT $'/*'.*'*/'$;

      DEFINE IDENTIFIER $('A'..'Z' | 'a'..'z'| '_' | '-' )('A'..'Z' | 'a'..'z' | '0'..'9' |

      DEFINE WHITESPACE $(' '|'\t'|'\f')$;
      DEFINE LINEBREAKS $('\r\n'|'\r'|'\n')$;

  }

  TOKENSTYLES {
      "ML_COMMENT" COLOR #008000, ITALIC;
      "SL_COMMENT" COLOR #000080, ITALIC;
      "place" COLOR #7F0055, BOLD;
      "transition" COLOR #7F0055, BOLD;
      "petrinet" COLOR #7F0055, BOLD;

  }

  RULES {
 ⊟    PetriNet ::= "petrinet" name[IDENTIFIER]?
                     "{" (components | arcs)* "}";

      Place ::= "place" name[IDENTIFIER];

      Transition ::= "transition" name[IDENTIFIER];

      Arc ::= in[IDENTIFIER] "->" out[IDENTIFIER] ;

  }
                                                                    ◄ ►
```

Fig. 11.10   Syntax specification for Petri nets language

an arrow (``->``), and the name of their out Node. For more details on the specification of textual syntax with EMFText, we refer to [92] and the EMFText documentation available online[2].

Semantic Constraint Specification

The specification of semantic constraints is the vital contribution of OWLText for ODMM. By metamodelling the semantic constraints for the Petri net language using OWLCL, an ontology expert enables consistency-preserving OIM for language users. Figure 11.11 shows the constraint specification using OWLCL.

In line 1, the specification refers to the metamodel it is defined for. The refinements section contains refinements for classes defined in the metamodel based on semantic properties. The example shows the definition of a class StartPlace that is identified as a refinement of Place with the name "Start". The specification of the semantic properties that identify a class refinement is made using OWL2 descriptions given in Manchester syntax. All descriptions refer to an ontology TBox that was automatically derived from the Petri net metamodel using the mapping of Ecore and OWL2 implemented in OWLizer (cf. Sect. 8.2). The rest of the specification contributes a set of semantic constraints that must be satisfied for

---

[2]http://www.emftext.org/index.php/EMFText_Documentation

```
  petrinets.owlcl  ⊠                                                    ▭ ▢
  1  import "./petrinets.text.ecore"
  2
  3  refinements: {
  4      type StartPlace refines Place : (NameableElement_name value "Start")
  5  }
  6
  7  StartPlace message "A Start Place is not allowed to have incoming Arcs."
  8      : (Component_incoming exactly 0 Arc);
  9
 10  Component message "Compoments need to be named."
 11      : (NameableElement_name exactly 1 xsd:string ) ;
 12
 13  Arc message "Arcs need to be either consuming or producing."
 14      : (Arc_in exactly 1 Transition and Arc_out exactly 1 Place)
 15          or (Arc_in exactly 1 Place and Arc_out exactly 1 Transition);
 16
 17  ConsumingArc message "Consuming Arcs need to have Places as input."
 18      : (Arc_in exactly 1 Place);
 19
 20  ConsumingArc message "Consuming Arcs need to have Transitions as output."
 21      : (Arc_out exactly 1 Transition);
 22
 23  ProducingArc message "Producing Arcs need to have Transitions as input."
 24      : (Arc_in exactly 1 Transition);
 25
 26  ProducingArc message "Producing Arcs need to have Places as output."
 27      : (Arc_out exactly 1 Place);
```

Fig. 11.11 Semantic constraints specification for Petri net language

a concrete Petri net to be consistent. Each constraint refers to a class from the Petri net metamodel, defines an error message to show for elements that violate a given constraint and provides a specification of the semantic properties that must hold for all instances of the constrained class to satisfy the constraint. Lines 7–8 define a constraint that says that StartPlaces are not allowed to have incoming arc. The other constraints define constraints for Arcs to be valid.

OIM with the Petri Nets Language

Given these three specifications, the language engineer uses the generators provided by OWLText to derive a language implementation. This implementation provides an advanced textual editor for Petri nets that integrates reasoning technology to enable OIM for language users. The application of the fully generated editor is demonstrated in Fig. 11.12. It shows an exemplary Petri net that contains inconsistencies. When language users specify a Petri net in the depicted editor, OWLText automatically translates the textual representation to a model and then to an ontology. A reasoner is used to find ontology concepts that invalidate the semantic constraints provided with OWLCL and annotates the given error messages to the corresponding model elements. These annotations are shown to language users as error markers in the Petri net editors. This example indicates the potential of a tight integration of several technical spaces provided by OWLText and the advanced tool support that can be provided for OIM.

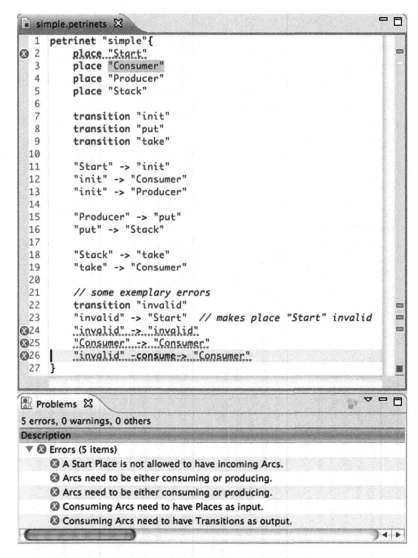

Fig. 11.12 Application of the generated Petri nets editor for OIM

11.3 Conclusion

In this chapter, we presented two metamodelling approaches that integrate ontology technology and metamodelling technology to ease the exploitation of ODSD when designing new modelling languages. Both approaches share a common vision but rely on different tools and integration approaches to achieve this vision. The following table compares both approaches by relating their distinguishing characteristics.

Concept	OntoDSL	OWLText
Abstract syntax combination	Core of OntoDSL is its integrated metametamodel being the merge of the Ecore metametamodel and the OWL 2 metamodel. It represents the abstract syntax component of a new *hybrid metamodelling* language which allows for designing Ecore-based metamodels with seamlessly integrated OWL 2-based annotations.	OWLText contributes OWLCL—an *external* metamodelling DSL to refine existing Ecore metamodel with addition types that are founded by semantic properties and to annotate metamodel classes with ontology-based constraints. Therefore, the abstract syntax for OWLCL refers to concepts of the Ecore metamodelling language.
Concrete syntax combination	OntoDSL provides a textual concrete syntax to design Ecore-based metamodels. The grammar of the textual syntax is extended with an adapted version of the OWL 2 Manchester syntax. It implements an *integrated textual DSL* for modelling metamodels and ontology-based constraints within one document.	OWLCL is implemented in an *external textual DSL*. The concrete syntax of OWLCL integrates OWL 2 Manchester syntax for the specification of type refinements and semantic constraints.
Inconsistency detection	Inconsistencies are detected using the ontology services for *consistency checking* (cf. Table 8.2). Before, the metamodel with all OWL-based annotations and a respective instance model are translated to an ontology. The metamodel is translated to the ontology TBox, and the instance model is translated to the ontology ABox.	To detect semantic inconsistencies, OWLText translates models, metamodels and semantic constraints to an ontology TBox and uses *classification* (cf. Table 8.6) to find all model elements which are equivalent to inconsistency classes that negate semantic constraints.
Inconsistency explanation	For the explanation of inconsistencies, OntoDSL uses an ontology service which computes for each inconsistency in an instance model a set of axioms explaining these inconsistencies. These sets of axioms are translated to human-readable text which is printed within a console.	In the OWLCL constraint specification, each constraint needs to be annotated with a custom, human readable error message. OWLText is seamlessly integrated with the EMFText-based textual editors that are used to edit language models. Using this integration, OWLText presents error annotations for text fragments representing inconsistent model elements.

Chapter 12
A Platform for ODSD: The MOST Workbench

Srdjan Zivkovic, Christian Wende, Edward Thomas,
Fernando Silva Parreiras, Tobias Walter, Krzysztof Miksa, Harald Kühn,
Hannes Schwarz, and Jeff Z. Pan

Abstract In this chapter, we discuss how scalable reasoning technologies (cf. Chap. 5) can be transparently integrated into the existing model-driven software development (MDSD) environments and how MDSD environments leverage reasoning technology, in order to provide scalable ontology-based MDSD services. The successful realisation of ontology-driven software development (ODSD) vision requires a tight coupling of the introduced ontology reasoning services with existing MDSD technology. The challenge of building ontology-enabled MDSD environments is raised by the technological clash between conventional MDSD technology and reasoning technology.

This chapter is organised as follows. In Sect. 12.1, we introduce the architecture of ODSD environments that support the vision of ODSD. In the subsequent sections, we refer to the key architectural components of such ODSD environments that either enable the reasoning services or make use of them. Therefore, in Sect. 12.2, the ontology reasoning infrastructure is introduced. Based on these ontology enabling components, we describe how the services of querying (Sect. 12.3), validation explanation (Sect. 12.4), and tracing support (Sect. 12.5) make use of the reasoning technology to contribute to the ODSD vision.

12.1 Towards ODSD Tool Environments

In this section, we elaborate how the common requirements on tool environments for software development can be addressed by extending current MDSD tools with ODSD technology.

J.Z. Pan et al. (eds.), *Ontology-Driven Software Development*,
DOI 10.1007/978-3-642-31226-7_12, © Springer-Verlag Berlin Heidelberg 2013

12.1.1 Current Tool Environments

Requirements on Tool Environments

In general, the following services are considered important for tool environments [46]:

Software Process Guidance

Environments should guide developers to help the effective execution [38] of a complex development process.

Development Methods Support

Tool environments need to provide means for creating, editing, and analysing specification artefacts in method-specific languages.

Repetitive Tasks Automation

Finally, tool environments are required to automate repetitive tasks. Such tasks typically involve the validation of specification artefacts or their transformation [200] when entering a new development phase, for example, the generation of implementation code from a design model.

Review of Current MDSD Tool Environments Architecture

MDSD tool environments already provide various technical means for productive model-driven software development. In the MDE community, such environments are known as language workbenches [71], software factories [80] or modelling frameworks [199]. We use the generic term *MDSD tool environment* to cover all those different cases. An MDSD tool environment supports, in the ideal case, all previously mentioned requirements translated to MDSD, such as language engineering, modelling (language application), and software process guidance. The main advantage of an MDSD environment compared to the traditional IDE is not only the development based on models (the M1 level support), but also the ability to engineer arbitrary software languages for the particular development problem (the M2 level support).

Regardless of the engineering level (M1 or M2), the following groups of tools can be distinguished within an MDSD tool environment:

Editors

Editors provide means for editing work products such as language specifications (abstract and concrete syntaxes, etc.), models, code, configurations, etc. Editors may be either text-based, tree-based, graphical, form-based or any combination of those.

Transformers/Translators

Transformation tools for language engineers and language users (modellers) allow a language or a model to be translated into another specification. Metamodel and model transformers, tool/code/text generators fall to this category.

Executors

Executors basically interpret language specifications or models according to defined semantics. Tools like debuggers, simulators, run-time engines, and test units are examples of executors. The simulation of business process models is an example of an executor on the M1 level.

Analysers

Analysers help language engineers and modellers to investigate language specifications and models. Such tools perform different types of static analyses according to defined set of constraints, such as consistency checking. Metamodel and model querying and tracing, syntax and static semantics validation of models and metamodels may be performed with the analysers.

Process Guidance Tools

Process guidance tools guide language engineers and modellers throughout the language engineering, i.e., MDSD process, respectively. In a collaboration with other tools mentioned before, a guidance tool computes the state of the system and tells the engineer what is the next step in the MDSD process.

Process Support Tools

Process support tools offer general support services such as collaborative work, versioning, user and security management, etc.

From an analysis of the current state of practice in MDSD, it becomes obvious that particularly MDSD tools such as analysers and process guidance tools an lack adequate level of maturity, for which the ODSD technology is expected to deliver improvements according to the ODSD vision (cf. Chap. 1).

12.1.2   ODSD Tool Environments

Addressing Requirements on Tool Environments with ODSD

ODSD tool environments are meant to adopt scalable ontology technology [40] to address current challenges of MDSD. Based on bridging infrastructure and the semantic services provided by ontology technology (cf. Chap. 8), the requirements introduced for MDSD tools in Sect. 12.1.1 can be addressed in the following way:

Ontology-Based Software Process Guidance

The process guidance provided for MDSD needs to be highly adaptive, since concrete tasks and steps depend on the concrete MDSD method, its target domain, the developed system and the dynamic development context. In ODSD tool environments, this service is meant to be provided by integrating ontology-driven process guidance. Chapter 13 presents an ontological process guidance engine. Using an ontological conceptualisation, the dependencies, requirements, and results of individual process steps can be formally defined. With this formalisation, ontology technology can be used to compute and suggest upcoming process steps and guide developers. Since the process definition is realised in the same technical space, ontologies help to connect the method execution with the specification artefacts and validation results. This enables the automatic derivation and adaptation of the task order in accordance to the developers' decisions and actions.

Ontology-Based Development Method Support

MDSD lacks a formal approach to precisely define metamodel semantics and ensure such semantics during modelling. In ODSD tool environments, this lack is meant to be addressed by exploiting means for ontology-based, consistency-preserving modelling as introduced in Chaps. 8–10. Sharing the abstraction level of MDSD metamodelling languages [88] (cf. Chap. 7), ontologies are easy to integrate and compose with existing metamodelling approaches [213] (cf. Chap. 11). This marriage enables the definition of metamodel semantics using logical axioms which facilitates a more precise and explicit definition of semantics, derived properties, and well-formedness constraints for MDSD languages.

Ontology-Based Repetitive Tasks Automation

The integration of ontology-based process guidance and ontology-based development method support enables automated validation of well-formedness and consistency rules in accordance to the current process status. Furthermore, MDSD methods which apply multiple languages and system specifications that are fragmented into several models often suffer from consistency problems. Here, ODSD

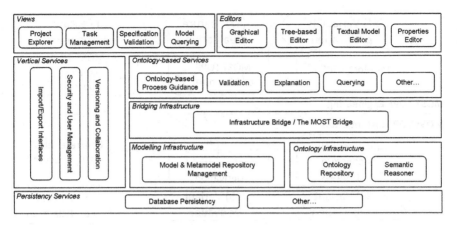

Fig. 12.1 The generic architecture for ontology-based MDSD environments

tool environments are meant to integrate the advanced capabilities of MDSD tool environments with the ODSD-tracing techniques introduced in Chap. 6. Using ontology-based tracing explicit and implicit interrelations between model artefacts can be queried and validated. Ontology explanation services can help to resolve inconsistencies and conflicts.

ODSD Tool Environments Architecture

The challenge of building ODSD tool environments results from the technological clash between *conventional* MDSD technology and reasoning technology. To address this challenge, ontology-enabled tool environments have to provide the bridging technology that can reconcile two different technical spaces. Figure 12.1 proposes a generic architecture for ODSD tool environments that integrates such bridging.

The central building block of the system is the Bridging infrastructure that makes the marriage between the Modelling infrastructure typically found in MDSD tools and the Ontology infrastructure possible. The bridging infrastructure addresses the technical problems of clashing technical spaces, by providing a set of dedicated transformation services. Ontology-based services such as Guidance, Validation, Explanation, Querying and others are, therefore, located in top of the Bridging Infrastructure. These services are exposed to the developers using the uppermost layer. This layer contributes various Editors to create and edit model-based system specifications and several Views informing developers of the current development status. The specifics of the ontology technology are be hidden to the upper-level components and consequently to the end users. Such abstraction enables seamless application ontology technology within the technological space of MDSD. In addition, the generic architecture contains

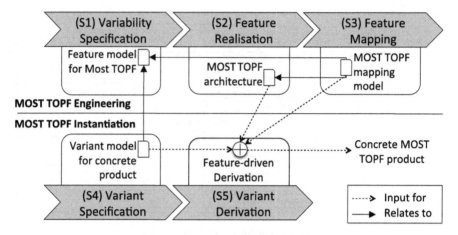

Fig. 12.2 The feature-based SPLE process for the MOST TOPF

`Vertical Services` such as user and rights management or versioning and `Persistency Services`.

12.1.3 Developing a Family of ODSD Tool Environments

To enable systematic reuse and variation of concrete ODSD tools in a family, we introduced the *MOST Tool Product Family (W3C)*. Figure 12.2 depicts our feature-based SPLE process for the development of the MOST TOPF and the customisation of specific ODSD tool environments.

The SPLE process consists of five steps (S1)–(S5) in two main phases. The first phase (*MOST TOPF Engineering*) is concerned with developing the MOST TOPF. The second phase (*MOST TOPF instantiation*) involves the derivation of a concrete MOST TOPF product. In the following, we discuss the individual steps of the introduced feature-based SPLE process.

(S1) Variability Specification: MOST TOPF Features

The development of an ODSD tool family requires a systematic specification of the commonalities and variability of all products. The Fig. 12.3 shows the feature model for the MOST TOPF. In accordance to the three common requirements for tool environments introduced in Sect. 12.1.1, the features are organised in three feature groups: `Software Process Guidance`, `Development Method`, and `Automation`. The features within these groups result from the variability found for the MOST case studies in Chap. 4. A fourth feature group relates to the `Ontology Technology` used to address the vision of ontology-based MDSD discussed in Sect. 12.1.2. This group provides features to customise different

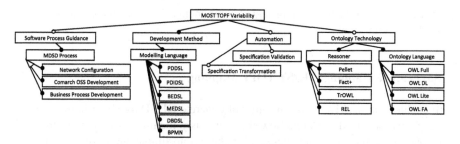

Fig. 12.3 Features of the MOST TOPF presented as a feature model [114]. From a group of features connected by a *filled arc* at least one feature needs to be selected. *Non-filled arcs* denote groups where exactly one feature has to be selected. A non-grouped feature connected by a line ending with a *filled circle* is mandatory. Features with *non-filled circles* are optional

Ontology Languages with a specific reasoning complexity and Reasoners with specific performance characteristics.

The feature model only represents cardinality-based restrictions on variant models. The configuration of a concrete Development Method and the according Modelling Language is mandatory, while the other feature groups are optional. There are also dependencies between features of the MOST TOPF that are more complex and cannot be directly expressed in the tree-shaped feature model. As an example, think of Specification Validation for the modelling language BPMN. As discussed in Chap. 13, such BPMN validation can be implemented by an transformation of BPMN models to an OWL-DL ontology. Consequently, the selection of the validation for BPMN requires to also include the according ontology language (OWL DL). To support such variability restrictions, we complemented the feature model with additional requires constraints. These are annotated on a specific feature and consist of the logical term describing the requirements of the annotated feature. The constraint for the above introduced example would be:

```
BPMN | requires
((Specification Validation and OWL-DL)
or
not (Specification Validation)) |
```

Further constraints used in the MOST TOPF are presented in [159].

(S2) Feature Realisation: MOST TOPF Architecture

For the realisation of the MOST TOPF, we rely on a generic, component-based architecture as described in Sect. 12.1.2). The MOST TOPF architecture was fully specified using UML component diagrams [154]. It consists of several standard components for ODSD tool environments such as graphical and textual editors, model and metamodel management tools, and a model transformation infrastructure. In addition, it provides components that contribute and integrate ontology technology.

(S3) Feature Mapping: MOST TOPF Mapping

To enable feature-driven customisation of concrete ODSD tool environments from the family, we need to define how the previously identified features are mapped to concrete realisation components. Often there is no simple one-to-one mapping of features to concrete components. Some features are only used to organise the feature model and may not be represented in the architecture directly, others may require the inclusion of several components, and again others may require the inclusion of a component only when used in special combinations. Therefore, we used FeatureMapper[1] to define mappings of features or logical feature expressions (AND, OR, NOT) to a UML component diagram specifying the concrete components of our MOST architecture. FeatureMapper provides an interactive, graphical mapping approach and stores the mappings in a dedicated model that supports arbitrary Ecore-based languages [39]. The mapping model is used to support the developer in understanding and analysing the complex interrelations of single components in the family by dedicated mapping validation [90] and visualisation techniques [91].

(S4) Variant Specification: Guided MOST TOPF Product Customisation

The customisation of a concrete ODSD tool environment for a specific ODSD scenario starts with the specification of a scenario-study specific variant model. The variant model is a subset of the original feature model, that only contains the features required for the specific MOST TOPF product. It has to conform to the cardinality constraints and feature dependencies defined by the feature model.

We use the approach presented in Sect. 9.2 to guide the specification and validation of variant models. Variant specification typically is a stepwise process. It involves intermediate variant models including and excluding a subset of the features found in the feature model. Such intermediate variant models are validated w.r.t. the feature model, and inconsistencies are reported to the user. Fixing these inconsistencies provides guidance for the stepwise refinement of the intermediate variant model to a valid variant.

(S5) Product Derivation: Automatic Deployment of MOST TOPF Products

If valid, the variant model is evaluated together with the specification of the MOST TOPF components and the mapping model. An automatic transformation task now

---

[1]http://www.featuremapper.org/.

removes all MOST TOPF components that are mapped to features not contained in the variant model. This results in a refined and customised MOST TOPF component model for the case-study specific requirements. Finally, the UML component model is used to deploy a physical MOST TOPF instance. Each component is associated to a set of physical realisation artefacts (i.e. files). The deployment task takes all physical artefacts for included components, bundles, and deploys them in an executable MOST TOPF instance.

12.2   Configurable and Tractable Ontology Reasoning Infrastructure for ODSD

Here, we discuss how the reasoning services described in Chap. 5 specifically relate to ODSD.

From this, we derive a set of simple requirements for reasoning in ODSD:

1. Support for closed-world reasoning
2. Support for justifications of reasoning results, including query answering results
3. Tractable reasoning
4. Configurability of reasoning services

12.2.1   Closed-World Reasoning in NBox

MDSD uses the *Closed-World Assumption (CWA)*: Anything not known to be true is assumed to be false; ontologies, and in particular the OWL language, use an open world assumption: Anything not known to be true is undefined. This allows a reasoner to infer new facts, as long as these facts are not contradicted by any existing knowledge. To effectively bridge ontologies and models, we can configure the reasoner to infer new facts about specific parts of the ontology, giving a local closed domain assumption, as we saw in Sect. 7.3.1.

In our reasoning infrastructure, we support this by closing some concepts and properties of a given ontology, preventing the reasoner from assuming new instances of these classes or properties, but instead, only considering the inferrable ones. This can be realised by using the NBox as we introduced in Sect. 5.1.5. This allows software developers to mark which parts of a specification are final and complete, and when this is translated into the ontology world, the resulting artefacts can be marked in this way, allowing additional inconsistencies to be identified which result from an erroneously incomplete model. In other parts of the model which are still under development and known to be incomplete, the reasoner remains free to create new implicit instances as necessary to resolve this incompleteness.

12.2.2 Justification and Explanation

When the ODSD workbench identifies an inconsistency, it is important to the developer that this is resolved as easy as possible. This implies that any ODSD reasoning service must be able to justify its reasoning results. As we have seen, a justification is the subset of some ontology which is the cause for some reasoning result, whether that result is an inconsistent model, an unsatisfiable class or property description, or a result to some query. By providing a set of ground axioms to the ODSD workbench which are the minimal justification, the bridge in the workbench can identify parts of a model which were translated into these axioms and therefore relate the reasoning result back into the model world. With CWA, the justification should also include the closure of related classes or properties, if they are responsible for the inconsistency.

12.2.3 Tractability

For expressive languages such as OWL, reasoning has exponential complexity. In the case of OWL2, which is required for the case studies we have considered in this book, the worst-case complexity is 2NEXPTIME. For even moderately complex models, this results in a lot of computations and a significant delay to any reasoning result. By using ontology language transformations described in Chap. 6, we can use expressive languages to represent a model and transform these into tractable ontology languages such as the EL and DL-Lite family to perform reasoning.

12.2.4 Configurability

There are many different reasoning tasks required to effectively support the software development lifecycle using ontologies. It can be shown that some of these tasks are mutually exclusive, it is not possible to support them all using a single reasoner. There is a complex interrelationship between reasoning requirements, in particular between different language expressive power, worst-case complexity of reasoning, and guaranteed soundness and completeness of the reasoning results. To prevent the need for a multitude of reasoners within the ODSD platform, we have introduced a configurable reasoner.

This allows different reasoning tasks to deploy different configurations of a reasoning framework. The result of this allows the workbench to dictate its requirements: language expressivity, level of performance, complex query answering, justification support, etc. And a reasoner will be configured that will support these requirements. By taking this approach, the complexity of the system is greatly reduced as there is a single black box reasoner. We can also take advantage of feature mapping services to aid in the configuration and the avoidance of unsatisfiable combinations of functional and non-functional requirements.

12.3   Integrated Queries for ODSD

The *Object Constraint Language (OCL)* language provides the definition of functions and the usage of built-in functions, whereas SPARQL-DL provides a powerful language to query resources in OWL, allowing for retrieving concepts, properties and individuals. While OCL assumes *Unique Name Assumption (UNA)*, OWL may mimic it using constructs like owl:AllDifferent and owl:distinctMembers.

A specific combination of these features reflects configurations for querying integrated models. We model these combinations in the feature model depicted in Fig. 12.4. The feature model reveals possible choices for querying integrated models and can also be used as a taxonomy to categorise existing approaches.

The relations between the features are constrained by the following composition rules:

```
SPARQL—DL requires OWL;
SPARQL—DL is mutually exclusive with UML class—based modelling;
OCL requires UML class—based modelling;
UML class—based modelling requires CWA;
UML class—based modelling is mutually exclusive with OWA.
```

We analyse these constraints as follows. SPARQL-DL queries require OWA reasoning with OWL and does not work with UML class-based modelling. In contrast, OCL queries requires UML class-based modelling and UML class-based modelling requires CWA exclusively. After ruling out the inconsistent configurations according to the constraints above, we have the following possible configurations for querying integrated models.

1. SPARQL-DL, OWL, OWA
2. SPARQL-DL, OWL, CWA
3. OCL, UML class-based modelling, CWA
4. OCL, UML class-based modelling, OWL, OWA, CWA

Figure 12.5 illustrates how these configurations for querying integrated models may be arranged in layers. Three out of four configurations can be found by adopting current approaches. One configuration involves a combination of different semantics and reasoning services. All these configurations are described in the following sections.

These four combinations cover the needs for querying integrated models considering the features aforementioned. They allow OWA as well as CWA and include capabilities for reasoning with OWL and UML class-based modelling.

Using SPARQL over OWL with OWA

Among existing RDF-based query languages for the semantic web, SPARQL is the W3C recommendation. It is based on triple patterns and allows for querying the vocabulary and the assertions of a given domain.

Restrictions on the SPARQL language, i.e., entailment regimes, allow for querying OWL ontologies, including TBox, RBox, and ABox. One implementation is

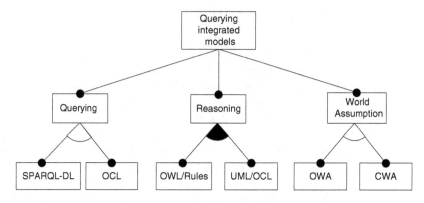

Fig. 12.4 Feature model of querying integrated models

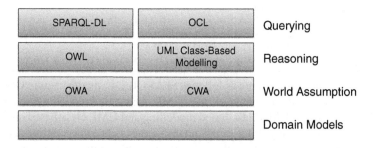

Fig. 12.5 Existing configurations for querying models, arranged in layers

SPARQL-DL [193]. SPARQL-DL enables querying OWL ontologies using the open world assumption. It is currently available together with the Pellet reasoner [195]. It offers a robust query language with DL reasoning support.

Using SPARQL over OWL with CWA

Polleres et al. [166] have explored the usage of the SPARQL language in combination with closed-world reasoning in SPARQL++. SPARQL++ extends SPARQL by supporting aggregate functions, CONSTRUCT query form, and built-ins. SPARQL++ queries can be formalised in HEX programs or description logic programs. SPARQL++ covers only a subset of RDF(S); how it could be extended towards OWL is still an open issue.

Using OCL over UML Class-Based Modelling with CWA

This is the standard application of OCL as query language. Query operations may be defined and used as helpers for OCL queries and constraints. Default values as well as initial and derived values can be defined by using UML and OCL.

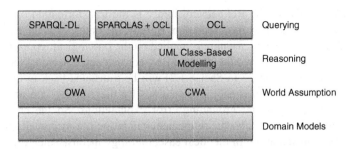

Fig. 12.6 Positioning SPARQL between existing approaches

UML class-based modelling rationale differs from OWL reasoning in the sense that the former includes behavioural features like operations whereas reasoning with OWL is strictly logical.

Using OCL and SPARQL over OWA and UML Class-Based Modelling

In some cases, a combination of UML class-based modelling and OWL is desired. For example, if one wants to define complex class descriptions or reuse existing ones. In contrast, to make usage of behavioural features like query operations, helpers and built-ins, UML class-based modelling may come into play.

In the next section, we present our approach for these combinations. Our approach allows for describing query operations using SPARQL-like syntax (such as the SPARQLAS used in TwoUse, see Sect. 9.4 for details). Figure 12.6 illustrates such a combination. Query operations are written in SPARQL-like notation and are translated into SPARQL and execute against an OWL knowledge base. The results are used as input for OCL query operations that allows the usage of helpers, query operations and built-ins defined in OCL.

12.4   Validation and Explanation in ODSD

12.4.1   Validation and Explanations for Process Refinements

The implementation of the process refinement validation techniques in the MOST ODSD workbench has been realised in the Java programming language. The outcome was a Java software library named *RefinementLibrary* that enables process refinement checks for refinement and grounding by utilising OWL reasoners. The reasoners that can be used with the library are *TrOWL* and *Pellet*, whereby *TrOWL* is the desired reasoner to be used because of the advantages described in Sect. 5.1.

The primary part of the RefinementLibrary is the transformation of a process model to an ontology TBox representation. Hereby, the ontology is the heart of the conceptual work since the reasoning is applied on the ontological representation of a process. Afterwards the results of the TBox consistency reasoning service (see the specification in Table 8.2 in Sect. 8.1.2) will be translated back to the original process model. The inconsistency explanations by the reasoner are an essential part for the refinement and grounding error explanations. So the challenge of precise error explanations after the refinement validation is conceptually related to the ontology representation. In the ideal case, ontology inconsistency explanations correspond directly to refinement inconsistency causes.

Additionally to the primary part various necessary debugging, process and error visualisation mechanisms were also implemented in order to simplify manual correctness checks for complex processes by the developers, specially in the case of library extensions. Furthermore, interfaces to the library are defined and documented for the ease of cooperation and collaboration and integration in the ODSD platform.

12.4.2 Validation and Explanations for Domain Engineering

The MOST workbench can also be used in the validation of constraints on domain models. For example, the use case UC-2: "Find wrongly configured instances of devices and explain errors" from domain engineering, introduced in Sect. 4.1, requires that the result of the validation service should be meaningful to the user. Specifically, the user should be informed which of the model elements are invalid and why. As described in Sect. 9.3.1, the model validation relies on the inconsistency checking. This service provides answers in terms of a Boolean value for whole ontology.

A more detailed answer can be retrieved using reasoning explanation. However, the reasoning explanations are still not meaningful to the user. The axioms forming the explanation need to be interpreted in the domain-specific manner. In the MOST workbench, this is done in two steps:

1. The set of individuals that occur in any of the object property assertion axioms involved in the explanation is extracted. These individuals are reported to the user as invalid.
2. In order to report to the user the reason for the inconsistency, we rely on the annotation mechanism of OWL2. The assumption is that every axiom which is meaningful to the user is annotated with a user friendly description of the error. If an axiom occurs in the explanation, its description is reported to the user.

Let us consider the instance of the device type Cisco_7603 from Listing 4.2 and the respective type model presented in Listing 4.1. A possible reasoning explanation for the inconsistency is given in Listing 12.1.

```
 1    Supervisor_Engine_2 SubClassOf Supervisor_Engine
 2    cisco_7603 pd_hasConfiguration cisco_7603_configuration
 3    cisco_7603_slot_1 pd_hasCard sip-400
 4    Supervisor_Engine_720 SubClassOf Supervisor_Engine
 5    cisco_7603_slot_1 pd_id 1
 6    Cisco_7603_Configuration_slot_1 SubClassOf pd_hasCard
 7      only Supervisor_Engine_2 or Supervisor_Engine_720
 8    sip-400 type 7600-SIP-400
 9    Functional pd_hasConfiguration
10    Cisco_7603 SubClassOf pd_hasConfiguration
11      exactly 1 Cisco_7603_Configuration
12    DisjointClasses(Catalyst_6500_Module Cisco_7600_SIP
13      Supervisor_Engine)
14    cisco_7603_configuration pd_hasSlot cisco_7603_slot_1
15    cisco_7603 type Cisco_7603
16    pd_hasSlot inverseOf pd_isInConfiguration
17    Cisco_7600_SIP-400 SubClassOf Cisco_7600_SIP
18    Cisco_7603_Configuration_slot_1 EquivalentTo pd_id
19      value 1 and
20        pd_isInConfiguration some Cisco_7603_Configuration
21    7600-SIP-400 SubClassOf Cisco_7600_SIP-400
```

Listing 12.1 Sample reasoning explanation

This raw form of explanation is not meaningful to the user. Even with some experience in OWL, the user is confused with the abundance of axioms which are irrelevant to detect error. On the other hand, from the user perspective, the reason for the error (i.e. the rule which does not hold in the user model) is related to just one axiom, describing the allowed cards in slot "1" (lines 6 and 7).

In order to discriminate axioms which are relevant to the user, the annotation mechanism of OWL2 is used. These annotations occur only when an axiom is relevant as a source of a potential error and it contains the respective error message. In the example model, the axiom contains the annotation: "Slot requires card from the following card categories: Supervisor_Engine_2, Supervisor_Engine_720" (Listing 12.2). This description is interpreted as the error message to be presented to the user.

```
Class: Cisco_7603_Configuration_slot_1
Annotations: rdfs:comment
  "Slot requires card from the following card categories:
  Supervisor_Engine_2, Supervisor_Engine_720."
SubClassOf: pd:Slot ,
        pd:hasCard only ( Supervisor_Engine_2 or
          Supervisor_Engine_720 ) ,
        pd:hasCard some pd:Card
EquivalentTo: pd:isInConfiguration some
  Cisco_7603_Configuration and pd:id value 1
```

Listing 12.2 Slot "1" of Cisco 7603.

12.4.3 Model Repair

In the sections above, we have highlighted some ontology explanation services that can be used to highlight the core erroneous axioms and concepts in a defect ontology. In an ODSD environment, the model repair is based on processing an ontology, resulting from the language metamodel and model.The next step for the developer is to resolve the errors by processing justifications that give her or him advice how to repair the ontology, respectively, the original metamodel and model.

In general, approaches for ontology repairing are presented by Kalyanpur et al., for example, in [110, 112]. Although there might be (semi-)automatic strategies for repairing ontologies and models, each repair step underlies the knowledge and proof of domain experts. Based on a set of justifications, different axiom rating strategies can be adopted. A simple one is to compute the frequency of an axiom. Here the number of times the axiom appears in each justification of the various unsatisfiable concepts in an ontology is counted. If an axiom appears in all justifications for n different unsatisfiable concepts removing the axiom from the ontology ensures that n concepts become satisfiable. Thus, the higher the frequency, the lower (better) the rank assigned to the axiom.

An excellent explanation, justification, and repair are of uttermost importance for ODSD. The MOST workbench has certainly taken only the first steps to this goal but shows that these ontology services are very helpful for modelling.

12.5   Traceability in ODSD

Since ODSD is based on two different technical spaces: the modelling space and the ontology space, three aspects concerning traceability have to be investigated:

1. The implementation of comprehensive traceability in the modelling space
2. The implementation of comprehensive traceability in the ontology space
3. The usage of bridging approaches to allow developers to seamlessly work with traceability information in both spaces

While the first two aspects have already been discussed in Chap. 6, the last one is covered in the following. Section 12.5.1 generally comments on the role the integration infrastructure of the ODSD tool environments' architecture plays for traceability. In Sect. 12.5.2, it illustrates how bridges between the two technical spaces, for example, transformations between query languages of both spaces, can ease developers' work.

12.5.1   Using the Integration Infrastructure for Traceability

As shown in Chap. 6, semantically rich traceability relationships can be defined and recorded using languages and technologies originating from either the modelling or the ontology space. Therefore, traceability information can be treated like any other artefact in the respective technical space. This also includes the transformation between the two spaces using the ODSD integration infrastructure.

With respect to retrieval problems, most of them are based on the CWA, as reflected by the three retrieval patterns *existence*, *reachable entities*, and *slice*. In the ontology space, this can be supported by having NAF (Negation as Failure) in ontologies themselves by using NBox or in the queries.

12.5.2 Benefiting from Transformations Between Modelling and Ontology Languages

It can be assumed that prospective users of ODSD are, in most cases, people with a software development background, i.e., who are mainly proficient in modelling technologies and programming languages, but who possibly lack a profound knowledge of the ontology technical space. These software developers can profit from the availability of bridging technologies between the technical spaces. Example approaches are given in [212], explaining how to transform GReQL constraints to OWL ontologies, and in [184], dealing with the mapping of GReQL queries to equivalent SPARQL queries and vice versa.

The employment of these approaches would allow developers to solely use languages stemming from the modelling space for the definition and retrieval of traceability information. Sticking to the approaches given in [212] and [184], for example, the specification of constraints and queries could be conducted with GReQL only. They are subsequently transformed to the ontology space if necessary. This accommodates the developers' skills and saves effort as constraints and queries have to be specified only once, thus avoiding costly manual rewriting if traceability information is transformed between the technical spaces. Furthermore, GReQL constraints and queries are, in general, more concise than their OWL or SPARQL counterparts, respectively [212]. Another application of the transformation of GReQL constraints to OWL is to use ontology-based reasoning to check the constraints' *satisfiability*, i.e., if some constraints are contradicting so that it is not possible to fulfil them all.

In the following, the bridging approaches presented in [212] and [184] are shortly introduced.

Transforming Constraints from GReQL to OWL

Roughly, the transformation described in [212] maps GReQL's universally and existentially quantified expressions, which are in most cases used for specifying constraints, to OWL SubClassOf axioms. The latter declare that the OWL class corresponding to the set of graph elements for which the GReQL constraint must be satisfied is a subclass of an anonymous class reflecting the constraint. By performing a consistency check on the ontology, it can be detected whether all instances of the subclass are also an instance of the superclass. If not, the constraint is not fulfilled.

The transformation approach is also able to convert logical operators (and, or, not) and regular path expressions.

Transforming Queries Between GReQL and SPARQL

Due to substantial differences between GReQL and SPARQL, the approach presented in [184] only allows to transform a very limited number of the available GReQL expressions. However, these include existentially quantified expressions as well as from-with-report expressions, which are both required for realising queries conforming to the three retrieval patterns. In short, while existentially quantified expressions are mapped to SPARQL ASK queries, FWR expressions are transformed to SELECT queries. For each variable declared in a quantified expression or in the from part of an FWR expression and used in the quantified expression's Boolean expression or in the with part, respectively, there is a corresponding variable in the SPARQL query's where clause. The variables used in the report part of an FWR expression are mapped to corresponding SPARQL variables specified after the SELECT keyword. However, it is not possible to transform *iterated path descriptions* to SPARQL. This severely limits the expressiveness of the path structures which may be specified, according to the retrieval patterns.

Concerning the transformation from SPARQL to GReQL, all kinds of SPARQL queries can be mapped, except for CONSTRUCT queries, involving the construction of a graph, and DESCRIBE queries, returning external descriptions for ontology entities.

12.6   Conclusion

As we have seen in this chapter, ontology-integrated services in the MOST ODSD workbench help to preserve the consistency of models. Since they also help to preserve the consistency of process models (behavioural models), they can also be used to guide developers through difficult software development processes, which is the topic of the next chapter.

Chapter 13
Ontology-Guided Software Engineering in the MOST Workbench

Uwe Aßmann, Srdjan Zivkovic, Krzysztof Miksa, Katja Siegemund, Andreas Bartho, Tirdad Rahmani, Edward Thomas, and Jeff Z. Pan

Abstract This chapter reports about the software process guidance in ontology-driven software development (ODSD), one of the core ontology-enabled services of the ODSD environments. Ontology-driven software process guidance amounts to a significant step forward in software engineering in general (cf. Fig. 1.1 on p. 3). Its role is to guide developers through a complex software development process by providing information about the consistency of artefacts and about the tasks to be accomplished to reach a particular development goal.

We start this chapter by providing an overview of the engine that enables ontology-based guidance (Sect. 13.1). In subsequent sections, we provide insights into four concrete domain-specific guidance ontologies that configure the guidance engine for the particular domain, all being designed for the MOST ODSD workbench. Some of these guidance engines are related to the case studies presented in Chap. 4, as well as related solutions presented in Chaps. 9 and 10. Section 13.2 provides a summary of the Guidance Ontology for Process Refinement in Sect. 13.3, designed for the purpose of the SAP. This is followed by Guidance Ontology for Domain Engineering, which has been created for the Comarch case study. In Sect. 13.4, we report on a Guidance Ontology for Requirements Engineering paving the way for a more systematic, consistency-preserving elicitation and analysis of requirements. Finally, Sect. 13.5 provides insights into the Guidance Ontology for Documentation Engineering, an essential step in any software development process.

13.1 Ontology-Based Guidance Engine

13.1.1 The Generic Guidance

The guidance engine of the MOST ODSD workbench relies heavily on the ontological representation of software development processes in order to compute

J.Z. Pan et al. (eds.), *Ontology-Driven Software Development*,
DOI 10.1007/978-3-642-31226-7_13, © Springer-Verlag Berlin Heidelberg 2013

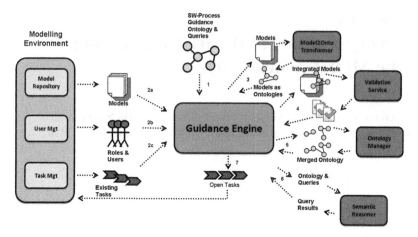

Fig. 13.1 Integrated guidance

tasks that need to be accomplished. We have called this kind of guidance *process guidance* in this book. In addition, the guidance engine considers the actual system state, i.e., the state of artefacts to reason about pre-condition and post-conditions of tasks. The state of the artefacts is computed by dedicated ontology-based validation services, which is what we have called in this book *consistency guidance*. For example, validating the refinement of two *Business Process Management Notation (BPMN)* process models can be considered as a consistency guidance. On the other hand, the fact that after and only after a *valid* process refinement, a grounding task can be performed is considered as a process guidance. The Guidance Engine combine these two kinds of guidance support into an *integrated guidance*.

A guidance engine is a central component of any ODSD tool environment. In order to tightly integrate it, the guidance engine has to communicate with different information providers. On the one hand, the guidance engine gathers the artefact information, i.e., models and their metamodels, from the modelling infrastructure. On the other hand, the guidance engine relies on the ontology infrastructure, in particular on the semantic reasoner, for the consistency checking and computation and inferring of the tasks. Figure 13.1 illustrates how the guidance engine computes the tasks by collaborating with both the modelling infrastructure and the semantic reasoner. The focus is on the information flow that takes place during the computation of tasks within the system.

Before we explain how the guidance engine performs at run time, it is important to note that the guidance engine needs to be configured at design time for a specific development process. By configuration, we mean the definition of the particular SW-Process Guidance Ontology together with a set of predefined Queries. This specific guidance ontology contains knowledge about the tasks, their preconditions and postconditions and how they are related to the modelling artefacts (see Sect. 13.1.2 for an explanation of the main concepts).

The computation of the tasks, which occurs at runtime in the guidance engine, can be divided into six major steps.

1. *Get Current Process State.* In this step, all needed information about the current state of the development process is retrieved from the (modelling) environment. This information is crucial for building the knowledge base for further processing. This includes getting the following elements:

   - `Models`. Models represent the current state of the development process. The guidance engine requests from the environment all models based on the underlying modelling language, for which the guidance ontology has been defined.
   - `Existing Tasks`. Existing tasks, if there are any, are retrieved from the task management component of the modelling environment, to infer the knowledge about already accomplished tasks. However, based on the state of artefacts, existing tasks may be reopened or even removed by the guidance engine.
   - `Roles and Users`. Since different roles may perform different types of tasks, it is important to supply the guidance engine with the currently active user and his role.

2. *Convert Models to Ontologies.* The guidance engine is based on semantic technology. In order to enable reasoning, model information needs to be converted into its ontological representation. For that purpose, the guidance engine relies on the integration infrastructure. The transformation itself is based on two basic rules:

   - The metamodel is transformed into the ontology `TBox`, thus representing the type information of the domain ontology.
   - The models become the ontology `ABox`, thus acting as instance data.

3. *Check Model Ontologies for Consistency.* Once the ontological representation of the models is available, the consistency check can be performed. For that purpose, the guidance engine relies on a dedicated semantic model validation component. Upon consistency check execution, for all models an additional axiom is added to the ontology stating whether the particular model is a *correct model* or an *incorrect model*. In addition, if the validation component also provides the validation information about the single objects in the model, axioms are added for model objects as well. However, if no validation information for objects has been retrieved, the validation state is taken from the containing model. Adding the axioms about the artefact state is important for the correct computation of pre-conditions and postconditions. For example, given some task *Fix Refinement Process* for some process model *P*, the precondition of such task is an *incorrect refinement process* and the postcondition is *correct refinement process*. Upon the validation, the process model *P*, as individual, may be classified either as *Incorrect* or *Correct* refinement process based on the

added axioms, which directly influences the satisfaction of related task pre- and postconditions.

4. *Merge Ontologies.* In this step, the guidance engine contains all necessary information, yet spread across several ontologies. Thus, this step makes sure that the complete knowledge base is merged into a single ontology before it is given to the reasoner. The ontology merge acts according to the mapping rules that have been defined during the guidance engine configuration. For this, metamodel element names relevant for the guidance have to be mapped to the artefact names defined in the guidance ontology. For example, the metamodel element `Task` from the BPMN metamodel is mapped to the `Activity` class which is a subtype of the class `Artefact` in the guidance ontology. The result of the merge step is a unified ontology consisting of the domain ontology (model and metamodel information) enriched by the consistency information and the task ontology enriched with the user and users' role information. The merge process relies on the basic ontology service `Merge` to found in OWL API.

5. *Compute Guidance Tasks.* Having the merged ontology on the one side and the predefined queries for inferring the guidance tasks on the other side, the process guidance actions can be computed. The query result retrieved from the semantic reasoner delivers all possible tasks based on the current state of the models. This set of tasks is then intersected with the already performed tasks, in order to show to the user only currently open tasks.

6. *Translate Results.* In the final step, the guidance engine translates the results into a format that the ODSD tool environment can handle, so they can be displayed to the user.

13.1.2 The Generic Guidance Ontology

The **generic guidance ontology** represents the core semantic data model of the guidance engine. It defines a set of generic concepts for software development, which abstracts from any specific software process methodology. Due to its generic design, the guidance ontology can be extended for any domain-specific software process. The process of extending the generic guidance ontology can at the same time be regarded as a configuration, respectively, instantiation process of the guidance engine.

Guidance Aspects

Software process methodologies distinguish three important aspects of software processes [93, 152]:

- *Work Units.* Work units subsume abstractions of processes, tasks, activities, steps but also builds, phases, milestones, cycles, etc.

- *Producers*. Producers describe persons or tools that act or enacted according to work units. Persons are usually represented as users that may have different roles in the process.
- *Work Products*. Work products represent abstractions of development artefacts. These can be source code files, requirement documents, models, documentation artefacts etc.

In essence, `work units` are performed by `producers`, which produce/work on `work products`.

Guidance Concepts

The generic guidance ontology covers all three main aspects of software processes by introducing three top level concepts and corresponding relationships, as we have described in Sect. 10.4:

- `TaskType`. A task type is a generic concept for representing any kind of a *work unit* in the process. There are no generic subtypes of this concept, i.e., its direct subtypes are concrete work units of some process (e.g. *Refine Process, Fix Device, Generate Source Code*, etc.). However, task types could be further differentiated on the generic level by introducing concepts such as *process, phase, activity* or *step*, all being subtypes of a TaskType class. In the generic guidance ontology, the TaskType is represented as an OWL class.
- `Role`. A role represents a *producer* in the process. Roles could be further differentiated between *persons* and *tools*. The latter are enacted by a guidance engine to automate the execution of certain tasks. However, the current implementation supports only person roles. The Role concept is represented in the guidance ontology by an OWL class.
- `Artefact`. An artefact represents a generalisation of all *work products* in the software process. These can be concepts such as model, requirement, documentation, source code etc. Each artefact can be in a state *correct* or *incorrect* reflecting its validity. We capture this fact in the generic guidance ontology by the subclass `ArtefactInState` and its subclasses `Correct` and `Incorrect`. These classes are used by the guidance engine to add appropriate axioms to the artefact ontology based on the results returned from the validation services. The artefact concept is represented by an OWL class.
- `preconditionOf`. Artefacts represent preconditions of certain task types. For example, a model artefact *correct refinement process* is a precondition of task type *Ground process*. In the generic guidance ontology, preconditions of task types are represented by the `preconditionOf` OWL object property, where the domain is some `Artefact` and the range some `TaskType`.
- `hasPostcondition`. Task types typically produce new artefacts, or change state of existing artefacts. For example, the result of the task type *Fix Device Type* is some *Correct Device Type*. Such constraints represent postconditions of task types and are used in the guidance engine to infer completed tasks.

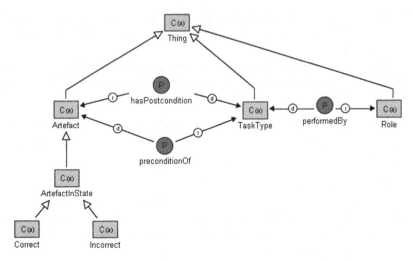

Fig. 13.2 Generic guidance ontology

Postconditions of task types are represented by the `hasPostcondition` OWL object property where the domain is some `TaskType` and the range is some `Artefact`.

- `performedBy`. Task types are performed by some roles. For example, the task type *Ground Process* can be performed only by the role *Developer*. Performing roles are represented by the `performedBy` object property, where the domain is some `TaskType` and the range some `Role`.

Figure 13.2 illustrates the generic guidance ontology using the prototypical BOC OWL2 graphical syntax[1].

13.1.3 Implementation Technologies

Following the generic architecture of ODSD tool environments introduced in Sect. 12.1.2, the guidance engine, the core of the *ontology-based process guidance*, belongs to the group of *ontology-based services*. It utilises the *modelling infrastructure* to retrieve model-relevant information and the *ontology infrastructure* to perform the reasoning.

---

[1]For the purpose of the integrated DSL+OWL modelling approach, BOC developed a prototypical graphical syntax for OWL2 in the ADOxx Platform, based on the abstract metamodel of the OWL2 Manchester syntax.

ODSD Tool Environment

In the MOST project, the prototype ODSD tool environment was built based on the ADOxx[2], an extensible, repository-based platform for building domain-specific modelling environments. ADOxx provides a common modelling infrastructure for the management of models and metamodels. In addition, *vertical services* such as *task management* and *user management*, relevant for the guidance engine are also available.

Ontology Infrastructure

In the MOST project, the guidance system utilises the REL reasoner [172], a reasoning component of the TrOWL framework[3] to do reasoning. The guidance ontologies are OWL2 EL [139] ontologies. Although the language expressive power of the guidance ontology may be extended by the domain ontology, the essential part that is responsible for describing the pre-condition and post-conditions of tasks will remain OWL2 EL. This restriction enables efficient online reasoning facilities for the guidance engine because the reasoning services of OWL2 EL are all of relatively low complexity.

The reasoning services used by the guidance engine are TBox classification and conjunctive query answering. The TBox classification service is used to retrieve the direct subclasses of the concept `TaskType` so that in the query phase, the system knows which task types can be retrieved. Similar reasoning service can be applied to role types. The conjunctive query answering service is used to retrieve tasks that should be performed, or could be performed with corresponding artefacts.

The reasoning time complexity of TBox classification is PTIME-Complete. The data complexity of conjunctive query answering is also PTIME-Complete. The query complexity is NP-Complete.

Guidance Engine

The *guidance engine* component implements and exposes a set of interfaces which represent core entities of the guidance engines such as *ITask*, *IArtefact* or *IRole*. These interfaces are implementations of the generic guidance ontology concepts. Furthermore, the guidance engine also implements and exposes the *IGuidanceEngine* interface which provides main functionalities of the guidance engine for triggering the computation and retrieval of the tasks. On the other side, the guidance engine relies on the ontology infrastructure components via the *IReasoner* interface for reasoning and on the OWL API for the ontology manipulation. An additional important aspect of the guidance engine design is the realisation of

---

[2]http://www.boc-group.com
[3]http://trowl.eu/

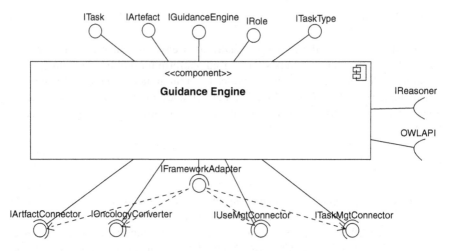

Fig. 13.3 The guidance engine interfaces

the loosely coupled connection to the particular ODSD tool environment. The connection has been realised by introducing the additional adapter layer between the guidance engine and the environment, where for each environment, such as ADOxx or Eclipse, a framework adapter has to be implemented. Following interfaces build up the adapter layer as depicted in Fig. 13.3:

- *The IArtefactConnector* is responsible for providing access to the artefacts coming from the environment, such as metamodels and models.
- *The IOntologyConverter* is the interface which retrieves the ontology representation of the given set of artefacts (models). The realisation for this interface is part of the integration infrastructure.
- *The IUserMgtConnector* provides access to user related information from the environment. It includes the information about the currently logged user and his role.
- *The ITaskMgtConnector* interface abstracts the connection to the particular task management component. This interface is used by the guidance engine to retrieve existing tasks and to issue the creation of the new tasks.
- *The IFrameworkAdapter* provides access to all of the previously mentioned interfaces.

The introduced adapter layer is a very important feature of the guidance engine, since it raises its portability for arbitrary ODSD tool environments.

13.2 Guidance for Process Refinement Engineering

The main concern of the case studies on *Process Refinement* and *Querying Tasks & Artefacts* is to provide guidance to software developers for better process modelling in the service consumption phase (see Sect. 4.2). The process refinement validation applied in the *Process Refinement* case study will help to apply the proposed process refinement methodology explained in Chap. 10 by preventing manual refinement checks. Furthermore, certain parts of the guidance ontology concerned with task management aspects enable developers to have adequate instant task lists at hand during the process modelling and refinement stage.

For a better understanding of what is concretely meant by guidance in process refinement engineering, we will demonstrate based on some examples how technologies addressing the case studies requirements could be utilised in a realistic guidance scenario.

13.2.1 Guidance as a Service for Refinement

The validation of process refinement is not easy. It consists of checking model constraints imposed by the behaviour of generic processes and also constraints which emerged during the refinement steps. Currently, such consistency checking is mainly done manually; not many methods have been investigated and implemented to help automation. Therefore, this validation task is error-prone, time-consuming and increases the costs during the development cycle.

In the example depicted in Fig. 13.4, there are three process models shown which are the refinements of each other. At the top of the figure, the most abstract process can be seen which corresponds to the view of the business process expert on the process. Then, the analyst process refines the abstract process. Last but not least, the most specific process is the developers process with the most detailed process description. The connectors in between the processes represent refinement connectors and are used for illustrating the refinement relation.

By having a closer look on the process models depicted in Fig. 13.4, it can be very hard to answer the following questions:

- Do some refinement errors exist between the expert and analyst view?
- Do some refinement errors exist between the analyst and developer view?

The role of guidance service—which is actually a process refinement validation service—is to enable a developer with better refinement flaw detection and refinement flaw resolution. This could either take place on the fly when the developer is still modelling or at one certain point of time when he decides to do the validation by activating some UI element like a button on a certain development screen. As an example, the screen could look like the Fig. 13.5, where on the top left side a special process refinement validation screen can be seen. There all existing refinement flaws could be shown to the developer. By clicking on one of these flaws, the process model entities and paths causing the error could be highlighted in the process model.

As a summary of the guidance example, one can conclude that any functionality delivered as an additional *service* to the software developer usable for better automated refinement checks is highly appreciated.

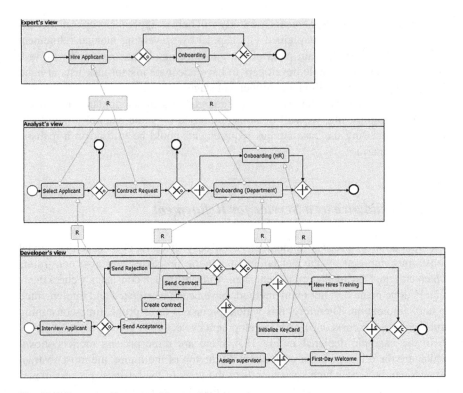

Fig. 13.4 Process refinement without guidance

13.2.2   Guidance as a Process for Refinement

As an introductory motivation to understand more precisely which problems we
are going to address, one should consider the case that the outcome of the model
validation together with the status of how modelling artefact influences the next
possible development steps resp. development tasks. In this situation, a developer
might want to know after a certain modelling step which other modelling tasks can
be performed on a certain artefact. Conversely, it might happen that modelling tasks
are categorised in order to delegate them appropriately to modelling teams with a
certain needed expertise. Consequently, it would be quite helpful to retrieve for a
specific modelling task type all artefacts on which the task can be applied or has to
be applied.

In order to address challenges mentioned in the motivation, obviously, there is
a need to relate tasks with artefacts and their status in the software development
lifecycle. The notion *artefact status* can thereby be understood as an abstract
placeholder for values that capture lifecycle important information and metadata
of an artefact. For example, a status of a process could be that some of his activities

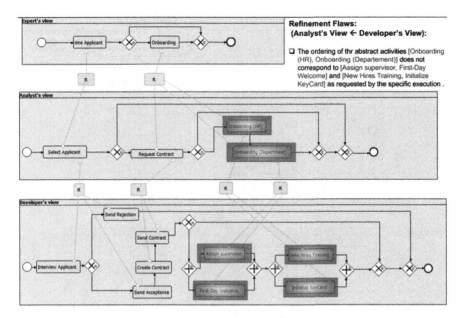

Fig. 13.5 Validation service as guidance for process refinement

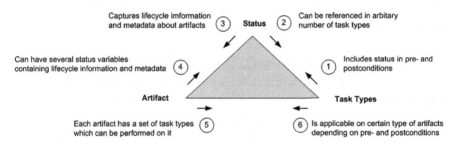

Fig. 13.6 Relations between artefact, status and task type

need still to be refined or that there exists a refinement flaw between this process and a more abstract or specific process. Some help addressing these requirements is provided by the guidance ontology and the methodology to create a guidance ontology described in Sects. 4.2.3 and 13.1.2.

To sum up, one can think of a triangle consisting of three points representing the artefact, the artefact status and the modelling task (Fig. 13.6). The edges depict relations that need to be known to provide an appropriate guidance solution. This guidance solution has the goal to guide a developer through the whole *process* of the refinement methodology until the process models can be deployed as a final outcome of the service consumption phase.

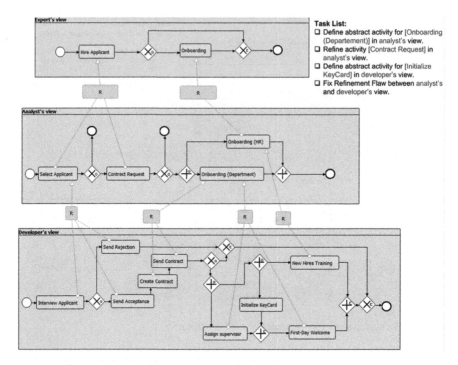

Fig. 13.7 Guidance example for task management

A developer with a certain role has to be able to easily answer the following questions in order to be productive in the service consumption phase and to have a high quality end result.

- Does some refinement errors exist in the refinement hierarchy that hinder the process to be deployed?
- Are there some not refined activities in the refinement hierarchy that hinder the process to be deployed?
- What kind of tasks can or have be performed next in order to come a step closer to deployment?

The availability of a guidance ontology as a data model containing all modelling artefacts and all modelling task types, together with the artefact statuses, would make it possible to utilise ontology query mechanisms to fill the developers task list appropriately with information. As an example to depict the role of guidance here, let's have a look at the process refinement hierarchy shown in Fig. 13.7. There one can see a special view presenting some hints to the developer. Of course, instead of hints the concrete development tasks to be performed could be in the list, but the statements show more clearly how the guidance ontology could help out here.

13.3   Guidance for Domain Engineering

The main concern of the case study on domain engineering (refer to Sect. 4.1 for the case study description) is to provide guidance for the users of *domain-specific language (DSL)*. The support is not limited to the post-change validation of models but also enables asking questions about possible next steps. These questions might involve both the fine grained actions, such as connecting the individual model elements, as well as suggesting next more coarse grained steps in the modelling process.

13.3.1   Consistency Guidance

The guidance services used in the case study are mainly used for the purpose of enforcing the semantics of the *ontological instantiation* (the *linguistic instantiation* semantics is already enforced by the MDE tools). For example, the instances of the devices which break the rules defined by their types are reported to the user (UC-2 in Sect. 4.1). Also, the user may proactively ask about the possible connections between the elements in order to avoid errors (UC-3 in Sect. 4.1). Both type of guidance services are realised by integrating the DSL with OWL2 and using reasoning services (as described in Sect. 9.3).

Validation services are triggered upon the committed changes in the model repository. The following error messages may be reported from the consistency guidance:

- Inconsistent artefact. An artefact (device, configuration, slot or card) may be inconsistent. An additional explanation is attached to the error message. The explanation is based on the annotations provided for the constraints.
- Inconsistent device type. A message for an incorrect device type is provided, if the constraints imposed by the type does are contradictory with some other semantic constraints.
- A model is malformed. There is an unexpected modelling error, for example, no devices or device type model exists.

In addition to the validation checks, the consistency guidance also provides the suggestions for correct modelling. The users may proactively ask the consistency guidance if certain connections between the artefacts are allowed in order to avoid errors. In the PDDSL Tool, the user can ask for:

- *Allowed card category suggestions.* By selecting a slot in a configuration of some device, one can ask for the possible card categories that can be inserted into this slot.
- *Allowed slots suggestions.* Conversely, one can select a card in the artefact repository and, for the active PDDSL device models, ask the system for the allowed slots, where the card can be inserted to.

13.3.2   Process Guidance

The users are also supported from the modelling process perspective. For instance, given that a device type is inconsistent the guidance engine will suggest to fix rather than to create an instance of it. The solution is based on the generic guidance engine which was configured with the generic guidance ontology extended for the PDDSL case. The following task types grouped by user roles are supported in the PDDSL tool:

- Domain Expert

  - *Fix Device Type*. This task occurs for the incorrect device types. As long as the validation service reports errors in device type definition, the task remains open.
  - *Check Device Type*. This task is always enabled for each device type.

- Domain User

  - *Create Device*. This task is created for all available correct device types.
  - *Set Type of Device*. If a device is created, this task ensures that the type of the device is set.
  - *Fix Device*. This task occurs for incorrect devices. As long as the validation service reports errors in the configuration of the device, the task remains open.
  - *Check Device*. This task is always enabled for each modelled device.

Guidance ontology for physical devices modelling extends the generic guidance ontology by the concepts specific to the domain of devices configuration. As introduced in Sect. 13.1 the generic ontology can be extended by adding specific task types, domain artefacts and domain roles. Figure 13.8 illustrates the complete asserted class hierarchy of the physical devices ontology using the BOC OWL2 graphical syntax.

In the diagram, boxes represent *OWL classes*. *Super class descriptions* are modelled using relations with white-filled arrows, whereas *equivalent class descriptions* are depicted using relations with black-filled arrows additionally signed with the E circle.

In addition to the extensions of the main guidance classes, generic object properties such as *preconditionOf* need to be extended as well. For each introduced task type, a specific object property representing the task-type precondition is defined. Figure 13.9 illustrates the object properties of the physical devices ontology. Again, *object properties* are represented using circles. *Super properties* relationships are modelled using relations with arrows. Object properties *domains* and *ranges* are specified using relations with black-filled arrows and marked with d and r circles, respectively.

Finally, the restrictions in the physical devices ontology are modelled using OWL expressions. First, for each task type we define roles that can perform the task. In the same way, postconditions of task types are defined. Figure 13.10 illustrates three definitions of OWL expressions using our graphical syntax. Expressions are defined

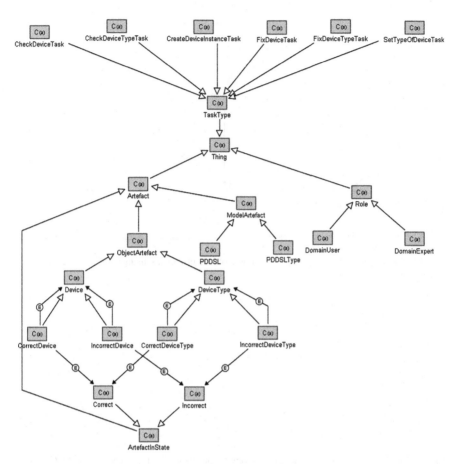

Fig. 13.8 Physical devices guidance ontology: asserted class hierarchy using BOC OWL2 graphical syntax

as description frames in a tree-like manner. This OWL expressions diagram can be read as follows. The first description defines that the class *SetTypeOfDeviceTask* is, on the one side, a *subclass* of a class that is *performedBy some* class *DomainUser*. On the other side, it is a *subclass* of a class that *hasPostcondition some* class *Device-Type*. The second description defines that the task-type class *FixDeviceTypeTask* is a *subclass* of a class, i.e., *performedBy some DomainExpert*. Similarly, the third description defines that the task type class *FixDeviceTask* is a *subclass* of a class, i.e., *performedBy some DomainUser*.

Figure 13.11 depicts expressions defined for the artefact *DeviceType*. For each task type where DeviceType participates as a precondition, we define one precondition expression. Since the task type *CheckDeviceTypeTask* can be performed for both correct and incorrect device types, we define that the class *DeviceType*

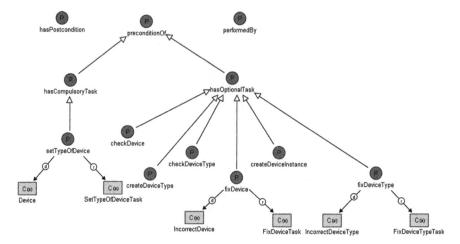

Fig. 13.9 Physical devices guidance ontology: object properties using BOC OWL2 graphical syntax

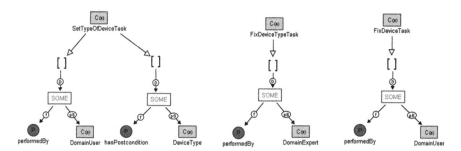

Fig. 13.10 Physical devices guidance ontology: expressions for task types using BOC OWL2 graphical syntax

is a *subclass* of class that is a *preconditionOf* some class *CheckDeviceType-Task*. However, we use the object property *checkDeviceType* as a subproperty of *preconditionOf*, since it holds exact property domain and ranges (see Fig. 13.9). Similarly, we define that the *CorrectDeviceType* is a *preconditionOf* of the task type *CreateDeviceInstanceTask*, whereas the *IncorrectDeviceType* is a *preconditionOf* the task type *FixDeviceTypeTask*.

The expressions for the artefact *Device* are defined in the same way (see Fig. 13.12). First, we define that the *Device* is a *preconditionOf* the task types *CheckDeviceTask* and *SetTypeOfDeviceTask*. Subsequently, we state that the *IncorrectDevice* is a *preconditionOf* the task type *FixDeviceTask*.

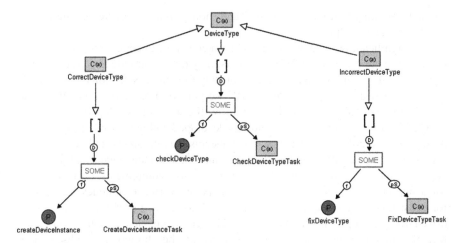

Fig. 13.11 Physical devices guidance ontology: expressions for the device type using BOC OWL2 graphical syntax

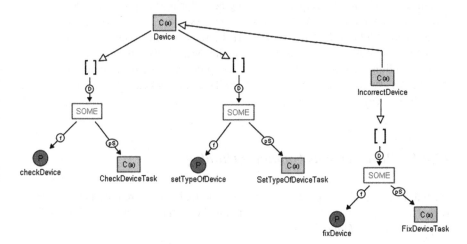

Fig. 13.12 Physical devices guidance ontology: expressions for the device using BOC OWL2 graphical syntax

13.4   Guidance for Requirements Engineering

Requirements engineering (RE) refers to the process of eliciting (identifying), evaluating, specifying, consolidating, and changing the objectives, functionalities, qualities, and constraints to be achieved by a software-intensive system [206]. Results are documented in a Requirement Specification that usually also serves as a contract between customer and developer. The importance of RE was already identified in several studies (e.g. [87]). Thus, an improved RE contributes to safer and better-quality software, safes time and money and also decreases the risk of overran budgets and project failures.

One significant problem requirement engineers have to cope with is the process itself. Although a variety of RE tools exists, they do not provide any process guidance. Thus, the requirement engineer is not supported in the selection of appropriate tasks. By providing assistance during RE we aim to improve the correctness and completeness of RE results, so that to improve the software developed.

The idea of the Requirements Ontology developed within the MOST Workbench is to use an ontology to structure the concepts, requirements and relationships captured during requirements elicitation. This domain independent ontology can be instantiated with the requirement artefacts (goals, requirements, obstacles, etc.) for a particular project. Reasoning and query answering techniques are applied for consistency and completeness checking. OntoReq is a prototype for ontology driven RE developed in the MOST Workbench. It enables reasoning based on formal semantics and aims to resolve many of the shortcomings observed in other approaches. However, even though the Requirements Ontology aims to overcome several deficiencies of today's RE tools, one major problem of RE remains: supporting the requirements engineer during the process of RE. Therefore, OntoReq includes guidance for the process of *goal-oriented requirements engineering (GORE)*. In order to support the requirements engineer OntoReq has a guidance engine like the one used in the MOST workbench, similar to the documentation guidance in Sect. 13.5. The guidance engine is configured by a specific SW-Process Guidance Ontology, the so-called Requirements Guidance Ontology.

13.4.1 Requirements Guidance Ontology

We will now explain the process of creating and maintaining requirements artefacts with OntoReq. Afterwards we will explain the *Artefact*s and *TaskType*s of the *Requirements Guidance Ontology*.

Documenting Requirements with OntoReq

OntoReq is a prototype for Requirement engineering. Requirements and other related artefacts (e.g. goals, obstacles, stakeholder, use-cases) are stored in the Requirements Ontology together with meaningful relationships between these artefacts (e.g. refinements, alternatives, influence). In order to avoid confusion with the guidance ontology concept *Artefact* they will from now on be called *requirement artefacts*. These requirement artefacts and relations as well as other data can be stored, manipulated and deleted in the Requirements Ontology by a Java GUI. The ontology itself is kept invisible to the user and only can be used in the background.

Guidance for Requirements Engineering

The guidance for the requirements engineering process is realised by a guidance engine. The guidance engine is configured by the *Requirements Guidance Ontology*, which extends the *Generic Guidance Ontology*.

The following *Artefact*s are used in the ontology.

ArtefactInState   It holds artefacts that are in a certain state (correct, incorrect) and can therefore provide additional tasks depending on the state an artefact is in.

Attribute   It contains additional data for requirement artefacts.

Identifier   Individuals of this class are placeholders for tasks that are not connected to any requirement artefact (this is the case for all identification tasks).

Metric   It Captures metrics for requirements.

RequirementArtefact   It Contains all requirement artefacts for GORE (Challenge, Goal, Requirement and Story).

Risk   It Represents all specified risks for requirement artefacts.

Stakeholder   It Represents all stakeholders for a project.

TestCase   It Represents TestCases for requirements.

Now we describe how the existence and the states of these *Artefacts* affect the guidance. If *Artefacts* exist in a specific state, the guidance engine infers an action to continue work. These actions are defined in the ontology as subclasses of *TaskType*. We have the following rules:

Identifier-rule   If the Requirement Ontology does not contain at least one of each RequirementArtefact, the guidance engine proposes the identification of each (*IdentifyChallengeTask, IdentifyGoalTask, IdentifyFunctionalRequirement-Task, IdentifyNonFunctionalRequirementTask, IdentifyPlatformRequirement-Task, IdentifyScenarioTask, IdentifyUseCaseTask* and *IdentifyStakeholderTask*).

RequirementArtefact   If a RequirementArtefact is not assigned to a Stakeholder, the guidance engine proposes to assign an author (*AssignAuthorOptionalTask*).

Requirement   If no Mandate is chosen for a Requirement, the guidance engine proposes to assign a Mandate(*AssignMandateTask*). If no Metric is connected to a Requirement, the guidance engine proposes to assign a Metric(*AssignMetricTask*). If no Priority is chosen, the guidance engine proposes to assign a Priority(*AssignPriorityTask*). If no Risk is chosen for a Requirement, the guidance engine proposes to assign a Risk(*AssignRiskTask*). If no Scenario is connected to a Requirement, the guidance engine proposes to assign a Scenario(*AssignScenarioTask*). If no TestCase is connected to a Requirement, the guidance engine proposes to assign a TestCase(*AssignTestCaseTask*).

Requirement   If a Requirement is not connected to any Goal, the guidance engine proposes to connect it to a Goal(*ConnectToGoalTask*).

Fig. 13.13 Step and flow
guidance for REG

Step Guidance

Task   Artefact

Flow Guidance

Requirement   If a `Requirement` is not related to any `UseCase`, the guidance
engine proposes to relate it to an `UseCase`(*RelateToUseCaseTask*).

Requirement   If a `Requirement` is not related to any `Artefact`, the guidance
engine proposes to relate it to an `Artefact`(*RelateToArtefactTask*).

Challenge   If a `Challenge` is defined, the guidance engine proposes to refine it
(*RefineChallengeTask*).

Goal   If a `Goal` is not related to any `UseCase`, the guidance engine proposes to
relate it to a `UseCase`(*RelateToUseCaseTask*).

Goal   If a `Goal` is not related to any `Challenge`, the guidance engine proposes
to relate it to a `Challenge`(*RelateToChallengeTask*).

Story   If a `Story` is not connected to any `Goal`, the guidance engine proposes to
connect it to a `Goal`(*ConnectToGoalTask*).

13.4.2   Guidance for Requirement Engineering

Guidance for RE provides two different kinds of guidance, *step guidance* and *flow
guidance*, illustrated in Fig. 13.13.

Step Guidance

Guidance can always be offered when the current intention of the user has been
recognised. Thus, *step guidance* is always related to a *step point* consisting of a
situation and an intention. The situation describes the actual artefact (e.g. a goal
or requirement), the intention describes which activity shall be executed regarding
this artefact, for example, goal refinement. The achievement of an intention causes
a change of that artefact. For this reason, step points are constructed from all
reasonable combinations of two sets: the set of all domain artefacts and the set of all
intentions. Step guidance provides guidance in means of guidelines. They include
instructions for every step point how to execute a certain intention. After executing
a certain activity the user is guided in the decision which task to accomplish next.
This is realised by the *flow guidance*.

Flow Guidance

The REG shows possible tasks to be executed depending on the available artefacts. These tasks are modelled according to the step guidance described in [191]. Therefore, we define *guidance points* as a tuple of an artefact and a task GP =< artefact; task >. The execution of the task can be optional or mandatory. Each guidance point will be assigned a textual guideline, describing how to complete this task. The execution of a task leads to a new guidance point in the guidance process. Thus, the execution of this guidance can be modelled as a successive relation in the form of the following: <artefact;task>,<artefact_i;task_i>. Whereas the step guidance is visible to the user by a represented list of artefact and actions, the flow guidance remains invisible and is only realisable by a refreshed list of tasks.

Optional vs. Mandatory Tasks

Generally, we differentiate between optional and mandatory tasks. This differentiation follows the completeness and consistency rules described in Sect. 9.1. Since these rules distinguish optional from mandatory information to be captured, we addressed this by suggesting optional and mandatory tasks.

Structured chronological vs. Flexible Guidance

One major problem arising during RE is which tasks to achieve in which order. It exists a huge amount of suggestions for the process of RE. So it was one of our aims to guide the Requirements Engineer through this process by displaying a chronological order of tasks to complete in order to accomplish a complete and consistent identification and specification of requirements. However, we did not want to ignore those requirements engineer that already found a RE process capable for their project, company, etc. Therefore, we realised the RE guidance also in such a way that it is possible to leave the recommended chronological path suggested by the guidance engine and to accomplish all the tasks in the order the requirements engineer intends to. Nevertheless he will still be supplied with all open tasks and can return to chronological guidance at any time. This is realised by a complete list of open tasks held by the guidance engine. This list can be filtered which results in recommending tasks following the structured guidance. Thus, the requirements engineer can always choose whether to accomplish any of the open tasks or the recommended tasks.

Connecting the Requirements Ontology with the Guidance Ontology

In order to generate meaningful guidance steps and tasks, the concepts of the Requirements Ontology need to be mapped to concepts of the guidance ontology.

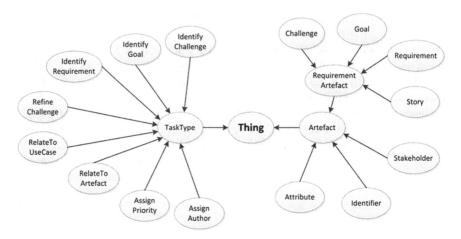

Fig. 13.14 Classification and consolidation of concepts of different ontologies

Figure 13.14 presents the current concept of consolidating both ontologies. The right part refers to the artefacts and the left one refers to the tasks that shall be presented by the REG. Arrows denote the separation of concepts into sub-concepts. In order to implement this concept, it will be necessary to extend the guidance ontology with the specialised task types (e.g. identify) and artefacts (e.g. goal).

We are currently working on connecting the requirements and guidance ontology with a Java interface that also processes the input of requirement artefacts and displays guidance and reasoning results as output. The guidance ontology will be accessed to compute all possible tasks depending on the actual state of the Requirements Ontology. A list of all tasks will be displayed to the user. In case the requirements ontology is changed, the guidance will be forced to update itself and new tasks will be displayed depending on the new status of the Requirements Ontology.

13.5 Guidance for Documentation Engineering

The results of the MOST project have been used for a tool-based documentation case study, which is based on Elucidative Programming [143].

Elucidative Programming is a documentation paradigm for the external documentation of source code. Documentation contains references to sections of code. When these references are resolved, the final documentation will contain embedded listings of the referenced code. If the documented code changes, the references from the documentation to the code can be resolved again. This ensures that the documentation is always up-to-date.

The approach can be extended to the external documentation of models. It is called Elucidative Development. The Elucidative Programming tool *Development Environment For Tutorials (DEFT)* [15] has been enhanced to support Elucidative Development. It can access the repository of the MOST workbench and is therefore suitable for the documentation of the models created with the workbench.

In order to support the documentation writer DEFT has a guidance engine like the one used in the MOST workbench. The guidance engine is configured by a specific SW-Process Guidance Ontology, the so-called Documentation Guidance Ontology.

We will now explain the process of creating and maintaining model documentation with DEFT. Afterwards we will explain the *Artefact*s and *TaskType*s of the *Documentation Guidance Ontology.*

Creating Documentation with DEFT

DEFT is a development environment for documentation. It has a repository, which stores the actual documentation text files (Chapters) and a copy or a symbolic links to the all the code files or the models which shall be documented (Artefacts or Artefact Links)[4]. The code or models are usually imported from the file system. However, the import mechanism is flexible enough to allow other sources. For the MOST project, a connector to the MOST workbench has been written. Models in the MOST workbench can be accessed in DEFT via DEFT Artefact Links, which are displayed in the Project View. There is also a Chapter editor to write the text. DEFT Artefacts can be added to the active Chapter, at the current cursor position. Internally, a Reference is created, but the user sees a concrete Representation of the DEFT Artefact. For models from the MOST workbench, the concrete Representation is an image. Other possible Representations of DEFT Artefacts are, for example, styled text or tables. The Representations are computed by parameterised transformation operations, which are encoded in the References.

Maintaining Documentation with DEFT

When the models in the MOST workbench are edited, the documentation becomes invalid. Fortunately, due to the References to the models, the documentation can be partially updated automatically. The model Representations in the Chapters are recomputed from the models in the MOST workbench. Sometimes the models change drastically, so that the Representation update is not enough. The explanatory text will also have to be updated.

---

[4]Artefacts and Artefact Links will from now on be called DEFT Artefacts and DEFT Artefact Links in order to avoid confusion with the guidance ontology concept *Artefact.*

DEFT is able to identify the models that have changed or even been deleted in the MOST workbench, and it also knows where these models are referenced in the Chapters. Thus, it is possible to generate a list of all positions where a Representation has changed or disappeared, and manual proofreading and correction of the documentation text is required. While the documentation writer will have to check the corresponding text manually, DEFT is still a great help here, because the writer can focus his attention on the important parts. Sections where the Representations have not changed need not be checked.

Guidance for the Documentation Process

The guidance for the documentation process is realised by a guidance engine. The guidance engine is configured by the *Documentation Guidance Ontology*, which extends the *Generic Guidance Ontology*. We will explain the used *Artefact*s and the *TaskType*s. *Role*s are not necessary for documentation guidance.

The following *Artefact*s are used in the ontology.

Workspace   It Represents the empty project workspace in DEFT
Project   It Comprises all the Chapters, DEFT Artefacts and References that somehow belong together
Chapter   It Represents a Chapter in DEFT, a document which contains both documentation text and the References to the DEFT Artefacts
Artefact   It Represents a DEFT Artefact, such as a code file, or a model from the MOST workbench
Reference   It Represents a Reference, which is embedded in a Chapter and points to a specific DEFT Artefact
Representation   It Represents a Representation of a DEFT Artefact after the corresponding Reference has been resolved. A Representation can be, for example, an image, a code listing, or a table.

Now we describe how the existence and the states of these *Artefacts* affect the guidance. If *Artefacts* exist in a specific state, the guidance engine infers an action to continue work or fix errors. These actions are defined in the ontology as subclasses of *TaskType*. We have following rules:

Workspace   If the workspace is empty, the guidance engine proposes the creation of a Project. (*CreateProjectTask*).
Project   If a Project contains no Chapters, the guidance engine proposes the creation of a Chapter (*CreateChapterTask*). Similarly, if no DEFT Artefacts have been imported into the Project, such an import is proposed (*ImportArtefactTask*).
ArtefactOutOfSync   If the original code or model in the filesystem or the MOST workbench have been edited or deleted, the documentation is not up to date. DEFT can discover such a change. The guidance engine proposes an update of the DEFT Artefact (*UpdateArtefactTask*). This also includes deletion.

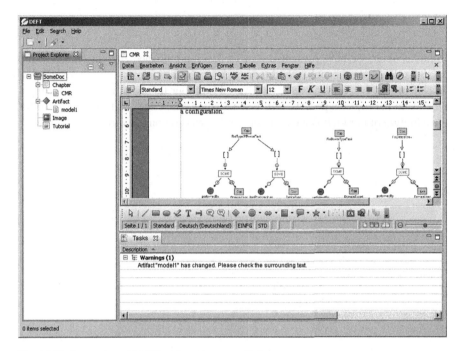

Fig. 13.15   Screenshot of DEFT with guidance enabled

ReferenceToDeletedArtefact   If a DEFT Artefact has been deleted, the References to the deleted DEFT Artefact are invalid. The guidance engine proposes to remove the References (*RemoveReferenceTask*).

ReferenceWithInvalidRepresentation   If the DEFT Artefact has changed drastically after an update, it might happen that the transformation into the Representation fails (e.g., an exception is thrown). The guidance engine proposes to fix the Reference (which, among others, contains the transformation parameters) (*RepairReferenceTask*).

RepresentationUpdatedButUnchecked   If a DEFT Artefact has been updated, all affected References must be reevaluated. In many cases the resulting new Representations are correct, but there is no certainty. In the end the documentation writer has to decide if he accepts the new Representations. The guidance engine proposes for each updated Representation that its correctness be checked (*CheckUpdatedRepresentationTask*).

Figure 13.15 shows a screenshot of DEFT with guidance enabled. The documented model comes from the MOST workbench and has been changed. This change has been detected by DEFT, and the guidance engine proposes to check the surrounding text if it is still consistent with the changed model.

13.6   Conclusion

In this chapter, we have presented how to develop guidance engines on top of the MOST ODSD Workbench, which conclude our discussions on the two stages of level 4 in Fig. 1.1. So far, we have covered both our theory of and a platform for ODSD. In the next chapter, we will discuss some challenges that we are facing for the adoption of our ODSD technologies and our vision on the way forward.

Chapter 14
Conclusion and Outlooks

Jeff Z. Pan, Steffen Staab, Uwe Aßmann, Jürgen Ebert, Yuting Zhao, and Daniel Oberle

Abstract Congratulations! We have covered a lot of ground of the ODSD infrastructure together, in the four parts that we have just walked over.

In Part I, you prepared yourself for this journey, with the state of the art on Model-Driven Software Development (Chap. 2), ontology languages and Description Logics (Chap. 3). You are also firstly exposed to the industrial case studies (Chap. 4) used in this book.

In Part II, you studied the key enabling technologies for Ontology-Driven Software Development (ODSD). Ontologies and metamodelling play important roles in integrating different software engineering models (Chap. 7). Such integration helps stakeholders to understand the associations and dependencies among software engineering models (Chap. 6). In order to exploit ontologies, efficient and scalable ontology reasoning services are necessary (Chap. 5).

In Part III, you learned the first feature of ODSD—exploiting ontology reasoning services. For structure models, ontology reasoning can be applied on extended models, i.e., structure models extended with ontologies (Chap. 9). For process models, task ontologies can be constructed so as to reduce process modelling problems into ontology reasoning problems against the task ontologies (Chap. 10). To integrate the ModelWare and OntologyWare technological spaces, transformation bridges and integration bridges are introduced (Chap. 8).

In Part IV, you learned the second feature of ODSD—Ontology-based guidance engines. This part binds all the previous parts together, by presenting the MOST workbench as a platform (Chap. 12) for ODSD and showing how to make use of the platform to build ontology-based guidance engines, with a few concrete guidance ontologies for the case studies presented earlier in the book (Chaps. 11 and 13).

J.Z. Pan et al. (eds.), *Ontology-Driven Software Development*,
DOI 10.1007/978-3-642-31226-7_14, © Springer-Verlag Berlin Heidelberg 2013

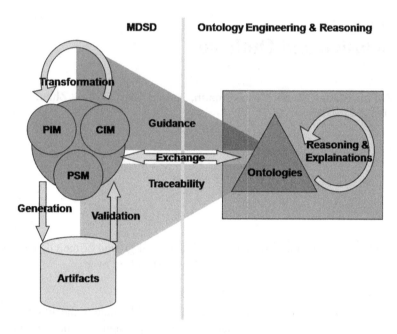

Fig. 14.1 Ontology-driven software development (ODSD)

14.1 Key questions for Ontology-Driven Software Development (ODSD)

You may find Fig. 14.1 helpful to provide a big picture of ODSD. This book addresses a few key questions that are related to this figure, namely:

- How to bridge software engineering models and ontologies
- How to reduce software engineering problems to reasoning and querying over ontologies
- How to combine closed world reasoning (typical in software engineering) and open world reasoning (typical in the Semantic Web)
- How to provide efficient reasoning and querying over ontologies
- How to explain the result of ontology reasoning and querying

14.2 Where to Go from Here?

At this point, you have the necessary context and background knowledge to explore how to apply ODSD in your application areas or investigate further interesting research issues. Here are some of our recommendations.

14.2.1 Things to Keep in Mind When Adopting ODSD

- *Technical Integration*: Technical integration means that ODSD needs to be embedded in the existing landscape of the adopting enterprise. Adaptors might need to be written for legacy codes and databases, versions of programming languages might have to switched, specific software components might have to be replaced because of licence incompatibilities, etc.
- *Constructing Ontologies*: How to construct ontologies properly might be a challenge for new comers. Existing developers/experts might not be familiar with semantic technologies. Educating them indicates training costs. Do not forget to check the web site of this book for the updated list of software engineering ontologies and ontology patterns.
- *Measuring the Benefits*: In addition to a sound scientific evaluation, one might also need to come up with a *business case*, which captures the rationale for initiating a project or task based on ODSD. The logic of the business case is that, whenever resources or effort is consumed, they should be in support of a specific business need. As an example, consider the exemplary business need of software company to increase the productivity of its 10.000 developers by one of the use cases presented in this book. An increase of productivity by 1 % would lead to an estimated cost saving of 15.000.000 Euro per year. A proper business case must clarify how this can be achieved by ODSD.
- *Benefit-Cost Ratio*: You might want to arrive at a positive overall benefit-cost ratio for adopting ODSD. On the one hand, ODSD promises increased productivity in software engineering as outlined above. On the other hand, the costs, due to, e.g., technical integration or constructing, have to be summed up and contrasted to the envisioned benefits.

14.2.2 Contributing to the Linked Software Data

Semantic technologies have been more and more widely accepted. There are more than 30 billion semantic data, also widely known as Linked Open Data, currently available online, not only contributed not only by academia, but also by government (such as data.gov.uk and data.gov), companies (such as BBC, New York Times, and BestBuy), and community efforts (such as DBpedia, the semantic version of Wikipedia).

When you successfully finish your first ODSD case study, please do consider contributing your semantic software data to the Web of Linked Open Data in our web site for this book.[1]

---

[1]http://book.odsd.eu/odsd/

14.2.3   Further Visions in Software Engineering

One of the software engineering's ultimate goals is to have programs that could understand and improve themselves. This is clearly relevant to the vision of the Semantic Web, which aims at improving machine understandability of data. Similarly, ODSD helps making programs more machine understandable. While it seems definitely possible to exploit ODSD to help achieve the above-mentioned goal, more work will be needed to find out all the interesting details.

We hope you have enjoyed learning about ODSD as much as we have enjoyed writing this book. Enjoy your journey onward!

References

1. Y. Guo, Z. Pan, and J. Heflin, LUBM: A benchmark for OWL knowledge base systems. Web Semant. Sci. Serv. Agents World Wide Web **3**(2–3), 158–182 (2005)
2. N. Aizenbud-Reshef, B.T. Nolan, J. Rubin, Y. Shaham-Gafni, Model traceability. IBM Syst. J. **45**(3), 515–526 (2006)
3. N. Aizenbud-Reshef, R.F. Paige, J. Rubin, Y. Shaham-Gafni, D.S. Kolovos, Operational semantics for traceability. in *ECMDA Traceability Workshop (ECMDA-TW) 2005 Proceedings, Nürnberg*, 2005, pp. 7–14
4. B. Amann, M. Scholl, Gram: a graph data model and query language. in *European Conference on Hypertext*, 1992
5. G. Antoniol, G. Canfora, G. Casazza, A. De Lucia, E. Merlo, Recovering traceability links between code and documentation. IEEE Trans. Software Eng. **28**(10), 970–983 (2002)
6. L. Apostel, Towards the formal study of models in a non formal science. Synthese **12**, 125–161 (1960)
7. C. Atkinson, T. Kühne, Model-driven development: a metamodeling foundation. Software, IEEE, vol. **20**(5), pp. 36–41 (2003)
8. C. Atkinson, M. Gutheil, B. Kennel, A flexible infrastructure for multilevel language engineering. IEEE Trans. Software Eng. **99**(RapidPosts), 742–755 (2009). ISSN 0098-5589. doi:http://doi.ieeecomputersociety.org/10.1109/TSE.2009.31
9. F. Baader, B. Suntisrivaraporn. Debugging SNOMED CT using axiom pinpointing in the description logic $\mathcal{EL}^+$. in *KR-MED'08*, vol. 410, CEUR-WS, 2008
10. F. Baader, S. Brandt, C. Lutz, Pushing the $\mathcal{EL}$ envelope. in *Proceedings of the 19th Joint International Conference on Artificial Intelligence (IJCAI 2005)*, 2005
11. F. Baader, D. Calvanese, D.L. McGuinness, D. Nardi, P.F. Patel-Schneider (eds.), *The Description Logic Handbook: Theory, Implementation, and Applications* (Cambridge University Press, Cambridge, 2003). ISBN 0-521-78176-0
12. F. Baader, C. Lutz, B. Suntisrivaraporn, Is tractable reasoning in extensions of the description logic EL useful in practice? in *Proceedings of the 2005 International Workshop on Methods for Modalities (M4M-05)*, 2005
13. F. Baader, R. Peñaloza, B. Suntisrivaraporn, Pinpointing in the description logic $\mathcal{EL}$. in *Proceedings of the 2007 International Workshop on Description Logics (DL2007)*, CEUR-WS, 2007
14. T. Baar, The definition of transitive closure with OCL—limitations and applications. in *Perspectives of System Informatics*, ed. by M. Broy, A.V. Zamulin. Lecture Notes in Computer Science, vol. 2890 (Springer, Berlin/Heidelberg, 2003), pp. 979–997. doi:http://dx.doi.org/10.1007/978-3-540-39866-0_36

J.Z. Pan et al. (eds.), *Ontology-Driven Software Development*,
DOI 10.1007/978-3-642-31226-7, © Springer-Verlag Berlin Heidelberg 2013

15. A. Bartho, Creating and maintaining tutorials with DEFT. in *Proceedings of the 17th IEEE International Conference on Program Comprehension (ICPC'09)*, May 2009, pp. 309–310
16. A. Bartho, S. Zivkovic, D2.2—modeled software guidance/engineering processes and systems. Project Deliverable ICT216691/TUD/WP2-D2/D/PU/b1.00, MOST Project, February 2009
17. A. Bartho, H. Kühn, S. Tinella, W. Utz, S. Zivkovic, D2.1—requirements definition of ontology-driven software process guidance system. Project Deliverable ICT216691/BOC/WP2-D1/D/PU/b1.00, MOST Project, 2008
18. D. Batory, Feature models, grammars, and propositional formulas. *Software Product Lines*, 2005, pp. 7–20
19. B. Beckert, U. Keller, P.H. Schmitt, Translating the object constraint language into first-order predicate logic. in *Proceedings of the Second Verification Workshop: VERIFY 2002, July 25–26, 2002, Copenhagen, Denmark*, vol. 02–07, ed. by S. Autexier, H. Mantel. DIKU technical report, DIKU, 2002
20. D. Beckett (ed.), RDF/XML Syntax Specification (Revised), W3C Recommendation, 10 February 2004, http://www.w3.org/TR/2004/REC-rdf-syntax-grammar-20040210/
21. A. Berglund, S. Boag, D. Chamberlin, M.F. Fernández, M. Kay, J. Robie, J. Siméon (eds.), XML Path Language (XPath) 2.0 (Second Edition), W3C Recommendation 14 December 2010, http://www.w3.org/TR/2010/REC-xpath20-20101214/
22. J. Bézivin, On the unification power of models. Software Syst. Model. **4**(2), 171–188 (2005)
23. J. Bézivin, O. Gerbe, Towards a precise definition of the OMG/MDA framework. *In: Proceedings of the 16th IEEE International Conference on Automated Software Engineering*, 2001, p. 273
24. J. Bézivin, I. Kurtev, Model-based Technology Integration with the Technical Space Concept, in *Proceedings of the Metainformatics Symposium, Springer*, 2005
25. J. Bézivin, F. Jouault, D. Touzet, An introduction to the atlas model management architecture. Research Report LINA, (05-01), 2005
26. D. Bildhauer, J. Ebert, V. Riediger, H. Schwarz, Using the TGraph approach for model fact repositories. in *Proceedings of the Second International Workshop MoRSe 2008: Model Reuse Strategies—Can requirements drive reuse of software models?* 2008, pp. 9–18
27. J. Bézivin, F. Jouault, I. Kurtev, P. Valduriez, Model-based DSL frameworks. in *OOPSLA* (ACM, New York, 2006), pp. 22–26
28. D. Bildhauer, T. Horn, V. Riediger, H. Schwarz, S. Strauß, grUML—A UML based modelling language for TGraphs. Technical report, University of Koblenz-Landau (2010)
29. B. Böhlen, *Ein Parametrisierbares Graph-Datenbanksystem für Entwicklungswerkzeuge*. (Shaker Verlag, Aachen, Germany, 2006)
30. H. Boley, G. Hallmark, M. Kifer, A. Paschke, A. Polleres, D. Reynolds (eds.), RIF Core Dialect, W3C Recommendation 22 June 2010. http://www.w3.org/TR/2010/REC-rif-core-20100622
31. G. Boudol, Towards a lambda-calculus for concurrent and communicating systems. in *TAPSOFT'89* (Springer, Berlin, 1989), pp. 149–161
32. R. Brcina, M. Riebisch, Defining a traceability link semantics for design decision support. In: ECMDA Traceability Workshop (ECMDA-TW) 2008 Proceedings, pp. 39–48. Sintef, Trondheim (2008)
33. S. Brockmans, P. Haase, P. Hitzler, R. Studer, A metamodel and UML profile for rule-extended OWL DL ontologies. in *3rd European Semantic Web Conference (ESWC)*. Lecture Notes in Computer Science, vol. 4011 (Springer, Berlin, 2006), pp. 303–316
34. S. Brockmans, R. Volz, A. Eberhart, P. Löffler, Visual modeling of OWL DL ontologies using UML. in *Proceedings of the Third International Semantic Web Conference*, ed. by S. McIlraith et al. (Springer, Hiroshima, Japan, 2004), pp. 198–213
35. J. Broekstra, A. Kampman, F. van Harmelen, Sesame: a generic architecture for storing and querying RDF and RDF schema. in *The Semantic Web—ISWC 2002*, vol. 2342/2002, 2002, pp. 54–68. doi:10.1007/3-540-48005-6_7. http://www.openrdf.org/doc/papers/Sesame-ISWC2002.pdf

36. A.D. Brucker, B. Wolff, A proposal for a formal ocl semantics in isabelle/hol. in *TPHOLs '02: Proceedings of the 15th International Conference on Theorem Proving in Higher Order Logics* (Springer, London, UK, 2002), pp. 99–114. ISBN 3-540-44039-9

37. A.D. Brucker, B. Wolff, The HOL-OCL book. Technical Report 525, ETH Zurich, 2006 http://www.brucker.ch/bibliography/abstract/brucker.ea-hol-ocl-book-2006

38. T. Bruckhaus, N. Madhavji, I. Janssen, J. Henshaw, The impact of tools on software productivity. IEEE Software **13**(5) (September 1996), Vol. **13**(5), pp. 29–38

39. F. Budinsky, S. Brodsky, E. Merks, *Eclipse Modeling Framework* (Pearson, New Jersey, 2003)

40. C. Calero, F. Ruiz, M. Piattini, *Ontologies for Software Engineering and Software Technology* (Springer, Berlin, 2006)

41. D. Calvanese, G. de Giacomo, D. Lembo, M. Lenzerini, R. Rosati, Tailoring owl for data intensive ontologies. in *Proceedings of the 1st OWL: Experiences and Directions Workshop (OWL-ED 2005)*, 2005

42. D. Calvanese, G.D. Giacomo, D. Lembo, M. Lenzerini, R. Rosati, DL-Lite: Tractable description logics for ontologies. in *Proceedings of AAAI 2005*, 2005

43. D. Calvanese, G.D. Giacomo, M. Lenzerini, R. Rosati, G. Vetere, DL-Lite: Practical reasoning for rich DLs. in *Proceedings of the DL2004 Workshop*, 2004

44. P. Carlshamre, K. Sandahl, M. Lindvall, B. Regnell, J. Natt och Dag, An industrial survey of requirements interdependencies in software product release planning. in *RE '01: Proceedings of the Fifth IEEE International Symposium on Requirements Engineering, Toronto* (IEEE Computer Society, USA, 2001)

45. J.J. Carroll, I. Dickinson, C. Dollin, D. Reynolds, A. Seaborne, K. Wilkinson, Jena: implementing the semantic web recommendations. Technical Report HPL-2003-146, Digital Media Systems Laboratory, HP Laboratories, Bristol, 2003. http://www.hpl.hp.com/techreports/2003/HPL-2003-146.pdf

46. R. Charette, *Software Engineering Environments: Concepts and Technology* (Intertext Publications/McGraw-Hill, New York, 1986)

47. X. Chen, Extraction and visualization of traceability relationships between documents and source code. in *Proceedings of the IEEE/ACM International Conference on Automated Software Engineering*, 2010, pp. 505–510

48. J. Cleland-Huang, C.K. Chang, M. Christensen, Event-based traceability for managing evolutionary change. IEEE Trans. Software Eng. **29**(9), 796–810 (2003). doi:http://dx.doi.org/10.1109/TSE.2003.1232285

49. P. Constantopoulos, M. Jarke, J. Mylopoulos, Y. Vassiliou, The software information base: a server for reuse. VLDB J. **4**(1), 1–43 (1995). ISSN 1066-8888. doi:http://dx.doi.org/10.1007/BF01232471

50. G. Cysneiros, A. Zisman, Traceability and completeness checking for agent-oriented systems. in *Proceedings of the 2008 ACM Symposium on Applied Computing (SAC '08)* (ACM, New York, 2008), pp. 71–77. doi:http://doi.acm.org/10.1145/1363686.1363706

51. K. Czarnecki, Generative Programming: Principles and Techniques of Software Engineering Based on Automated Configuration and Fragment-Based Componet Models, Ph.D. thesis, Technical University of Ilmenau, 1998

52. K. Czarnecki, C. Kim, Cardinality-based feature modeling and constraints: a progress report. in *International Workshop on Software Factories*, Citeseer, 2005

53. K. Czarnecki, S. Helsen, U. Eisenecker, Formalizing cardinality-based feature models and their specialization. Software Process. Improv. Pract. **10**(1), 7–29 (2005)

54. Å.G. Dahlstedt, A. Persson, Requirements interdependencies—moulding the state of research into a research agenda. in *Requirements Engineering Forum on Software Quality (REFSQ), Klagenfurt/Velden*, 2003, pp. 71–80

55. C.V. Damásio, A. Analyti, G. Antoniou, G. Wagner, Supporting open and closed world reasoning on the web. in *Proceedings of 4th Workshop on Principles and Practice of Semantic Web Reasoning, Budva, Montenegro (10–11 June 2006)*, Lecture Notes in Computer Science REWERSE, 2006, pp. 149–163

56. A. De Lucia, R. Oliveto, G. Tortora, ADAMS re-trace: traceability link recovery via latent semantic indexing. in *Proceedings of the 30th International Conference on Software Engineering (ICSE '08)* (ACM, New York, NY, USA, 2008), pp. 839–842. doi:http://doi. acm.org/10.1145/1368088.1368216

57. J. Dick, Rich traceability. in *Proceedings of the 1st International Workshop on Traceability in Emerging Forms of Software Engineering, Edinburgh*, 2002

58. F.M. Donini, D. Nardi, R. Rosati, Description logics of minimal knowledge and negation as failure. ACM Trans. Comput. Log. **3**(2), 177–225 (2002)

59. N. Drivalos, D.S. Kolovos, R.F. Paige, K.J. Fernandes, Engineering a DSL for software traceability. in *Software Language Engineering: First International Conference, SLE 2008, Toulouse, France, September 29–30, 2008. Revised Selected Papers*, Lecture Notes in Computer Science, 2008, pp. 151–167

60. N. Drivalos-Matragkas, D.S. Kolovos, R.F. Paige, K.J. Fernandes, A state-based approach to traceability maintenance. in *Proceedings of the 6th ECMFA Traceability Workshop 2010 (ECMFA-TW)*, ed. by J. Oldevik, G.K. Olsen, D.S. Kolovos, 2010, pp. 23–30

61. J. Ebert, D. Bildhauer, Reverse Engineering Using Graph Queries. In: Andy Schürr, Claus Lewerentz, Gregor Engels, Wilhelm Schäfer, Bernhard Westfechtel: Graph Transformations and Model Driven Engineering. 335–362, Springer Verlag. 2010

62. J. Ebert, A. Franzke, A declarative approach to graph based modeling. in *Graphtheoretic Concepts in Computer Science*, ed. by E. Mayr, G. Schmidt, G. Tinhofer, Lecture Notes in Computer Science, vol. 903 (Springer, Berlin, 1995), pp. 38–50.

63. J. Ebert, V. Riediger, A. Winter, Graph technology in reverse engineering, the TGraph approach. in *Proceedings of the 10th Workshop Software Reengineering (WSR 2008)*, ed. by R. Gimnich, U. Kaiser, J. Quante, A. Winter. GI Lecture Notes in Informatics, vol. 126, pp. 67–81 GI, Bonn, 2008.

64. J. Ebert, R. Süttenbach, I. Uhe, Meta-CASE in practice: a case for KOGGE. in *Advanced Information Systems Engineering* (Springer, Berlin, 1997), pp. 203–216

65. J. Ebert, B. Kullbach, V. Riediger, A. Winter, GUPRO. Generic understanding of programs— an overview. Electr. Notes Theor. Comput. Sci. **72**(2) (2002), pp. 47–56

66. A. Espinoza, P.P. Alarcón, J. Garbajosa, Analyzing and systematizing current traceability schemas. in *SEW '06: 30th Annual IEEE/NASA Software Engineering Workshop SEW-30*, 2006, pp. 21–32. doi:http://doi.ieeecomputersociety.org/10.1109/SEW.2006.12

67. J.-M. Favre, T. Nguyen, Towards a megamodel to model software evolution through transformations. Electr. Notes Theor. Comput. Sci. **127**(3), 59–74 (2005)

68. D. Firesmith, Are your requirements complete? J. Object Tech. **4**(1), 27–44 (2005)

69. J.J. Fleck, Overview of the Structure of the NGOSS Architecture. White paper (Hewlett-Packard Company, Palo Alto, May 2003)

70. D. Forum, DSM forum web page, 2010. http://www.dsmforum.org/

71. M. Fowler, Language workbenches: the killer-app for domain specific languages? Online Web Page, http://martinfowler.com/articles/languageWorkbench.html, 2005

72. A. Friesen, J. Lemcke, D. Oberle, T. Rahmani, D6.1—description of functional and non-functional requirements. Project Deliverable ICT216691/SAP/WP6-D1/D/PU/b1, MOST Project, 2008

73. A. Friesen, J. Lemcke, D. Oberle, T. Rahmani, D6.2—case studies design. Project Deliverable ICT216691/SAP/WP6-D2/D/RE/b1, MOST Project, 2009

74. E. Gamma, R. Helm, R. Johnson, J. Vlissides, *Design Patterns: Elements Of Reusable Object-Oriented Software* (Addison-Wesley, Boston, MA, 1995)

75. A. Goknil, I. Kurtev, K. van den Berg, Change impact analysis based on formalization of trace relations for requirements. in *ECMDA Traceability Workshop (ECMDA-TW) 2008 Proceedings*, ed. by J. Oldevik, G.K. Olsen, T. Neple, R. Paige, 2008, pp. 59–75

76. A. Goknil, I. Kurtev, K. van den Berg, J.-W. Veldhuis, Semantics of trace relations in requirements models for consistency checking and inferencing. Software Syst. Model. December 2009. doi:10.1007/s10270-009-0142-3. Available online at http://springerlink. metapress.com/link.asp?id=109378

77. B.C. Grau, A possible simplification of the semantic web architecture. in *Proceedings of the 13th International Conference on World Wide Web, WWW 2004, New York, NY, USA, May 17–20, 2004* (ACM, New York, 2004), pp. 704–713

78. B.C. Grau, B. Motik, Z. Wu, A. Fokoue, C. Lutz, Owl 2 web ontology language tractable fragments. W3C Working Draft, 11 April 2008. Available at http://www.w3.org/2007/OWL/wiki/Tractable_Fragments. Accessed 14 June 2008

79. M. Grechanik, K.S. McKinley, D.E. Perry, Recovering and Using Use-Case-Diagram-To-Source-Code Traceability Links. in *ESEC-FSE '07: Proceedings of the 6th Joint Meeting of the European Software Engineering Conference and the ACM SIGSOFT Symposium on The Foundations of Software Engineering*, 2007

80. J. Greenfield, K. Short, *Software Factories: Assembling Applications with Patterns, Models, Frameworks and Tools*, 1st edn. (Wiley, Indiana, 2004)

81. S. Grimm, B. Motik, Closed world reasoning in the semantic web through epistemic operators. in *OWLED Workshop on OWL: Experiences and Directions*, CEUR Workshop Proceedings, vol. 188. CEUR-WS.org, 2005

82. G. Groener, S. Staab, Modeling and query pattern for process retrieval in OWL. in *Proceedings of 8th International Semantic Web Conference (ISWC)*. Lecture Notes in Computer Science, vol. 5823 (Springer, Berlin, 2009), pp. 243–259

83. P. Groot, H. Stuckenschmidt, H. Wache, Approximating description logic classification for semantic web reasoning. in *Proceedings of ESWC2005*, 2005

84. G.M. Gwyner, J. Lee, Defining specialization for process models. Technical report, Boston University School of Management, 1995

85. V. Haarslev, R. Moller, M. Wessel, Querying the semantic web with racer + nRQL. in *Proceedings of the KI-04 Workshop on Applications of Description Logics*, 2004

86. P. Haase, G. Qi, An Analysis of Approaches to Resolving Inconsistencies in DL-based Ontologies, in *Proceedings of International Workshop on Ontology Dynamics* (IWOD'07), Innsbruck, Austria, 2007

87. T. Hall, S. Beecham, A. Rainer, Requirements problems in twelve software companies: An empirical analysis. IEE Proc. Software **149**(5), 153–160 (2002)

88. H. Happel, S. Seedorf, Applications of ontologies in software engineering. *Workshop on Sematic-Web Enabled Software Engineering (SWESE)*, 2006

89. H. He, A.K. Singh, Graphs-at-a-time: query language and access methods for graph databases. in *Proceedings of the 2008 International Conference on Management of Data (SIGMOD '08)* (ACM, New York, 2008), pp. 405–418. ISBN 978-1-60558-102-6

90. F. Heidenreich, Towards systematic ensuring well-formedness of software product lines. *1st Workshop on Feature-Oriented Software Development*, 2009

91. F. Heidenreich, J. Kopcsek, C. Wende, FeatureMapper: mapping features to models. *30th International Conference on Software Engineering*, 2008

92. F. Heidenreich, J. Johannes, S. Karol, M. Seifert, C. Wende, Derivation and refinement of textual syntax for models. in *Model Driven Architecture-Foundations and Applications*, Lecture Notes in Computer Science, vol. 5562 (Springer, Berlin, 2009), pp. 114–129

93. B. Henderson-Sellers, C. Gonzalez-Perez, A comparison of four process metamodels and the creation of a new generic standard. Inform. Software Tech. **47**(1), 49–65 (2005)

94. P. Hitzler, D. Vrandecic, Resolution-based approximate reasoning for OWL DL. in *Proceedings of the 4th International Semantic Web Conference (ISWC2005)*, 2005

95. D.A. Holland, PQL language guide and reference. Web document, Harvard School of Engineering and Applied Sciences, 2009. http://www.eecs.harvard.edu/syrah/pql/docs/guide.pdf

96. T. Horn, J. Ebert, The GReTL transformation language. ICMT 183–197 (2011)

97. M. Horridge, N. Drummond, J. Goodwin, A.L. Rector, R. Stevens, H. Wang, The manchester owl syntax. in *OWLED*, ed. by B.C. Grau, P. Hitzler, C. Shankey, E. Wallace, B.C. Grau, P. Hitzler, C. Shankey, E. Wallace. CEUR Workshop Proceedings, vol. 216. CEUR-WS.org, 2006

98. I. Horrocks, P. Patel-Schneider, Reducing OWL entailment to description logic satisfiability. J. Web Semant. **1**(4), 345–357 (2004). ISSN 1570-8268.

99. I. Horrocks, O. Kutz, U. Sattler, The even more irresistible sroiq. in *Proceedings of the 10th International Conference on Principles of Knowledge Representation and Reasoning (KR 2006)* (AAAI Press, USA, 2006), pp. 57–67

100. I. Horrocks, P.F. Patel-Schneider, H. Boley, S. Tabet, B. Grosof, M. Dean, SWRL: A Semantic Web Rule Language Combining OWL and RuleML, W3C Member Submission 21 May 2004. http://www.w3.org/Submission/2004/SUBM-SWRL-20040521, 2004.

101. J. Huffman Hayes, A. Dekhtyar, S.K. Sundaram, Advancing candidate link generation for requirements tracing: the study of methods. IEEE Trans. Software Eng. **32**(1), 4–19 (2006). doi:http://dx.doi.org/10.1109/TSE.2006.3

102. C. Hurtado, A. Poulovassilis, P. Wood, A relaxed approach to RDF querying. in Proceedings of the 5th International Semantic Web Conference (ISWC-2006), 2006

103. U. Hustadt, B. Motik, U. Sattler, Reducing $\mathcal{SHIQ}^-$ description logic to disjunctive datalog programs. in *Proceedings of KR2004*, 2004, pp. 152–162

104. M. Jarke, Requirements tracing. Comm. ACM **41**(12), 32–36 (1998). doi:http://doi.acm.org/10.1145/290133.290145

105. W. Jirapanthong, A. Zisman, XTraQue: traceability for product line systems. Software Syst. Model. **8**(1), 117–144 (2009). doi:10.1007/s10270-007-0066-8

106. F. Jouault, Loosely coupled traceability for ATL. in *ECMDA Traceability Workshop (ECMDA-TW) 2005 Proceedings, Nürnberg* (2005), pp. 29–37

107. F. Jouault, J. Bézivin, Km3: a dsl for metamodel specification, in *Proceedings of 8th FMOODS*. Lecture Notes in Computer Science, vol. 4037 (Springer, Berlin, 2006), pp. 171–185

108. F. Jouault, F. Allilaire, J. Bézivin, I. Kurtev, ATL: A model transformation tool. Sci. Comput. Program. **72**(1–2), 31–39 (2008)

109. H. Kaindl, The missing link in requirements engineering. SIGSOFT Software Eng. Notes **18**(2), 30–39 (1993). doi:http://doi.acm.org/10.1145/159420.155836

110. A. Kalyanpur, Debugging and repair of OWL ontologies. Ph.D. thesis, University of Maryland, College Park, 2006

111. A. Kalyanpur, B. Parsia, M. Horridge, E. Sirin, Finding all justifications of OWL DL entailments. Lecture Notes Comput. Sci. **4825**, 267 (2007)

112. A. Kalyanpur, B. Parsia, E. Sirin, B. Cuenca-Grau, Repairing unsatisfiable concepts in OWL ontologies. *The Semantic Web: Research and Applications*, 2006, pp. 170–184

113. A. Kalyanpur, B. Parsia, E. Sirin, J. Hendler, Debugging unsatisfiable classes in OWL ontologies. Web Semant. Sci. Serv. Agents World Wide Web **3**(4), 268–293 (2005)

114. K. Kang, S. Cohen, J. Hess, W. Nowak, S. Peterson, Feature-oriented domain analysis (FODA) feasibility study. Technical Report CMU/SEI-90-TR-21, Software Engineering Institute, Pittsburgh, PA, 1990

115. M. Kasztelnik, K.M. Miksa, P. Sabina, D5.2—case study design. Project Deliverable ICT216691/CMR/WP5-D2/D/RE/b1, MOST Project, February 2009

116. S. Kelly, J. Tolvanen, *Domain-Specific Modeling: Enabling Full Code Generation* (Wiley-IEEE Computer Society Press, New York, 2008)

117. S. Kent, Model driven engineering, in *Proceedings of Third International Conference on Integrated Formal Methods*, Lecture Notes in Computer Science, vol. 2335 (Springer, Berlin, 2002), pp. 286–298

118. N. Kiesel, A. Schürr, B. Westfechtel, GRAS, a graph oriented (software) engineering database system. Information Systems **20**(1), 21–51 (1995). ISSN 0306-4379. doi:http://dx.doi.org/10.1016/0306-4379(95)00002-L

119. A.G. Kleppe, J.B. Warmer, W. Bast, *MDA Explained, The Model Driven Architecture: Practice and Promise* (Addison-Wesley, Boston, 2002)

120. H. Knublauch, R. Fergerson, N. Noy, M. Musen. The Protégé OWL plugin: An open development environment for semantic web applications. In ISWC-2004, Lecture notes in computer science, 2004, Vol. 3298, pp. 229–243

121. M. Krötzsch, S. Rudolph, P. Hitzler, Conjunctive queries for a tractable fragment of owl 1.1, in *ISWC/ASWC*, 2007, pp. 310–323

122. B. Kullbach, A. Winter, Querying as an enabling technology in software reengineering, in *Proceedings of the 3rd Euromicro Conference on Software Maintenance & Reengineering*, ed. by C. Verhoef, P. Nesi (IEEE Computer Society, Los Alamitos, 1999), pp. 42–50. http://www.uni-koblenz.de/~ist/documents/Kullbach1999QAA.pdf

123. B. Liskov, Data abstraction and hierarchy, in *OOPSLA '87: Addendum to the Proceedings on Object-Oriented Programming Systems, Languages and Applications (Addendum)* (ACM, New York, 1987), pp. 17–34. ISBN 0-89791-266-7. doi:http://doi.acm.org/10.1145/62138.62141

124. P. Mäder, O. Gotel, I. Philippow, Rule-based maintenance of post-requirements traceability relations, in *Proceedings of the 16th IEEE International Requirements Engineering Conference*, 2008, pp. 23–32

125. J.I. Maletic, M.L. Collard, TQL: A query language to support traceability, in *Proceedings of 5th ACM International Workshop on Traceability in Emerging Forms of Software Engineering (TEFSE'09), Vancouver, BC, Canada, May 18* (2009), pp. 16–20

126. J.I. Maletic, M.L. Collard, B. Simoes, An XML based approach to support the evolution of model-to-model traceability links, in *Proceedings of 3rd International Workshop on Traceability in Emerging Forms of Software Engineering, Long Beach*, 2005, pp. 67–72

127. J.I. Maletic, E.V. Munson, A. Marcus, T.N. Nguyen, Using a hypertext model for traceability link conformance analysis, in *Proceedings of the 2nd International Workshop on Traceability in Emerging Forms of Software Engineering, Montreal*, 2003

128. M. Mannion, B. Keepence, Smart requirements. ACM Software Eng. Notes **20**, 42 (2005)

129. D.L. McGuinness, F. van Harmelen, Owl web ontology language overview. W3C Working Draft, 10 February 2004

130. K. Mehlhorn, S. Näher, C. Uhrig, The LEDA platform of combinatorial and geometric computing, in *Proceedings of the 24th International Colloquium on Automata, Languages and Programming (ICALP '97)*, 1997, pp. 7–16. ISBN 3-540-63165-8

131. K. Miksa, M. Kasztelnik, D5.1—definition of the case study requirements. Project Deliverable ICT216691/CMR/WP5-D1/D/PU/b1, MOST Project, September 2008

132. K. Miksa, M. Kasztelnik, P. Sabina, T. Walter, Towards semantic modelling of network physical devices, in *Models in Software Engineering*, Lecture Notes in Computer Science, vol. 6002 (Springer, Berlin, 2010), pp. 329–343

133. J. Miller, J. Mukerji, Mda guide version 1.0.1. Technical report, OMG, 2003

134. R. Milner, *A Calculus of Communicating Systems*, Springer Lecture Notes in Computer Science (Springer, Berlin, 1980)

135. R. Milner, *Communication and Concurrency* (Prentice Hall, New Jersey, 1989)

136. R. Milner, J. Parrow, D. Walker, A calculus of mobile processes, I Inform. Comput. **100**(1), 1–40 (1992)

137. M. Moon, H.S. Chae, T. Nam, K. Yeom, A metamodeling approach to tracing variability between requirements and architecture in software product lines, in *Proceedings of the 7th IEEE International Conference on Computer and Information Technology* (IEEE Computer Society, Washington, DC, USA, 2007), pp. 927–933

138. B. Motik, On the properties of metamodeling in OWL. J. Log. Comput. **17**(4), 617–637 (2007)

139. B. Motik, B.C. Grau, I. Horrocks, Z. Wu, A. Fokoue, C. Lutz, Owl 2 web ontology language profiles. W3C Recommendation, 27 October 2009. Available at http://www.w3.org/TR/owl2-profiles/

140. B. Motik, P.F. Patel-Schneider, I. Horrocks, OWL 2 Web Ontology Language—Structural Specification and Functional-Style Syntax. Working draft, W3C, April 2008

141. M. Nagl, An incremental compiler as component of a system for software generation, in *Programmiersprachen und Programmentwicklung, 6. Fachtagung des Fachausschusses Programmiersprachen der GI* (Springer, London, UK, 1980), pp. 29–44

142. T.N. Nguyen, E.V. Munson, A model for conformance analysis of software documents, in *Proceedings of the 6th International Workshop on Principles of Software Evolution (IWPSE)*, 2003

143. K. Nørmark, Elucidative programming. Nord. J. Comput. **7**(2):87–105 (2000)

144. I. Ober, A. Prinz, What do we need metamodels for? in *Proceedings of the 4th Nordic Workshop on UML and Software Modelling* (NWUML'06), Norway, 2006

145. OMG, Business Process Modeling Notation (BPMN), Version 1.2, Object Management Group, 2009

146. G.K. Olsen, J. Oldevik, Scenarios of traceability in model to text transformations, in *Proceedings of the 3rd European Conference on Model-Driven Architecture—Foundation and Applications (ECMDA-FA 2007)*, ed. by D.H. Akehurst, R. Vogel, R.F. Paige, 2007

147. OMG. MOF QVT Final Adopted Specification, Object Management Group, 2005. http://www.omg.org/docs/ptc/05-11-01.pdf

148. OMG. Object Constraint Language Specification, version 2.0. Object Modeling Group, 2005. http://fparreiras/specs/OCLSpec06-05-01.pdf

149. OMG. Meta Object Facility (MOF) Core Specification. Object Management Group, 2006

150. OMG. Ontology Definition Metamodel. Object Modeling Group 2007

151. OMG. Unified Modeling Language: Superstructure, version 2.1.2. Object Modeling Group, 2007. http://fparreiras/specs/UML2.1.1.formal07-02-03.pdf

152. OMG. Software Process Engineering Metamodel (spem) Specification—Version 2.0 Object Management Group, 2008. http://www.omg.org/docs/formal/08-04-01.pdf

153. OMG, OMG Unified Modeling Language (OMG UML) Infrastructure. Version 2.2, Object Management Group, 2009. http://www.omg.org/spec/UML/2.2/Infrastructure

154. OMG. Unified Modeling Language™, OMG Available Specification, Version 2.2. Object Management Group (OMG), 2009. http://www.omg.org/spec/UML/2.2/

155. J.Z. Pan, I. Horrocks, RDFS(FA) and RDF MT: two semantics for RDFS, in *Proceedings of the 2nd International Semantic Web Conference (ISWC2003)*, 2003

156. J.Z. Pan, E. Thomas, Approximating OWL-DL ontologies, in *AAAI-2007*, 2007, pp. 1434–1439

157. J.Z. Pan, I. Horrocks, G. Schreiber, OWL FA: A metamodeling extension of OWL DL, in *Proceedings of the First International OWL Experience and Directions Workshop (OWLED-2005)*, 2005

158. F.S. Parreiras, S. Staab, Using ontologies with uml class-based modeling: The twouse approach. Data Knowl. Eng. **69**(11), 1194–1207 (2010)

159. F.S. Parreiras, T. Walter, C. Wende, D1.3—report on transformation patterns. Project Deliverable ICT216691/UoKL/WP1-D3/D/PU/a1, MOST Project, (2009)

160. P.F. Patel-Schneider, B. Motik, (eds.), OWL 2 Web Ontology Language Mapping to RDF Graphs, W3C Recommendation 27 October 2009, http://www.w3.org/TR/2009/REC-owl2-mapping-to-rdf-20091027

161. B. Pierce, in *Foundational Calculi for Programming Languages*, ed. by A.B. Tucker. Handbook of Computer Science and Engineering, chapter 139 (CRC Press, Boca Raton, 1996), pp. 2190–2207

162. F.A. Pinheiro, An object-oriented library for tracing requirements. in Anais do WER99—Workshop em Engenharia de Requisitos, Buenos Aires, 1999

163. F.A. Pinheiro, Requirements traceability, in *Perspectives on Software Requirements*, chapter 5, ed. by J.C. Sampaio do Prado Leite, J.H. Doorn (Kluwer Academic, New York, 2003), pp. 91–113

164. K. Pohl, *Process-Centered Requirements Engineering*. Advanced Software Development Series (Research Studies Press, Taunton, Somerset, England, 1996)

165. K. Pohl, G. Böckle, F. Van Der Linden, *Software Product Line Engineering: Foundations, Principles, and Techniques* (Springer, Berlin, 2005). ISBN 978-3540243724

166. A. Polleres, F. Scharffe, R. Schindlauer, Sparql++ for mapping between rdf vocabularies, in *OTM Conferences (1)*, ed. by R. Meersman, Z. Tari. Lecture Notes in Computer Science, vol. 4803 (Springer, Berlin, 2007), pp. 878–896. ISBN 978-3-540-76846-3

167. E. Prud'hommeaux, A. Seaborne, SPARQL Query Language for RDF, W3C Recommendation, 15 January 2008. http://www.w3.org/TR/2008/REC-rdf-sparql-query-20080115/

168. B. Ramesh, M. Jarke, Toward reference models for requirements traceability. IEEE Trans. Software Eng. **27**(1), 58–93 (2001). doi:http://dx.doi.org/10.1109/32.895989

169. R. Reiter, A theory of diagnosis from first principles. Artif. Intell. **32**(1), 57–95 (1987)
170. Y. Ren, Syntactic approximation in PDDSL: A completeness guarantee. Technical report, University of Aberdeen, 2010. Http://www.abdn.ac.uk/~csc280/TR/pddsl.pdf
171. Y. Ren, J.Z. Pan, Y. Zhao, Closed world reasoning for OWL2 with NBox. J. Tsinghua Sci. Tech. Vol. 15(6), December (2010) pp. 692–701
172. Y. Ren, J.Z. Pan, Y. Zhao, Soundness preserving approximation for TBox reasoning, in *Proceedings of the 25th AAAI Conference Conference (AAAI2010)*, 2010
173. Y. Ren, J.Z. Pan, Y. Zhao, Towards soundness preserving approximation for abox reasoning of owl2, in *Description Logics Workshop 2010 (DL2010)*, 2010
174. Y. Ren, J.Z. Pan, Y. Zhao, Abox syntactic approximation: A technical report. Technical report, University of Aberdeen, 2011. Http://www.abdn.ac.uk/~csc280/TR/aboxapprox.pdf
175. Y. Ren, G. Gröner, J. Lemcke, T. Rahmani, A. Friesen, Y. Zhao, J.Z. Pan, S. Staab, Validating process refinement with ontologies, in *Description Logics*, ed. by B.C. Grau, I. Horrocks, B. Motik, U. Sattler. CEUR Workshop Proceedings, vol. 477. CEUR-WS.org, 2009
176. Y. Ren, G. Gröner, J. Lemcke, T. Rahmani, A. Friesen, Y. Zhao, J.Z. Pan, S. Staab, Process refinement validation and explanation with ontology reasoning. Technical report, University of Aberdeen, University of Koblenz-Landau and AP AG, 2011. http://www.abdn.ac.uk/~csc280/pub/ProcessRefinement.pdf
177. M. Richters, A Precise Approach to Validating UML Models and OCL Constraints. Ph.D. thesis, Universität Bremen, 2002
178. D. Roe, K. Broda, A. Russo, Mapping UML Models incorporating OCL Constraints into Object-Z. Technical report, August 2003. http://pubs.doc.ic.ac.uk/UMLtoObjecZ2003/
179. D. Sangiorgi, Bisimulation for higher-order process calculi. Inform. Comput. **131**, 141–178 (1996)
180. D.C. Schmidt, Guest editor's introduction: model-driven engineering. Computer **39**, 25–31 (2006), ISSN 0018-9162
181. P.H. Schmitt, A Model Theoretic Semantics for OCL, in *Proceedings of IJCAR Workshop on Precise Modelling and Deduction for Object-oriented Software Development*, Siena, Italy, 2001
182. H. Schwarz, D4.2—report on traceability information extracting and using traceability information during the developement process. Project Deliverable ICT216691/UoKL/WP4-D2/D/PU/b1, MOST Project, January 2009
183. H. Schwarz, Taxonomy and definition of the explicit traceability information suppliable for guiding model-driven, ontology-supported development. Project Deliverable ICT216691/UoKL/WP4-D1/D/PU/b1, MOST Project, January 2009
184. H. Schwarz, J. Ebert, Bridging query languages in semantic and graph technologies, in *Reasoning Web—6th International Summer School 2010* (Springer, Berlin, 2010)
185. H. Schwarz, J. Ebert, A. Winter, Graph-based traceability: a comprehensive approach. Software Syst. Model., November 2009 doi:10.1007/s10270-009-0141-4
186. H. Schwarz, J. Ebert, V. Riediger, A. Winter, Towards querying of traceability information in the context of software evolution, in *10th Workshop Software Reengineering (WSR 2008)*, ed. by R. Gimnich, U. Kaiser, J. Quante, A. Winter. GI Lecture Notes in Informatics, vol. 126. GI, 2008
187. E. Seidewitz, What models mean. IEEE Software **20**(5), 26–32 (2003). ISSN 0740-7459. doi:http://dx.doi.org/10.1109/MS.2003.1231147
188. B. Selman, H. Kautz, Knowledge compilation and theory approximation. J. ACM **43**(2), 193–224 (1996)
189. I. Seylan, E. Franconi, J. De Bruijn, Effective query rewriting with ontologies over dboxes, in *IJCAI'09: Proceedings of the 21st International Joint Conference on Artifical Intelligence* (Morgan Kaufmann Publishers, San Francisco, CA, USA, 2009), pp. 923–929
190. S.A. Sherba, K.M. Anderson, M. Faisal, A framework for mapping traceability relationships, in *Proceedings of the 2nd International Workshop on Traceability in Emerging Forms of Software Engineering, Montreal*, 2003

191. S. Si-Said, C. Rolland, Formalising guidance for the crews goal-scenario approach to requirements engineering, in *8th European-Japanese Conference on Information Modelling and Knowledge Bases*, 1998, pp. 172–190

192. F. Silva Parreiras, S. Staab, S. Schenk, A. Winter, Model driven specification of ontology translations, in *Conceptual Modeling—ER 2008*. Lecture Notes in Computer Science (Springer, Berlin, 2008)

193. E. Sirin, B. Parsia, Sparql-dl: Sparql query for owl-dl, in *OWLED*, ed. by C. Golbreich, A. Kalyanpur, B. Parsia. CEUR Workshop Proceedings, vol. 258. CEUR-WS.org, 2007

194. E. Sirin, J. Tao, Towards integrity constraints in OWL, in *OWL: Experiences and Directions, Sixth International Workshop (OWLED 2009)*, 2009

195. E. Sirin, B. Parsia, B. Grau, A. Kalyanpur, Y. Katz, Pellet: A practical owl-dl reasoner. Web Semant. Sci. Serv. Agents World Wide Web **5**(2), 51–53 (2007)

196. M. Śmiałek, Towards a requirements driven software development system. Poster presentation at MoDELS, Genova, Italy, 2006

197. G. Smith, *The Object-Z Specification Language* (Kluwer Academic, Norwell, MA, USA, 2000). ISBN 0-7923-8684-1

198. X. Song, W.M. Hasling, G. Mangla, B. Sherman, Lessons learned from building a web-based requirements tracing system, in *ICRE '98: Proceedings of the 3rd International Conference on Requirements Engineering* (IEEE Computer Society, Washington, DC, USA, 1998), pp. 41–50. ISBN 0-8186-8356-2

199. D. Steinberg, F. Budinsky, M. Paternostro, E. Merks, *EMF: Eclipse Modeling Framework*, 2nd edn. (Addison-Wesley Professional, Boston, 2008)

200. W. Stinson, Views of Software Development Environments: Automation of Engineering and Engineering of Automation. In ACM SIGSOFT, Software Engineering Notes, Vol. 14(5) July 1989, pp. 108–117, ACM

201. H. Stuckenschmidt, F. van Harmelen, Approximating terminological queries, in *Proceedings of FQAS2002*, 2002, pp. 329–343

202. B. Suntisrivaraporn, Module extraction and incremental classification: a pragmatic aApproach for $\mathcal{EL}^+$ ontologies, in *Proceedings of the 5th European Semantic Web Conference (ESWC'08)*, ed. by S. Bechhofer, M. Hauswirth, J. Hoffmann, M. Koubarakis, Lecture Notes in Computer Science, vol. 5021 (Springer, Berlin, 2008), pp. 230–244

203. E. Thomas, J.Z. Pan, Y. Ren, TrOWL: Tractable OWL 2 reasoning infrastructure, in *Proceedings of the Extended Semantic Web Conference (ESWC2010)*, 2010

204. E. Tryggeseth, Ø. Nytrø, Dynamic traceability links supported by a system architecture description, in *ICSM '97: Proceedings of the International Conference on Software Maintenance*, 1997, pp. 180–187

205. A. von Knethen, B. Paech, A survey on tracing approaches in theory and practice. Technical Report 095.01/E, Fraunhofer IESE, 2002

206. A. van Lamsweerde, Reasoning about alternative requirements options, in *Conceptual Modeling: Foundations and Applications*, ed. by A. Borgida, V.K. Chaudhri, P. Giorgini, E.S.K. Yu Lecture Notes in Computer Science, vol. 5600 (Springer, Berlin, 2009), pp. 380–397

207. A. Van Lamsweerde, R. Darimont, E. Letier, Managing conflicts in goal-driven requirements engineering. IEEE Trans. Software Eng. **24**(11), 908–926 (1998). ISSN 0098-5589

208. H. Wache, P. Groot, H. Stuckenschmidt, Scalable instance retrieval for the semantic web by approximation, in *Proceedings of WISE-2005 Workshop on Scalable Semantic Web Knowledge Base Systems*, 2005

209. S. Walderhaug, U. Johansen, E. Stav, J. Aagedal, Towards a generic solution for traceability in MDD, in *ECMDA Traceability Workshop (ECMDA-TW) 2006 Proceedings, Bilbao*, 2006

210. T. Walter, J. Ebert, Combining DSLs and ontologies using metamodel integration, in *Domain-Specific Languages*. Lecture Notes in Computer Science, vol. 5658 (Springer, Berlin, 2009), pp. 148–169

211. T. Walter, J. Ebert, Combining ontology-enriched domain-specific languages, in *Proceedings of the Second Workshop on Transforming and Weaving Ontologies in Model Driven Engineering (TWOMDE) at MoDELS*, 2009

212. T. Walter, H. Schwarz, Y. Ren, Establishing a bridge from graph-based modeling languages to ontology languages, in *Proceedings of the 3rd Workshop on Transforming and Weaving OWL Ontologies and MDE/MDA (TWOMDE 2010)*, 2010

213. T. Walter, F. Silva Parreiras, S. Staab, OntoDSL: An ontology-based framework for domain-specific languages, in *Model Driven Engineering Languages and Systems, 12th International Conference, MODELS 2009*, vol. 5795 (Springer, Berlin, 2009), pp. 408–422

214. T. Walter, F. Silva Parreiras, S. Staab, J. Ebert, Joint language and domain engineering, in *Proceedings of 6th European Conference on Modelling Foundations and Applications, ECMFA 2010, Paris*. Lecture Notes in Computer Science, vol. 6138 (Springer, Berlin, 2010)

215. H. Wang, Y. Li, J. Sun, H. Zhang, J. Pan, A semantic web approach to feature modeling and verification, in *1st Workshop on Semantic Web Enabled Software Engineering (SWESE'05)*, 2005

216. C.A. Welty, D.A. Ferrucci, What's in an instance. Technical Report 94/18, RPI Computer Science Department, NY, 1994

217. C. Wende, S. Zivkovic, U. Aßmann, H. Kühn, Feature-based customisation of MDSD tool environments. Technical Report TUD-FI10-05-Juli 2010, Technische Universität Dresden, July 2010

218. R. Wieringa, An introduction to requirements traceability. Technical Report IR-389, Faculty of Mathematics and Computer Science, Amsterdam, 1995

219. S. Winkler, J. von Pilgrim, A survey of traceability in requirements engineering and model-driven development. Software Syst. Model. **9**(4), 529–565 (2010). doi:10.1007/s10270-009-0141-4

220. A. Winter, Referenz-metaschema für visuelle modellierungssprachen. DUV Informatik. Deutscher Universitätsverlag, 2000

221. R. Witte, Y. Zhang, J. Rilling, Empowering software maintainers with semantic web technologies, in *Proceedings of the 4th European Semantic Web Conference (ESCW 2007)*. Lecture Notes in Computer Science, vol. 4519, 2007, pp. 37–52. doi:10.1007/978-3-540-72667-8_5

222. G.M. Wyner, J. Lee, Defining specialization for process models, in *Organizing Business Knowledge: The MIT Process Handbook*, chapter 5 (MIT, Cambridge, 2003), pp. 131–174

223. A. Yie, D. Wagelaar, Advanced traceability with ATL, in *Proceedings of the 1st International Workshop on Model Transformation with ATL* (2009)

224. R. Yuan, J.Z. Pan, Y. Zhao, Soundness Preserving Approximation for TBox Reasoning. In *Proc. of the 24th AAAI Conference on Artificial Intelligence (AAAI2010)*, 2010

225. Y. Zhao, J.Z. Pan, Y. Ren, Implementing and evaluating a rule-based approach to querying regular el+ ontologies, in *Proceedings of the International Conference on Hybrid Intelligent Systems (HIS2009)*, 2009

226. S. Zivkovic, C. Wende, A. Bartho, B. Gregorcic, D2.3—initial prototype of ontology-driven software process guidance system. Project Deliverable ICT216691/TUD/WP2-D3/D/PU/b1.00, MOST Project, 2009

Index

ABox reasoning, 55
AMMA, 38
API, 5
ARIS, 26
ATL, 38, 42
Axiom explanation, 182

BPMN, 26, 100, 132, 219, 224, 294

Case study, 69, 74, 78, 87, 91
CDA, 170, 206
Change management, 122
CIM, 5, 76
Classification, 182
Comarch, 70, 293
Combined complexity, 56
Completeness checking, 197
Computational complexity, 55
Consistency, 305
Consistency checking, 181, 194
CPSD, 10
CRM, 77
CWA, 168, 206, 283

Data complexity, 56
DAWG, 55
DEFT, 315, 317
DL, 180
DL-Lite, 60, 61
Documentation engineering, 314
DRAGOS, 32
DSL, 28, 69, 305
DSML, 22

EBNF, 258
Ecore, 258, 259
EL^{++}, 60
EMF, 4, 132
EMOF, 5, 24
Entity-Relationship, 23
EPC, 26

Feature analysis, 35, 201
Feature model notation, 34
Feature models, 33, 199

GCI, 52, 100
GPML, 22
Graph UML, 29
GRAS, 32
GReQL, 44, 137, 149, 291
GReTL, 39, 42, 137, 150
Grounding, 231, 237
Grounding refinement, 225
grUML, 31, 137
GSD, 11
Guidance, 293, 300, 305, 309, 314

ICT, 1
Inconsistency explanation, 182
ISM-dimension, 23
ISV, 75

Justification, 113, 166

KM3, 258, 259

LEDA, 32
Lifecycle, 75

M0, 6, 8, 22, 28, 76
M1, 6, 8, 22, 28, 76, 263
M2, 6, 8, 22, 28, 76, 183, 258, 263, 267
M3, 8, 9, 22, 28, 76, 184, 190, 191, 259, 261,
       267
MDA, 1, 22
MDE, 21, 23
MDSD, 1, 121
Metamodel, 22, 28, 152, 154–157, 172, 186,
       257
Metamodeling, 24, 151, 174, 258
Model, 22
ModelWare, 6
MOF, 6, 22, 24, 167
MOST, 1, 292

NBox, 283
NeOn metamodel, 154

OCL, 2, 43, 149, 285
ODM, 152
ODRE, 194, 195, 199
ODSD, 1, 67, 94, 290, 292
OIM, 257, 272
OIS, 6, 8
OMG, 23, 76
OMG OWL metamodel, 152
OMG RDF metamodel, 152
Ontology, 180, 232, 237
Ontology reasoning, 240, 242
Ontology service, 179
OntologyWare, 6
OntoReq, 310
OSGS, 93
OWA, 169, 206
OWL, 4, 57
OWL 2, 57, 204, 206, 207, 211, 214, 259
OWLCL, 266
OWL DL, 64, 221
OWL FA, 157, 168
OWLizer, 184
OWLText, 257, 265
OWL metamodel, 153
OWL 2 metamodel, 156

Parallel gateway, 234, 235
PDDSL, 70, 204, 207, 208, 211, 214, 262, 263

Pellet, 73, 287
Petri Nets, 272
Petri nets, 27
PIM, 5, 22, 76
Pinpointing, 240
Process algebra, 48
Process guidance, 244
Process model, 221
Process modelling language, 26
Process refinement, 78, 224, 287, 300
Process retrieval, 223
PSM, 5, 22, 76

Query answering, 55, 182
Query complexity, 56
Quill, 102
QVTO, 43, 209

RDF metamodel, 153
RDFS, 6
RE. *See* Requirements Engineering (RE)
Reasoning, 244
Reasoning services, 73
Refinement, 225, 232, 234
REL, 102, 299
Requirements Engineering (RE), 9, 194,
       309
Requirements management, 123
Requirements ontology, 310
Reuse, 123
RI, 52
RSB, 9

SaaS, 75
SAP, 74, 293
Satisfiability checking, 181
SCM, 77
Semantic approximation, 103
SOA, 75
SPARQL, 55, 143, 148, 149, 198, 292
SPLE, 93
Subsumption checking, 182

Taxonomic complexity, 56
TBox reasoning, 55
TGraphs, 29, 39, 137, 150
Tool environment, 275
Traceability, 290
Traceability retrieval patterns, 149
Transformation, 183

TrOWL, 73, 99, 198, 287, 299
TRTT, 127–129, 132
TwoUse, 214, 217
2-Dimensional modelling, 36

UML, 22, 23, 214, 285
UNA, 170, 206, 285
Unsatisfiability, 181

Use case, 73

W3C, 4, 55, 92, 280

XML, 23

YAWL, 26